JOURNEY TO CARITH

JOURNEY TO CARITH

THE STORY OF
THE CARMELITE ORDER

PETER-THOMAS ROHRBACH

O.C.D.

Imprimi potest: Christopher Latimer, o.c.d., Provincial
Nihil obstat: Jerome Flynn, o.c.d., Censor Deputatus
Imprimatur: Patrick A. O'Boyle, Archbishop of Washington
March 21, 1966

The nihil obstat and imprimatur are official declarations
that a book or pamphlet is free of doctrinal or moral error.
No implication is contained therein that those who have
granted the nihil obstat and the imprimatur agree with the
content, opinions, or statements expressed.

FIRST EDITION

Library of Congress Catalog Card Number 66–20942

Preface

When *Journey to Carith* was first published by Doubleday & Co. in 1966, it was praised for its broad scope and felicitous style. In an engaging narrative of less than 400 pages, Peter-Thomas Rohrbach had somehow managed to survey a full eight centuries of the Carmelite tradition. One reviewer even proposed the book as a new model for histories of other religious orders.

Decades have passed since the appearance of this work and important new discoveries in the study of Carmelite history have come to the fore. Unfortunately, such scholarly research is not yet readily accessible to the general public. Readers are still awaiting a new single-volume popular history of the Discalced Carmelite tradition that incorporates the latest findings. In the meantime, despite its limitations, *Journey to Carith* remains unsurpassed as a concise and readable overview.

Responding to numerous requests, therefore, ICS Publications has arranged with the author for this reprint edition. We have changed the subtitle to reflect the fact that the book is really about the people and events associated with the "discalced" branch of the Carmelite family as well as the first four centuries of the Carmelite tradition out of which St. Teresa's reform grew.

Readers should be aware that the author's account of the origins of Carmel in the first chapter has been superseded. Carmelite historians now believe that our first hermit community in the wadi-es-Siah on the slopes of Mount Carmel could not have begun much before the beginning of the thirteenth century, and that figures such as "Aymeric" and "Berthold" are largely mythological. In fact, the earliest historical document concerning this original hermit community is the Rule given to them by Albert, the patriarch of Jerusalem, around the year 1209. This rule mentions a prior with the initial "B," about whom nothing else is known.

Again, current studies of sixteenth-century Carmel suggest a more nuanced picture of the beginnings of the Teresian Reform. The Carmelites of Castile were in fact considered relatively observant at the time Teresa of Avila began her foundations there, and all parties shared responsibility for the painful conflicts that erupted.

For other works on Carmelite origins, readers are encouraged to consult historian Joachim Smet's multivolume work, *The Carmelites: A History of the Brothers of Our Lady of Mount Carmel* (Darien, IL.: Carmelite Spiritual Center, 1976-85), as well as John Welch's *The Carmelite Way* (New York: Paulist Press, 1996).

Despite the need for some updating, *Journey to Carith* remains a fascinating account of one of the oldest religious families in the Christian West, with a uniquely important spiritual tradition. This book that has inspired so many in the past, we hope, will continue to fire readers with an interest in the order of Carmel.

Kieran Kavanaugh, OCD

Carith was a wadi, a small watering place, where the Lord God sent the prophet Elijah—"Depart from here and turn eastward, and hide yourself by the torrent of Carith, which is east of the Jordan." (I Kings 17:3)

The medieval Carmelites, who proposed themselves as followers and imitators of Elijah, found in this one episode in the prophet's life a symbol of their entire life and dedication. Playing on the phonetic similarity between Carith and the Latin word *caritas* (love), they envisioned the trip to Carith as a journey to love.

TABLE OF CONTENTS

FORENOTE: PERSPECTIVE OF A CHRONICLE

This is the chronicle of a family. Granted, a family of enormous proportions, a family of long historical traditions and vast membership, embracing territories and cultures around the world—but for all of that, a family. It is in this light that any religious order must be seen: not so much as an institution or an apostolic mechanism, but as a divinely oriented grouping of people into an association of mutual love and common objectives. A religious order is the family of God in the truest sense of the term, with its own origin, its own history, its own spirit, its own people.

This is the story of the Carmelites, one family in the Church of God, like other religious families in many respects, but unique and individual as every family must be. Carmel—as the Carmelite order is called—originated in the Eastern world of Palestine, and found its flourishing in western Europe. It became a part of the popular mendicant movement of the thirteenth century. It succumbed to the nadir of the religious orders of the fourteenth and fifteenth centuries. It was resuscitated by the sixteenth-century reformers, St. John of the Cross and St. Teresa of Ávila, who articulated and restated its deep contemplative and mystical tradition. Then it spread to the New World and to the Indies and the Orient. It was devastated by the upheavals following the French Revolution, and then regrouped itself for a strong continuance into the twentieth century. Like all families, Carmel has had its bright moments and its dark moments, its days of great prosperity and purpose and its days when it seemed to be confused and stumbling; it has known strife and disagreement from within, persecution and misunderstanding from without. But it survived—because it had that basic human dynamism that all families have, and because it was divinely inspired and divinely protected.

This chronicle, however, must not be merely a report of historical movements and grand epochs; it must be a story of people. Matthew Arnold said that history is the essence of innumerable biographies. And so this must be: an honest account of the people of Carmel, products of their own lineage, but involved in the instant historical moment, similar from country to country and epoch to epoch, but different and individual as only people can be.

A family history has inherent value because it is a human document recording the story of men and women. An account of Carmel's story has wider implications because of the impact this family has had on Christianity and Western culture. The story cannot be told in all its ramifications and details; that would necessitate too wide a canvas. But it can be told in survey, outlining the principal movements, describing the more important and interesting personages, underscoring the pivotal events. Large and unwieldy volumes, bristling with footnotes, would be necessary to give a completely satisfactory historical analysis of Carmel, but there might be some value in a narrative account of this family's history.

This is what this chronicle proposes to do.

PETER-THOMAS ROHRBACH, O.C.D.
Washington, D.C.

JOURNEY TO CARITH

– I –
THE BIRTH OF AN ORDER

THE mountain seems to rise directly from the sea. It begins abruptly at the water's edge, climbs rapidly to a height of eighteen hundred feet, and then joins itself to a chain of hills stretching fifteen miles down into the Palestinian countryside. The Mediterranean, its waters astonishingly blue, washes in at the mountain's base, while to the west down the coast lies the city of 'Atlit; immediately beneath the mountain is the modern port of Haifa, and across the bay the historic beleaguered city of Acre.

Mount Carmel! Tall, massive, brooding at the water's edge. The site of innumerable Biblical scenes. The home of the fiery prophet Elijah, the mountain dwelling of Elisha and his school of prophets. The image used by Solomon in his Song of Songs to describe the bride's alluring beauty. The mountain retreat of early Christian monks who prayed there and lived in its caves. The scene of battle and bloodshed for marauding armies which climbed its steeps: Saracens and Turks, Crusaders and the French armies of Napoleon. Rich with history, venerable with age, confidante of a thousand stories of personal human drama. Part mountain, part symbol, it stands in the new Israeli state, evocative of the past, but an enduring and tangible testimony that the spirit of the great realities enacted there, Judaic and Christian, will never die or be lost.

On top of the gray limestone of modern Mount Carmel, rising from the promontory like a rugged outcropping of stone, stands a large rectangular building surmounted by a Byzantine cupola. It could readily be mistaken for a fortress peering out over the sea, but it is, in fact, a monastery of Carmelite friars. This building represents another dimension in the history of Mount Carmel: the story of a religious order founded on that mountain and nurtured in the contemplative traditions of prayer and solitude by the hermits who lived there over the centuries. The present monastery, constructed in 1836, is the fifth Carmelite monastery constructed on that site, and it can trace its lineage back to the first chapel of St. Berthold in the twelfth century, and by a type of synthetic ancestry, back to the cave dwellings of Elijah and Elisha.

The Carmelite story spans centuries and reaches around the world, but it has its beginnings on this Palestinian mountain which must always remain the homeland of the heart for every Carmelite. It is here we must begin the chronicle.

Elijah, the Old Testament prophet from Mount Carmel, appears abruptly on the scene of Jewish history in the ninth century B.C. Without offering any preliminary information, the scriptures suddenly introduce him as he stands uncompromisingly before the Israelic king Ahab, upbraiding him for his sins and predicting a three-year punitive drought. "As the Lord God of Israel lives, before whose face I stand," Elijah exclaims, "there shall be neither dew nor rain these years, except by my word." And thus begins the narrative of that towering figure of salvation history, Elijah the prophet.

Elijah's story is recounted in the first and second Book of Kings. It is an epic, dramatic narrative, filled with sharply drawn personalities and colorful events, depicting the odyssey of a man of God whose mission was to bear witness to the living God. Elijah has had an enduring impact on the history of God's people. He was revered in the Old Testament as the great prophet, the man of God, the living witness of God's reality, the fearless champion of true belief and worship. John the Baptist is introduced as coming in "the spirit and the power of Elijah," and then the prophet is mentioned twenty-nine times more in the pages of the New Testament. And in his most impressive moment, he appeared at the transfiguration of Jesus, together with Moses, giving witness that Christ was the fulfillment of the law and the prophets. Veneration for Elijah continued in the early Christian Church, and he is mentioned frequently in the patristic literature. The Church Fathers wrote extensively about Elijah, examining his life, proposing him as a model of virtue and source of inspiration, and several of them—notably Basil, John Chrysostom, Gregory Nazianzen, and Jerome—present him as the model of religious perfection and the patron of hermits and monks. And even today he survives as a particularly appealing ecumenical figure, in that he is revered by Christians, Jews, and Moslems.

Elijah's relevance to this chronicle lies in the fact that the Carmelite Order regards him as its founder.

And with that statement we immediately encounter a historical dilemma. There is no evidence in Scripture of any such foundation, nor of a permanent religious organization founded by Elijah which continued until the time of Christ. Granted, Elisha followed in the footsteps of his master and maintained the sons of the prophets which Elijah had grouped together, but these schools of the prophets, a frequent phenomenon in that era of Jewish history, began to disappear at the breakup of the Israelite kingdom and we find no further trace of them after the fifth century B.C. On the other hand, valid historical evidence can place the foundation of the Carmelite Order no earlier than 1150 A.D. After the Holy Land had been reopened to Christians during the time of the Crusades, a number of pilgrims and crusaders settled on Mount Carmel in the latter part of the twelfth century to lead an eremitical life in imitation of the prophet Elijah, who had dwelt there two thousand years before. In the year 1209, the Latin patriarch of Jerusalem, Albert of Vercelli, composed a rule for them, and in 1226 Pope Honorius III gave official confirmation for the rule. That is the point of origin of the Carmelite Order, and it certainly precludes a legendary foundation by Elijah nine hundred years before the birth of Christ.

Nevertheless, despite these incontestable historical facts, the Carmelites of the late Middle Ages stoutly defended the thesis that Elijah had actually founded an order and that his successors had lived on Mount Carmel in a line of unbroken succession throughout the Old Testament and New Testament eras. The Carmelite Constitutions of 1324 accordingly claim:

Therefore we state, in evidence of the truth, that since the time of the Prophets Elijah and Elisha who piously lived on Mount Carmel, holy fathers of the Ancient and New Testament, true lovers of the solitude of that mountain for the contemplation of heavenly things, have undoubtedly and worthily dwelt near the fountain of St. Elijah in holy penance, continuing a holy succession. Their successors, after the Incarnation of Jesus Christ, built a church there in honor of the Blessed Virgin Mary, and they took Her name for title, and were consequently called by Apostolic privileges the Brothers of the Blessed Virgin Mary of Mount Carmel.

Carmelite writers and theologians propounded this thesis with great energy and growing tenacity, and it became a critically important point for them. Elijah was called *Dux et pater Carmelitarum* —the leader and father of Carmelites. The Order celebrated a special

Mass and office (July 20) in honor of its founder, Elijah. Even some of the popes accepted this legend, and in the bull *Dominici Gregis cura* of 1604, Clement VIII wrote to the Order: "You are the disciples of St. Elijah, the founder of your institute." In 1725, Benedict XIII in a rescript written in his own hand allowed the Carmelites to erect a statue of Elijah in St. Peter's basilica bearing the inscription: "*Universus ordo Carmelitarum fundatori suo sancto Eliae prophetae erexit. MDCCXXVII.*" (The entire Order of Carmelites erected this to the Holy Prophet Elijah its founder. 1727.) This massive statue of Elijah, sword in his hand, flames licking at his side, still stands in St. Peter's under the great dome of Michelangelo a few yards from the main papal altar.

Of course the legend was disputed by historians who reviewed the evidence objectively and dispassionately, and there ensued centuries of heated and wearisome debate. In 1374, for example, a major disputation was conducted before the University of Cambridge between the Dominican John Stokes and the Carmelite John of Horneby. Stokes based his argument on historical evidence, while John of Horneby appealed to statements from papal briefs and juridical proceedings. Unfortunately, John of Horneby was declared the victor, and members of the university were summarily forbidden to question the antiquity of the Carmelite Order or the Elijahan foundation. Not all the defenders of the legend, however, were Carmelites. Other distinguished churchmen came to their defense, particularly the eminent Jesuit theologian Suarez, who wrote: "I esteem the tradition a true one . . . that the Order descends by hereditary succession from the Prophets Elijah and Elisha and other Fathers who have dwelt on the holy mount of Carmel." The argument reached its peak of intensity in 1668 with the publication of Daniel Papebroch's treatise on the Carmelites in the Bollandists' *Acta sanctorum*. Papebroch maintained that the Order was founded in 1155 when a group of Christians gathered on Mount Carmel to begin an eremitical life in imitation of Elijah. The respect which the Bollandists had gained for their historical work lent special prestige to this argument, and the proponents of the Elijahan legend sprang to a vigorous and sometimes violent defense. Papebroch's work was placed on the Spanish Index, but the Holy See, appealing to both sides for a cessation of the controversy, refused to place it on the Roman Index. Finally, in exasperation, the Holy See imposed silence on both parties in 1698, forbidding any further public discussion or debate until Rome gave a definitive decision on the matter.

To this day no decision has been handed down by the Holy See. But it is hardly necessary now, because calmer and saner heads ultimately prevailed and the Elijahan foundation of the Carmelite Order has been firmly rejected. An objective and scientific review of history clearly showed that the Order was indeed established in the middle of the twelfth century, but it also demonstrated that the original Carmelites of the twelfth century regarded Elijah as the model of their religious life, the person whose example and philosophy of life they would follow. These original Carmelites and their successors considered themselves true followers of Elijah, new sons of the prophets, faithful heirs of the prophetic vocation. In this extenuated and spiritual sense can Elijah be called the founder of the Carmelite Order.

But the obvious question asserts itself: How could this insupportable legend possibly be proposed for so long a time? For four principal reasons. First, the Middle Ages was a time of easy legend and almost no scientific history. A story merely had to be recounted a few times and it quickly passed into the area of the firmly accepted fact. Historians are still attempting to untangle the facts and legends which became so hopelessly intertwined during the Middle Ages. Thus the credulous mood of the times plus the uncritical belief in legend and hero-story contrived to perpetuate the pious tale of the Elijahan foundation.

Secondly, the Carmelites themselves were searching for a positive, actual founder for their order. If the Dominicans had their St. Dominic, the Franciscans their St. Francis, and the Benedictines their St. Benedict, then surely the Carmelite Order must have its prestigious founder, someone stamped in the noble proportions of these great saints. There was more than mere competitiveness involved in this attitude: there was an intrusion of juridical and scholastic thinking—every major religious order must have a legal and efficient cause. This again was erroneous and naïve, because Elijah was, in the language of Scholasticism, not the efficient cause of the Order, but the exemplary cause, the person upon whom the Carmelites modeled their way of life.

Thirdly, the early documentation about the first seventy-five years of the Order, from the time of the original Carmelites on Mount Carmel in the middle of the twelfth century until after the composition of the rule in the early thirteenth century, is meager and scarce. No written records were kept during those primitive years, and much of the information we do possess must be taken from fragmentary accounts and secondary sources. This paucity of documentation gave ample room for the creation of legends and fables.

Fourthly, and most important, the Elijahan tradition was essential to the inner life of the Order. The Carmelites called Elijah their father and leader not in a metaphorical sense, nor in a mood of wistful recollection that they were inhabiting the same site he had sanctified two millennia previously. Rather, they considered Elijah the archetype of the true Carmelite—Elijah the prophet, Elijah the solitary, Elijah the witness. Elijah loomed so large in their eyes that it was fairly easy for them to accept the legend that he had legally and juridically established a religious order almost a thousand years before Christ.

This fourth reason for accepting the Elijahan legend brings us to the core concept of the Carmelite story: The early Carmelites, and their successors through the centuries, committed themselves to what they called "the prophetic vocation." *The Institution of the First Monks,* a Carmelite book which was originally presented as a work composed in the fifth century A.D., but which was later discovered to be a medieval composition, bases its entire argument on the contention that all members of the Order are called to this prophetic vocation in imitation of Elijah. The book uses the terms "prophetic vocation" and "prophetic discipline" and "prophetic perfection" as a constant refrain, and despite the book's historical invalidity it has exercised an extraordinary influence in molding and forming Carmelites for six hundred years. No adequate understanding of the force that drove the Carmelites of the ages—from Simon Stock, to John of the Cross, to the two Teresas—is possible without an appreciation of the Order's enduring commitment to the prophetic vocation.

The Hebrew word for prophet is *nabi,* which means "an enthusiastic (that is, possessed by God) proclaimer of God's praises and announcer of God's revelation." The usual meaning of the word *prophet* suggests a man who foretells future events under the inspiration of God, but that function is quite accidental and secondary to his basic vocation. While occasionally some of the prophets predicted the future, and sometimes in great length and great detail, their principal role in Israel was to bear witness to the living God. This act of witness took the form of the prophet's own personal experience with God and his proclamation of God's message. It was therefore the combination of intense religious experience and fearless preaching which produced the phenomenon of the Israelite prophet.

There were occasional *nabis* in Israel as early as the time of Moses, but it was not until the time of Samuel that organized groups of prophets began to appear, men who had a precise vocation and a distinct status in the Jewish community. They lived in groups or communities, most often isolated and separated from the rest of the Jewish people, in the deserts, on mountains, in caves. One of their number was appointed leader, and he was often called "master" or "father." These "enthusiasts" gathered for ritual prayers and religious chanting, but the main characteristic of their lives was their solitary experience of God. Thus when Elijah appeared before Ahab he expressed the essence of the prophet's vocation— "As the Lord God of Israel lives, before whose face I stand." The *nabi* was a man who experienced God in an unusual and immediate way.

The prophet was easily identifiable by his garb, a leather loincloth wrapped around him and a hairy mantle draped over his shoulders, and when these bearded men came striding into town or village, usually carrying staffs in their hands, they presented a striking image. The immediacy of their relationship with God and the austerity of their life gave tremendous urgency and impact to whatever they said. The *nabis'* preaching was a mission that almost necessarily resulted from their life of union with God. They were not career preachers or teachers in the manner of the rabbis, nor did they even attempt, in the traditional language of Christian religious life, to combine the contemplative and active vocations. They only appeared occasionally in the urban community when the situation demanded it, and they came as exponents of the living Yahweh. In an age when Israel was surrounded by pagan cultures, when Canaanite philosophy was making constant assaults upon the people of God, they preached the reality of God. Yahweh lives, they said. We know Him, we serve Him, we love Him, we experience Him.

Throughout the epoch of Israelite prophetism the *nabis* preached insistently and vigorously and authoritatively about monotheism, the true worship of Yahweh, the nature of the covenant, revelation, eschatology, and messianism. Modern Biblical scholars have called them "the conscience of Israel." They appeared surprisingly and suddenly in the Jewish town or village, preached the message of Yahweh to a forgetful people, and then retired swiftly to their solitary places to be alone with their Yahweh. And they prepared the Jewish people for Christ's momentous act of prophetic witness to the reality and the power of the Father. Jesus came in the full stream of this ancient prophetic tradition, and Luke calls Him "a great prophet," while Matthew notes that "the people looked upon him as a prophet."

The prophetic vocation is personified and dramatized in the chronicle of Elijah. Carmelites of the ages have read and reread this chronicle to discover in human form, in flesh-and-blood situations, the nature of the *nabi's* vocation. Because the figure of Elijah so dominated the lives of the Carmelites, and because they attempted to imitate him so carefully, his biography is an integral part of Carmelite history. The story of Elijah is the biography primeval of the Carmelite Order.

Elijah's name in Hebrew is *eliyyah*, which means "my God is Yahweh." He came from Thisbe in Galaad, but his initial appearance in the pages of salvation history takes place, as we have noted, at his confrontation with Ahab. Subsequently in the narrative we learn that he had organized a group of *nabis*, a "school of prophets" which inhabited the caves and rock formations of Mount Carmel. Elisha, the son of Saphat from Abelmeula, became his chief lieutenant and eventual successor.

The drought that Elijah had predicted came over the land, and the Lord spoke to his prophet: "Depart from here and turn eastward, and hide yourself by the torrent of Carith, which is east of the Jordan." Accordingly he made the journey from Samaria and then across the river Jordan to the wadi, the small watering place, known as Carith. This incident, recounted in chapter 17 of I Kings, was employed in an allegorical sense by the medieval Carmelites, as we shall see, to epitomize their vocation and way of life. Carith was one of the many wadis in the area, the tiny brooks which frequently ran dry in the summer months, and today we have no way of knowing which of these wadis was the one designated as Carith in the ninth century B.C. As Elijah sat by his wadi, the Lord sent ravens to bring him bread and meat to eat twice a day, both in the morning and in the evening.

Then, after the word of the Lord had spoken to him again, he journeyed to Sidon, where he encountered the widow of Sarepta at the city gate. "Bring me a little water in a vessel that I may drink," he asked her. And when she started to get it for him, he added: "Bring me a morsel of bread in your hand."

"As the Lord your God lives," she said, "I have nothing baked, only a handful of meal in a jar and a little oil in a cruse; and now, I am gathering a couple of sticks, that I may go in and prepare it for myself and my son, that we may eat it, and die."

"Fear not," Elijah answered, "because thus says the Lord God of Israel, 'The jar of meal shall not be spent, and the cruse of oil shall not fail until the day that the Lord sends rain upon the earth.'" Elijah remained with the widow and her son, and the Scriptures tell us that there was a daily sufficiency of meal and oil for the three of them.

The widow's son became grievously ill, and when the boy ceased breathing the widow said to Elijah: "What have you against me, man of God? Have you come to me that my sins should be remembered, and that you should cause the death of my son?"

"Give me your son," he said to her, and he carried the dead child to the upper chamber where he was living. Laying the boy on his bed, he prayed aloud: "O Lord, my God, have you brought calamity even upon the widow with whom I am staying by slaying her son?" And then stretching himself over the corpse, he continued: "O Lord, my God, let the soul of this child, I beseech you, return into his body."

The child stirred, began to breathe, and returned to life again. Elijah brought him downstairs to his mother. "See, your son lives."

"Now I know that you are a man of God," she said, "and that the word of the Lord in your mouth is true."

This concludes the scriptural account of Elijah and the widow of Sarepta, that intriguing interlude in the prophet's career. The episode is important for understanding the full dimension of the prophetic vocation, particularly in light of the spectacular and sometimes unnerving events of Elijah's turbulent life. A cursory reading of the Scriptures can possibly give the false impression that Elijah was a religious fanatic, an uncompromising zealot, cold, rigid, unbending. The sojourn at Sarepta disproves that. Here we see him demonstrating those human, compassionate, responsive qualities that we later associate with Christ. He reacts immediately to the widow's hunger, he provides food for her, and he remains to guarantee continued help. In the moment of her maximum crisis, he prays with all the fervor at his disposal and restores her child to life, thus providing the first act of resurrection in recorded salvation history.

After leaving Sarepta, Elijah again presented himself to Ahab. "Is it you, you troubler of Israel?" the king asked.

"I have not troubled Israel, but you have, and your father's house, because you have forsaken the commandments of the Lord and followed the Baals. Now therefore send and gather all Israel to me at Mount Carmel, and the four hundred and fifty prophets of Baal and the four hundred prophets of the groves who eat at Jezabel's table."

Thus the stage was set for that dramatic contest between the true and false prophets. Queen Jezabel, the Phoenician, had introduced the worship of Baal, the sun god, into Israel and had imported large numbers of pagan priests whom she supported and encouraged. Pagan worship had made alarming inroads among the Jewish people, particularly since it was sponsored by the royal court. Elijah therefore decided upon a spectacular and irrefutable test of truth, and chose Mount Carmel for the contest, the mountain which in Hebrew means "garden" and which even today is called by the Arabs *Gebel Mar Elyas*, Mount St. Elijah. On the crown of the mountain he challenged the pagan priests to construct an altar of sacrifice to their god while he constructed one to Yahweh. They were to place two young bulls on the altar, prepare the wood for holocaust but not light the fire. "Put no fire to it," he said. "And you call on the name of your god and I will call on the name of the Lord and the God who answers by fire He is God."

The pagan priests placed the bull on their altar, praying aloud to Baal. They leaped around the altar, did ritual dances, bending and contorting themselves, and continued their invocations all morning. Elijah watched them calmly until at noon he indulged in some sharp irony. "Cry aloud," he said to them, "for he is a god; either he is musing, or has stepped outside, or is on a journey, or perhaps he is asleep and must be wakened." The priests of Baal intensified their prayers, and even cut themselves with swords and lances until their blood flowed on the ground. Finally in the middle of the afternoon Elijah prepared his altar. After he had laid the bull on the wood, he dug a trench around the entire altar and then poured water over it three times until the trench was filled with water.

"O Lord God of Abraham, Isaac, and Israel," he prayed, "show this day that you are God in Israel and that I have done all these things at your word. Hear me, O Lord, hear me, that this people may know that you are the Lord God and that you have turned their hearts again."

The altar broke into a roar of flames, consuming the entire holocaust and evaporating the water in the trench. The people fell to their knees, crying, "The Lord he is God, the Lord he is God." At Elijah's command the prophets of Baal were executed. The incident at Mount Carmel presents a remarkable demonstration of the prophet's faith and his trust in the power of prayer. Calmly and confidently, Elijah watched the rabid contortions of the pagan priests; and his own prayer, phrased simply and humbly, is in marked contrast to the furious incantations of the pagans. Elijah bore spectacular witness to Yahweh; but more important, he demonstrated the prophet's approach to God: faith, humility, trust. These three qualities are basic elements of the prophetic personality.

One more incident transpired that same day on Mount Carmel, an incident that has been frequently commented on by Carmelite writers. Elijah promised an end to the drought, and then went to the highest summit of the mountain and sat down with his head between his knees. He sent a servant to the edge of the mountain to look out over the sea for rain clouds, but seven times he returned without seeing any. Finally he reported to Elijah: "Behold, a little cloud like a man's head is rising out of the sea." The heavens grew black with rain clouds, the wind whipped furiously, and a torrential downpour ensued. Carmelite writers have seen a figure of the Blessed Virgin in the small cloud, in that she was the small, grace-filled cloud which preceded the torrent of God's love in the Incarnation of His Son. This is an entirely spiritual and metaphorical interpretation of the text, and it is credulous to suggest, as some Carmelites have, that Elijah actually understood the small cloud to represent a virgin who would inaugurate a rain of grace. The text says nothing for Elijah's evaluation of the cloud, but it does say a great deal for the mentality of the thirteenth-century Carmelites who, as we shall see, adopted a Marian life as an integral part of the Christian prophetic vocation.

When Ahab returned to Jezabel after his harrowing experience at

Mount Carmel he related the entire course of events to her. She was violently angry at Elijah for executing her priests, and sent a message to him: "So may the gods do to me, and more also, if I do not make your life as one of them by this time tomorrow." The Scriptures relate that Elijah became afraid and fled for his life into a desert at Bersabee. He collapsed under a juniper tree and prayed the Lord to take away his life: "It is enough. Now, O Lord, take away my life, for I am no better than my fathers." This was Elijah's nadir, the moment of his profound discouragement and fear. The prophet who had stood so serenely on Mount Carmel before Ahab and the pagan priests was now crumpled and defeated and despondent. The people of Israel were apparently not converted by the fantastic miracle on the mountain, and Jezabel was now hunting him down. St. John of the Cross later called this state of anguish "the dark night of the soul," a period of inner desolation which God sends to deeply spiritual persons for the purpose of purifying them and leading them to a fuller love and trust.

But the dark night, if patiently and trustfully endured, culminates in a new strength and nearness to God. An angel of the Lord appeared at Elijah's side, touched him, and told him to eat the loaf of bread and water which he suddenly noticed on the ground beside him. The angel commanded him to eat and drink a second time, "for you have yet a great way to go." Strengthened and sustained by the food, Elijah hiked forty days and nights until he reached Mount Horeb. There, in one of the mountain caves, the prophet entered into a dramatic dialogue with the Lord.

"What are you doing here, Elijah?" the Lord asked.

"With zeal I have been zealous for the Lord God of hosts; for the people of Israel have forsaken your covenant, thrown down your altars, and slain your prophets with the sword. And I alone am left, and they seek to take away my life." (The phrase "with zeal I have been zealous for the Lord God of hosts" was later adopted as the motto of the Carmelite Order and is emblazoned across the Order's escutcheon.)

"Go forth," the Lord said, "and stand upon the mount before the Lord."

As Elijah emerged from the cave a mighty wind began to blow, and then the mountain quivered while an earthquake tore apart the rock formations, and finally a raging fire broke out. He drew his mantle over his head until he heard the voice of the Lord again. "Go, return on your way through the desert to Damascus. And when you arrive you shall anoint Hazel to be king over Syria; and you shall anoint Jehu the son of Namsi to be king over Israel. And Elisha, the son of Saphat of Abelmeula, you shall anoint to be prophet in your place."

The Lord had commissioned the prophet to anoint two kings and to select Elisha, whom he had never met, as his successor in the school of the prophets. Interestingly, Elijah did not accomplish the anointing of Hazel and Jehu during his lifetime: Elisha anointed Hazel and he sent another one of the sons of the prophets to anoint Jehu.

Elijah encountered Elisha for the first time on the return journey from Mount Horeb. Elisha was plowing a field when Elijah approached him, threw his mantle around him, and invited him to become a follower. Elisha immediately left the oxen he was using to plow the field and began to walk away with Elijah. Then he remembered: "Let me kiss my mother and my father and then I will follow you."

"What have I done to you?" Elijah answered sympathetically. "Go, and return back."

Elisha summoned his family and they killed the oxen and had a great feast, and when the meal was concluded the new prophet said his farewells and departed with Elijah. And thus was established that close friendship between the two men whom God had called to direct the activities of the prophets of Mount Carmel.

Elijah had one final meeting with Ahab, occasioned by the king's treacherous conduct in obtaining Naboth's vineyard. Naboth, a faithful Israelite, owned an attractive vineyard and garden near Ahab's palace. The king asked him to sell it to him or accept another and superior vineyard in exchange for it, but Naboth refused, claiming that it was a family inheritance which according to Mosaic law could not be sold except in case of the most extreme necessity. Ahab was sulking in the palace over his failure to obtain the vineyard when the devious Queen Jezabel noticed his sadness. She pried the story out of him, and promised to get the garden for him. She arranged for two men to offer false testimony before the chiefs of the people that Naboth had blasphemed God and cursed the king. The testimony was accepted and Naboth was stoned to death. Elijah heard about the incident and descended from his solitude on Mount Carmel to upbraid the king and queen.

"You have killed," Elijah said to the king. "Moreover you have taken possession. Thus says the Lord: In the place where the dogs have licked the blood of Naboth, they shall also lick your blood."

"Have you made me your enemy?" the king asked.

"I have made you so because you have sold yourself to do what is evil in the sight of the Lord. Behold I will bring evil upon you. I will utterly sweep you away, and will cut off from Ahab every male, bond or free, in Israel."

And, turning to Jezabel, he added: "The dogs shall eat Jezabel within the boundaries of Jezabul."

Ahab, apparently terrified by the dire prediction, did penance for his sin by fasting and wearing sackcloth. The Lord accepted his atonement and said to Elijah: "Because he has humbled himself for my sake, I will not bring the evil in his days; but in his son's days I will bring the evil upon his house." The prediction about Jezabel, however, was fulfilled literally after Elijah's death. During Jehu's rebellion, Jezabel attempted to entice the young chieftain by adorning herself in heavy cosmetics and attractive clothing, but Jehu had her thrown from a window and then he ran his chariot over her. Afterward her corpse was devoured by dogs.

The last public act in Elijah's life was his encounter with King Ahaziah, Ahab's son and heir. During his short, two-year reign Ahaziah sponsored the idolatrous worship of the pagan gods and he himself became a devotee of Beelzebub, "the lord of the flies." After a serious accident when he fell to the ground from an upper-story window in his palace, he sent messengers to consult the pagan priests to learn whether he would recover from the accident. The word of the Lord inspired Elijah to confront the messengers en route before they reached the pagan shrine.

"Go and return to the king who sent you," Elijah announced to the startled messengers. "And say to him: Thus says the Lord: Is it because there is no God in Israel that you sent to Beelzebub, the god of Accaron? Therefore you shall not come down from the bed to which you have gone, but you shall surely die."

The messengers returned immediately to the palace without visiting the pagan shrine and reported the incident to the king. "What kind of man was he who met you and spoke these words?" Ahaziah asked.

"He wore a garment of haircloth, with a girdle of leather about his loins."

"It is Elijah the Thesbite," the king said.

Ahaziah sent a military captain with fifty soldiers to Mount Carmel for the purpose of taking Elijah into custody and bringing him to the palace. "Man of God," the captain said contemptuously to the prophet, "the king has commanded you to come down."

Elijah responded promptly to this arrogant and unjust command. "If I am a man of God, let fire come down from heaven and consume you and your fifty." A flash of flame cracked from the sky and consumed the entire patrol. The king sent another contingent of fifty men to apprehend the prophet, and again the group was destroyed by fire. The third group that climbed the mountain was led by a frightened and chastened captain who fell on his knees before Elijah, pleading: "Man of God, I pray you, spare my life and the lives of your servants who are with me." The captain's request was sincere and respectful, far different than the earlier contemptuous and pre-emptory commands, and Elijah agreed to see the king.

Standing before Ahaziah, he said: "Thus says the Lord: Because you have sent messengers to consult Beelzebub the god of Accaron, as though there were not a God in Israel, of whom you might inquire the word, therefore you shall not come down from the bed to which you have gone, but you shall surely die."

Ahaziah did die, and with that the prophet's public life comes to a close in the pages of Scripture. The intrepid defender of Yahweh finishes his career in the same way he started it—demonstrating the reality and the power of the living God. While the execution of the prophets of Baal on Mount Carmel and the slaughter of Ahaziah's troops might strike us in the Christian age as cruel and hardly religious, we must remember that these were harsh and primitive days in the world's history and that such demonstrations were the only kind the people really understood. Elijah in the context of his times was not considered cruel and intemperate by the people of that eye-for-an-eye epoch; he was, instead, hailed and revered as the magnificent champion of Yahweh.

The death scene of Elijah in the scriptural account is both poignant and dramatized: poignant, because it depicts the moving farewell to Elisha; dramatized, because the Jewish author could not write about the death of this tremendous *nabi* as he would about the death of other men, and thus he narrated it by means of an imaginary fiery chariot and fiery horses which carried Elijah aloft in a whirlwind. The entire death scene is presented as a journey beyond the river Jordan, and what the author is dramatizing is the fact that Elijah in his final illness was slipping away from his life and friends.

Elijah is pictured as journeying from Galgal. "Stay here," the prophet says to Elisha, "because the Lord has sent me as far as Bethel."

"As the Lord lives, and as you yourself, I will not leave you," Elisha answered, declaring his firm intention of remaining with his friend until the end.

The sons of the prophets tell Elisha quietly: "Do you know that today the Lord will take away your master from you?"

"Yes, I know it. Hold your peace."

The same scene is repeated again as Elijah announces a further journey to Jericho, and the same dialogue is repeated with the sons of the prophets again commenting to Elisha that the Lord will take *your* master from *you*. Elijah and Elisha then cross over the river Jordan while, as the Scriptures note, fifty sons of the prophets stand at a distance watching them.

"Ask what I can do for you before I am taken away from you," Elijah says.

"I beseech you that your double spirit may be in me."

"You have asked a hard thing. Nevertheless if you see me when I am taken from you, you shall have what you have asked. But if you do not see me, you shall not have it."

Elijah then dies, and the scriptural author describes it metaphorically: "Behold a fiery chariot and fiery horses separated the two of them, and Elijah went up by a whirlwind into heaven." Elisha cries out: "My father, my father! The chariot of Israel and its driver!" He tore his garments in sorrow, picked up the mantle of Elijah, and returned to the sons of the prophets.

"The spirit of Elijah rests on Elisha," they said as he approached.

The Carmelite tradition makes frequent allusion to the double spirit which Elisha inherited from Elijah, interpreting it as a symbol of the prophetic vocation: the spirit of solitude and the spirit of prophetic preaching. Elisha himself imbued his followers with this double spirit and his sons of the prophets were true disciples of Elijah. The exploits and adventures of Elisha and his sons of the prophets are related in 4 Kings, but it is difficult to follow the Elijahan tradition with any precision after the death of Elisha. At any rate, organized prophetism disappeared completely in Israel, as we have mentioned, after the exile in the fifth century B.C. It was not until the twelfth century of the Christian epoch that Elijahan prophetism was revived by the first Carmelites on Mount Carmel.

When the original Carmelites began to inhabit the caves and slopes of Mount Carmel they turned to the enduring image of the great *nabi* Elijah for their inspiration and ideal. Elijah the solitary hermit, who dwelt on Mount Carmel, standing before the face of the living God, talking with the Lord. Elijah the fearless preacher, proclaiming to king and commoner the truths of the Lord. Elijah the man of faith and humility and trust, whose prayer caused the altar to burst into flames during his contest with the priests of Baal. Elijah the compassionate man, who tarried in his journey to provide meal and oil for the widow of Sarepta. Elijah the faithful servant of the Lord, who was plunged into fear and despondency in the desert at Bersabee; and who was eventually comforted by an angel of the Lord. Elijah the contemporary, relevant man, involved in the pressing situations of his time. Elijah the community man, dedicated to his sons of the prophets. Elijah the true and loving friend of Elisha.

For those first Carmelites, and for their successors throughout the centuries, Elijah was truly their leader and father, and the image of his life can be seen clearly in theirs.

The Carmelite Order had its origin and early development during the period of the Latin domination of the Near East, that uneasy and never completely successful occupation which began with the Crusaders' capture of Jerusalem in 1099 and collapsed completely with the fall of Acre in 1291. Prior to the eleventh century, European Christians were able to make pilgrimages to the Holy Land, due to the more or less tolerant attitude of the Moslem Arabs, but in the eleventh century the nomadic Seljuk Turks began their conquest of Asia Minor and the situation changed radically. Migrating from their homeland of Turkestan in Central Asia, the Seljuk Turks overran Moslem Persia, became Mohammedans themselves, and extended their sway into Syria and Palestine, bringing a resurgent Islam to the very gates of eastern Europe. Although the Seljuks were only a ruling minority in the conquered territories, they fired the Moslem community with a burning animosity for Christians, and

34 JOURNEY TO CARITH

particularly for Christian pilgrims, whom they harassed and persecuted.

The situation provided the catalysis for the Crusades, the "holy
war" which unleashed and offered an excuse for a variety of forces,
most of which were not religious, and many of which were not even
Christian. Pope Urban II, a Frenchman and former Cluniac monk,
delivered one of the great demagogic speeches of history at Cler-
mont, France, in November of 1095, and the response all over Europe was immediate and enthusiastic. "God wills it" was the cry; and
the curious phenomenon of the Crusades was under way. The
avowed purpose of the Crusade movement was religious: the rescue
and veneration of the holy places inhabited by Jesus, now inaccessible and neglected. But other motives eventually seemed to overshadow the religious motive—the attempt to drive the Turks from
the edge of Europe and prevent any threat of future invasion; the
grasping desire of extending feudalism into the Near East and
thereby acquiring more territory; the hope of opening new economic
markets and establishing trade relations with the Moslem people.

Two abortive and ill-prepared bands of Crusaders were hastily
organized—one by the fanatical preacher Peter the Hermit, and the
other by Walter the Penniless—but they were quickly decimated by
Turks in Asia Minor. But then a large and well-equipped force of
soldiers was mounted and a determined military invasion began. The
original Crusaders were mostly French, and consequently the Crusaders became known as "Franks." They marched to Constantinople,
crossed through Syria, then captured Edessa, and in July of 1099
they took Jerusalem after a six-week siege.

The victorious Crusaders established a Latin kingdom in the Near
East, divided into the four states of Edessa, Antioch, Tripoli, and
Jerusalem. The kingdom of Jerusalem included the holy towns of
Jerusalem, Bethlehem, and Nazareth; the important ports of Tyre
and Acre; and the territory of Mount Carmel. Godfrey of Bouillon
was the first ruler of the kingdom, and in 1100 he was succeeded by
his brother Baldwin I. The kingdom was quickly organized in the
typical Western feudal fashion of fiefs and baronies, and the Moslems became subservient to their Western lords. At the outset it
seemed as if the arrangement might work. Baldwin ruled the kingdom carefully and attempted to maintain the peace. Trade routes
were immediately opened with Europe, and the kingdom enjoyed

a sudden prosperity. Europeans poured into the Holy Land: Italian merchants and traders who settled along the coast; pilgrims who visited the Christian shrines; settlers from England and France and the Holy Roman Empire; ecclesiastics who established a Latin hierarchy; monks and religious who founded monasteries and religious houses.

But the Turks never really accepted the arrangement, and beneath the façade of an efficiently operated colonial state there smoldered seething discontent and a determined resolution to drive out the invader. In 1144 the Turks revolted and captured Edessa, and new Crusaders, inspired by the preaching of St. Bernard of Clairvaux, marched into Asia Minor, but they were roundly defeated. An armed truce prevailed until the rise of Saladin, Sultan of Egypt, who was able to organize Moslems all over the Near East for a major uprising. He defeated a Christian army in a decisive battle at Hattin near the Lake of Tiberias in 1187, and Moslems swept all over the Latin kingdom. In succeeding months the major cities of Palestine fell: Acre, Sidon, Nazareth, and finally Jerusalem.

The famous Third Crusade was convoked in 1189 under the direction of kings Richard I of England and Philip Augustus of France. They recaptured Acre and the coastal regions, but were unable to take Jerusalem. A new epoch in the Latin domination of Palestine followed: the Christians occupied Acre and the coastal regions, now called the Kingdom of Acre, while the Moslems occupied and controlled the inland regions. This condition lasted for a century, but the final outcome was never in doubt. The Christians hung tenuously to their coastal territories, while the Turks maintained an almost continual series of raids and skirmishes. Occasional expeditions set out from Europe to recapture lost territory and subdue the Turks, such as the Crusade of St. Louis IX and the tragic Children's Crusade, but Christian Europe had lost its interest in crusading. The Moslem leader Bibars finally eradicated the Latin kingdom with his fierce Egyptian soldiers, the Mamelukes. In 1291, he took Acre, the last Christian stronghold in Palestine, and the era of the Crusades was over.

That was the milieu in which the Carmelite Order had its origin.

The original Carmelites began to live on Mount Carmel in the middle of the twelfth century, probably in the year 1155. They were former crusaders and nobles and pilgrims, both clerics and laymen, who came to Palestine with the inauguration of the Latin kingdom. A great number of religious communities and monasteries had sprung up in Palestine during those first prosperous days of the Latin kingdom, but the men who settled on Mount Carmel declined to enter those established organizations because they had a precise and distinct vision: they wanted to revive the Elijahan prophetic vocation in a Christian context.

James of Vitry, the bishop of Acre who wrote his *Historia Orientalis* in the early thirteenth century, describes the situation in Palestine after the first Crusades:

From that time the Eastern Church started to flower and flourish, the Faith to spread in the East, and the Lord's vine to produce new fruit. . . . From the different regions of the world, from every tribe, tongue and every nation under the sky, devout pilgrims and men of faith flocked to the Holy Land, attracted by the atmosphere of the holy and venerable places. Old churches were repaired and new ones built. Due to the generosity of the princes and the alms of the faithful, religious monasteries were constructed in suitable places; everywhere ministers for the churches and the other things pertaining to the divine cult and worship were provided for adequately and completely. . . . Others, after the example and in imitation of the holy solitary, the prophet Elijah, led a life of solitude in the hives of their tiny cells on Mount Carmel like bees of the Lord gathering spiritual honey; and especially in that section which overlooks the city of Porphiry, today known as Caiffa, near the fountain which is called the fountain of Elijah, and which is not far from the monastery of the virgin St. Margaret.

An earlier and more detailed account of the first Carmelites is given by John Phocas, a Greek monk from the island of Patmos, who wrote his *De locis sanctis* after a pilgrimage to the Holy Land in 1185:

At the extreme point [of Mount Carmel] which faces the sea we find the cave of the prophet Elijah. Here after an angelic life, this man was miraculously taken up into heaven. In olden days there was a large building for many men, as the ruins still testify. . . . But some years ago a white-haired monk, who was also a priest and a Calabrian, was called to the mountain by means of a revelation from the prophet Elijah; and he has constructed a little wall around the ruins and built a tower and a modest little church, and gathered about ten companions to live with him. He is still living there today.

Another chronicle, by a Spanish Jew, Benjamin of Tudela, who visited the Holy Land in 1163, adds the note that the chapel of which Phocas writes was dedicated to Saint Elijah.

From these fragmentary reports, and other similar sources, we can construct at least a dim outline of those early Carmelite days. First, the white-haired Calabrian monk. This is the man we know as St. Berthold, the first prior (superior) of Mount Carmel. The name Berthold is arbitrary, since Phocas does not name him, nor does any other contemporary source, and the name is first attributed to him, as far as we can determine, in the fourteenth century. He was a Calabrian, a literary euphemism for "Western," and tradition claims that he was a Frenchman from Malifaye in West-Central France. He was a nephew of Aymeric of Malifaye, the Latin patriarch of Antioch, a man to whom the Carmelite writers of the fourteenth century paid much attention. Aymeric was a controversial figure in Antioch, and after an altercation with Reynald, the ruler of Antioch, he was thrown into prison. At the intercession of Baldwin, king of Jerusalem, he was released and given refuge in Jerusalem. The patriarch resided in exile at Jerusalem from 1153 to 1159, and during that time visited Mount Carmel and helped his nephew organize the primitive Carmelite community. The date of Aymeric's residence in Palestine helps us to establish the date of the foundation of the Carmelite Order. The fourteenth-century Carmelites tended to overemphasize Aymeric's role in establishing the Carmelite community, and some have even considered him the first legislator. However, Aymeric's assistance was in the nature of advice, encouragement, and perhaps even financial support. When he was able to return to his See it is reported that he took a few Carmelites with him and founded two small communities in the neighborhood of Antioch.

The Phocas account is the only source which cites a revelation from the prophet Elijah, and we have no more information about it. Unfortunately, it must remain one of those obscurities of history. At any rate, Berthold did gather a small group of ten companions on Mount Carmel, and he did proceed to revive the Elijahan prophetic vocation. The most curious facet in the story of the man we now call St. Berthold is that nowhere in any of the early chronicles of the Order is a name attributed to him. Even the document which connects him with Aymeric merely calls him "a nephew in the Order of Carmelites, a holy and famous man." There is such an impenetrable anonymity about the man that it suggests an intriguing possibility. None of the early chroniclers or Carmelite writers ever call him the founder of the Order, despite the fact that he was the first prior of Mount Carmel. That title is reserved for Elijah alone. Perhaps there was a tacit conspiracy among the chroniclers to keep him anonymous lest he ever be revered as the founder of the Order. For those early Carmelites, Elijah was the inspiration and the dominating influence on their lives. And Berthold was merely the man who, at Elijah's command, had organized the monks on Mount Carmel. Even the date of Berthold's death is uncertain. It has been placed as early as 1187 and at late as 1198. Only in the sixteenth century do we find Berthold venerated as a saint, and his liturgical cult in the Carmelite Order started in 1525.

We know nothing about the identity of the ten or so original Carmelites beyond the fact that they were Europeans who had come to Palestine in the wake of the Crusades. They were a mixture of priests and laymen, and there is good probability that the majority were laymen. They lived in the mountain caves near the chapel which Berthold constructed, and as their number increased they built huts and small hermitages for the individual monks. The actual location of the chapel was near the cave of Elijah, the modern *el-chadr*, a traditional pilgrimage spot where Elijah purportedly lived in his solitude on the mountain. This site is on the extreme northern section of the mountain on a slope which veers down toward the sea. James of Vitry's account mentions the presence of another monastery on the mountain, the monastery of St. Margaret. This was a Greek monastery, probably a Benedictine one, situated at a higher spot on the mountain precisely on the site of the present-day Carmelite monastery. The Greek institution soon disappeared from history, but historians must keep it carefully in focus so that they can distinguish whether twelfth-century references pertain to it or to the Carmelite community.

Carmelite life on Mount Carmel for the first fifty years of the Order's existence presents a picture of a loosely knit, formless organization. The monks lived scattered over the hill in the region of *el-chadr*, and assembled only for the celebration of Mass in the small chapel. The liturgical rite they followed was the rite of the province of Jerusalem, the so-called rite of the Holy Sepulcher which Godfrey of Bouillon sponsored throughout the kingdom of Jerusalem. This was the rite employed by the canons in the metropolitan church of the Holy Sepulcher, and it belonged to the Gallican family of the

Roman rite which had in all probability come from Île-de-France. The Carmelites initially recited the Divine Office privately, and only in the time of St. Berthold's successor, St. Brocard, did they begin to assemble for the public chanting of the office.

The Carmelites, however, did leave their mountain retreat occasionally, to be of Christian service to the people of Palestine. They preached; and they performed works of charitable assistance. The documents of the thirteenth century give ample testimony of this. *The Institution of the First Monks* recalls the preaching and charitable works of Elijah and Elisha, and then states that such activity was a proper and integral part of the prophetic vocation. Even *The Fiery Arrow*, the vigorous defense of the contemplative life by Nicholas the Frenchman, admits that the original Carmelites descended from their mountain to be "of service to their neighbor." Those who were priests preached the truths of God in the Elijahan tradition, and those who were not priests performed charitable works in the spirit of Elijah's ministrations to the widow of Sarepta. This activity was, of course, subordinated to and inspired by their life of solitude on the mountain. They were, in the prophetic tradition, witnesses; and their role of witness was accomplished by manifesting the face of God in their own person.

Some commentators on the Carmelite Order have misinterpreted the eremitical life of the original Carmelites and therefore concluded that there was a radical change of spirit in the Order when it migrated to Europe. The confusion centers around the use of the word "hermit." True, the Carmelites were hermits, but not in the restricted, legal, Western use of the word. They were hermits in the Eastern and prophetic sense of the word, and as such were able to coordinate their apostolic enterprises with a life of solitude in a cave or hermitage separated from their brethren. The Elijahan tradition demanded that the hermit, under the inspiration of the Spirit and at the direction of the prior, leave his solitary retreat for the precise apostolic business at hand. It was a freer, more inspired type of eremitism than the hermit's life in other traditions.

After Berthold's death sometime in the last quarter of the twelfth century, he was succeeded in the office of prior by Brocard, a native of Jerusalem who was born of one of the European families which had settled there. Although there is not much factual documentation about his life, we do know that he came onto the scene of Carmelite history at a decisive moment and accomplished some vitally important things.

The Carmelite community of hermits in their separate cells had grown in numbers over the years, and Brocard had to provide a larger chapel. Accordingly, he moved the center of the community from the cave of Elijah to the fountain of Elijah, the present *wadi 'ain es-sich*, a site in a chasm of the mountain some miles south of *el-chadr*. The fountain was supposedly a watering spot which Elijah used when he lived on the mountain, and beginning with the time of Brocard it became the focal point of the Carmelite Order. The rule of Carmel is, in fact, addressed to Brocard and to "the other brother hermits who live with him near the fountain of Mount Carmel."

The most significant element about the development at *wadi 'ain es-sich* was the fact that the chapel constructed around the turn of the century was dedicated to Our Lady. There are frequent and authoritative citations in the contemporary documents about this "small church of Our Lady." This is the first public act of demonstration of the important Marian character of the Order, a tradition which manifested itself more clearly throughout the thirteenth century. The recent excavations undertaken by the Carmelite Order on Mount Carmel in 1959 unearthed the remains of this small rectangular church, as well as some of the original caves of the hermits.

Brocard was also responsible for the spread of the Order throughout the Holy Land. Hermits were sent from Mount Carmel to establish other Carmelite communities, which were arranged according to the general pattern of life on Mount Carmel—a group of individual and separated hermitages situated around a small chapel. It is difficult to determine precisely how many of these initial daughter foundations existed because the early twelfth century was a turbulent time in the Near East. The Turks were restive and their marauding parties were constantly attacking the Christian communities. Some of the early Carmelite daughter communities were short-lived; others were destroyed almost as soon as they were built. In a number of instances the Carmelites were murdered.

Some commentators claim that there were as many as fifteen of these foundations, and others contend that there were almost a thousand Carmelite hermits in the Near East by the time of Brocard's death. There is no way of proving these assertions. It does seem fairly certain that by the first half of the thirteenth century there were foundations in Acre, Tyre, Sarepta, Tripoli, in the Lebanese city of Beaulieu, and perhaps even in Jerusalem. All of these foundations were successively destroyed by the Turks, and no trace of them remains. What is important about the foundations, however, is that they represent a vital dimension of the early Carmelites' mentality: namely, that they intended to propagate the Elijahan prophetic vocation, make additional foundations, and not restrict it to the single site on Mount Carmel.

Brocard's major accomplishment was the promulgation of a written rule for the Carmelites. Until his time the hermits on Mount Carmel followed an oral tradition based principally on their understanding of the Elijahan prophetic vocation. But with the increase of numbers and the development of daughter houses it became apparent that some kind of precise written legislation was necessary for the growing Order.

The Carmelite rule of 1209 was not written by a Carmelite, at least not in its final form. It was presented to the Order by the Latin patriarch of Jerusalem, Albert of Avogadro, at the request of Brocard. Albert was an Italian, born in the diocese of Parma sometime in the middle of the twelfth century. He entered the Augustinian monastery of the Holy Cross at Mortara as a young man, made his religious profession in the canons regular of St. Augustine, and was eventually elected prior of the monastery in the year 1180. Four years later he was made bishop of the diocese of Bobbio, and one year after that he was transferred to the diocese of Vercelli, which he governed for twenty years. He had a wide reputation as a man of holiness and prudence, and in 1205 Pope Innocent III appointed him the Latin patriarch of Jerusalem and papal legate. Albert arrived in the Holy Land the following year, but with the permission of the pope he established his residence at Acre because Jerusalem was occupied by hostile Moslems. He died tragically in 1214 during a religious procession when he was stabbed to death by the former Master of the Hospital of the Holy Spirit whom he had deposed from office because of public immorality. He is venerated as a saint in the Carmelite Order with a liturgical feast on September 25, but in one of those ironies of history he is not venerated as a saint in the Augustinian Order of which he was a member.

Albert of Avogadro was the papal legate in Palestine; thus when

Brocard approached him for a rule he was seeking what was considered at the time the highest kind of ecclesiastical approbation. The rule, therefore, was considered to be definitively approved and only sent to Rome some fifteen years later when doubts were voiced about the Carmelites' status as a result of the Lateran Council. In addition to Albert's ecclesiastical position, he was a man who was admirably equipped to evaluate proper legislation for the Carmelites: he had long experience in ecclesiastical administration, he himself was a member of a religious order, and he was a saintly man. Furthermore, he lived at Acre, some fifteen miles away from Mount Carmel across the Bay of Caiffa, and was undoubtedly in close contact with the hermits.

Some historians of the Order claim that Brocard himself wrote the rule in collaboration with his hermits, and then presented it to Albert for approbation and formulation into a final draft. This procedure has been frequently employed in ecclesiastical affairs— as, for example, when documents are presented to popes for approbation and are then issued as papal documents over the papal signature—and it is not inconceivable that this is exactly what happened in the case of the Carmelite rule. At the very least, it seems reasonable to assume that Albert was in close consultation with Brocard, that he studied the actual mode of life of the hermits on Mount Carmel, and that he followed Brocard's suggestions as to precise legislation. In fact, Albert writes in the third sentence of the text that he is presenting a rule of life to Brocard "according to your proposal" (*juxta propositum vestrum*).

The Carmelite rule begins with Albert's salutation:

Albert, by God's grace called to be the Patriarch of the church of Jerusalem, bids health in the Lord and the blessing of the Holy Spirit to his beloved sons in Christ, Brocard and the other hermit brothers who live under his obedience near the fountain on Mount Carmel.

And it continues for about two thousand words which succinctly lay the outline for the Carmelites' life. The essence of all religious life is stated at the outset: "Each one . . . ought to live in dedication to Jesus Christ, and faithfully serve Him with a pure heart and a good conscience." A prior was to be elected to whom the hermits would promise obedience. They were to remain in separate cells, meditating day and night on the law of the Lord, unless "they are engaged in some other just occupations." The Divine Office was to be recited, except by those who were unable to read, and in that case an office composed of Pater Nosters was outlined for them. An oratory was to be constructed where they would assemble for daily Mass and for Sunday meetings at which they would discuss the business of the Order and whatever disciplinary matters might be necessary. They would have no personal property, and they were to abstain completely from meat, except in the case of illness, and they would fast each year from September 14 to Easter. They were to avoid idleness, keeping themselves always occupied. An absolute silence was to be maintained from late afternoon until nine o'clock the following morning; and a less strict silence was to be observed during the day. The prior was exhorted to practice humility, and the hermits were encouraged to reverence their prior as the representative of Christ.

The rule is brief, unlegalistic, and scripturally oriented. Despite its brevity there are thirty-seven citations from the pages of Scripture, either in the form of direct quotations or Biblical allusions. The rule is deeply impregnated with the flavor of Easter monasticism, and as such it represented a radical departure from the complex, juridical rules that were flourishing in the West. The influence of the rules of Basil and Cassian can be discerned in the insistence on continual prayer, asceticism, silence, and simplicity of life. It has been called a "Rule of Mysticism."

There are three principal factors which framed the composition of the Carmelite rule and made it unique: the historical moment in which it was written, the place where it was written, and the tradition it sought to codify. The high Middle Ages was a period of renewal of interest in religious life, a time when recruits were flocking to the established orders, when new religious orders were being founded. It was also a period of reaction against many of the established traditions of Western monasticism. During the Dark Ages the great monasteries had been the conservatories of Western culture as well as of Christian religion, but they had also become landed estates with vast territorial holdings and huge abbey churches. Serfs worked the monastery properties and supplied revenue for the lord abbot. The monks chanted the Divine Office ornately in the abbey church, and then spent the remainder of their time either in the scriptorium or the refectory or in their private studies. It was not decadence, but it was decidedly a comfortable way of life. The reaction movement of the Middle Ages sought to return to a more austere form of monastic life with greater emphasis on poverty, manual labor, asceticism, and apostolic work, and the Carmelite rule reflects these aspirations of the historical moment. The hermits are to live in poor huts and hermitages. They must fast long months. They must keep themselves busy with manual work. They must recapture the simplicity of the evangelical life. In this sense, the Carmelite rule is a rule of renewal, a return to the unfettered spirituality of the Gospels.

The rule furthermore reflects the more contemplative, more mystical traditions of Eastern monasticism. With the establishment of the Latin kingdom the world of western Europe came into close contact with the thinking of the East from which it had been blocked for centuries. Westerners became acquainted with the culture, the philosophy, the science, and even the religious values of the East. The monasteries of Europe had become feudal manors where a man tranquilly and comfortably served the interests of the Christian religion. But the monasteries of the desert tradition were sanctuaries where a man could experientially meet the living God. This is the pervading spirit of the Carmelite Order.

Finally, the rule is an articulation of the prophetic tradition, placing on paper the pattern of Elijah's life as the hermits on Mount Carmel understood it. Carmelites of all ages have always regarded one sentence of the text as the heart of the rule: "Let them remain alone in their own cells, or near them, meditating day and night on the law of the Lord and watching in prayer, unless they are engaged in some other just occupations." This statement embodies the core of the prophetic vocation: the unremitting life of solitude with God, and a provision whereby the prophet can break his solitude for the inspirational work of the moment. The rule does not specify the precise kind of apostolic work for which the hermit could leave his solitude, except to stipulate that all things must be done at the prior's direction. This is in the finest tradition of the *nabi*'s vocation—when the word of the Lord comes to the *nabi* he must follow its direction, and that cannot be preordained or foreseen by precise legislation.

The Carmelite rule, notwithstanding its brevity, must certainly be regarded as one of the great rules of the Church and as one of the important documents of Christianity. It has molded saints and apostles for almost eight hundred years, producing religious figures of an astonishing variety who are nevertheless stamped in the unmistakable image of the original *nabis* on Mount Carmel. Carmelites of every age and nationality have based their mode of life upon it, turning to it for inspiration and direction. And whenever they have strayed from this simple piece of legislation they have stumbled and become confused. It was to this rule of St. Albert that St. Teresa instinctively returned after the Order had weakened its spirit and intent by fifteenth-century additions to the text.

Constitutions and additional regulations have been drafted by the Carmelites over the centuries to amplify the spirit of the original rule and direct its broad prescriptions to changing situations. The first constitutions were drawn up probably in 1247, and there have been numerous new versions down the ages. Some of the constitutions have been excellent documents, well written and practical, while others have been poorly conceived, prolix, and highly legalistic. The genius of the Carmelite rule is in its simplicity, its unerring instinct for the essence of the *nabi's* life, and whenever complex legislation has been added to it, drowning it in a sea of Roman law, the impact of the rule has been diminished and weakened.

The initial crisis over the rule developed after the Fourth Lateran Council at Rome in 1215. The Council had firmly decreed that no new religious orders could be founded, and that if any new institutes were established they had to adopt one of the religious rules approved before that date. This was the age of the proliferation of new orders, the Dominicans and Franciscans among them, and there was a justified fear that an unending succession of new rules and orders would appear unless a halt were called. The Carmelites were at first unconcerned about the decree since they felt that the authorization of the patriarch of Jerusalem in 1209 constituted sufficient approval, but soon questions were raised by a number of prelates in the Holy Land about the Carmelites' status. No official document had been granted by Rome prior to 1214, they argued, and according to the explicit decree *Ne nimium religionum diversitas* of the Lateran Council the Carmelites had no juridical right to exist in the Church. St. Albert was no longer alive to defend the Carmelites; thus Brocard appealed directly to the pope for protection. Accordingly, Pope Honorius III responded with his bull *Ut vivendi normam* on January 30, 1226, which settled the issue in these curious words:

Honorius, Bishop, Servant of the Servants of God—to his beloved sons, the prior and the brother hermits of Mount Carmel, health and

the apostolic blessing. We enjoin you and your successors, for the re-
mission of your sins, to observe in the future, as faithfully as you can
with the help of God, the rule which was given to you by the Patriarch
of Jerusalem of happy memory, and which, as you have humbly contended, you received before the General Council.

The rule was confirmed again in 1229 in the bull *Ex officii nostri*
of Pope Gregory IX, who included in the document a stipulation
that the hermits should not only observe individual poverty but also
collective poverty. The hermits should not possess, the bull commanded, any revenue-producing properties nor possessions from
which they might receive a regular income; they could only own
"some mules and other domestic animals, and poultry for food."
This papal directive was inspired by the reaction movement of the
times against the manorial establishments of the old monasteries
which derived their income from their vast property holdings. All
of the orders founded in the thirteenth century received similar instructions from the Holy See.

The construction of the chapel on Mount Carmel consecrated to
Our Lady gave articulation and physical presence to a Carmelite
tradition that was as fundamental and as important as the Elijahan
heritage. The Carmelites were reviving the prophetic vocation in a
Christian context—and for the Carmelites the structure of that
Christian context embraced a deep dedication and devotion to the
Blessed Virgin. Elijah and Mary are together the inspiration for
Carmel. In the words of the fifteenth-century Belgian Carmelite,
Arnold Bostius, Elijah is the father of Carmel and Mary is its mother.

The reason for the early Carmelites' deep and instinctive devotion
for the Blessed Virgin lay in their contention that Mary's life was the
perfect Christian expression of the prophetic vocation and that
through her they could Christianize the ancient *nabi*'s role in their
medieval environment. There were three principal elements in the
Carmelites' relationship to the Blessed Virgin: (1) She was the
model of the prophet's life, and they must conform to the ideal she
presented; (2) they belonged to her by a unique dedication and
title; (3) she had consequently pledged herself to watch and protect
her Carmelites in a close and special way. We can trace the historical
aspects of that relationship through the thirteenth century, but we
find the best written expression and explanation of it in the Carmelite writers of the following century.

In the earliest historical documentation we discover that the Carmelites were originally addressed as "the hermit brothers of Mount Carmel." But by the year 1227 they were called "the hermit brothers of St. Mary of Mount Carmel." In 1253 Innocent IV addressed them in his bull *Sacrosanctae Romanae ecclesiae* as "the hermit brothers of the Blessed Virgin Mary of Mount Carmel," and that title was used exclusively in official documents from that time forward. In fact, Pope Urban VI granted an unusually substantial indulgence in 1379 to whomever would call the Carmelites by this title, and the indulgence was ratified two centuries later by Gregory XIII.

In the earliest extant profession ceremony of vows, that of 1281, we find the Carmelite promising his vows to "God and the Blessed Virgin Mary of Mount Carmel." This profession ceremony had a particular significance for the medieval mind, schooled as it was in the tradition of feudalism: it was an act of vassalage in which the man placed himself completely at the service and under the protection of his liege lord and master. The words of the Carmelite profession ceremony are, therefore, more than mere formula or pietism; they express a pledge of unusual commitment to God and the Blessed Virgin. When the Carmelite recited his vows he felt he was making the same pledge of loyalty and donation to the Blessed Virgin as the contemporary vassal made to his king or lord, and consequently he emerged from the ceremony with the conviction that he belonged to the Blessed Virgin and had a unique claim to her protection.

The acts of the Carmelite chapter (the name used by religious communities for the assembly at which they elect their superiors) at Montpellier in 1287 contain the statement: "Let us implore the suffrage of the Virgin Mary, Mother of Jesus, for whose service and honor our Order of Mount Carmel was founded." And Pope Clement V continues the same theme in a bull of 1311 when he writes of the Carmelite Order, which was "divinely instituted in honor of the glorious and Blessed Virgin Mary."

It remained, however, to the three outstanding Carmelite Marian writers of the fourteenth century to explain the inner dimensions of this commitment—the celebrated *Doctor Resolutus* of the University of Paris, John Baconthorpe, an Englishman who was both scholar and religious administrator; the German, John of Hildesheim; and the Frenchman, John of Cimentho. These Carmelites explained the three aspects of the thirteenth-century Marian life and thus established the pattern for the centuries to come.

1. Mary the Model. Baconthorpe adopts a fundamental theme from *The Institution of the First Monks* when he describes Mary as the Carmelites' *sister*. This unusual and somewhat startling appellation is developed from the premise that Mary is the exemplification of Elijah's life, and the Carmelites are accordingly joined to her in a brother-sister enterprise by reason of their commitment to the prophetic vocation. *The Institution of the First Monks* employs the word "conformity" to express the similarity between Mary's life and theirs. In his *Analogical Exposition of the Carmelite Rule*, Baconthorpe analyzes the rule point by point, contending that the Carmelite legislation closely resembles the life of the Blessed Virgin as it appears in the pages of Scripture. He emphasizes her virginity, her obedience, her poverty, and above all, her spirit of silence and solitude and recollection. "We are called the Brothers of the Order of the Blessed Virgin Mary," he concludes, "because we have chosen a Rule which closely resembles the life which she lived." John of Hildesheim and John of Cimentho amplified the same idea in their writings.

We also find the frequent use of the term "mother of Carmel" in the fourteenth century (John of Cimentho writes: "Brethren, you are . . . honored with the title of the Virgin Mary, the source of mercy, our mother"), but this is something independent of the sister relationship. Mary is the mother of all Christians, and since the Carmelites have vowed themselves especially to her she must be their mother in a very significant way, but this does not diminish the unique relationship they possess by their commitment to the prophetic vocation. John of Hildesheim expresses it simply: "Mary is their sister by religious profession, their mother through devotion."

2. Mary the Owner. The fourteenth-century writers lay heavy stress on the official title "the brothers of the Blessed Virgin Mary of Mount Carmel" to demonstrate Mary's ownership of the Order. Medieval feudalism placed utmost importance on a title or designation—if the Carmelites were called brothers of the Blessed Virgin, then they surely belonged to her in a legal and contractual way. Baconthorpe expands this concept by calling Carmel the Blessed Virgin's *fief*, the community she legally owned. John of Hildesheim

writes that the Carmelites belong to Mary by reason of their profession of vows, and he claims that if they did not in actuality belong to Mary their vows would be invalid.

3. Mary the Protector. Consequent upon Mary's ownership of the Order is her obligation to take care of it. If the Order belongs to her, the writers of the fourteenth century said, then she must protect it and the individual members in it. The Carmelites, therefore, have a particular claim and right to her continuing assistance. John of Cimentho calls it Mary's "governorship" of the Order. The writers of the fourteenth century based their contention of Mary's protection on the fact of legal ownership, without adverting significantly to the scapular revelation. But the fifteenth-century writers, notably Bostius, use the scapular as both a title to Mary's protection and a proof of her concern for the Order.

Into this pure stream of Marian devotion the medieval Carmelites unfortunately inserted a number of legends and fables. They adopted the legend of Elijah's actual foundation of the Order and its continuance through the ages of the Old Testament, and the fable that Mary visited these first-century Carmelites on Mount Carmel. They recounted the story of a dream that Pope Honorius III had in 1226 during which the Blessed Virgin appeared to him, urging him to grant his bull certifying that the Order had been duly founded before the Lateran Council. (This story bears remarkable resemblance to one recounted by the medieval Franciscans about a dream which Honorius had encouraging him to support the Franciscans.) But the legend most frequently employed was the interpretation of the episode when Elijah saw the small cloud on Mount Carmel after his victory over the prophets of Baal. In their attempt to unite the Elijahan and Marian elements in the Carmelite tradition the medieval Carmelites unhesitatingly claimed that Elijah immediately recognized the cloud as a prefigure of the Blessed Virgin. These idyllic stories found their way into the liturgy for the feast of Our Lady of Mount Carmel, which was composed in the middle of the fourteenth century. Even Pope Pius X in his encyclical *Ad diem illum* perpetuates the fable about the cloud on Mount Carmel when he writes: "Mary is the object of Elijah's thought as he watches the cloud rising from the sea."

Despite the medieval legends, a profound and authentic Marian tradition emerges from the Carmelite history of the twelfth and thirteenth centuries: the Blessed Virgin was for the Carmelites their model, their owner, and their protector. The resulting relationship between Carmel and the Blessed Virgin throughout the centuries has been both important and intimate. However, Carmel's devotion to Mary, rooted as it is in the deepest historical tradition of the Order, has always been characterized by its simplicity, its lack of ostentation, its profound interior quality; and it has consisted fundamentally in a life of inner dependence on Mary, worked out in prayer and solitude, in close association and union with the woman whom those medieval Carmelites called their sister and mother.

Elijah and Mary, therefore, occupy equally prominent positions in the original Carmelite tradition. The sixteenth-century Dutch Carmelite, John Paleonydor, accordingly described the Order in a succinct phrase as "the Marian and Elijahan Carmelite Order."

New foundations, as we have noted, were being established in Palestine in the early thirteenth century. Brocard, in his position of prior of Mount Carmel, served as the superior general of all the daughter foundations, and the prior of Mount Carmel soon became known as the prior general. This tradition of the primacy of the prior of Mount Carmel has endured in the Order, and even today the superior general of the Discalced Carmelites who resides in Rome is automatically the prior of the monastery on Mount Carmel in Palestine.

A large part of the membership of the Order during the first half of the thirteenth century was composed of men who were not priests. These former crusaders and pilgrims led the same life as their priest brothers, except of course that their contacts with people were in the nonsacramental realm. The priests and the nonclerical members had equal voice in the administration of the community, both enjoying the right to vote in the election of the prior. In fact, the nonclerics could themselves be elected to office, a condition that existed until the chapter at Trèves in 1291 when the Order adopted the European custom of restricting the right of voting and holding office to the priest members of the community. For this reason, the Carmelite Order was not, in the terminology of Church law, a clerical order until 1291.

The original Carmelites attempted in their mode of dress to approximate the costume worn by Elijah and the ninth-century *nabis*.

They wore a long black tunic reaching to the ground, girded by a leather belt at the waist. Over this they wore a cloak in imitation of Elijah's mantle. From the European tradition of religious dress they added a cowl, a cloth headpiece which was hung over the shoulders and could be pulled up over the head; and attached to the cowl they appended a scapular, two panels of cloth which hung down to the knees in front and back. The scapular was a practical garment in the history of monasticism, serving as a kind of apron to protect the monks' habits while they worked, but it was to become, as we shall see, a garment of deep religious significance in the Carmelite tradition. The habit was originally made of local Palestinian material, undoubtedly sheepskin, but when the Order migrated to Europe wool was substituted as the accepted material.

The color of the habit went through a series of fluctuations for the next three hundred years, alternating between black and brown. The Constitutions of 1324 decreed that the habit was to be brown, but the Constitutions of 1394 stipulated black again. In the early sixteenth century brown was worn in Italy, and by the middle of the sixteenth century brown became the universal and definitive color of the habit all over the Order. The mantle presents an even more picturesque history. The original mantle was composed of seven wide vertical stripes, four white and three black. The image these religious presented in their long striped mantles was so bizarre when they appeared in the West that the Europeans, in their medieval penchant for Latin sobriquets, called the Carmelites *fratres barrati* (the barred brothers) or *fratres virgulati* (the striped brothers). The unusual costume worn by the Carmelites was one of the contributing factors to their lack of acceptance in Europe, and thus in the chapter at Montpellier in 1287 the color of the mantle was changed to a solid white wool. Some of the medieval chroniclers of the Order claim that the reason for the striped cloak was to commemorate the marks produced by the flames of the fiery chariot when Elijah threw his mantle on Elisha, but this is a pietistic viewpoint. The true significance of the stripes was that it constituted the typical mode of dress in the East, and as such was merely the custom of the country. During the sixteenth century a number of Carmelites carried staffs in their hands, in imitation of the staffs carried by the ancient *nabis*, but the practice was soon abandoned.

Detailed information about St. Brocard's life is unavailable, as our earliest biographies of him derive from the fourteenth century and they are far from reliable. These chronicles indicate that Brocard had a distinguished reputation in the Palestine of his day and was very much involved in contemporary ecclesiastical affairs. He died at Mount Carmel about the year 1231, purportedly at eighty-one years of age. A liturgical feast in his honor originated in the fifteenth century, and in the sixteenth century it was made mandatory for the entire Order. According to the traditional biographies, his last words to his brethren as he lay dying were: "Model your life on the pattern of Mary and Elijah."

Brocard's immediate successors in the priorship of Mount Carmel during those primitive Carmelite days of the first half of the thirteenth century come down to us in history as little more than mere names. Cyril. Berthold II. Alan. According to the traditional account Cyril was originally from Constantinople, Berthold II from the Lombard region of Italy, and Alan from Brittany in France. They governed the Order on Mount Carmel in the turbulent years in Palestine leading up to the election of St. Simon Stock as general of the Order in 1247. According to the tenets of the rule, they were duly elected to the priorship, and as was the custom of the age, they held that office until their deaths.

Life for the Carmelites in Palestine was becoming increasingly difficult because of almost constant Moslem uprisings, but, as we shall see in the following chapter, the Order had been largely relocated in Europe by the time of St. Simon's election. One by one the Carmelite foundations in the Holy Land were destroyed until only the communities at Acre and Mount Carmel remained. The Acre community was secure because it was located in the area of the large military concentration which had withdrawn to that city to protect it as the last foothold of the Latin kingdom. Mount Carmel, at first, enjoyed a privileged position with the Moslems because of their veneration for the prophet Elijah, but even that community became less secure in face of the mounting Turkish desire to drive out every westerner from Palestine. In fact, the elections of 1247 were held at Aylesford in England, the first election ever conducted away from Mount Carmel; and from that time the superior generals of the Order resided in Europe. In 1263 the Moslems raided the community on Mount Carmel and vandalized the small chapel at *wadi 'ain es-sich*, without, however, destroying it.

Pope Urban IV granted an indulgence to whomever would contribute for the restoration of the chapel, and in 1264 the chapel was repaired and enlarged. The additions of 1264 are also visible in the 1959 excavations on Mount Carmel.

In March of 1291 Bibars led his Mamelukes to the gates of Acre and laid siege on the city. The European defenders joined themselves in a heroic defense, but on May 18, after two months of fighting, the walls of Acre fell and by nightfall the city was in Moslem hands. The Mamelukes, in their frenzy, massacred all the inhabitants and set fire to the city. So systematic was the destruction that forty years later only a few poor peasants could be found living in the ruins of this once prosperous city.

With the fall of Acre the Latin kingdom collapsed and the Moslems proceeded to rid the country of the last vestige of the westerners. They turned up the coast and eradicated the groups at Tyre and Sidon, then turned down the coast again and took the city of Caiffa on July 30. Upon capturing Caiffa, they immediately climbed Mount Carmel and massacred the Carmelites and destroyed their building. The unreliable chronicle of William of Sanvico claims that the hermits were chanting the *Salve Regina* when they were set upon by the Moslems. The massacre of 1291 marked the end of an epoch: the Latin kingdom was forever finished, the westerner was excluded from Palestine for centuries, and no Carmelite was to live on Mount Carmel until Prosper of the Holy Spirit returned the Order to its homeland in 1631.

When the shadows of evening played across the *wadi 'ain es-sich* that July 30, 1291, they fell on an eerie scene—the blood-splattered corpses of men dressed in black robes and white mantles, their eyes open and vacant in death; the smoldering ruins of a small chapel; the horror of senseless ravage. And there was stillness on Mount Carmel.

– II –
CARMEL IN THE WEST

W̲E HAVE observed that in the early part of the thirteenth century new foundations were established in the Near East. It was inevitable that this development would carry to western Europe, the homeland of so many of those original Carmelites. The basic motive for Carmel's migration to western Europe emanated from its own inner vitality: the Order was a family, and as such it must grow and develop and spread. Where there is no growth, there is decay and eventually death.

The migration was quickened and made imperative by the unsettled conditions in Palestine. The Moslem threat was not, as some authors have suggested, the prime reason for the Carmelites' move to Europe, but it definitely made that move appear more prudent and urgent as the decades of the thirteenth century rolled on. When the Carmelites were reduced to the two foundations at Acre and Mount Carmel, they realized that their immediate future and growth rested on the European foundations.

The Carmelites did not stage a massive exodus to Europe, but instead they migrated in small groups as individual foundations became available. Their relocation in the West, therefore, was accomplished gradually, step by step, in the manner of normal, healthy growth. The first European foundation about which we have incontestable historical documentation was made in 1235 at Valenciennes, a city in the extreme northern part of modern France, although there are reports of other earlier foundations at Cologne, Cyprus, and Sicily. It is from the fragmentary and inconclusive report about the early foundation in Sicily that there appears the story of St. Angelus, the first Carmelite celebrated as a martyr by the Order. The entire account of St. Angelus is sketchy, most of it derived from fifteenth- and sixteenth-century reports. The liturgical feast, composed in 1458, represents him as a native of Jerusalem, a convert to Christianity, and a hermit on Mount Carmel.

Later he was said to have been a convert from Judaism. He appeared in Sicily sometime in the 1220s (on an individual mission? as part of an early foundation?), and preached the Christian faith there. He was assassinated in Sicily, supposedly by Manichean heretics, and has since been venerated as the protomartyr of the Carmelite Order. St. Angelus' story, however, remains largely buried in the inaccessible reaches of history.

The foundation at Valenciennes rests on more stable documentation. The extant city records relate that two Carmelites, Peter of Corbie and an unnamed companion, appeared at Valenciennes in 1235 for the purpose of founding a Carmelite community. They were sponsored by Jeanne, the Countess of Flanders and Hainault, from whom they had previously received permission to establish themselves in her realm and build a church and monastery. Joachim Tupain, apparently a wealthy merchant of Valenciennes, had already given them a piece of property for their foundation in the tanners' quarter of the city. The two Carmelites proceeded to build a chapel surrounded by a number of hermitages in the manner of the Carmelite establishments in the East.

The succeeding Carmelite foundations in Europe fairly well follow the pattern of the community at Valenciennes. First, they were made by only a few Carmelites in most instances—there were only two Carmelites who originally came to Valenciennes; only two at the foundation in Pisa, Italy; six at Paris; and eight at the foundation at Hulne near the Scottish border. Secondly, the monastic arrangement was the same as the original one in Palestine: the central chapel with adjacent individual hermitages. Thirdly, the community was most often sponsored by some person of political prominence who was acquainted with the Carmelites in Palestine and wished to establish them in his own particular jurisdiction in Europe. The majority of the Carmelites in Palestine were either European or of European extraction, and they possessed contacts and means of communication with influential people in Europe. Furthermore, it must be remembered that the thirteenth century was an age of increasing commerce and international travel, and as long as the cities of Acre and Caiffa maintained their independence there was a steady passage of European travelers to these areas near Mount Carmel.

The English foundations, for example, were sponsored by two English barons, Lord Richard Grey and Lord William de Vescy, who brought the Carmelites to England when they returned home in 1241 after the unsuccessful crusade led by Richard, Earl of Cornwall. The two barons had discovered some Englishmen among the hermits on Mount Carmel, and asked permission from the prior to bring a group of Carmelites back to England with them. The group was led by Ralph Fresburn, a Carmelite of considerable years, and the community located itself at Hulne close to Scotland. Successive foundations were quickly made at Aylesford and Lossenham, both in Kent, and Bradmer in Norfolk. In 1247, with the permission of the king, they established a community on the left bank of the Cam River at Newnham near Cambridge. Lord Richard Grey also sponsored the foundation in London sometime in the early 1250s.

The most prestigious sponsor the Carmelites had during their migration was St. Louis IX, king of France, who when he returned from his abortive crusade in 1254 brought six Carmelites with him. The king gave to these Carmelites, all of whom were Frenchmen, a piece of property at Charenton on the Seine near Paris. He continued his interest and financial support throughout his lifetime, and bequeathed the community an inheritance in his will. The Carmelites of Charenton maintained a deep affection for the saintly king, and after his canonization in 1297 they celebrated his feast in their own liturgy.

It is difficult to ascertain with any certainty precisely how many foundations were established in the early period of the Carmelites' migration. We definitely know of communities in Sicily, in Cyprus, at the desert of Les Aygalades near Marseille, in Pisa and Siena in Italy, in addition to the foundations we have already mentioned. At the elections of 1247, the Order seems to have been divided into the four provinces of the Holy Land, Sicily, England, and Provence (France). Whatever the exact number of foundations, the Carmelites were neither numerous nor influential in the first epoch of the migration before the time of St. Simon Stock. They possessed a number of small foundations staffed by a few men in each instance; and while they increased the number of men in each foundation by additional members from Palestine and the recruitment of vocations from Europe, they soon experienced, as we shall see, an alarming amount of defections to other religious orders.

The original Carmelite foundations in Europe were mostly in rural areas where there was adequate space for their particular kind of establishment and where they could find the necessary solitude for the prophetic vocation. The chapels were private oratories in which they could celebrate Mass but which had to remain closed to the faithful on Sundays and feast days. The Carmelites, therefore, were in the uncomfortable position of guests of their sponsors: they had no official ecclesiastical status in Europe, nor were they allowed to participate in the ministry for souls, except in an occasional and accidental way. They even had to bring their deceased to a local parish church for burial, since they did not possess the right of conducting funeral services in their own chapels. They existed as protégés of their sponsors, restricted and limited by tight ecclesiastical legislation, and therefore insularly excluded from the mainstream of the vital European life which swirled around them. It was a vastly different situation from the freedom and liberty they enjoyed in Palestine. And it almost brought the Order to extinction before it had time to establish itself in the West.

Carmel in Europe immediately found itself in a perilous state: hampered, restricted, ineffectual, on the verge of falling into obsolescence. Many factors contributed to the Carmelites' unhappy condition, but the principal reason for the crisis was the Order's lack of relevancy to the world of the West. The original Carmelites had revived the prophetic vocation in the particular cultural and geographical situation of the Latin kingdom in Palestine, and their legislation and customs were designed for that environment. But the world of Europe in the thirteenth century was a different world than the quixotic Latin kingdom.

Thirteenth-century Europe was in the process of one of the major changes in the entire course of history—the shift from an essentially rural, agrarian culture to an urban, commercial culture. Feudalism, the basic framework of Western society for centuries, was breaking up and being replaced by that phenomenon of the twelfth and thirteenth centuries: the medieval city. Prior to the economic revolution of the Middle Ages, the Western world was basically an agrarian society structured around the individual feudal manor, which was the center of existence for the local community, producing all that was necessary for life and sustenance. Commerce was almost nonexistent, and hard currency was used sparingly. Whatever cities did exist were merely centers of administration or armed fortresses where people could flee in time of emergency; and their permanent population was small, most often no more than three or four thousand people. But in the eleventh and twelfth centuries radical economic changes took place which affected every aspect of society. People began to cluster in urban centers, and merchants and artisans emerged as the nucleus of the new and developing middle class.

Commerce became the stable and fundamental support of the new society, and feudalism was regarded as both an anachronism and an impracticality. Hard currency was adopted as the medium of exchange. People lived in closer contact, and new human values were discovered. The great medieval universities developed, and by the end of the twelfth century there were universities at Bologna, Paris, Oxford, and Salerno. It was also a time of religious revival, a period in which the new and free middle-class man expressed his enthusiasm and exuberance for authentic Christianity and, in addition, almost every kind of bizarre religious excess. The great mendicant Orders of St. Francis and St. Dominic sprang up to meet this challenge of the new bourgeoisie, the new city, the new commerce, and the new intellectual life in the universities; and with their mobility and particular adaptability the mendicants were magnificently equipped to face the contemporary situation.

Onto this new and exciting and somewhat bewildering scene entered the Carmelite hermits. They dutifully established themselves in rural areas, built their chapels and small hermitages, and proceeded to follow their rule. But unlike the situation in Palestine, they were not enthusiastically received as the sons of Elijah. They were outside the mainstream of European life. They remained largely unnoticed, and when they did attract attention it was only to incite the antagonism of the parochial clergy. The Carmelites in their peculiar striped mantles even appeared strange to the European eye: they seemed to be estranged and uprooted Orientals wandering in a foreign land.

Legally the Carmelites had no ecclesiastical status in Europe. They possessed no sprawling abbatial territories where they could exercise their activities. They had no parochial churches in which they could operate. And they did not have the privileges of the Franciscan and Dominican mendicants, who could roam over their large provincial territories administering the sacraments. In Palestine they had experienced no such difficulties: they were the sons of the prophets and they could follow the inspiration of the moment to engage in whatever pressing need presented itself. But the Church in Europe operated on a more juridical and legalistic basis: jurisdiction was

carefully apportioned, and rights were systematically divided. The
Carmelites thus found themselves ecclesiastical outcasts in Europe.

Financially the Carmelites were in an even more abysmal state.
In Palestine life had been more simple and the climate was more
temperate. The hermits had been able to subsist on their own few
animals and the alms that the pilgrims to the Holy Land gave them.
But life in Europe was much more complex, and the climate more
severe. The Carmelites required sturdier hermitages and warmer
clothing and more substantial food. But they had little money to
use in the new era of hard currency. They did receive benefactions
from their sponsors but these were occasional and sporadic gifts,
hardly enough to support them on a sustained basis, and certainly
not enough to allow for any development of the Order. Ecclesiastics
in Europe received their financial support from three sources: the
monks in the grand abbeys were supported from the monastery
holdings, the properties and farm lands which produced revenue
for them; the parochial priests obtained their income from their
parishes, some of it in the nature of freewill offerings, but most of
it from the endowments and benefices which had been willed to the
parishes over the years; and the mendicants were given adequate
offerings and donations by the people they served in the apostolate.
However, the Carmelites were juridically blocked from these three
principal sources of ecclesiastical income—they had no abbatial holdings, they possessed no parochial rights, and they did not have the
right to engage in the apostolate. They soon found themselves in a
state of dire poverty, almost approaching penury.

As a final indignity, they found themselves the object of a mounting animosity on the part of the parochial clergy. These emigrants
from the East were an unnecessary addition to the Church in
Europe, many of the parish priests felt, serving no recognizable
purpose in the new developing society. In that age of religious enthusiasm there was a marked tendency to multiply religious orders
and, as we have noticed, the Fourth Lateran Council had to forbid
the creation of any new orders after 1215. Despite the Council's
prohibition, new orders were nevertheless established during those
years, and at the Council of Lyons in 1274 twenty-two of these
orders were suppressed because they had been founded after 1215.
The Carmelites were regarded suspiciously as one of these illegitimate orders, and even when they produced the bull of Honorius III

of 1226 the further objection was made that the bull only allowed them to exist in Palestine and said nothing about migrating to Europe. Return to Palestine, many ecclesiastics in Europe said to the Carmelites. But they could not return to Palestine: the Moslems were slowly but systematically pushing the Latin kingdom back into the Mediterranean Sea. They must remain in Europe or perish. And it appeared as if they very well might perish.

The net result of the Order's condition in Europe was a profound discouragement and dispiritedness among the individual Carmelites. Living in their small and isolated hermitages in rural European countrysides, they had no opportunity to contact the new bourgeoisie, no chance to exercise the full dimension of the prophetic vocation. They had no financial resources, and there seemed to be no way to further the development of the Order in Europe. They were regarded as useless anachronisms in the new society, and there was a determined effort to suppress the whole Carmelite movement. The inevitable happened: Carmelites—at first only a few, and then in growing numbers—began to request transfers to other religious orders, until it seemed that in addition to the Order's external problems it would now be irreparably weakened by defection from within.

When a religious order is unable to identify itself with the environment in which it operates, it is a time for a searching interior reappraisal. The order which discovers itself to lack relevancy to its own times must necessarily embark on the risky but unavoidable road of adaptation. Adaptation implies the intelligence and courage to preserve essential qualities while directing and adjusting them to the actual situation in which the order exists. Such adaptation is not an infidelity to original traditions, but rather an attempt to preserve these traditions and make them operational in the instant moment. When an order does not possess the wisdom to adapt its traditions to environmental conditions, it will then surely become a historical relic, lifeless, ineffective, and decaying.

The process of adaptation, the attempt to make authentic and timeless values viable in timely situations, demands a leader of extraordinary ability—he must be a man of sanctity, a man who loves and respects the traditions of his order, a man who understands the contemporary scene, and a man of wisdom and prudence. Such a man was St. Simon Stock, who entered the scene of Carmelite history at that critical moment in the middle of the thirteenth century.

St. Simon Stock was so monumental a figure in Carmelite history that his story has become easy prey for the legend makers; and their task was made more simple by the fact that we do not possess much precise documentation about his life, particularly the early part of it. He must unfortunately remain one of those important historical figures whose portrait is sketched more from his works and accomplishments than from an abundance of personal biographical data.

Simon Stock was an Englishman, and his birthplace has traditionally been given as Kent. John Grossi, writing in the fifteenth century, claims he was born in 1165, but this would make him an old man when he was engaged in the vigorous years of Carmelite adaptation and a centenarian when he died. As a young man he became a hermit in the English countryside, fashioning a primitive cell for himself in the hollow of a tree—and this is the derivation of his surname, Stock. Simon Stock's mode of life was not as bizarre nor erratic as it might seem in another age: in that age of religious enthusiasm the English countryside was peopled with a great number of these hermits, many of them priests, who lived solitary lives under the general direction of the local bishop. Sometime in the early twelfth century he joined the Carmelite Order, probably after a pilgrimage to the Holy Land. He returned to England with the group of Carmelites led by Ralph Fresburn, as the traditional story has it, and after the initial foundation at Hulne he was sent with the original group to Aylesford.

When the chapter assembled on Pentecost Sunday at Aylesford in 1247, the Order was at its nadir: it was conducting its first elections in the West because of the turbulent situation in Palestine, and the situation in Europe seemed hopeless. At this chapter Simon Stock was elected prior general, and the great work of adaptation was inaugurated.[1] He commissioned two Carmelites to ap-

[1] A recent historical theory contends that Simon Stock was not elected prior general until 1254. This argument is based on some documents recently discovered in Pisa concerning the foundation of the Carmelite monastery in that city. The documents seem to indicate that a hitherto unknown Godfrey was the prior general in 1249. The argument is hardly conclusive, particularly in the light of all the medieval documentation to the contrary, but even if it should be true it would not diminish Simon Stock's role or unique contribution at that moment of history: he would still be the prior general who put into operation the adaptations in the rule of 1247, thereby launching the Order into a new epoch.

proach Pope Innocent IV, who was then residing at Lyons, and request adaptations in the rule which had been undoubtedly approved by the chapter at Aylesford.

Reginald and Peter of Folsham were the two Carmelites commissioned to present the request for adaptation to the pope at Lyons. Pope Innocent IV received the request favorably and appointed two Dominican bishops to study the petition and incorporate it into the text of the rule of 1209. The Dominicans—Hugh of St. Cher, who was the Cardinal of St. Sabina in Rome; and William, bishop of Antera in Syria—completed their work on September 2, 1247, and on October 4 of the same year Innocent IV promulgated the adapted rule. He also wrote letters of recommendation for the Carmelites to a number of dioceses in which they had foundations.

The adaptations written into the rule constitute only a few lines but they had a profound effect upon the Carmelite way of life. The two most significant changes concern the physical arrangement of the individual Carmelite establishment: the Order was able to locate in urban centers ("You may accept foundations in deserts, or in any other place which is given to you, provided that in the opinion of the prior and the brethren it be suitable and fitting for the way of life proper to your Order"); and provision was made for a community refectory, thus enabling the Carmelites to dwell in a single building in the city, rather than the individual hermitages they occupied in the uninhabited countryside. The time of the strict night silence was shortened to last from early evening until early the next morning; and while the rule of abstinence remained unchanged, allowance was made for the Carmelite when he traveled ("You are to abstain from eating meat, except as a remedy for sickness or weakness. But since you are usually required to beg while you are on your journeys, you may outside your own houses eat food cooked with meat, so that you will not be bothersome to your various hosts"). The statement about common poverty from the bull of Gregory IX in 1229 was incorporated into the text, and explicit mention was made of the vows of chastity and poverty, which in the rule of 1209 had been tacitly included under the vow of obedience.

The spirit and tenor of these adaptations were an attempt to make the Carmelite way of life practicable in the new society. There was no desire to change the essentials of the life, nor to detract from the prophetic vocation. The essence of the rule which stipulated that the Carmelites should remain alone in their cells, meditating day and night on the law of the Lord and watching in prayer, remained unchanged. But instead of following their way of life in an agrarian setting, they would now move into urban areas; and instead of dwelling in separate hermitages, they would now all occupy the same building. Without these adaptations the Order could not have survived, or at least it could not have survived in a manner faithful to the original traditions of the prophetic vocation. And such is the genius and purpose of adaptation.

But the historical question asserts itself: Did the Carmelites then become mendicants, indistinguishable from the other mendicant orders? Assuredly, the Carmelites became identified with the vital mendicant movement of the thirteenth century, and they were henceforth called friars instead of the original title of hermits. And gradually over the course of the next one hundred years they gained all the privileges possessed by the mendicants. However, it is too simplistic a view of history to state that the Carmelites were simply swallowed into the mendicant movement and lost their own identity.

We must remember the Eastern tradition of the hermitic life which the Carmelites practiced in Palestine and which they unsuccessfully tried to practice when they first came to Europe: the hermit who lives his life of solitude, but who can follow the inspirational apostolic need which presents itself. And we must also remember the difficulty the Order had in finding any juridical category in the Church in Europe where they could properly function in this manner. The closest approximation to the prophetic vocation as they understood it was the mendicant movement, the appearance of those dynamic orders which combined the religious features of the old monastic orders with the mobility and apostolic commitment of missionary organizations. The Carmelites had to find some kind of ecclesiastical category to satisfy the anxious canonists, and if there was any European category in which they could feel comfortable it was surely the mendicant movement.

Moreover, the mendicant movement was not so strictured a category that it included a group of orders indistinguishable from each other; rather, each mendicant order possessed its own traditions and its own identity. In fact, the mendicants represented a major breakthrough in organized religious institutes in the Church, and became the general pattern for most of the varied orders founded since that time. The Carmelites thus became mendicants in the sense that they participated in the movement and possessed the particular status enjoyed by these new orders. Interestingly, nowhere in the medieval papal decrees granted to the Carmelites does it state that they were mendicants. We only find phrases to the effect that they were to be placed alongside the mendicants and enjoy the mendicants' privileges. It was apparently not the intention of the Holy See to force the Carmelites into a determined category, but rather to grant them the opportunity to function on the European scene along the broad outlines of the mendicant vocation.

And this is the way the Carmelites themselves understood the sweeping adaptations of 1247. They were still firmly committed to the prophetic vocation and the Elijahan tradition, and the literature of the fourteenth and fifteenth centuries is even more insistent on that point than is the literature of the thirteenth century, but now they would operate in the new free patterns established by the mendicants—monastic priests not permanently assigned to any one monastery or diocese, but able to travel over all of Europe exercising their apostolate. In this aspect the Carmelites were mendicants in the full sense of the term, but they nevertheless possessed their own particular modality, their own unique spirit and tradition—the prophetic vocation.

In their new urban environment the Carmelites still followed their lives of solitude in their cells, their program of austerity, their long hours of prayer, their subordination of any apostolic activity to their life of aloneness with God, but they were also able to contact and influence the world in which they lived. There were inevitable dissenters among the Carmelites themselves who charged that the changes were too drastic and detrimental to the prophetic spirit; but although they were quite vocal in the period immediately following St. Simon's death, within fifty years these dissenting voices had fairly well died out. The authentic prophet must necessarily be a witness, and the adaptations approved by Innocent IV enabled the Carmelite to be a witness to his own age and to the ages which followed.

St. Simon began to move the Carmelite foundations into the cities, and he obtained ecclesiastical permission for his men to preach and administer the sacraments. He also involved the Carmelites in the important university movement of the thirteenth century, so that they could contact this vital area of European life and also equip themselves intellectually to cope with the better-educated medieval citizen. The Carmelites were suddenly in the mainstream of European life. It would be naïve to conclude that the Carmelites, especially after their unhappy beginning in Europe, won complete and immediate acceptance. Almost a century passed before the Order gained all the ecclesiastical rights and privileges enjoyed by the Franciscans and Dominicans, but the foundation was laid by St. Simon Stock and the cause could not fail. St. Simon had to appeal continually to the pope for protection against the Order's antagonists: in 1252 he obtained a decree from the pope which threatened ecclesiastical censure to those who harmed the Carmelites; in 1254 he received a papal bull protecting the foundations at Aylesford and London from opposition; and in the years 1261 and 1262 he appealed to the Holy See three separate times for protection against some prelates, notably the Archbishop of Canterbury. Even the Carmelites themselves were not unanimously in favor of the adaptations, and St. Simon's successor, Nicholas the Frenchman, wrote a scorching indictment of the changes before he retired from office. But despite these initial difficulties, St. Simon had launched the Order into a new epoch, and a golden age was inaugurated for the Carmelites which would last for a century and a half.

From this moment in history we find the Carmelites actively participating in the Church's work in Europe. They were able to preach and administer the sacraments in their own churches, and they occasionally staffed the parochial church of an area; they became itinerant preachers, teachers in the great universities, and were sent on special missions by the Holy See. They were engaged in works of social and corporal mercy, responding to human need when the problem presented itself. But their whole apostolate was individual and inspirational, rather than organized and institutional. We notice a definite pattern to avoid an involvement with an organized school or hospital or parochial arrangement, despite a few isolated cases. The prophetic tradition demanded a freer and less institutional approach to human problems—the prophet emerging from his solitude to preach the instant and necessary message, to give aid and comfort where and when it was needed.

The stature of St. Simon himself played no small part in the growing acceptation of the Order in the West. Here was a wise and fearless and intrepid fighter for his cause. And a holy man, too. The medieval chronicles are replete with pious stories of his austerities and fasts and incessant prayers and his miracles (he was said to have changed water into wine by the sign of the cross!), but these are the typical legend stories found so frequently in the hagiography of that era. We do know, however, that he was particularly devoted to the Blessed Virgin, and that he received the scapular vision, probably in 1251. The scapular also contributed significantly to the Carmelites' growing prestige.

St. Simon Stock was making a visitation of the Carmelite foundation at Bordeaux in France when he was taken ill and died in 1265. He was buried in the cathedral at Bordeaux, but a year later the archbishop, Pierre de Roncevaux, transferred the remains back to the room in the monastery where he died. He also allowed the room to be converted into a chapel, and soon there were reports of numerous miracles effected there. In 1276, only eleven years after St. Simon Stock's death, the Holy See permitted the celebration of a Mass in his honor by the Carmelites of Bordeaux, and this feast was ultimately extended to the entire Carmelite Order.

The scapular devotion inaugurated by St. Simon soon became widespread and a prominent feature of Carmelite activities. The first official hagiographical notice about St. Simon Stock is contained in the *Viridarium*, the Sanctology of Carmelite saints composed by John Grossi sometime in the middle of the fourteenth century, and the account in the Sanctology relates one of the earliest and most authentic descriptions of the scapular vision:

The ninth [saint] was St. Simon of England, the sixth General of the Order. He continually pleaded with the most glorious Mother of God to grant some special privilege to the Order of Carmelites, which enjoys the special title of the Virgin. He prayed devoutly:

> *Flower of Carmel, fruitful vine,*
> *Splendor of heaven, Mother divine—*
> *None like to thee;*
> *Mother of meekness, spotless virgin,*
> *To the Carmelites a favor impart,*
> *Star of the Sea.*

Surrounded by a multitude of angels, the Blessed Virgin appeared to him, holding in her blessed hands the scapular of the Order. She said: "This shall be a privilege for you and for all Carmelites, that whoever dies clothed in this shall not suffer eternal fire; rather, he shall be saved."

The said Simon died in the province of Bordeaux while on a visitation to the province of Vasconia. . . .

The author of this notice, John Grossi, was a distinguished and saintly Carmelite who served as general of the Avignon faction during the Great Western Schism and who was unanimously elected general of the whole Order when the breach was healed in 1411. He claims in the *Viridarium* that he is quoting only from ancient documents, but he does not cite any of them explicitly, nor do we possess any of these documents today. However, we can trace a very clear scapular tradition emanating from the Carmelites of the thirteenth century, testifying to their belief that the Blessed Virgin appeared to St. Simon Stock and promised him that the scapular would be the sign of her ultimate protection of the individual Carmelites. The Constitutions of 1281 command all Carmelites to wear the scapular continually, even while they sleep, under threat of serious ecclesiastical censure; and by the time of the chapter of Montpellier in 1287 the terms *habit* and *scapular* are used interchangeably. The Constitutions of 1357 state that the scapular "is to be regarded as the special habit of the Order." And in 1369 the penalty of automatic excommunication was levied against any Carmelite who celebrated Mass without wearing his scapular. This solemn reverence for the scapular in the thirteenth and fourteenth centuries is even more astonishing and convincing when we recall that it was directed toward an insignificant part of the habit which only a few decades earlier was merely an apron the hermits wore to keep the habit itself neat and clean.

The earliest Carmelite authors who wrote about the scapular—notably John of Cimentho and John of Hildesheim—cite only the fact of the vision to St. Simon Stock without offering any explanation of the startling promise contained in the revelation. Apparently no explanation was necessary at that time because the historical setting of the vision made it both logical and understandable. The Carmelites had already proposed themselves as an order particularly devoted to the Blessed Virgin, her own special fief; and it seemed a logical consequence that those men who persevered until their death in loyalty to the Blessed Virgin would obtain assistance from her to save their souls. And the symbol employed in the vision was readily accepted by a medieval mentality that reveled in symbol and sign—the common scapular of religious life which was employed to protect the hermit was now elevated to a symbol of a higher and more important protection.

In the fifteenth century, however, a precise and definite scapular literature began to evolve in the Carmelite Order. Thomas Bradley, who was named bishop of Dromore, Ireland, in 1450 explains the scapular as a manifestation of Mary's maternal love and powerful mediation. Nicholas Calciuri, a Sicilian writing in the middle of the century, sees the scapular as a sign of Mary's continuing protection and the cause of numerous miracles. Baldwin Leersius, a Frenchman, also cites the protecting intervention of the Blessed Virgin in the lives of scapular wearers. But the most incisive and influential scapular writer of that epoch was the Belgian Carmelite, Arnold Bostius, who wrote *De patronatu et patrocinio B.V.M.*, a careful exposition of Mary's relationship to the Carmelite Order. Bostius' work was popularized by the Fleming John Paleonydor in his *Fasciculus tripartitus*, originally published in 1495 and frequently reprinted in the sixteenth and seventeenth centuries.

Arnold Bostius (1445–1499) was born at Ghent and entered the Carmelite Order as a youth. He ultimately became subprior, and probably prior, of the monastery in Ghent, but his outstanding achievements were in the field of the burgeoning humanist movement in Europe. The middle fifteenth century was witnessing an electrifying rediscovery of the Greek and early Latin classics, both Christian and profane, and Bostius was engaged in the full stream of the movement. His correspondence with Erasmus is still extant, and the circle of his friends included many other outstanding humanists, among them Robert Gaguin and Trithemius. He was a skillful writer, a clever debater, and was intimately involved in the raging controversy about the doctrine of the Immaculate Conception. When one of the friends of the community at Ghent submitted a scholastic proposition inquiring about the Blessed Virgin's patronage of the Carmelite Order, Bostius was assigned to offer a reply. The expert Latin stylist composed the *Patronatu* of thirteen chapters, completing it in 1479, and the work both articulated and molded scapular doctrine for the centuries to follow.

Bostius' fundamental point about the scapular is that it constitutes a symbol of reciprocity on the part of the Blessed Virgin—in return for the Carmelite's love and loyalty she reciprocates with her love and protection. He writes:

All Carmelites, encouraged by the dignity of the honor and grace of Mary, rejoice to wear this gift of Our Lady night and day as an impenetrable shield. It reminds them that they must always consider the holy life of Mary as their model, that they must engrave her image, along with her Son's, on the shield of their faith, and that they must place all their trust in the all-powerful protection of this sovereign queen who is always ready to come to their aid. Happy are they who affectionately receive the gifts of Mary in the embrace of reciprocal spiritual love. They can look at this habit and joyfully remember the special love their most loving benefactor bestows on them, and thus know that they have been selected by her for so great an inheritance.

His thesis of "reciprocal spiritual love" is based on the original Carmelite tradition of Mary's ownership of the Order, and he compares the scapular to the medieval Order of the Golden Fleece, the insignia of the house of Burgundy which was a coveted honor and a sure defense against molestation and harassment. Pius XII adopted the same analogy five centuries later when he wrote: "Whoever wears [the scapular] professes to belong to Our Lady, just as the knight of the thirteenth century—the era to which the scapular traces its origin—was inspired to bravery and confidence in combat under the eyes of his lady."

Bostius also underscores the theological implications of the scapular. He describes Mary's role in the history of salvation, calling her the "Mother of grace and Mother of mercy," and he explains her posture of mediation, her ability to impetrate graces from God. And he reminds the scapular wearer of his obligation and commitment to Mary: "to invoke her in all our necessities, to contemplate her life and virtues, keeping her always in our memory, to imitate her, to live in continual dependence on her."

Finally, Bostius comments on a custom which had developed sometime in the late fourteenth century:

Many devout persons . . . well aware that it would be most advantageous to be enrolled in the family of Mary . . . were anxious to have the protection of the armor of Mary, the scapular of our Order. They secretly wore the scapular during life that they might be able to resist in the evil day and remain perfect in all things; and they ultimately died holy deaths wearing this garment.

The practice of giving small scapulars to laymen to wear under their regular clothing can be traced back no farther than the late fourteenth century, and it presents another development in scapular history: the affiliation of lay people into the Carmelite Order so that they might enjoy the benefits of the scapular promise. The practice of affiliation to a religious order was a frequent medieval custom, and we find it being employed by the Dominicans and Franciscans. The Carmelites adopted this custom of affiliation, and when they had invested a lay person in the scapular—"the special habit of the Order"—they actually considered him a member of the Order and thus eligible for the scapular promise. Pius XII, commenting on the practice, wrote that "all who wear the scapular, whether they live in a monastery or not, belong to the same family of the Blessed Mother Mary through a special kind of love."

In the beginning of the sixteenth century the prior general, Nicholas Audet, organized the scapular confraternity, the association of lay people who wear the scapular, and the popes through the centuries have frequently recommended the confraternity and the wearing of the scapular. The papal decrees, however, inserted one word in the narrative of the Blessed Virgin's promise to St. Simon Stock: ". . . whoever dies piously clothed in this . . ." The addition of the word *piously* was an attempt to obviate any flavor of superstition in the wearing of the scapular, and to underscore the fact that it is a symbol, rooted deeply in the authentic Carmelite tradition of a "reciprocal spiritual love," of fidelity meeting fidelity, of the Blessed Virgin's promise to help those who have confidence and loyalty for her. The scapular confraternity developed dramatically during the seventeenth and eighteenth centuries and the scapular gradually assumed a position as one of Catholicism's most popular forms of Marian devotion.

In the fifteenth century another phase of scapular history was inaugurated with the dissemination of a papal bull, *Sacratissimo uti culmine*, purportedly issued by Pope John XXII in 1322. The bull reports a vision to Pope John, the Frenchman who established a permanent papal court at Avignon, in which the Blessed Virgin promised that scapular wearers would be liberated from purgatory on the Saturday following their deaths, provided they either recited the Divine Office or practiced some additional abstinence from meat. The bull is mentioned by Nicholas Calciuri in 1461 and Baldwin Leersius in 1465, and the Carmelite chapter of 1517 makes reference to it. The bull contains a detailed account of the alleged vision and a rather wordy statement of the Blessed Virgin; and because of the

Saturday promise it became known as the Sabbatine (from *sabbato*, Latin for Saturday) bull. There is, however, no record of the bull in the official registers of the Roman Curia, and the historicity of the document is clearly vulnerable. But in 1530 Clement VII did issue the authentic bull *Ex clementi sedis apostolicae* in which he stated that the Blessed Virgin would help the confreres of Carmel after their deaths "with her continued intercession, with her prayers, and with special protection to insure their speedy release from purgatory."

At length, in 1613 the Holy Office under Pope Paul V issued a decree which formulated and regulated the Church's position about the Sabbatine aspect of the scapular devotion. Without mentioning the bull of John XXII or the vision of the Blessed Virgin, the decree states:

> The Carmelite Fathers may preach that the Christian people can piously believe in the aid of the souls of the brethren and confreres of the sodality of the Most Blessed Virgin of Mount Carmel. Through her continuous intercessions, pious sufferages, merits, and special protection the Most Blessed Virgin, especially on Saturday, the day dedicated to her by the Church, she will help after their death the brethren and members of the sodality who die in charity. In life they must have recited the Little Office. If they do not know how to recite it, they are to observe the fast of the Church and to abstain from meat on Wednesdays and Saturdays, except for the feast of Christmas.

In 1890, Pope Leo XIII granted the faculty to confessors to commute the obligation of recitation of office or abstinence into other prayers or good works for obtaining the Sabbatine privilege. Thus the Sabbatine privilege acquired a theological justification entirely independent of the question of the authenticity of the original Sabbatine bull, and in the light of the papal documentation over the centuries the Order was clearly justified in teaching that scapular wearers who observe the requirements of the Holy Office's decree of 1613 can expect special help from the Blessed Virgin after their deaths, particularly on Saturday. The problem of the historicity of John XXII's bull will probably never be solved, nor need it be solved, but it should be noted that the absence of a papal document from the medieval registers is not necessarily a conclusive argument against its authenticity. As recently as 1959, Pope John XXIII, recalling that John XXII was the last pope to bear the same name, stated: "Above all he was very devoted to Mary. It is to him that history attributes the paternity of the Sabbatine privilege—so precious and dear to those who wear the scapular of Our Lady of Mount Carmel."

In 1653, John Launoy, a priest and doctor of the University of Paris, published his *De visione Simonis Stochii*, an attack on the historicity of the original scapular vision to St. Simon Stock, which caused decades of controversy about the question. Launoy's work was valuable because it was written in the spirit of the new scientific approach to history being formulated in his age, and he thus called attention to the dubious authenticity of some scapular documentation. His conclusions against the historicity of St. Simon's vision, however, are groundless, particularly in view of the scholarship and scientific discoveries since his time. Launoy based his attack on the doubtful nature of two documents then widely quoted in defense of the scapular: the chronicle of William of Sanvico; and the Swanington fragments, remnants of a letter purportedly written by Peter Swanington, secretary to St. Simon Stock. The Swanington fragment has since been judged spurious, and the Sanvico chronicle very unreliable. Launoy also rejected the tradition that the small scapular was worn by lay people in the thirteenth century, and his theory has since been proved correct. The modern foundation for affirmation of the historicity of the scapular vision is composed of an undeniable scapular tradition among the Carmelites dating back to the thirteenth century, the fourteenth-century documentation, particularly the Sanctology of John Grossi, and the ensuing papal documentation over the centuries.

St. Simon's vision occupies a pre-eminent position in the history of the Carmelite Order, and it profoundly influenced its fortunes. It took place at the nadir moment in the Order's migration to the West, and helped re-establish its pride and confidence in itself, providing a tangible symbol of Carmel's original tradition and continuing relevance. (Bostius said that the scapular was a symbol of family unity within the Carmelite Order.) The scapular also helped the Order gain prestige in the medieval world of Europe. And it increased the Order's sphere of influence by eventually incorporating millions of lay people throughout the centuries into the Carmelite family. As Pope Pius IX said:

This most extraordinary gift of the Scapular . . . from the Mother of God to Saint Simon Stock . . . brings its great usefulness not only to the Carmelite family of Mary, but also to all the rest of the faithful who, affiliated to that family, wish to follow Mary with a very special devotion.

The most prominent spokesman of the faction in the Carmelite Order which opposed the adaptations and changes of St. Simon Stock was his immediate successor as prior general, Nicholas the Frenchman, author of the stinging document *Ignea sagitta* (*The Fiery Arrow*). Nicholas was a native of Narbonne, who joined the Carmelites on Mount Carmel in Palestine and spent his entire religious life in the East until his election as general. In 1250 he was made provincial of the Holy Land, and after St. Simon's death he traveled to the chapter at Toulouse where he was elected the saint's successor. As prior general, he first made a careful visitation of the monasteries in the West, and he discovered that he did not like what St. Simon had done in the years since the adaptation of the rule by Innocent IV: he did not approve of the monasteries in the cities, nor the Carmelites dwelling in the same building, and he was opposed to the foundations near the large universities. In brief, he was a hermit who had spent all his life in a solitary hermitage on Mount Carmel, and he was unwilling to admit the necessity for any kind of adaptation or change in that mode of life when the Order migrated to the West. Nicholas convoked a general chapter at Messina in Sicily in 1267, and voiced his disapproval of Carmel in the West in strong and biting terms, but his remarks went unheeded. Three years later he issued the *Ignea sagitta*, a fierce statement of his misgivings about the whole situation, and then promptly tendered his resignation as general, retiring to a monastery in Provence. The date of his death is unknown.

The *Ignea sagitta* is a puzzling document: it is the testimony of a man who yearns for the solitary slopes of Mount Carmel, who wants a life of solitude with God, and yet it is a bitter castigation of the Carmelites in the West, couched in harsh and sometimes crude language. The argument itself is uneven, lacking in logical precision or proper arrangement of thought, almost as if it were an angry tirade dashed off in white heat. Commentators on this monograph have noted that its style is typical of the fervent and polemic and intemperate kind of writing done so frequently in the Middle Ages, the kind of writing in which a man desperately wants to make his point regardless of acerbate language or trampled sensitivities. But yet we find it disconcerting as we read it today.

Nicholas writes about the new arrangement of the cells:

The Holy Spirit, knowing what is fitting for each one of us, inspired, not without reason, that part of our rule which directs each one of us to have his separate cell. It is not a question of neighboring cells, but of cells which are distinct from each other, so that the heavenly Bridegroom and His bride, the contemplative soul, may be able to converse there in the tranquillity of an intimate conversation. . . . But you, city dwellers, you have turned the separate cells into a house where you live in common: how can you prepare yourselves for those holy occupations which should be yours? At what hours do you meditate on the law of the Lord in reflection and prayer? Are not your nights troubled by the remembrance of your vanity, since you pass your day in gossiping, running around, listening, speaking, and acting? Your memory is filled with forbidden and impure thoughts to such an extent that your mind is incapable of meditating on anything else.

Nicholas admits that the Carmelite hermits of old did participate in the apostolate:

Conscious of their own imperfection, our predecessors lived continually in the solitude of the desert. But for the benefit of other souls, as well as their own, they occasionally—but rarely—descended from the mountain to disseminate by their preaching what they had reaped in the desert with the sickle of contemplation.

But there is a vast difference for him between the original Carmelites and the men he now sees in the West:

The Order does not lack preachers, but they are presumptuous men, lovers of vain show who make a virtue of chirruping forth before the people things they have discovered in books, men who claim to instruct others on matters of which they themselves are ignorant.

Are we, then, to dismiss Nicholas as a religious crank, a man hopelessly out of tune with his times, an old hermit yearning for the untroubled past, heaping reproaches on those who seek progress? Not entirely. Admittedly, he is unaware of the mood of medieval Europe and the need to adapt the prophetic vocation to the real situation, and he is certainly caustic and unfair in his evaluation of the Carmelites in the West, but nevertheless he must stand as a lone and cautioning figure in the medieval epoch, reminding the Carmelite of his desert origins and his primary commitment to see the face of the living God. The prophet's abiding temptation is to forget the God of the mountain when he descends into the valley of men. This was not a pressing or imminent danger in Nicholas' time, and unfortunately most of his violent reactions must be ascribed to a mere human reluctance to any form of change, but a time was to come a century and a half later when the somber warnings of Nicholas the Frenchman would be fulfilled.

Nicholas' successor, Ralph the German, was apparently similarly disposed to a life of almost absolute solitude because after serving in the office of general for three years he resigned, retiring to the ancient foundation of Hulne at the Scottish border. Despite the Order's move to urban locations the original foundations at Hulne, and Les Aygalades near Marseille were preserved in their pristine condition, and they soon became houses of absolute contemplation and strict solitude. This tradition of a few select houses of solitude in the Order endured during a greater part of the medieval period, thus providing the opportunity for individual Carmelites who desired a completely eremitical life with no apostolate to retire to these establishments, either for a short time or a number of years, or in some cases for a major part of their lives. Another such house was founded at La Selve near Florence in Italy in 1343; and in 1428 the Carmelites took possession of an ancient Benedictine monastery, La Geronde, in the Swiss canton of Valais and turned it into one of their contemplative houses. All of these houses disappeared during the years of decline in the late fifteenth and sixteenth centuries, but they were re-established, as we shall see, on a more organized basis after the reformation movement of St. Teresa.

Peter Amilian, a Frenchman from Rodez, was next elected general, governing the Order for nineteen years with a stable and calm administration. The adaptations of 1247 and the efforts of St. Simon Stock to solidify the Carmelites' position in Europe had proven eminently successful, and the Order was enjoying a phenomenal development. At the chapter of 1247 the Order had numbered only four provinces, but by the chapter of Montpellier in 1287 the provinces of Rome, Paris, Lombardy, Germany, and Aquitania had been added, bringing the total to nine. In 1318 the number of provinces increased to twelve, Spain and Ireland being among the new provinces. The Scottish province was inaugurated in 1324, and by the end of the century there were nineteen provinces. In 1472 at the height of Carmel's numerical strength before the Protestant Reformation, the Order was divided into thirty-three provinces. Despite the fact that the Carmelites were able to stabilize their legal position in Europe by participating in the mendicant movement, they quickly and ironically found themselves involved in the mendicants' own struggle for survival. The mendicant orders were regarded as dangerous innovations by many ecclesiastics and bishops because of the independence and freedom they enjoyed to travel from diocese to diocese, and there was strong sentiment in Europe to either suppress these new orders or make them subject to the local bishops. The conflict was exacerbated by the inflammatory writing of William of St. Amour, a professor of theology at the University of Paris, who in 1256 published a tract vigorously indicting the mendicants. Ten years later he composed an even more savage attack, *Liber de antichristo*, in which he stated that the mendicant movement was the spirit of the antichrist.

The issue came to a head at the Second Council of Lyons in 1274, that magnificent medieval assembly of more than one thousand participants under the presidency of Pope Gregory X. The mendicant orders marshaled their forces to bring the matter to a point of final resolution. St. Thomas Aquinas died on his journey to the council, and St. Bonaventure died during its sessions, but the mendicant cause prevailed. The Dominicans and Franciscans were granted full and final approval, while all other orders founded after 1215 were suppressed. The Carmelites and Augustinians, however, found themselves in a peculiar position: they were permitted "to remain in their present state," but a definitive decision about them would be given later after a study of their usefulness to the universal Church and the salvation of souls.

The Carmelites remained in that unresolved and vulnerable position for twenty-five years, and a spirit of further adaptation and a desire to conform more completely to European customs is reflected in some of the legislative decisions in the Order during that time. In the chapter at Montpellier in 1287 they decided to substitute a white mantle for the traditional striped mantle they had been wearing, and they accordingly became known as the Whitefriars, in distinction to the Dominicans who were called Blackfriars. At the chapter of Trèves in 1291 the Order adopted the traditional and juridical distinction in its membership between cleric and lay brother. The position of the lay brother was an ancient one in the history of Western religious life, although it became more clearly defined in the eleventh century. Prior to that time the religious monks were generally divided into two categories: the ordained, lettered monks (*literati*) and the lay, unlettered monks (*illiterati*). In the writings of St. John Gualbertus, who founded the Vallombrosans in 1038, we first find the lay brothers called *conversi*, a term which was employed in a different sense in early Christianity to signify the difference between those who were converted to the practice of religion at a later age in life (the *conversi*, literally the converted ones) and those who practiced the faith from their youth (the *oblati*, literally the oblated or consecrated ones). The word endured, and to this day lay brothers are designated in church law as *conversi*, although the term is imprecise and lacking in etymological significance. In the first half of the twelfth century the Cistercians drew up a separate set of instructions for the lay brother, the *Usus conversorum*, which described the form of life of these men who lived in the monastery, performed the manual labor of the institute, but who were largely separated and segregated from the cleric monks, almost forming a distinct institute within the order. The *conversi* were an important part of the old monasticism because they participated in the agricultural development of the vast monastic estates.

The mendicant movement of the thirteenth century established the lay brotherhood as part of its membership, although the more democratic spirit of the mendicants attempted to unite the clerics and lay brothers into a single familial unit. The mendicant lay brother, like his counterpart in earlier monasticism, performed the manual work of the monastery, but since the mendicants did not possess the estates and farm lands of the old monasteries their work was of a more domestic nature. Both St. Francis and his successor, Brother Elijah, were not priests, and until 1239 the lay brother in the Franciscans could both vote in community elections and hold office. That was the tradition of the Carmelites until 1291 when they decided to conform to the prevailing monastic custom and create a sharp juridical difference between cleric and lay brother: the Carmelite lay brother was deprived of his right to vote and his legal capacity to hold office. A compromise was arranged, however, to the effect that any lay brother who had entered the Order before 1291 could retain his right to vote and hold office for the duration of his life.

We find this mentioned in the Constitutions of 1324, but it is omitted by the Constitutions of 1357 since all the old lay brothers were presumably dead by that time.

A saintly Carmelite lay brother died in that very year of the Trèves chapter in 1291, Blessed Frank, who was beatified sixteen years later by Clement V. Blessed Frank was born at Orosio, near Siena, in 1201, and spent the greater part of his first sixty years in a life of dissipation. At the age of sixty he repented and made a pilgrimage to St. James of Compostella, and then proceeded to Rome where he sought the absolution of Pope Gregory X. He petitioned the Carmelites of Siena for admission, but they insisted on public reparation for the scandal he had given during his life. He was seventy years old when he was finally admitted to the Order as a lay brother, but he lived to the age of ninety as a holy penitent.

The Carmelite Order obtained its final and definitive approval from Boniface VIII in 1299, and in 1317 John XXII issued the bull *Sacer ordo vester* in which he granted the Carmelites the full rights of religious exemption enjoyed by the mendicant orders. Religious exemption, which frees the members of an order from the jurisdiction of any local bishop and makes them responsible only to the order's superiors and ultimately to the pope, has been a point of contention in the Church from the thirteenth century until the present day. There have been strong movements within the Church, particularly at the time of general councils, to abrogate the privilege of exemption and make exempt religious subject to the local bishops, but these movements have never succeeded, principally because the privilege of exemption is too valuable for the Church at large. The purpose of exemption is to provide the religious priest the necessary mobility to be effective in a cosmopolitan society. In the thirteenth century, Western society underwent a vast and permanent change: it broke out of the small, isolated, provincial world of the feudal state into the large world of commerce and urban life and international travel. The mendicant was particularly equipped to cope with this world: he was not ascribed to a single diocese or a single monastery, but he was assigned to a religious province, a large territory embracing sometimes a whole nation or a significant part of one. He could be immediately moved anywhere in this territory at the command of his superior as a particular need or opportunity presented itself. Without denying the absolute necessity and value of diocesan priests in their parishes, the Church also needs these mobile and adaptable priests to serve the requirements of Christianity. Another major benefit of exemption is that it provided the Church in an international age with priests who were not dependent on any local ruler, lay or ecclesiastic, and who could not therefore be intimidated or hampered by them. These exempt religious, subject directly to the pope, were the Church's international priests.

The charge has been frequently levied that the privilege of exemption is contrary to the revealed nature of the Church by which every priest should be subject to his bishop. Pope Paul VI answered this objection in 1964 when he wrote:

The exemption of religious Orders is in no conflict whatsoever with the divinely given constitution of the Church, by force of which every priest, particularly in the performance of the sacred ministry, must obey the sacred hierarchy. For the members of these religious institutes are, at all times and in all places, subject principally to the Roman Pontiff, as to their highest superior. For this reason, the religious institutes are at the service of the Roman Pontiff in those works which pertain to the welfare of the universal church.

The Carmelite constitutions were subjected to numerous changes: almost every chapter in that medieval age with its fascination for laws and regulations made additions to existing legislation, which were frequently qualified or abrogated by subsequent chapters. The main genius, however, of the mendicants' legislation was that it provided one of the earliest democratic systems in the Western world. Superiors were elected, legislation was voted upon, and every priest in good standing had a representative voice in government. To be sure, many of the ceremonies and trappings of monarchical rule infiltrated themselves into the customs of the mendicants' regime, but there was nevertheless a radical departure from the ancient system of the lord abbot who ruled his monastery for life or the feudal bishop permanently appointed either by Rome or sometimes by the local temporal ruler. The democratic spirit of the mendicants further unnerved some anxious, ecclesiastics who were inexorably committed to the regal spirit in the Church.

From 1247 until the end of the fourteenth century the Carmelites assembled for a general chapter almost every third year, but in the fifteenth and sixteenth centuries the intervals became longer: six, ten, and even as much as sixteen years. At these general chapters the prior general was elected by delegates who had in turn been elected from each of the provinces. There was no stated limit to the number of years the prior general could serve in office: he was elected at one chapter, and in succeeding chapters he was either confirmed in office until the next chapter or rejected by the electors. Most of the prior generals continued in office until they either died or resigned or were appointed to some bishopric, in which case they necessarily had to resign their office. The prior general chose his own residence, usually someplace in the province of which he was originally a member, but after 1472 the general's residence was ordinarily in Rome. Each of the provinces correspondingly conducted their own elections, which in the thirteenth century were convened every year and then in the later Middle Ages every two or three years. The provincial and his definitory (his board of advisors) were elected at these elections, as well as the priors of the various monasteries of the provinces. Each monastery was represented at the provincial chapter by the prior of the monastery, and another priest elected by the remainder of the cleric members of the community. As in the case of the prior general, the prior of the monastery was not limited to the number of years he could serve in the same office, but later legislation finally restricted both these offices to terms of incumbency of three or six years.

At the turn of the fourteenth century the Order was distinguished by the celebrated St. Albert of Sicily. He was born near Mount Trapani in Sicily of parents who had been childless for many years and who finally vowed to consecrate any child they might have to the Blessed Virgin. Albert was the fruit of that union and that vow, and as a youth he entered the Carmelite monastery at Trapani. He became a priest and eventually provincial of the Sicilian province, acquiring a wide reputation as a holy man and a wonder worker. The medieval accounts are replete with stories of his miracles, but they can hardly stand the scrutiny of scientific history. His shining hour occurred in 1282 during the popular revolt against the Angevin regime in Sicily—the famous "Sicilian Vespers," so named because the revolt began on Easter Tuesday about the hour of vespers after a French soldier had allegedly molested a woman near a church in Palermo. A wholesale massacre of any Frenchman, man or woman, raged across the island, and the Sicilians declared their independence from the French. However, Charles I of Anjou retaliated immediately, landing his troops on the eastern end of the island and laying siege to Messina. St. Albert was in Messina at the time, helping the sick and wounded while the battle was in progress. As the siege dragged into the summer months the food and water in Messina became depleted, and starvation set in among the civilian population. Albert crossed the enemy lines and pleaded with the French to allow some supplies to enter for the starving people of the city. He obtained his request, and three ships loaded with provisions were allowed to pass the blockade and enter the port. After the Sicilians had finally repelled the French with the help of Peter of Aragon, Albert was acclaimed as a national hero because of his efforts during the siege. Perhaps his reputation as a wonder worker derived from a sentiment among the Sicilians that anyone who could obtain an act of mercy from the hated French must surely be able to work miracles. St. Albert died in Messina on August 7, 1306, and although he was never formally canonized his feast was introduced in 1411.

One of St. Simon Stock's most important achievements was the introduction of the Carmelites into the great medieval universities. He established monasteries in the university cities of Cambridge, Oxford, Paris, and Bologna, thereby insuring that his men would be in contact with the intellectual revolution that was transpiring in the Middle Ages. The appearance of the medieval university was the product of the development of the new urban civilization. As people began to congregate in cities they made more use of the traditional cathedral schools, and the burgeoning population caused these schools to develop all out of proportion to their original size and purpose. New teachers were recruited and classes were conducted anyplace in the city where space was available. The medieval universities, therefore, were never actually "founded," but they grew out of the sociological phenomenon of the age. Eventually the teachers and students of these outsized cathedral schools adopted the organizational structure of the medieval guilds: the teachers and students both became federated, and the whole organization of scholars was called a university—from the Latin word *universitas*, corporation. Before the twelfth century the best educational institutions in Europe had been the monastic schools, but they were invariably located in rural areas, and the type of scholarship was of a custodial, historical nature. However, the new city university attracted scholars from all over Europe, who were able to engage in free discussion and investigation with other scholars and thereby increase the content of human knowledge.

The mendicants quickly and wisely established monasteries in the university cities, particularly at Paris, the greatest of the thirteenth-century universities. The young mendicant students attended the various schools, and ultimately gained important professorial and faculty positions. This was a daring innovation in ecclesiastical education, a bold departure from the narrow, confined education that was given to prospective priests in the old monastery system. The mendicants found themselves in the middle of the intellectual revolution and their students were in vital contact with the cultural and educational achievements of the age. Unfortunately the post-Tridentine history of the ecclesiastical seminary tended to reverse this position and drive the seminarians back into an isolated church school which was almost totally unrelated to the educational and cultural world around it.

Carmelite monasteries began to appear in all of the European cities with a university of any importance in the late thirteenth and early fourteenth centuries, and soon a few of them were designated as *studia generalia*, monasteries which could receive men from any province for the purpose of attending the university. After the tyro Carmelite completed his novitiate, the year of basic spiritual training, he was usually educated in grammar and rhetoric in one of the monasteries of his own province, but for his higher studies he was often sent to one of the *studia generalia*. By the year 1324 there were eight of these *studia generalia* in the Carmelite Order: Paris, Toulouse, Bologna, Florence, Montpellier, Cologne, London, and Avignon. During the fourteenth century the number of students in the Carmelite monastery in Paris averaged about three hundred, and in London over one hundred.

Carmel is dedicated to prayer and contemplation and it is also committed to preaching the word of God. For both aspects of the Order's life intellectual competence is essential. St. Teresa of Ávila was to write at a later epoch: "Those who walk in the way of prayer have need of learning, and the more spiritual they are, the greater their need." When contemplation is practiced without intelligent direction there is always danger of falling into illuminism or fanaticism, as the history of the Church has sadly demonstrated. The Order's early and continued insistence on the cultivation of intellect has provided the Church with a contemplative tradition that is firmly integrated with a sound theology and a healthy psychology. The monasteries situated near the universities guaranteed that the Order would maintain the necessary union between spirituality and intellect, and despite the abuses that developed in the Carmelite *studia generalia* during the fifteenth century, Carmel would always be at home in the academic environment.

A number of Carmelites distinguished themselves in the academic field during the period of Carmel's first golden age. The first doctor of theology in the Order was Gerard of Bologna, who obtained his degree at Paris in 1295, two years before he was elected prior general. In 1318 he was succeeded in that office by Guy of Perpignan, also a doctor of Paris, known by the sobriquet *Doctor Breviloquius* (the Doctor of Few Words). Sigbert Van Bieck, a German, obtained his doctorate at Paris and later became provincial of the German province and led the Carmelites to Holland. He wrote *Quodlibets*, a profound discussion of the rule and the contemplative life, phrased in the technical scholastic language of the age; and he composed the Ordinal, a codification of the Carmelite liturgy.

The most celebrated of the Carmelite doctors at Paris was John Baconthorpe, the *Doctor Resolutus*, a native of Norfolk in England. He entered the Order at Snitterly and was later sent to Oxford and Paris. At the Sorbonne he was the recipient of great adulation, and was called "Most Learned Philosopher, Resolute Doctor." In 1329 he was elected provincial of the English province, but he resigned after four years so that he could devote more time to his studies and research. He was small of stature but a man of great physical energy, producing a prodigious number of writings. He was an intrepid defender of the doctrine of the Immaculate Conception, and the resolution of that theological question is due in no small part to his efforts. Baconthorpe died and was buried at the Carmelite monastery at London in 1348.

Another Englishman, John Cunningham, distinguished himself in the violent Wyclif controversy. He was born at Suffolk *circa* 1320, entered the monastery at Ipswich, and obtained his doctorate at Oxford. He was one of the earliest to oppose the teaching of John Wyclif, the priest who denied papal supremacy and the doctrine of transubstantiation and who has been called "the Morning Star of the Reformation." Cunningham frequently attacked the assertions of Wyclif and his followers, and in turn was the object of their argumentation and sarcasm. When Wyclif was condemned at the Council of Blackfriars in 1382, Cunningham preached the closing address at St. Paul's Cross. He died at York in 1399.

The earliest historians of the Order were John of Cimentho, John of Hildesheim, and a Spaniard, Philip Riboti, who first presented the manuscript of *The Institution of the First Monks*. Riboti, the provincial of the Catalonian province, published a textual compendium of Carmelite documentation in 1370 under the title *Decem libri de institutione et peculiaribus gestis religiosorum Carmelitarum*. He wrote that his purpose in compiling the documentation was ". . . to prepare a practical manual for the instruction of my brethren in religion, thus placing at their disposal, in compact form, the authentic sources of information relating to the origin and progress of their Order." His book included: an epistle of Cyril of Constantinople, the third prior general; the chronicle of William of Sanvico, who was purportedly a Carmelite on Mount Carmel at the time of the massacre of 1291, but who escaped from the Turks after witnessing the murder of his brethren; an excerpt from a commentary of the rule by Sigbert Van Bieck; and the *Institution* by John the Forty-fourth, patriarch of Jerusalem in the year 412. Only the work by Sigbert is of proven authenticity: the other three monographs are spurious, written by unknown authors. But, notwithstanding the *Institution*'s historical invalidity, the book has exercised an enormous influence on the inner spirit and character of the Order from the time of its appearance until modern days.

The epistle of Cyril of Constantinople states that the *Institution* was composed in Greek in 412 by John, the Forty-fourth patriarch of Jerusalem, and was translated into Latin about 1154, or at the command of Aymeric, patriarch of Antioch. John of Jerusalem was an authentic historical figure; in fact he was accused by St. Jerome of following the teachings of Origen, and in the late fourteenth century the Carmelites placed him in their catalogue of saints. However, the Roman Index of 1688 forbade the further use of the word "saint" in editions of the *Institution*. Cardinal Baronius, that eminent historian of the sixteenth century, was the first scholar of any note to attack the authenticity of the book, and his arguments were continued and developed by Daniel Papebroch in the following century. From an analysis of style, content, word structure, and scriptural quotation he was able to prove that the monograph was clearly a medieval document, definitely something that was not composed in the fifth century.

The first recorded reference to the document was in a sermon by James Fitzralph, bishop of Armagh, delivered at Avignon before the papal Curia when it assembled at the Carmelite monastery to celebrate the feast of the Immaculate Conception in the year 1342. The book had apparently been known for some years at that time. This fact, plus the internal evidence, have inclined scholars to place the time of composition at the end of the thirteenth or the beginning of the fourteenth century. Some historians claim that parts of the book derive from the twelfth century, and others have suggested that Riboti himself composed parts of it.

The *Institution* is fundamentally a discussion of the Order's inner spirit, based on the Elijahan tradition and the prophetic vocation. It adopts the erroneous history of the Elijahan foundation of the Order and the continuance of the Order through the Old Testament and the first millennium of the Christian epoch; however, the value of the book does not lie in this bad history, but rather in its careful delineation of the Order's contemplative spirit.

The author writes of the Elijahan character of the Order:

God decreed that the perfection of the prophetic life consists in the imitation of Elijah. Thus Elijah gave to the members of the Order the great models of the prophetic discipline and the monastic life: namely, his actions and good words, according to which they should adorn their hearts, so that, in his spirit, all the monks on Carmel and in the other deserts and places, should advance to that goal, completely forsaking the world and all earthly things, crucifying their carnal concupiscences by continence and abstinence, denying their will and humbly subjecting it to their superior, hidden from the sight of men and living the eremitical life of a prophet—which Elijah himself had lived in the desert and especially on Mount Carmel. The closer they approach this goal, the more willingly should they unite their hearts with God in perfect love.

The *Institution* claims that the fundamental aim of all Carmelites should be union with God—"to taste, in some manner, in our heart, and to experience in our soul the intensity of the divine presence and the sweetness of the glory from on high, not only after death, but even in this mortal life." And this is obtained by "our labor and effort, when we offer God a pure heart, free from every stain of sin." The theme of ascetical effort which produces contemplative union was later developed in greater depth and with greater clarity by St. John of the Cross, but it had its original expression in this early monograph. The author of the *Institution* presents the process of contemplation in the Elijahan context:

This prophet of God, Elijah, was the chief of the monks, from whom the holy and ancient Order took its origin. For it was he who, desirous of greater progress in the pursuit of divine contemplation, withdrew far from the cities and, divesting himself of all earthly and mundane things, was the first to adopt the holy and solitary life of a prophet which he had established at the inspiration and command of the Spirit. In a vision God had ordered him to depart from the ordinary dwelling place of men and to hide himself in the desert, away from the crowd, and thus live alone in solitude in the manner of life he followed. This is proved from the clear testimony of holy Scripture. We read what was written on this matter in the book of Kings: "And the word of the Lord came to him [Elijah] saying: 'Depart from here and turn eastward and hide yourself by the torrent of Carith, which is east of the Jordan. And I have commanded the ravens to feed you there.'"

Elijah's journey to Carith is a figure that was frequently adopted by the medieval Carmelites to express the soul's journey to love. The author of the *Institution* interprets Carith as love, and plays on the phonetic similarity between the words *Carith* and *caritas* (Latin for "love" in the original text). Indeed, one of the internal criteria for rejecting the Greek origin of the book is the author's insistence on the similarity between the two words: had the book originally been written in Greek, then the word for love would have been *agape*, and the literary comparison would have been meaningless. The author continues:

Therefore, my son, if you wish to be perfect and to arrive at the goal of the eremitic monastic life, and "east of the Jordan," that is away from the degradation of sin, you must hide in Carith, that is, in charity, and there drink of the torrent—you shall love the Lord your God with your whole heart, and with your whole soul and with your whole mind. When you have done this, you shall be perfect and "by the torrent of Carith which is the Jordan," that is, hidden in charity.

The book comments on the other features of Carmel's life. The apostolic dimension:

Although Elijah and Elisha, and the other religious of the Order, remained mostly in the deserts at God's command, for the sake of the people they sometimes went into the towns and villages, working miracles among the people, foretelling the future, reproving men's vices, recalling them to God, and drawing many to the prophetic Order. Therefore, in the surrounding districts of certain towns and villages of the Promised Land, especially in Galgal, Bethel, Jericho, and Samaria, they established the schools for religious men, sons of the prophets (as we read in the book of Kings), where the monks lodged when they came to the towns and villages.

The Marian tradition is underscored with a narration of the legend of Elijah's vision of Mary in the cloud, and then the author develops the theme of the similarity of vocation between Mary and the Carmelite, particularly in the vow of virginity, the sign of complete dedication, which establishes a conformity between them.

Because of this conformity, the religious of Carmel called the Virgin Mary their sister even in the times of the Apostles, and for the same reason called themselves the Brothers of the Blessed Virgin Mary. . . . These followers dedicated themselves to her, and assembled there every day to offer their continual prayers, supplications and praises to the Virgin and her Son.

There is a haunting charm about the book, redolent of the quiet mysticism of the East, and despite its prolix and repetitious style and its faulty history, the *Institution* has had a forceful and enduring impact on the Carmelite Order. It was used consistently throughout the medieval period for the instruction of novices, and it was proposed as the fundamental ascetical work of the Order and the depository of its ancient traditions. It was still being used when St. John of the Cross was instructed in the Carmelite life, and after the Teresian reform it enjoyed a new popularity. Thomas of Jesus edited it in 1599 and again in 1617, and it was published among his collected works in 1684. The book has remained in use until today, providing an unbroken link with the aspirations and inspirations of the twelfth and thirteenth centuries. The most recent edition was in 1941.

Commentators, recognizing the book's impact, have sometimes overemphasized its position in history. It has been called "the Magna Charta of the Carmelites" and "the essential basis of the Carmelite tradition," but those are exaggerations—the rule must remain the essential basis of the Carmelite life. However, the *Institution* does occupy a unique place in Carmelite history: it is a powerful and enduring medieval document, providing clear testimony to the Order's necessary commitment to the prophetic vocation.

At the apogee moment of its golden age in the middle of the fourteenth century, the Order was graced with two attractive and appealing saints: St. Andrew Corsini and St. Peter Thomas.

Andrew was born in Florence in 1301 of the titled Corsini family. His early biographies state that he was well-educated, but as a young man he gradually fell into a life of vice and profligacy and was the despair of his family. After a few years he decided to amend his ways and enter the Carmelite monastery in the city. The medieval biographies quaintly relate that in the monastery he was immediately subjected to "various temptations provoked by the devil, but he could not be dissuaded from his intention to remain in the Order"—which can only mean that the burden of his former escapades was weighing upon him, calling him to return. However, Andrew made the necessary adjustment, was professed in the Order, and sent to the University of Paris where he received a doctorate in theology. One of the Corsinis was a cardinal in the papal retinue at Avignon, and for a short time Andrew was attached to his suite, but he soon returned to the monastery in Florence and was eventually elected prior. Over his objections, he was elevated to the bishopric of Fiesole, and he remained in that office for the rest of his life. Urban V commissioned him to act as arbitrator in the city of Bologna during a period of civic uprisings which threatened to break into a civil war, and despite the disaffection of the Milanese for the foreign arbitrator, he was able to bring both factions together and terminate the strife. St. Andrew Corsini died quietly at Florence in 1373 at the age of seventy-two, and his feast is celebrated by the universal Church on February 4.

St. Peter Thomas, whom the ecclesiastical historian Rhorbacher calls "one of the greatest glories of the Church of France," had a less conventional career and a more important place in Carmelite history: he was particularly revered by medieval members of his Order who regarded him as the ideal Carmelite, combining in his life the two prophetic elements of contemplation and apostolic engagement. He also benefited from an excellent biographer: Philip de Mezières, a layman, aide of Peter of Lusignan, king of Cyprus, whom he met during his assignment as papal legate to the Christian East. Mezières became a close personal friend of the saint and recorded his life from his own experiences with him and from Peter Thomas' statements about his earlier life. The biography is almost unique for a book of that epoch: it is candid, honest, singularly lacking in the fables and pietisms so common in medieval hagiography, and it presents a sincere account of an authentic human being. Mezières' book has been called "one of the gems of medieval literature."

Peter Thomas was born in a small town in the province of Périgord in Aquitaine about the year 1305.[2] His father was a farm laborer, and the family was wretchedly poor. He had one brother and one sister, but the brother died as a small child. Peter was a brilliant student, and as a young boy, probably an adolescent, he left his impoverished home to tutor other children in the neighboring villages. He then went to Agen where he studied grammar, logic, and dialectic, working as a laborer to support himself through school. After completing his studies, he began teaching again and the prior of the Carmelite monastery at Lectoure employed him as a professor for his young clerics. He had worked in this employment for one year when, through the influence and encouragement of the prior of the monastery at Condom, he entered the Carmelite Order. Peter was sent back to Agen after his profession to study philosophy and theology, and then was ordained to the priesthood. Assigned to the monastery in Paris for the purpose of acquiring a higher degree in theology, he encountered a vexing and shameful problem—a growing abuse in the Order, which we will discuss in the following chapter, required that the university student obtain for himself the money to finance his education, either from his preaching, or his tutoring, or, most often, from his own relatives. Therefore Carmelites who came from affluent families were easily able to get the required money, while students from poorer backgrounds had to struggle. Peter's family was impecunious, and with the pressure of his religious duties and his studies he felt for a time that he would have to discontinue his studies. He later recounted to Mezières an episode which happened as he paced the cloister corridor late one night, worrying about his problem. The Blessed Virgin appeared to him, saying: "My son, do not worry about your lack of money, for I will not forsake you. Work hard at your studies and so you will serve my son and me." The next morning he received a large and unexpected donation with which he was able to continue his studies.

He obtained his doctorate in theology, and was assigned to the important monastery at Avignon, where the papal court was located.

---

[2] His place of birth was first thought to be the town of Condom, but since the seventeenth century the cult of St. Peter Thomas has been associated with the village of Lebreil. One modern commentator notes that Mezières and other contemporary documents always refer to the saint as Peter or Peter *of* Thomas, and that perhaps Thomas refers to his birthplace.

An excellent preacher and a man with a wide circle of friends, he soon came to the attention of the papal court and was entrusted with a succession of important missions. It is here at Avignon that we can obtain a clear portrait of this fourteenth-century saint. Physically, he was an extremely small man, and one of his Spanish biographers says "people wondered much that such a small vase could carry such large treasures of wisdom." He was, of course, a saintly man, spending long hours at prayer each day, and praying alone at night before the tabernacle after the rest of his community had retired. But he was also an extremely convivial person, quite witty, warm, outgoing, with a fantastic ability to attract people to himself. Mezières furthermore recounts that he could be very caustic and ironic, and he frequently made oblique remarks about the luxury at papal court from his pulpit. About his preaching Mezières says that "in the middle of his sermon he usually made his hearers laugh." And again: "He made them weep and laugh as he chose." His tenacity of purpose was already demonstrated during his struggle to educate himself, both before and after he entered the Order, and it would be seen again in his subsequent career.

At Avignon there also occurred the celebrated vision of the Blessed Virgin's promise concerning the Carmelite Order. Peter had apparently been praying to her—late at night again—in behalf of the Order when he heard these words from her: "Have confidence, Peter, for the Carmelite Order will last until the end of the world. Elijah, its founder, obtained it a long time ago from my Son."

Peter Thomas gradually became one of the confidential advisors to the Avignon Popes Clement VI and Innocent VI, and Innocent entrusted him with fourteen different diplomatic missions for the Holy See. When he was sent on a mission to the Holy Roman Emperor, Charles IV, he was consecrated bishop of Patti in Sicily so that he would have sufficient diplomatic stature at the German court. Mezières records another mission, a hazardous one, to the Serbian court when Peter was sent to affect a settlement with the schismatic king, Stephen Dushan. Mezières depicts Stephen in grotesque terms, presenting him as almost a barbarian—"among all the men in the world at that time he was possessed of the largest body and the most terrible countenance." When Peter entered the court he disregarded the king's order that all who approach the throne must kiss the king's feet under penalty of death, and there was a silent, eye-to-eye confrontation between the two men, the towering king and the diminutive papal legate. Peter's associates in his entourage "were certain that he and they were dead men." But the king relented, and Mezières states that "friar Peter received so many marks of respect and reverence from the king that it would be impossible to record all the details."

In 1356 Peter Thomas was appointed emissary to John V Palaeologus, emperor of Constantinople, and he brought about the emperor's submission to the pope. Since Palaeologus was under pressure from the Turks and needed Western help, the sincerity of his conversion has been questioned; but for a few years, at least, there was a certain measure of unity between East and West, and the personality of Peter Thomas seems to have been an important factor in this peace of convenience. In 1359 he was made legate to the entire Christian East with full powers, "general and special," and one of these powers was the typically medieval one of "making war on the enemies of the faith."

It was at this time of Peter Thomas' life that he met Philip de Mezières. The saint was in his middle fifties, and Mezières was a younger man, the chancellor of the king of Cyprus and a frequent visitor to the papal court. Mezières called the saint his "most beloved father and shepherd," and Peter Thomas called the chancellor his "most loving son." But their relationship was more than just a professional association between priest and layman—they became close personal friends, and Peter confided that he cherished Mezières more than anyone else in the world. They seemed to be of similar temperaments: they both were extremely intelligent, both men of determination who knew what they wanted, and they both had friendly and happy dispositions.

In the autumn of 1359, Pope Innocent VI dispatched a military force, composed of French knights, mercenary soldiers, and probably some Venetians and Cypriots, to aid Palaeologus by attacking the Turkish concentration in the Dardanelles. Peter Thomas was placed in charge of the expedition, and, sword in hand, he participated as an active combatant. From the vantage point of the twentieth century we are appalled to witness a professed man of God waging war and wielding a sword. But this was the fourteenth century, and another mentality prevailed. The strange spirit of the crusades had come alive again, and the Turks still appeared as the foes of Christianity, holding the Holy Land, constantly threatening to pour into Europe. The holy war, however much we might deplore it, was an integral part of medieval thinking, and the Christian dream was to reopen the Holy Land. The warrior ecclesiastic was part of that mood, too: the priest, as much as any other citizen, was historically and emotionally involved in wresting Palestine from the Turks and restoring free access to the shrine places in Palestine. In this, St. Peter Thomas was a man of his times.

The expeditionary force of 1359 attacked the Turkish camp at Lampsacus in the Dardanelles. They routed the Turks, burned the installation, and began the journey back to the coast, which lay a few miles from the Turkish camp. But before the Christian force could reach the ships the Turks had regrouped themselves, quickly recruited extra troops, and now waited in ambush. They swept down on the papal troops, shouting and screaming, and cut the line of march. The Christian troops broke ranks, dropped their standards, and began to run toward the ships, only to be met by more Turks. Peter Thomas rallied a group of fifty Knights Hospitalers and with sword and mace they opened a passageway through the Turkish soldiers and led the troops back to their ships. Mezières relates that a number of Peter's personal followers were killed, but that three hundred Turks were slain.

In 1361 Peter Thomas was on the island of Cyprus when a serious plague broke out, probably a species of the Black Death which had ravaged Europe a few years previously. He ministered to the sick, caring for them, consoling them, burying the dead. As a result of his efforts during this plague and the reputation he acquired for assisting the sick, St. Peter Thomas was particularly invoked during the succeeding ages in time of pestilence. The liturgical prayer for his feast beseeches that "we may be preserved from the illness of pestilence."

Pope Urban V, who acceded the papacy in 1362, tried to revive the futile hope of toppling the Turkish empire. He attempted to enlist the Christian princes of Europe, but after many promises the only help he could obtain came from Peter I of Lusignan, king of Cyprus. A fleet was assembled at Rhodes under the leadership of the king, and Peter Thomas was appointed papal legate to the expedition and given the title of patriarch of Constantinople. Mezières was in command of the galley which carried the saint, and was therefore able to observe him closely during the entire operation. In port before sailing, Peter Thomas visited each of the nobles and knights and soldiers, talking with them, hearing confessions, encouraging them. The saint's charm and rare human magnetism was at work again, and Mezières states that even the rough mercenary soldiers came under his spell—"they almost adored him, and those who kissed his hand felt they were thereby insured against all dangers." Every man in the fleet received the Eucharist from his hand before setting sail.

The fleet left Rhodes on October 4, 1365, bound for the Moslem stronghold of Alexandria. It could hardly be called a crusade: it was more a marauding party, and a badly executed one at that. Peter Thomas had long confided to Mezières his desire for martyrdom, and he felt that he might obtain his desire on this expedition. When the fleet reached the harbor at Alexandria, the king allowed the ships to drift idly in the water, apparently undecided about the proper moment of attack. Peter Thomas impatiently urged Mezières to forge ahead, but his friend told him he had to obey the king. Finally the king gave the attack order, and the Christian troops landed and Peter Thomas went with them. Mezières records his conduct:

> Did he fear the arrows that rained on him? Not in the least. As God is my witness, I did not see his expression change, nor could I discover any least motion of fear in him, either on the sea or on land. So great was his desire to get on shore that although innumerable arrows were flying about him he would not even use the shelter of a shield, although I begged him to do so several times.

The attack was successful, and Alexandria was taken. Peter Thomas, carrying a cross, led the men through the city. However, the perennial problem of the crusaders ensued, the problem that had beset this quixotic movement almost since its origin: the crusading nobles began to argue and disagree among themselves. Some wanted to carry on the fight, pursuing the Turk through the Near East, while others, having gotten their plunder and spoil, wanted to return home. Eventually the expedition was abandoned and the fleet returned to Rhodes. Peter Thomas was bitterly disappointed at the failure to continue the expedition, and he complained about it in a letter when he arrived back at the island of Cyprus: "Whom God joined together for the task of taking the city, iniquity divided."

Peter Thomas returned to Cyprus a sick and broken man. Worn out by years of travel, exhausted from his military expeditions, and now dispirited that his last great enterprise had ended in a fiasco, he was taken ill at the Carmelite monastery at Famagusta on the island.

He died a few days later, January 6, 1366, and great crowds came to view his body, acclaiming him a saint. Mezières eulogizes him in the final section of his book in a moving lament. He remembers the saint's letters, "sent to me so often, written in his own hand, containing words of such holiness that they seemed to proceed from the mouth of God." And he recalls his bravery—"a strong fighter whose sword never turned aside in battle." And yet his final recollection is of an approachable, unpretentious man in whom there was "neither austerity of manner nor pomposity." He had lost a true friend.

St. Peter Thomas was venerated as a saint, a bishop and confessor, during the fourteenth century, but in the year 1564 we discover that he is curiously venerated as a martyr. This strange elevation of a man to the state of martyrdom two centuries after he died of natural causes affords an illuminating insight into the pious manner in which the early hagiographers rewrote history. Mezières notes in his book that Peter Thomas desired martyrdom, and that it would be entirely proper to regard him as a martyr because he exposed himself to danger so frequently and he was accordingly a martyr in spirit. But Mezières' statement is a literary comment and hardly a factual report of a martyr's death. Nevertheless, a liturgical cult to St. Peter Thomas as a martyr endured from the seventeenth century until recent times. The fable was embellished, and the liturgical lessons for his feast relate that he was wounded by the arrows at the siege of Alexandria and was then carried back to Famagusta where he died from these injuries shortly afterward. None of that, of course, is historical, and finally in 1958 the Congregation of Rites directed that all references to St. Peter Thomas' martyrdom be stricken from his feast and that he be venerated as a bishop and confessor.

St. Peter Thomas exercised a unique fascination for the late medieval Carmelite, someone cast in the mold of the prophet Elijah. There was something overwhelmingly Elijahan about the saint—the man of prayer, the forceful preacher, the courageous warrior for the cause of God. These qualities, plus his particular devotion to the Blessed Virgin, made him an image of the ideal Carmelite. He became a hero for the members of his Order. And he entered the scene of history at a moment when the Order desperately needed a hero, someone to look up to, because the Order was beginning its period of descent and decline, the epoch of abuses and scandals, the time of decadence.

– III –
DECLINE AND MITIGATION

During the late fourteenth century and the entire fifteenth century the Carmelite Order slipped into a state of severe decline, a period characterized by a loss of original religious fervor and shocking abuses. Partisan historians have been quick to point out that these were particularly unsettled times in Europe, and that in those pre-Reformation years of the high Renaissance the identical problem was shared by most of the religious orders. These nervous statements are undoubtedly meant to minimize the Order's guilt for allowing the situation to develop, but they hardly do that: they simply indicate the historical context in which the problems did occur and the imminent evils the Order should have resisted. While no religious order lives in a vacuum, untouched by the secular conditions around it, and while it certainly must be profoundly affected by contemporary conditions, it must still not submit or be submerged by attitudes which are diametrically opposed to its very purpose. An epoch of inimical conditions is a call to struggle, a summons to greater effort; it is not a time for capitulation. Carmel's situation, as we will see, was not entirely black: there was much that was good; but there was much that was bad. The forebodings of Nicholas the Frenchman had been realized.

In 1347 the most devastating plague in European history made its grim appearance, the Black Death, the bubonic plague which is estimated to have killed almost a third of the entire European population in the four years of its duration. The disease apparently originated in the Orient and was carried back to Europe along the trade routes to Italy by small animals, particularly rats. The highly infectious disease caused an inflammatory swelling in the victim's lymph glands, especially in the groin (*boubon*, Greek for groin), which quickly resulted in chills, fever, and prostration. The victim's skin turned black, and he suffered excruciating pain, usually dying in a matter of hours after the disease struck. The plague reached catastrophic proportions, and the terror was increased by the terribly infectious nature of the disease and the rapidity with which it felled its victims. In some cities more than half the population perished, and there were not sufficient people to bury the infected corpses as they piled in the streets.

The Black Death was a major catastrophe in European history: it decimated the population, caused severe economic hardships, and depleted the labor force for economic recovery. There was famine, hunger, massive looting, and the almost inevitable moral decay. Understandably, the plague wreaked immense havoc in the monastic life of the fourteenth century, killing off great segments of its membership. In a single day, for example, seventy Carmelites died in the monastery at Avignon. In the wake of this disaster the Order found itself dangerously depopulated: there were not enough men to fulfill the religious observances of the monastic regime in the many monasteries throughout Europe, and the number of new vocations declined radically. One unfortunate result was that the Order, like many of the contemporary religious orders, began to recruit and accept young boys into the monastery for the purpose of educating them into a religious vocation, a practice that had drastic consequences. Carmel also suffered economically as the amount of donations and freewill offerings decreased alarmingly in that time of famine and economic disaster. Many monasteries found themselves in extreme financial need. With few men and slender financial resources, the monasteries had difficulty in maintaining proper religious observance and providing adequate intellectual and spiritual formation for their members. For almost seventy-five years the Order struggled to recover from the tragedy of the Black Death.

Another grievous problem of that epoch was the Hundred Years' War, that protracted struggle of intermittent skirmishes and battles which spanned the years from 1340 to 1453. This "war" between England and France was not, of course, an uninterrupted period of actual fighting, but rather a long epoch of hostility in which the French eventually drove the English from the Continent. Beginning with the English victory at the naval battle of Sluys in 1340 and ending with their defeat at Bordeaux in 1453, the struggle saw a gallery of romantic figures: the English Black Prince, and Henry V; and the French Philip the Bold, and the Dauphin, Charles VII; and *La Pucelle,* Joan of Arc. And the historic battles: Crécy, Agincourt, Orléans. The English introduced the use of the longbow at Crécy, and before the end of the conflict gunpowder was being used as a kind of primitive artillery. But for all the romanticism involved in this last great medieval war, it was a time of tragedy and misery for the people in the duchies of France. Armies roamed the countryside, attacking each other, destroying towns and villages, causing inestimable damage. As a result of the destruction and the havoc and the constant fear of raiding armies, the people became pathetically dispirited, despairing that a final settlement would ever come. Joan of Arc's major contribution was to rally the people, restore their morale, and ultimately to crystallize an incipient French patriotism which laid the foundation for a true French nation in that age of developing nationalism.

The religious orders suffered immensely during the long struggle. Many monasteries were destroyed in the path of the fighting armies, usually by fire. Records are inexact, but we do know some of the Carmelite monasteries which were destroyed: Bergerac, Caen, La Rochelle, Angers, Bordeaux, Carcassonne, Montpellier, Arras, Tours, Orléans, Chalon-sur-Saône. It has been estimated that as many as fifty Carmelite monasteries were lost during the hundred-year period. But more tragic than the actual loss of buildings was the general demoralization the war caused in religious life. During the various battles the religious of the town or city, the Carmelites among them, frequently fought with the townspeople against the detested English, and sometimes they even were placed in charge of the raiding parties which sallied forth to harass the enemy. It unfortunately created a bellicose mood in the monastic life, something hardly conducive to the original Carmelite ideal of prayer and solitude. Thus for almost a hundred years the monasteries of France lived in a spirit of insecurity, preparedness for battle, occasional famine, financial need, and consequently a deterioration of monastic discipline. And the impact and ramifications of France's problems, both in the secular and religious life, was felt all over Europe during the time of the Hundred Years' War.

Another damaging influence on late medieval religious life was the emergence and distortion of the new humanism and the Renaissance. The rebirth of the culture of ancient Greece and Rome which the Renaissance represented was not a new phenomenon which originated in the fourteenth and fifteenth centuries: Latin literature had formed the basis of most medieval education, and Aquinas and his followers in the thirteenth century had restored the pre-eminence of Greek philosophy in scholastic circles. But there was a new penetration and a new emphasis on the entire ancient culture and language and art during the late Middle Ages. Thus the humanism of the period denoted an enthusiastic rebirth, or "renaissance," of interest in the culture of the ancient Greco-Roman world, with special emphasis on its literature, the *litterae humaniores* (the humane letters). Francesco Petrarch (1304-1374) is commonly regarded as the father of humanism, and he inspired others to follow in his path, notably Giovanni Boccaccio, Cardinal Bessarion, and Cosimo de' Medici. Soon the impact of this movement was felt all over Europe, and there was a rush to delve deeply into the human treasures of the ancient world. The new humanism was sponsored particularly at the courts of the local princes, who patronized the new culturists and made them tutors for their children, training their charges not only in classical literature but also in art, music, athletics, dancing, military skill, and gentlemanly bearing. The "universal man," as he came to be called, was then the humanist ideal.

With the invention of the printing press sometime in the middle of the fifteenth century, probably by Johann Gutenberg of Mainz, the movement was given a new impetus. Printed material became available, and ideas were communicated more easily. In the early sixteenth century, humanism found such ardent followers and eloquent spokesmen as Desiderius Erasmus in Rotterdam, John Colet and Thomas More in England, Juan Luis Vives in Spain, and François Rabelais in France.

From its earliest beginnings the Renaissance had been patronized by the popes. At Avignon Pope Clement VI (1342-1352) was an enthusiastic devotee, and he sponsored a number of humanists. Capable Latinists were always in demand in the Curia, and we find such outstanding figures as Salutati, Poggio Bracciolini, and Bruni working as papal secretaries. When the papacy was re-established at Rome after the confusion and neglect of the Avignon residence and the Great Western Schism, the popes commissioned painters, architects, and sculptors to refurbish and embellish the city. And the cardinals emulated the popes in patronizing the humanists in order to lend luster to their own entourage. Pope Nicholas V (1447-1455), who founded the Vatican Library, assembled scholars and artists from all over Europe at the papal court in an attempt to make Rome the capital of the Renaissance. He has been called the humanists' greatest patron.

The religious problem in the Renaissance developed with the growth of an unfortunate tendency to imitate not only the culture and wisdom of the ancient past, but also its paganism and hedonism. The presence of authentic Christian humanists seemed to be more and more overshadowed by a growing number of neopagans, who lacked any Christian frame of reference and were intent only on celebrating the physical. Gatherings at the various courts began to descend from assemblies of scholars into scenes of orgies and revels, and this was true also at the papal and ecclesiastical courts. We can note a definite and perceptible decline of morality at the papal court throughout the fifteenth century, until Innocent VIII (1484–1492) became the first pope to recognize his illegitimate children publicly. His successor, Alexander VI, obtained the papacy by open simony, and fathered the infamous Cesare and Lucrezia Borgia. The papacy seemed to be at a moment of depravity, and pious people in Rome prayed aloud in the streets, fearing that God would destroy the world.

It is unfortunate that so much of the blame for the moral disintegration at the papal court has been ascribed to the humanist revival. Although the Renaissance did create a boundless enthusiasm to imitate the ancient pagan world, and although it did occasion the collection of many disreputable persons at the papal court, it is nevertheless an oversimplification to state that the Renaissance itself must bear the principal responsibility. Too many other factors intervened—the Avignon papacy, the Great Schism, and not the least of all, simple human corruption. There were many dedicated and enthusiastic humanists who were simultaneously sincerely Christian. The Carmelites Arnold Bostius and Blessed Baptist Spagnoli were both gifted and respected humanists, yet they were both saintly men, conscious of their Christian vocation and yet equally conscious of their obligation to discover and penetrate the human condition. However, many ecclesiastics over the centuries have retained an irrational fear and suspicion of human culture precisely because of the immoralities at the papal court during the Renaissance.

The moral decline in Rome was witnessed by Christian Europe, and it had its understandable influence in weakening moral responsibility throughout the entire Church. And the religious orders participated in this decline: there were abuses, irregularities, a breakdown in religious discipline, a failure to keep the religious vows, and flagrant immoralities. The Carmelite Order, as we shall see, was no exception.

As a final indignity in this time of enormous trouble, the Church found itself split wide open by perhaps the most grievous problem in its entire history—the Great Western Schism.

From the year 1309 until 1376 the popes resided in southern France at the city of Avignon during what has been euphemistically called the Babylonian captivity of the papacy. This prolonged residency began with the pontificate of Clement V, the former archbishop of Bordeaux who was elected pope in 1305. After his election he was crowned in Lyons, but pleading ill health and the pressure of negotiations with the French king, Philip the Fair, he tarried in France, finally taking up residence with the Dominicans in Avignon in 1309. During his nine-year reign he provided substance to the suspicion throughout Europe that the papacy was being converted into a French institution: he allowed Philip to appropriate Church funds, he agreed to suppress the Knights Templars, he appointed seven French cardinals, and at the Fifteenth General Council held at Vienne all recent decrees not acceptable to the French king were annulled. There was a two-year interval after his death before King Philip allowed the conclave to assemble at Lyons in 1316. The conclave of twenty-three cardinals, two-thirds of them French, elected another Frenchman, John XXII, a native of Cahors. John permanently established the papacy at Avignon, and set up the Curia and the complex, efficient machinery of government which characterized the Avignon residence of the popes. Throughout the almost seventy years at Avignon there was a constant effort and urging among European churchmen to restore the papacy to Rome. The Avignon papacy was not a bad papacy, but it was far from a satisfactory one. The elaborate and insistent system of taxation which was constructed caused an understandable amount of criticism, and there was considerable indignation against the venality and luxury, however much exaggerated by contemporary critics, of the pope, his cardinals, and their retinues. But the main complaint against the Avignon papacy was its subservience to the French crown and the growing loss of identity with the original See of Peter. Finally in late 1376 Pope Gregory XI, prodded by the exhortations and encouragement of St. Catherine of Siena, who had journeyed to Avignon in person, sent a mercenary force ahead of him in late 1376 to quell the strife and civil battles waging in Rome, and he himself traveled to Genoa and then set sail for the Eternal City. He was in the Vatican by January, 1377.

But the problem was not really resolved. Pope Gregory XI unfortunately died a year later, in March of 1378, and a conclave of comic opera proportions ensued. Ten days after Gregory's death, the sixteen cardinals of the conclave—eleven Frenchmen, four Italians, and a Spaniard—assembled to elect a successor. The Roman populace, milling outside the conclave, clamored for the election of a Roman pope: they did not want to lose the papacy to Avignon again, having regained it after a seventy years' absence. Throughout the entire period of the conclave the unruly mob roamed the area, drinking wine stolen from the papal cellars and shouting for a Roman pope. On the afternoon of the eighth of April the crowd forced its way past the guards and surged into the conclave chambers. In the meantime the cardinals had found themselves deadlocked between two French candidates, and had decided to compromise on an Italian: they chose Bartolomeo Prignano, the archbishop of Bari, who was not even present at the conclave. He was not a Roman, but at least he was an Italian. However, the cardinals were uncertain of the crowd's possible reaction to Prignano, so they quickly placed the papal robes on Cardinal Tebaldeschi, the aged archpriest of St. Peter's, and presented him to the Romans as their new pope. Then they took to hiding while awaiting the arrival of Prignano in Rome. His reception was remarkably peaceful: the people accepted him enthusiastically, after learning of the deception with Tebaldeschi; the cardinals reassembled and reaffirmed their election; and Prignano took the name of Urban VI, and celebrated the Holy Week services with his cardinals.

But the cardinals apparently did not know what they had purchased in Prignano. As Urban VI he set to work immediately to cleanse the Curia of many abuses that had developed in Avignon, and he began to engage in public disputes with the cardinals, calling them to their face liars, traitors, and simoniacs. Whatever good Urban was attempting to accomplish, he greatly impaired it by his extraordinary lack of tact and prudence. Some historians have even suggested that he became mentally unbalanced in the process of using the mighty power of the papacy. When the cardinals began to leave Rome at the end of May because of the hot weather, they gradually assembled at Anagni in the kingdom of Naples, and engaged in some long soul-searching about the election of Urban VI. They concluded that the freedom of the conclave was destroyed by the fear of violence from the threatening mob outside, and that consequently Urban was not validly elected. They issued a manifesto to that effect on August 2, and on September 20 they went into conclave again, electing a Frenchman, Cardinal Robert of Geneva, who took the name of Clement VII. Urban promptly excommunicated Clement and the entire college of cardinals, and appointed another whole college. Clement in turn excommunicated Urban. The Great Western Schism had begun.

Clement took up his residence with his college of cardinals at Avignon, and Urban remained in Rome with his group, and for the next thirty-nine years the Church was submitted to the sorry spectacle of two men with considerable followings, each claiming to be the true pontiff. And after the Council of Pisa in 1409 attempted to end the schism, there were three claimants to the papacy. The Church was split down the middle, with two Curias, two sets of legates, conflicting bulls of excommunication, and two organizations for the collection of money. The various religious orders followed suit and they were divided according to their allegiance to one or the other of the two claimants, and thus there were two superior generals for each order and two different administrations. The nations of Europe followed their political interests rather than an appraisal of the facts in selecting their allegiance. Accordingly France and her allied nations, the Spanish kingdoms, Naples, Sicily, and Scotland followed the popes at Avignon. On the other hand, Rome, England, Flanders, and the Scandinavian kingdoms supported the popes at Rome. Only Germany and northern Italy were divided in their allegiance. The religious orders followed the same principle, and thus individual religious were not given any choice in the matter: they simply followed the allegiance of their nation.

The Carmelite general in 1378 at the outbreak of the schism was Bernard Oller, a native of Catalonia and consequently a sympathizer of the Clementist faction. However, at Rome he prudently tried to hold the Order together and prevent a division. While allowing his sympathies to be known to the Clementist countries, he managed to retain the loyalty of the Urbanist faction in Rome. This fragile regime endured for two years until finally the suspicions of Urban VI were confirmed and he deposed Oller from office. Michael of Bologna, whom Oller had already assigned as vicar general for

"Urbanist affairs," was placed in the office of general by Urban, and in the following year he was duly elected at a chapter held in Rome. Oller retired to Avignon where he continued as general of the Clementist faction. The split in the Carmelite Order had been accomplished.

Michael of Bologna already possessed an outstanding reputation as a scholar. A doctor from the University of Paris, he spent most of his subsequent academic career as a professor at the University of Bologna, where he composed his theological and scriptural works. Michael became one of the two leading Carmelite theologians of the late Middle Ages—the other was John Baconthorpe—and beginning with the fifteenth century the constitutions prescribed that theological studies in the Order were to follow the doctors of the Order, "especially Baconthorpe and Michael of Bologna." However, Michael was less successful as an administrator in Rome. He allowed the financial situation to deteriorate, and the truculent Urban VI began to suspect him of Clementist tendencies and general malfeasance in office. After a long, tedious canonical trial, the pope had Michael deposed from office in 1386. He was succeeded by John of Palude, and he in turn was followed by Matthew of Bologna.

The Avignon section of the Order fared better in its administration. Bernard Oller governed until 1383 when Clement VII appointed him to a bishopric. He was followed first by Raymond Vaquerius, and four years later by John Grossi, a saintly man of exceptional ability. Grossi, a native of Toulouse, traveled extensively during his administration, encouraging his men, attempting to bolster their spirits and maintain discipline despite the upheavals of the Schism and the Hundred Years' War in France. When the breach in the Order was finally healed in 1411 he was unanimously elected general by both factions.

The period of the Great Schism was a time of confusion and uncertainty, as well as a time of bitter hostility. Viewing the Schism from the dispassionate viewpoint of the twentieth century and examining all the documentation, historians generally agree that Urban VI was the legitimate pope. But the average citizen of the fourteenth century lacked the evidence we now possess: all he knew was that Prignano had been declared the pope, only to be unanimously repudiated three months later by the very men who elected him. Sincere and honest men were to be found on both sides of the question: St. Vincent Ferrer and St. Collette supported Avignon;

and St. Catherine of Siena and St. Catherine of Sweden supported Rome. The net result was a general bewilderment which did nothing to further the interests of the Christian religion.

As effort after effort to unite the two papal factions failed, a new theory was broadcast abroad in the Church: the conciliar theory, which contended that when the head of the Church was in default the entire Church must assert itself through the instrumentality of a general council. The conciliar theory, which harassed the Church for almost forty years, was the spirit behind the convocation of the Council of Pisa in 1409. Accordingly, Gregory XII, who was the fourth Roman pope, and Benedict XIII, the second Avignon pope, both approached the council reluctantly. When no resolution of the conflict between the two claimants seemed possible, the council fathers, composed of twenty-two cardinals and eighty-four bishops, deposed them both and proceeded to elect the Milanese cardinal as Alexander V. Neither Gregory nor Benedict accepted the council's decision, and the final result of the council was the creation of a third pope, the Pisan claimant. Alexander V died after one year, and in his place was elected John XXIII, a less than attractive personality. Finally the new German king, Sigismund, recalling the role that the ancient emperors played in ecumenical councils, forced the convocation of another council at Constance in 1414. This remarkable assembly lasted in almost continuous session for three and a half years, and was able to bring the Great Schism to a close. The Pisan pope, John XXIII, fled in the middle of the proceedings, hoping to disrupt the council, but Sigismund pursued him to Schaffhausen where he had him imprisoned. The council then declared him deposed. The Roman claimant, Gregory XII, was more tractable: he resigned voluntarily. But the Avignon claimant, Benedict XIII, now a very stubborn old Spaniard, defied the council and refused to resign, even after the Spanish monarchs withdrew their support. In July of 1417, after a lengthy process, the council declared him deposed, and the old man retired to Spain where he futilely continued to proclaim himself pope for the remainder of his life. In November of that year the council fathers elected the Roman Cardinal Colonna, who took the name of Martin V, and was the first universally acknowledged pope in forty years.

The one happy factor for the Carmelite Order in the confusion of the Pisan Council in 1409 was that it prepared the way for the reunification of the Order. The Pisan pope, Alexander V, was a

Franciscan, and was thus concerned about the divided condition of the religious orders. In an attempt to unite the Carmelites, he named the Avignon general, John Grossi, as general of the entire Order. This nomination was not, of course, accepted by the Roman faction, but it did serve to alert the whole Order to two facts: the Order desperately needed to reunite; and John Grossi was the most prestigious Carmelite of his day, the only one who could command respect from both parties. Negotiations were inaugurated between Grossi and the Roman Carmelites, and in 1411 a chapter assembled at Bologna. The Romans, who had suffered from bad administration, gladly accepted Grossi, and after both Grossi and Michael of Bologna had resigned their offices to heal the division, the chapter unanimously elected John Grossi as general of the now reunited Order. Thus the Order solved its problems of division six years before the Council of Constance was able to end the papal schism.

Grossi remained in office for nineteen years; he resigned in 1430 because of old age and ill health. During his vigorous administration he attempted to pull the Order out of its continuing descent: he made numerous visitations, enacted disciplinary decrees, convoked a series of general chapters, founded more monasteries, and even established the new provinces of Touraine and Bohemia. But he had no more than limited success in his efforts, and was not able to dispel the general mood of decadence within the Order. A man of intelligence and tact and sensitivity, Grossi distinguished himself during the long deliberations at the Council of Constance, and despite his inability to effect a radical change of spirit within the Order, he must nevertheless be regarded in history as one of its outstanding generals. After resigning from office, he retired to the monastery of Pamiers, where he died in 1437.

Among the many personal abuses of the Carmelites in this age of decline, one of the most fundamental was a general relaxation in the practice of the vow of poverty. Technically, the religious were obliged to relinquish all moneys when they entered the Order, and from that point in their lives all moneys which came to them in any way should have been given to the Order; and the Order had the concomitant obligation of providing for its members. But grave abuses in these obligations began to be accepted as common practice. Many Carmelites continued to participate in the revenues from their family estates, and in inheritances, and in regular financial assistance from their relatives. The superiors, in turn, allowed their men to retain moneys they acquired through preaching, teaching, and the copying of books. An unhealthy class system thus developed between the affluent and the poor Carmelites, which almost inevitably engendered a spirit of avariciousness. Some of the Carmelites led comfortable lives with an abundance of material possessions, while others who came from poorer backgrounds or who were less enterprising were reduced to an almost impoverished state. The lay brothers, for instance, frequently adopted the practice of selling in the market place the vegetables they had secretly taken from the monastery garden so they could provide themselves with what they needed.

The teachers and university professors furthermore acquired a host of privileges which placed them on a special plane elevated above their confreres. In addition to retaining their salaries, they were for all practical purposes dispensed from most of the community acts of the monastic schedule, even from the recitation of the office. They were allowed to purchase their own food and eat in their rooms, rather than in the community refectory. And they could hire a servant to clean their rooms, prepare their meals, and wait on them.

In that age of easy dispensation a little money could induce a variety of privileges from Rome. Those Carmelites who had not obtained an academic degree could apply for an indult from Rome, accompanied by an appropriate honorarium, and in turn receive a document which declared that they were doctors. These so-called *Doctores Bullati* (doctors by papal bull) could then teach and participate in the excessive privileges of the professors. Another interesting document could also be readily obtained from Rome: a titular bishopric, in actuality merely a piece of paper which declared that the holder was a titular bishop of some distant and usually underdeveloped mission territory. Sometimes these documents were presented to obliging bishops who then consecrated the holders, but most often they were merely retained as papers of privilege which could be used to dispense oneself from any obligation to community or superior.

Europe was dotted with many thousands of benefices, those revenue-producing churches and chapels and estates which returned an income to their holders from their endowments or testamentary foundations. After the Black Death many of these smaller benefices fell vacant, and religious priests, Carmelites among them, eagerly applied for the title to these sources of income. They were willingly granted in the form of pontifical chaplaincies, for which the priest had to offer some usually insignificant service such as the occasional celebration of a Mass; but more often than not, there was no service required of any kind, and the chaplain merely collected his income. The religious were furthermore able to hold multiple benefices at the same time, and one English Carmelite in the early fifteenth century received permission to have simultaneous possession of fifty different benefices.

The practice introduced after the Black Death of bringing young boys into the monastery began to pay grim dividends. These boys, some of them as young as eight or nine years of age, were presented to the monasteries for the purpose of educating them into a religious vocation. They pronounced their religious vows at a ridiculously immature age, without an accurate understanding of the religious life or the dimensions of their commitment. When they reached a more mature age they frequently discovered that they had no vocation at all, but they were unfortunately obligated by serious and binding vows. This produced generations of less than adequate and dedicated Carmelites, and thus lowered the whole tone and spirit of dedication in the Order. Another sad effect was the reduction of the number of competent men to hold the office of superior, and consequently many of the numerous monasteries in Europe were governed by inadequate and grossly incapable men.

The cumulative result of all these irregularities was a vast breakdown in monastic discipline and an amazing infidelity to the original aspirations of the prophetic vocation. The fasts and abstinence of the Order were not maintained. Silence and solitude became a thing of the past as the friars left the monastery on any pretext and immersed themselves in the amusements and entertainments of the day. There were reports of concubinage and illicit affairs, and some Carmelites used to place a ladder against the monastery wall so they could climb over at night to reach their assignations. In Seville two Carmelites were apprehended by the police when a brothel was raided.

Throughout this long, shameful period of more than a century and a half there were almost constant admonitions by the general chapters pleading with the men for a return to regular observance. These admonitions, as unsuccessful as they were, indicate that there was a wiser and saner segment in the Order which deplored the current conditions; they also afforded detailed information about some of the abuses. In addition to the expected warnings about solitude, communal life, eating in the refectory, choral attendance, and poverty, the acts of the general chapters during the fourteenth and fifteenth centuries prohibit the use of fine linen clothes, the wearing of silver buckles on the habits, and the carrying of swords with ivory and silver handles. There is an injunction for the Carmelites to cease cultivating their hair and wear the monastic tonsure, and a prescription against wearing secular clothes, and for those who were apparently circumventing this legislation, a further admonition not to wear secular clothes under their habits when they left the monastery. Another prescription forbids the Carmelites to sing and dance to the profane songs. But the most frequent exhortation during that period was a plaintive plea for the Carmelites to avoid idleness and indolence, and to get busy.

The late medieval Carmelites had degenerated a far degree from those original austere hermits who lived with Berthold and Brocard on Mount Carmel.

When John Grossi resigned in 1430, the chapter convened at Nantes to elect his successor, Bartholomew Roquali. But after the election some Carmelites began to protest its validity because of legal irregularities in the electoral procedure. There were appeals to the pope about the question, and at length in 1433 Eugene IV solved the question delicately and diplomatically by appointing Roquali bishop of Marseille where he served until his death in 1445. The pope also appointed Natale Bencesi of Venice to act as vicar general of the Order until a new chapter could be convened, and in the following year the general chapter elected John Faci of Avignon as prior general.

Roquali's major work during his short and contested tenure of office was the implementation of a major decision of enormous consequence agreed upon at the chapter of Nantes: the mitigation of the Carmelite rule. The chapter fathers, confronted by the general breakdown in monastic discipline, chose to seek a solution by that most hazardous of routes: an expedient compromise born out of fear and uncertainty. Since so many of the Carmelites were not following the rule, they argued, a solution might be found by mitigating the rule and lessening its severity, thereby making legal and official that which was already being done in practice. They felt this would present a minimum goal to the members of the order and thus make its life more palatable. If the Carmelites could or would not follow the rule, they claimed, then we must change the rule and modify it down to a level where there was no excuse for infidelity.

This was thinking which emanated from panic, and it only further complicated an already extremely difficult situation. The men who were not following the original rule did not, of course, practice the new mitigated one with any greater fidelity; and the men who were attempting to be faithful to the rule deplored and contested this further deterioration of the Order because, in effect, the new legislation struck a lethal blow at the very essence of the Carmelite life: it was a radical departure from the prophetic vocation.

The actual changes suggested by the chapter fathers at Nantes were concerned with only the three items of solitude, fast, and abstinence, and upon reading the simple text of the mitigations one might wonder at the furor and violent reaction caused by this new legislation. But the contemporary Carmelites and their successors realized what the changes implied: these reductions in solitude and austerity were a major divorcement from Carmel's historical traditions, practices which profoundly changed the inner spirit of the Order and its original vision. The prophetic vocation, the imitation of the prophet Elijah, demanded solitude and an intensive program of penance, and with an abandonment of this tradition the Order was beginning a further confused descent.

John Faci, who served as the procurator general in Rome during the uneasy administration of Bartholomew Roquali, was assigned to formulate the petition to the Holy See and work out the details of obtaining permission for the mitigation. A brief was prepared and submitted to Eugene IV on February 15, 1432, but three years passed before a favorable response was received, and by that time Faci was himself the prior general. Eugene IV's bull *Romani pontificis* was granted in 1435, but it bore the date of the original petition of 1432. (This strange practice of issuing a decree over the date of the petition rather than the actual date of the document was common curial procedure in that epoch, and it has confused many historians and caused a number of serious historical errors.) Eugene IV seemed to have some misgivings about the whole affair when he wrote in his decree that the mitigations were being granted "due to the fact that some professed members of the Order were unable to observe the rule because of its severity and rigor, and because of human frailty (*ex humana fragilitate*) and bodily weak-

ness." Then he allowed the Carmelites to remain outside their cells
and to walk in the general area of their churches and cloister gardens,
and he permitted the abstinence from meat to be restricted to three
days a week. These mitigations were added to the text of the original
rule as footnotes.

There was no explicit mention in Eugene IV's text about a
mitigation of the rule of fasting, but it was commonly interpreted
by the Order that the long fast from September 14 to Easter was
similarly reduced to three days a week. To clarify the matter, Pius II
in 1459 issued the bull *Ad hoc divina miseratio,* allowing the prior
general to dispense from the fast for three days a week. And in 1476
Sixtus IV confirmed this permission and granted the prior general
even wider latitude in dispensing from prescriptions of the rule.

A large segment of the Carmelites in every province objected
strenuously to the mitigation, claiming that it had destroyed the
essence of the Carmelite life. Spain was the only country which
accepted it without any dissent. The objectors to the mitigation
argued that Carmelites had traditionally regarded as the heart of the
rule the text which enjoined them to remain in their cells day and
night meditating on the law of the Lord; but now Carmelites were
free to leave their cells and walk around the precincts of the monastery, presumably talking and conversing freely. All of this, they
contended, was in addition to the legitimate apostolic reasons they
had for relinquishing their solitude, and thus a true spirit of solitude
and prayer was now destroyed. What the mitigation had done to the
Order, they felt, was to reduce it to a community of active clerics
who were only tenuously and historically united to the old prophets
of Mount Carmel, but who did not realistically and effectively re-
incarnate these ancient men of prayer and solitude and prophetic
preaching. For almost a century and a half the Carmelites who were
trying to preserve intact the nature of the original vocation struggled
to overcome the new burdens placed upon them by the mitigation.
But their efforts were largely unsuccessful, because in addition to the
Order's own disintegration in that age of confusion and moral decay,
it now had the formidable hurdle of an approved and legal conces-
sion to the spirit of decline.

From almost the very moment of the mitigation a number of vigorous reform movements developed in the Order, attempting to recapture the original spirit and ideals. Three things, however, should

be noted about these reform movements of the fifteenth and early sixteenth centuries: first, they were all ultimately unsuccessful, notwithstanding the initial enthusiasm they generated and the good they did accomplish; secondly, these movements included a great number of dedicated and saintly Carmelites; and thirdly, they gave clear indication and expression of the fact that the original spirit was not dead —it only required something or someone to revive it and revitalize it.

The most influential and enduring of the reform groups actually had its origins a few years before the mitigation of the rule. In 1413 Jacob d'Alberto was elected prior of the monastery of La Selve near Florence, one of the houses which had attempted to preserve the purely eremitical life but which had fallen from its original ideal in the late fourteenth century. D'Alberto instituted an energetic campaign against the major abuses of the age: he re-established regular monastic observance and fidelity to the prescriptions of the rule; he abolished all private sources of revenue for the religious; and he forbade the acceptation of any offices or obligations which would habitually keep the religious outside the monastery. His efforts at reform were continued by his successor, Angelus Mazzinghi, a holy and learned man who had become a celebrated preacher in Florence. The monasteries at La Geronde in Switzerland and Mantua in Italy adopted the practices of the La Selve community, and thus the three monasteries existed as a reformed group within the Order. The group was ultimately called the reform of Mantua, taking its name from the Mantua house, which contributed the most illustrious members to the movement. In 1442 the group petitioned Pope Eugene IV to be allowed to follow the primitive rule without the mitigations of 1432 and to govern itself under its own vicar general. Both petitions were granted, and the group then assumed the position of a self-governing, semiautonomous congregation within the Order. A number of other houses quickly aligned themselves with the Mantuan congregation in a surge of enthusiasm: Ferrara, Brescia, Parma, Bologna, Bergamo, Genoa, Milan, Venice, Padua, among others. Perhaps the sudden numerical growth plus the independence it enjoyed from the prior general had something to do with the congregation's inability to persevere in its original ideals, for in 1465 it adopted the mitigated rule, and in the following century a general spirit of relaxation developed. The congregation did persevere, however, in resisting the major abuses of the epoch and maintaining a better religious observance, particularly in the areas of poverty and communal living. But the Mantuan congregation had no real impact on the Order at large, particularly after it adopted the mitigated rule. It became more insular and isolated, until it finally was merely a grouping of a few Italian monasteries dedicated to a more responsible religious observance. This Italian congregation lasted for three centuries, but in 1783 Pope Pius VI suppressed the group, incorporating it with the remaining Carmelites who still followed the mitigated rule.

The two most distinguished members of the Mantuan reform were Blessed Bartholomew Fanti and Blessed John Baptist Spagnoli.[1] Fanti was a prior of the monastery at Mantua and one of its foremost exponents of dedicated observance. A man particularly devoted to the Blessed Sacrament, he is depicted in ecclesiastical art holding a sanctuary light in his hand. He died in 1495. Spagnoli is a better-known and more important character. Born at Mantua in 1447 of an Italian mother and a Spanish father, he acquired the sobriquet Spagnoli (Spanish). He joined the reformed Carmelite community when he was seventeen, and ultimately served as vicar general of the congregation six times. In 1513 he was elected prior general of the whole Order. He was a saintly man, and Pope Pius X proposed him as a special model of virtue for young students. But his unique claim to fame is that he was not only a holy Carmelite and an incessant worker for ecclesiastical reform, but that he was also recognized as one of Europe's outstanding humanists and perhaps the greatest Latin poet of the Renaissance. He studied science at the University of Milan, philosophy at Padua, and received his doctorate in theology from Bologna. He was a friend of the leading humanists of his day, especially Erasmus, who wrote of him: "The Order produced in our times a man exceptionally well versed in theology and belles-

[1] During the age of the high Renaissance in the fifteenth century there was a liberal and excessive use of the term "Blessed" for people who had led upright lives and died saintly deaths. The practice was part of the Renaissance mentality, which reveled in a fulsome and effusive vocabulary and which enjoyed attributing titles to people. These "Blessed" were usually declared by popular acclaim, but sometimes all that was required was pressure from a small and interested group. A number of these Renaissance "Blessed" were later officially recognized by the Church as a result of the precise procedures of beatification and canonization established after the Council of Trent. Bartholomew Fanti, for example, is recognized as a Blessed only in the Carmelite Order, while John Baptist Spagnoli was officially beatified by Leo XIII.

lettres, Baptist of Mantua, whose poetry is only slightly inferior to that of Virgil." Known in the artistic circles of Europe as "The Mantuan," he produced a fantastic amount of literary work—it has been estimated that he wrote almost a hundred thousand Latin verses. His literary style was the typical wordy, prolix presentation of that period of the Renaissance, and it soon went out of fashion. But for one brief moment in literary history this sincere Carmelite occupied the spotlight of European letters, thus giving eloquent testimony to the fact that humanism and sanctity were not at all incompatible, that one helped the other, and that the excesses and pagan distortions of many humanists did not have to be so. When Spagnoli was elected general of the entire Order in 1513 he was sixty-six years old and in quite poor health. There were high hopes at his election that this energetic and vigorous and saintly man with his background of ecclesiastical reform would bring about effective reform measures in the Order, but it was too late in the day for him. His administration was insignificant, and the ailing prior general lived only three years, dying at his home monastery in Mantua in 1516. He was acclaimed a Blessed in the Carmelite Order, and during Pope Pius X's early career as bishop of Mantua the future saint sponsored his cause with Leo XIII and had him declared a Blessed in the universal Church.

Another reform group sprung up on the other side of the Alps, at Albi in the Aquitaine province of France. The impulse for this reform came from outside the Order: the bishop of the diocese, Louis d'Amboise, an enlightened prelate who had interested himself in the reform of a number of religious communities in his diocese, wanted to reform the Carmelites of Albi, but he apparently was having little success in his efforts. In 1499, the bishop accomplished his objective by means of a plot that had an intriguing Machiavellian twist. He requested Baptist Spagnoli at Mantua to send him two of his men for the purpose of introducing the Mantuan customs in Albi. Spagnoli agreed, and commissioned two men: one of them died before leaving Italy, but the other one, Elijah Denis, a Frenchman and former merchant who had entered the Order on a business trip to Parma, presented himself to the bishop. D'Amboise now had his reform leader, but he felt he needed a whole new community at Albi if he were to have any success. Accordingly he recruited twenty-two men from the Montaigu College in Paris, brought them to the episcopal palace in Albi, and invested them with the Carmelite habit in his private chapel. Then he invited the entire Carmelite community at Albi to dine with him. The men cheerfully accepted, and while they were at dinner, Elijah Denis secretly led the new recruits to the monastery and occupied the building. At the conclusion of the meal in the palace, d'Amboise informed his guests of what he had done and gave them the option of either joining his now reformed monastery or transferring to other monasteries of the Order. Surprisingly, a number of them chose the reform.

The reform of Albi quickly spread to other monasteries in France: Meaux, Rouen, Toulouse, and Paris. However, the reform was unfavorably received by the prior general in Rome, both because of the abortive, unauthorized nature of its origin and because of the reform's leading figure, Louis de Lire, a Carmelite from Rouen who sought the protection of the French king against the general in Rome. Years of hostility ensued, and finally in 1504 the general excommunicated de Lire. Peace was only restored with the election of Baptist Spagnoli in 1513 when the reform group of Albi was given the right to elect its own vicar general, as was done in the Mantua reform. But the Albi group soon lost its first fervor, and the religious wars in France during the second half of the sixteenth century completely devitalized the operation. In 1584 there remained only three monasteries in the Albi reform, containing a total of thirty religious, most of whom were too old to carry out the regular observance. In that same year Gregory XIII suppressed the entire congregation.

A reform of a somewhat different nature took place at the monastery of Mount Olivet near Genoa in Italy. In 1516 Hugo Marengo from the Lombard province of the Order founded this monastery for the observance of a completely eremitical life according to the primitive rule. He sought to bring his monastery under the jurisdiction of the Mantua reform, but Mantua rejected the proposal because the congregation was then following the mitigated rule. The single monastery of this reform was then placed under the direct supervision of the prior general. Mount Olivet was characterized initially by a harsh and austere form of life, but it only endured until 1599 when Clement VIII joined it to the Lombard province of the Carmelites following practicing the mitigated rule.

In addition to these organized reform movements which established themselves as more or less independent and separated congregations within the Order, there was a continuing concern at the

general's office in Rome for universal reform of the Order. John
Faci's successor was Blessed John Soreth, a native of Caen in
Normandy and a graduate of the University of Paris. Elected general
in 1451, he embarked on a strenuous program to encourage reform
"at least according to the mitigation of Eugene IV." In 1462 he
issued new constitutions for the Order, stressing the obligations of
poverty, solitude, and fidelity to the religious vows. Soreth was an
indefatigable traveler for the cause of reform, visiting the monasteries
all over Europe, preaching against abuses and excessive privileges
which were destroying community life. He stated:

> The goal of every religious and the perfection of his soul consists in
> striving for a continual state of prayer, uninterrupted and persevering as
> far as human weakness permits, and in advancing with effort toward
> permanent peace and perpetual purity of soul.

Soreth was a gentle and sympathetic person, quietly urging his
men, encouraging them to a more dedicated form of life. But despite
his compassion and his vigorous efforts at reform, his admonitions
were generally unheeded. His most enduring accomplishment, as we
shall see, was the foundation of the Carmelite nuns. When he died
at Angers in 1481 a false rumor was circulated that he had been
poisoned by Carmelites hostile to his program of reform.

By the year 1523, when the Cypriot Nicholas Audet became prior
general, no substantial change had taken place in the mood of
decadence which was so prevalent in the Order. Audet published
his *Isagogicon* in 1524, a book which outlined the principal abuses
of the Order and the lamentable state into which it had fallen. He
suggested the same basic areas of reform as his successors, but again
this voice of renewal fell on deaf ears. It was during Audet's long
administration of almost forty years that the catastrophe which had
been feared by many churchmen took place in Europe when the
Church and its religious Orders were dealt a crippling blow by the
Protestant Reformation.

For more than a century and a half the Carmelite Order groaned
beneath the weight of severe abuses, fighting an almost helpless
battle against decadence and a forfeiture of the original Carmelite
vocation. There were bright spots in that epoch, though. In the
worst of times there are always unaccountably present the best of
men. In addition to the sincere Carmelites we have already men-

tioned, there were men like Blessed Louis Rabata (1430–1490), a Sicilian, prior of the monastery at Randazzo, a faithful follower of the rule, renowned for his work with the poor, who died from a serious arrow wound inflicted by a man who bore him a grudge but whose identity he refused to reveal. In England there was Thomas Netter of Walden (1375–1431), a graduate of Oxford, one of the most celebrated theologians of his day, confessor to Kings Henry V and Henry VI; in an unusual gesture for that epoch, he refused the bishopric a number of times when it was offered by Henry V. In Portugal the national military hero, Nuno Álvares Pereira, entered the Order as a lay brother following a brilliant career in the army. Born in 1360, he first served as a page at the Portuguese court, and eventually married a childless widow by whom he had three children. He was only twenty-three years of age when he was made field marshal of the Portuguese army, leading his troops against the invading Castilians. His victories at Aljubarrota and Valverde in 1385 consolidated the Portuguese throne for King John I. Called "the Constable" and "the Messiah of Portugal," he campaigned tirelessly for the maintenance of a standing army to act as a deterrent to aggression. At the age of sixty-two, after the death of his wife and children, he entered the Carmelite monastery at Lisbon, which he had previously endowed from his own funds. He received the habit in 1423, and spent the remaining eight years of his life in the quiet, unassuming role of a lay brother. During his years as a Carmelite he curiously kept his sword and lance in his monastic cell as a reminder of past exploits. Nuno Pereira is regarded as a national hero in Portugal and a Blessed in the Carmelite Order.

More characteristic, though, of the general caliber of men during that difficult and troubled age were two personalities who typified the strange excesses of the times: Thomas Connecte and Filippo Lippi. Connecte was born at Rennes in Brittany sometime near the end of the fourteenth century. He entered the Carmelite monastery at La Geronde in Switzerland and was one of the leaders in the reformation movement which ultimately linked his community with the other two monasteries of the original Mantuan group. A forceful and dynamic preacher, he soon obtained a large following throughout southern France, vigorously denouncing the evils of the day. But he was a fanatic, and he attracted the popular, noisy throngs that usually congregate around a demagogue. He attacked profane amusements, gambling, card playing, and his special target, the prevailing fashion of women's coiffure, which at that time was to pile hair extravagantly high on the head in an enormous structure of combs and false hair. When he had whipped his congregation into a frenzy he usually concluded his sermon by building a bonfire into which were thrown playing cards, dice, and the ladies' hairpieces. He drew enormous crowds, and it was reported that on some occasions he preached while dangling from a rope hung in the middle of the church so that he could be seen and heard by his entire audience.

As so often happens with zealots, Connecte became more and more impressed with his own mission and the sound of his own voice. He turned his fury on the prevalent clerical abuses in celibacy, castigating priests who lived in concubinage or had mistresses, and he decided to carry his cause to Rome and reform the entire Roman Curia. He embarked on a bizarre pilgrimage down through Italy, accompanied by a number of Carmelites and a huge, clamoring crowd of followers. He proceeded through the towns of northern Italy, usually entering these towns riding on a donkey, and then to Venice where he made some impassioned speeches, and finally to Rome. He preached in the public squares in Rome, and announced his particular solution to the problem of clerical failures in chastity: Latin priests should be allowed to marry like the Greek priests. Finally Pope Eugene IV summoned Connecte to appear before him, but a sudden and unexpected timidity came over Connecte and he refused to go. After a second summons went unheeded, the pope sent a delegation to bring him forcefully if necessary. Connecte fled through the window of the room where he was staying, but he was quickly apprehended and brought before Eugene IV. At the insistence of Cardinal de la Roche-Taille, archbishop of Rouen and cardinal protector of the Carmelite Order, the pope handed him over to the Inquisition. Examined by de la Roche-Taille and the Cardinal of Navarre, he was found guilty of heresy and condemned to death. Toward the end of the year 1433 he was burned at the stake in Rome.

Thomas Connecte has been called "a Carmelite Savonarola," and the English Carmelite historian, John Bale, even called him a saint, but Bale had his own personal interest in the career of Thomas Connecte, as we shall see. Connecte was certainly a fanatic, but there is nothing to support the contention that he was a heretic. The only charge that the Inquisition seemed to have against him was his advocacy of clerical marriage. Historians are agreed that the

Inquisition acted cruelly and intemperately in Connecte's case, providing one more sorry episode in its strange and bloody history. Thomas Connecte must ultimately be judged as a peculiar man in a peculiar age.

Filippo Lippi (1406–1469), a Carmelite and one of the most renowned painters in the Italian quattrocento, was a classic case of the profligate Renaissance monk. Born at Florence, he was orphaned at the age of two and was cared for by an aunt who, being too poor to keep him, placed him in the Carmelite monastery when he was eight years old. He made his profession of vows when he was fifteen, but he had little aptitude or inclination for the religious life. At that time Masolino and Masaccio were painting their frescoes in the Carmelite church in Florence, and the work of these masters seems to have had a profound influence on the young Carmelite. He studied painting and design—Bernhard Berenson suggests that his master was Lorenzo Monaco—and did his first cameo frescoes on the walls of the Carmelite cloister. His reputation spread rapidly, and at the age of thirty-three he was already hailed as one of the great talents of the age. He was sponsored by Cosimo de' Medici, who commissioned him for a number of important paintings. But Filippo was far less successful as a religious: his life was scandalous, he was involved in constant escapades, and at one point he was brought before an ecclesiastical court for forgery. However, in that Renaissance epoch genius excused everything, and not much concern was paid for the friar's riotous life. Cosimo de' Medici dismissed it airily as the "folly of the friar."

In 1452 Filippo was appointed chaplain of the Augustinian convent at Prato, and from that time his economic fortunes improved considerably. He began work on one of his masterpieces, the dome of the cathedral of Prato, and he purchased a house for himself in the city. While painting a picture of the Madonna, he requested the nuns at the convent to allow a young girl who was a boarder at the convent, Lucrezia Buti, to sit as a model for him. He fell in love with the girl and abducted her to his house where she eventually gave birth to his illegitimate son, Filippino Lippi, who became a famous painter in his own right. Lucrezia lived with Filippo for three years, but then curiously returned to the convent where she received the habit as a nun. But the affair must have continued, because three years later Cosimo de' Medici petitioned Pope Pius II to allow Filippo to marry Lucrezia. The pope granted the petition, but at

this point in Filippo's unhappy career the records are confusing, and
many historians say that he never did use the permission to marry
the girl. At any rate, a second child, a girl, was born when Filippo
was sixty years of age. In 1466 he began work on the cathedral at
Spoleto, but he died there before he could complete the task. His
name is inscribed in the list of the deceased Carmelites at the monastery in Florence.

Filippo Lippi is regarded as one of the masters of his artistic age,
a powerful naturalist, and a genius at coloring. His output was prodigious, and his paintings today hang in the great gallerys of the world,
in the Louvre, the Metropolitan Museum in New York, and in the
national galleries in London and Washington. Lippi invariably
painted himself somewhere into his pictures as a minor figure, and
we are left with a permanent portrait of this Renaissance painter: a
flat-nosed, thick-lipped man with a jesting but rather vicious look—
a great artist, but a poor Carmelite.

On October 31, 1517, a thirty-four-year-old Augustinian friar named
Martin Luther tacked a list of ninety-five theses on the church door
at Wittenberg in Saxony, attacking the doctrine of indulgences and
the taxes levied on the Germans by the Italian Curia. Luther's
action was catalytic, unleashing a vast and far-reaching series of reactions with such force and rapidity that some prominent churchmen
refused for a long time to believe what was really happening. The
momentous Protestant Reformation was under way, and because of
it Europe and the Church would never be the same again.

The indulgence controversy which Luther fomented put the spark
to a fire which had been smoldering beneath the European surface
for many years, enabling churchmen and statesmen to turn their
grievances against the Church into the form of an open revolt. The
age of the national state and the absolute prince was under way, and
these new national princes found the power of Rome and the
Church's taxation system both restrictive and oppressive. Newly developed national sentiment in many countries reacted with strong
aversion to the Italianism of the papacy and the Curia, regarding
the Church as basically an Italian-directed operation. There were
also present healthy religious movements which were opposed to the
mechanical and sometimes superstitious aspects of medieval piety
and wished to return to a more simple evangelical spirituality with
a greater emphasis on experiential contact with God. And there were

the grievous evils in the Renaissance Church: the moral faults, nepotism, the Inquisition, monetary abuses, the absentee bishops, the juridicism of the Roman Curia. These multiple forces worked in concatenation to produce the Protestant Reformation. Within seventy-five years half of Europe was lost to the Catholic faith, and the Church was almost totally destroyed in large regions of Europe: most of the northern German states, the Scandinavian countries, Holland, England, Scotland, and large parts of France and Switzerland. Churches and ecclesiastical properties were either destroyed or confiscated, priests and nuns were either interdicted or forced to flee, and the practice of the Catholic religion was forbidden by state decree.

The Carmelite Order fell with the Church in the defecting areas, and in a matter of decades the Order was completely eradicated in the Protestant territories. The Order had its vigorous defenders of the faith: Eberhard Billick and Alexander Blankart in Germany, Paul Helie in Denmark, Lawrence Cook in England, and Peter Lupus in Holland. But Europe was now firmly divided into two Christian camps, and their efforts were ultimately unfruitful. In England, for instance, the Carmelite province of almost three hundred men just disappeared. During the reign of Henry VIII the monasteries were confiscated, and the men were turned into the streets with no compensation. Many of them signed the Oath of Supremacy, returning to lay life as Anglicans; some became Anglican ecclesiastics; and many others went underground as "outlaw priests," conferring the sacraments secretly until the time of their deaths. Only two English Carmelites are known to have suffered death: Lawrence Cook and Reginald Pecock. The Order did not return to England until 1615 when Carmel opened its clandestine English mission.

The most famous of the English apostates was John Bale. He was born at Suffolk, and entered the Carmelites at Norwich. He was educated at Cambridge, and eventually served as prior of the monasteries at Doncaster, Norwich, and Ipswich. He distinguished himself as a historian, and his *Catalogus* of British authors will always remain a valuable work. In 1536 he signed the Oath of Supremacy, entered marriage in the same year, and began a career of bitter writing against the Church. During the reign of Edward VI he was named Anglican bishop of Dublin, but he was afraid of the temper of the Irish people and he hesitated to go. Ultimately, he took up residence in Dublin, but harassment by the Irish unnerved him and he returned to England. During the reaction period of Mary Tudor's reign he fled to the Continent for safety, living for a while in Holland and Geneva. When Elizabeth I came to the English throne, he returned home, spending the years until his death in 1563 as a canon in the now Anglican Canterbury Cathedral.

Carmel's already staggering problems were thus compounded immeasurably by the Protestant Reformation. In one gigantic blow almost half the Order suddenly disappeared. Some of the men fled to other provinces in the Catholic countries, some of them defected to the new Protestantism in its various forms, and some remained to work as clandestine missionary priests in their own countries. But without the usual slow and agonizing pains of imminent death, the Order was swiftly and astonishingly dead in the Protestant countries. And still the agonizing need for reform remained—and still nothing was accomplished.

Beginning with the general chapter at Venice in 1524—the chapter at which Nicholas Audet was elected—there is a continuing and plaintive plea for reform throughout the subsequent chapters for the next twenty-five years. In 1524 there is a call for "universal reform in the Order" and a decree that "the life of all our brothers in the entire Order be reformed for the honor of God and the Blessed Virgin and the preservation and growth of our holy Order." A reform is urged even more strongly in the chapter of 1532, and in 1539 the priors of the Order are commanded "to use all their energy to introduce and promote, sincerely and honestly, a true reformation of the monasteries and the brethren, extirpating every impropriety and scandal." And in 1548 the priors are again urged to maintain religious observance and adherence to the law "in all things which pertain to the reformation of our Order and the regular life."

There is a shrill and tragic tone in these decrees, as they plaintively and unsuccessfully cry for reform. Carmel, miserably mutilated by the upheaval of the Protestant Reformation, and still burdened by the weight of its decadence, was looking for the road back to its original vision. And there seemed to be no one to show them the way and lead them up the ascent.

The restoration of the pristine Carmelite spirit, that urgent task which could not be accomplished by Grossi, Soreth, Audet, and the other sincere reformers, was finally achieved by that most improbable of persons: an unschooled Carmelite nun from the walled city of Ávila in Spain.

– IV –
THE NUNS

THE tradition of women who dedicate their lives to God's service by a special commitment dates from the beginning of Christianity. St. Paul speaks of the virgins and widows who were consecrated for a particular and distinct devotion to the Lord and for various kinds of Church work. By the third century we find these dedicated women living a communal form of life, with obedience to a superioress and specified hours of prayer and religious observance. The great founders of the monastic life—Pachomius, Augustine, Benedict—sponsored the adoption of their rules by women, who then practiced the same rule as their male counterparts, with the necessary adaptations and adjustments for female community life. The nuns in the East traditionally practiced a strict enclosure, an inviolable cloister which prohibited them from leaving the confines of their convent, while the nuns in the West did not consider the enclosure indispensable and many groups were thus able to leave their convents for apostolic or charitable works. But by the twelfth century the rigorous enclosure of the East was gradually extended to convents in the West, and the only apostolic work the nuns could then do was the education of young girls in the convent proper. It was not until the seventeenth century that St. Vincent de Paul, working in conjunction with Louise de Marillac, made a radical break with this tradition by founding his Daughters of Charity, a community of religious women without cloister who could engage in apostolic works.

Both St. Dominic and St. Francis in the thirteenth century founded groups of nuns which followed the rules they had written: they were called members of the second order, in distinction to the friars who were then called members of the first order. In 1212 St. Francis started his second order when he encouraged an eighteen-year-old heiress, Clare of Assisi, to steal away from her father's house at night and meet him at the church of the Porziuncola where he personally cut off her hair and invested her in a Franciscan habit. St.

Dominic instituted his nuns and gave them a set of constitutions even before he inaugurated his friars. These second order groups existed, of course, as strictly cloistered nuns. However, the Carmelites had no second order or affiliated Carmelite nuns, at least in the organized, juridical form of the Franciscans and Dominicans, until the middle of the fifteenth century.

During the thirteenth and fourteenth centuries a number of pious women placed themselves under the direction of the Carmelites, and individually attempted to follow the Carmelite rule in some fashion. Many of them even wore a religious habit fashioned on the general pattern of the friars' habit. Most frequently these women lived by themselves as recluses in a hut or tiny cell constructed near a church or monastery. Their life, then, was one of absolute solitude and prayer. This was not an unusual form of life in the Middle Ages, and we have already seen that it was practiced by St. Simon Stock before he entered the Carmelite Order.

But many other groups of pious women lived a form of communal life, wearing a kind of Carmelite habit, and following the broad outlines of the Carmelite rule. We find groups of this nature in Lombardy, Spain, Sicily, Flanders, and the Low Countries. This, again, was not an unusual phenomenon, and it brings us to a unique religious situation in medieval Europe: the tradition of the Beguines, women who lived together without vows, and without official status, in a very loosely knit pious association, something resembling a home for Christian ladies. These groups were called Beguines in France and in the Lowlands, the name that is most commonly used to designate them in history; Beatas in Spain; Mantellate in southern Italy and Sicily; and Humiliates in Lombardy. The Beguines had no apostolate whatsoever, and the movement cannot be interpreted as an attempt to circumvent the contemporary ecclesiastical legislation, since the general mood of medieval Europe, which was definitely anti-feminist in many ways, was opposed to female apostolic endeavors. These Beguines simply led quiet Christian lives: they said their prayers, did their knitting, could receive visitors freely, and could come and go as they pleased. They retained their own moneys, and some of them lived rather comfortably with a suite of rooms and a provision of fine foods. The life was not demanding, and it provided a pleasant residence for Christian ladies, both virgins and widows, who wanted to make an open profession of their Christian faith.

We possess little accurate information about the Beguine groups that attempted to associate themselves with the Carmelite tradition of prayer and solitude; we only know that there were a number of such groups, and that they were under the direction of individual Carmelite priests. But the spirit of the Beguines is an important factor in this chronicle because it exercised a definite influence on some convents of early Carmelite nuns.[1]

John Soreth was extremely interested in the condition of the Beguines who were affiliated to the Order, and after his election as general in 1451 he began to work for a closer relationship of these groups with the Order and for the ultimate establishment of a Second Order. Although the impetus for the foundation of a Second Order came from a number of different quarters in Europe, John Soreth sponsored the movement, obtained official approval for it, directed many of the original convents personally, and he therefore can be rightly called the founder of the Second Order.

The first two Carmelite convents were at Florence in Italy and Gueldre in Holland, and they were originally communities of Beguines which were elevated and organized into second order convents. In 1451 Cardinal Nicholas de Cues made an apostolic visitation for the Holy See in the ecclesiastical territories of Germany and the Lowlands, and he encouraged the various communities of Beguines he encountered to affiliate themselves to an existing religious order as members of a second order. He made this recommendation to the Beguines at Gueldre, who were already under the direction of some Carmelite friars, and accordingly in May of 1452 these women petitioned the provincial chapter held at Cologne to seek affiliation from the general in Rome. John Soreth responded by letter in the same month, granting an affiliation which, although it did not bestow the official status of a second order, was still the first recognition of a Beguine group by a prior general from Rome. Then in October of that same year (1452), John Soreth presided at the provincial chapter of Florence, and one of the questions before the chapter was a similar petition from a Beguine group in Florence for

[1] In the European tradition, religious houses of men are called convents, and houses of cloistered religious women are called monasteries. In America, of course, we use the inverse terminology—convents for women, and monasteries for men. This book will follow the American terminology, with the understanding that whenever documents are quoted directly I have made the necessary inversion of terms in the actual text.

admittance into the Order. The group in Florence, like the one in Gueldre, was under the direction of the Carmelites, and had been founded in 1450 by a widow named Innocenza de Bartoli. Apparently at the suggestion of Soreth, this petition was forwarded directly to the Holy See with a request for permission to establish convents of a second order.

Less than five months later, on October 5, Pope Nicholas V issued the bull *Cum nulla*, which granted the Carmelites permission to organize a second order. However, the bull was a curious document because, in addition to granting all the privileges that other second orders enjoyed, it allowed the Carmelites to admit into the Order "pious virgins, widows, Beguines, Mantellate, or others who wear the habit and are under the protection of the Order of the Blessed Virgin Mary of Mount Carmel." This obscurely worded document was interpreted in the fifteenth and sixteenth centuries as permitting the various Second Order convents to continue the general spirit of the Beguines, if they desired, without strict enclosure and without too exacting a schedule; and a great many of the convents did just that. The bull also directed the nuns to follow the mitigated rule of Eugene IV. The Carmelite convents were organized in the same juridical system employed by the Franciscans and Dominicans and other second order groups: each convent was autonomous in itself, completely independent of the other convents; but the local provincial of the First Order served as the major superior of the individual convent; he was consulted on more important matters of administration and he provided the single step in the chain of command between the convent and the general in Rome.

Soreth used the bull immediately in 1452 to elevate the community at Florence into the initial Second Order convent, and in the following year he did the same for the community at Gueldre. During the next twenty-five years there was a rapid growth of Carmelite convents in Europe, especially in France, the Lowlands, Italy, and Spain. Soreth was particularly interested in the groups in France and the Lowlands, and he worked closely with them, but he seems to have had little impact or influence on the Italian and Spanish convents.

He ordered the prior of the monastery at Gueldre to adapt the constitutions of the friars for the new convent of the nuns, and he himself wrote the constitutions for the later foundations in the Lowlands and Brittany. His constitutions provided for a strict cloister, although there was allowance for a few extern nuns who could live outside the cloister and perform the business transactions of the community; and there was insistence upon prayer, solitude, silence, and penance. But above all, Soreth's constitutions echoed his traditional theme: union with God by means of continual prayer.

The Carmelite nuns throughout Europe gained immense prestige when the duchess of Brittany, Blessed Frances d'Amboise, joined one of the convents she herself had endowed. The daughter of Louis d'Amboise, she had been betrothed at the age of four to Peter the duke of Brittany, and was married at the age of fifteen. The marriage was not a happy one, owing largely to the melancholic temperament of the duke, who occasionally beat her. Despite her problems with her husband and interminable family feuds, she distinguished herself as an enlightened and dedicated regent, aiding the poor of her district and liberally bestowing alms from her ample fortune. She was a devout woman, spending long hours in prayer before the Blessed Sacrament, and she endowed the convents of Dominicans and Franciscans at Nantes. The Duke died in 1457 when she was thirty years of age, leaving no heir, but testifying in his will to his wife's goodness and devotedness.

Frances met John Soreth in 1459 at Nantes when he was making a visitation of the Carmelite monasteries in Brittany. She invited him to her chateau and confided her desire to enter a convent. She wanted to join the Franciscan community at Nantes, she said, but she felt that the life of these "Poor Clares" was too austere for her in light of her almost continuous illnesses. Soreth explained the new Second Order of Carmelites he was sponsoring, and the young widow found it immediately appealing. She volunteered to endow a convent of this new Second Order at Vannes and then join it as one of its members. Soreth made all the arrangements for the foundation, and prepared to obtain a group of Carmelite nuns from the recently founded convent at Liége. But the operation met formidable opposition from the new duke of Brittany and Frances' family: they wanted her to remarry, and they were searching for some suitor who would provide a politically advantageous marriage for the duchy of Brittany. Frances would have no part of it; but the duke refused to relent, and he forbade both the establishment of the convent in his kingdom and Frances' entrance into the religious life.

That state of impasse endured for almost three years. Finally

Frances made a bold and dramatic gesture that resolved the situation. During a public Mass in church one day, she rose in her place and as the priest turned to distribute Communion she recited in a loud voice a personal vow of perpetual chastity, and she added her firm intention to enter a convent. Faced with this determined and apparently invincible woman, Francis II, the duke of Brittany, was forced to relent: he allowed the foundation of the Carmelite convent at Vannes, and he gave his permission for Frances to join when she had concluded her business affairs.

John Soreth personally conducted nine nuns from Liége, and solemnly installed them in a small building which was constructed immediately adjacent to the monastery of Carmelite friars. Frances joined the community a few years later, receiving the habit from the hands of John Soreth. She was first assigned as infirmarian in the convent, but after she had impressed the nuns by her holiness and kindness, she was elected prioress in 1473. When the convent at Vannes proved too small she moved it to a former convent of Benedictine nuns in Nantes. Soreth maintained a close association with Frances, and her convent remained under the direct jurisdiction of the prior general in Rome, a unique arrangement in that era. She continued as prioress until 1484 when she resigned the office so that she could serve God as an ordinary religious. She died in the following year, giving as her last recommendation to the sisters one of her favorite phrases: "Above all things, let God be loved the most." Pius IX beatified the duchess of Brittany on July 16, 1863.

Because of the diverse interpretations of the bull *Cum nulla* of 1452, and because of the independent status of each Carmelite convent, there existed a vast dissimilarity among the various groups of convents in Europe. Those convents which were under the influence of John Soreth—those in the Lowlands, in northern France, and in Brittany—followed his ideals of the Carmelite life, and were accordingly carefully cloistered convents with great fidelity to prayer, solitude, poverty, and practice of the Carmelite rule.

The Italian Carmels presented a different picture. The original convent at Florence was more a group of Beguines than a group of Carmelite nuns: the cloister was not strictly observed, and the nuns were permitted to go out of the convent and maintain close contact with the people of the city. Like the Beguines of a former epoch, their life was not particularly demanding, and while it was still a virtuous Christian life, it was far removed from Soreth's inspiration for a group of cloistered nuns who would have prayerful contact with God as their chief preoccupation. Most of the other convents of Italy followed this same spirit of the Beguines, except for those which came under the influence of the friars in the Mantuan reform: Parma, Reggio, Brescia, and Ferrara. The convent at Reggio was distinguished by Jane Scopelli, and that at Parma by the prioress Archangela Girlani, who ultimately made an additional foundation at Mantua. These convents under the Mantuan friars were a closer approximation of Soreth's ideal, and although they did not observe a strict cloister they were far superior to the other Italian convents.

The Second Order enjoyed a rapid growth in Spain, especially in Andalusia and Castile, and eventually in Portugal. But from the outset these convents were dominated by the spirit of the Beguines, and while there were numerous convents, sometimes with unbelievably large numbers of nuns, the lack of challenge in the life attracted many women who did not have an authentic religious vocation. Most of the Spanish convents were originally Beaterios (communities of Beatas, as the Beguines were called in Spain) and their affiliation to the Order implied little real change in their status.

The Second Order was founded during the worst of all possible times for the Church and the Carmelite Order: the age of the high Renaissance preceding the Protestant Reformation, the time when severe abuses were rampant in the Church and when ecclesiastics were helplessly attempting to renew the pure spirit of Christ among the Christian people. It is astonishing that the Second Order could be established at all in that milieu, and not surprising that it was confused and diversified, with different theories of religious life and different levels of commitment. There were no shocking abuses among the nuns of that epoch as there were among the friars, but in many quarters the Second Order was far removed from the form of life which should have been practiced by religious women who had pledged themselves to follow in the footsteps of those ancient prophets of Mount Carmel who stood before the face of the Lord. The Second Order, as well as the First Order, needed a reformer.

In the tradition of the Western church a third order is an association of lay people who, while retaining their lay status, affiliate themselves to a religious order for the purpose of practicing the order's essential spirit and participating in some of the order's privileges. These tertiaries, as members of a third order are commonly called, may wear the habit of the parent order, and they follow a specially written rule of life which is compatible with their lay status and responsibilities but which seeks to capture the distinct religious tradition and commitment of the first order.

The custom of affiliating lay people to a religious order is an ancient one in Western Christianity, and may be traced back to the Benedictines and their oblates, but the inauguration of third orders, properly so called, must be placed in the thirteenth century, particularly at the time of St. Francis, who wrote a rule for men and women which was animated by the Franciscan tradition. The tertiary who pledged himself to that rule continued his ordinary secular occupations, but added to them a number of additional religious obligations, principally prayer, penance, and attendance at meetings. Sometimes these tertiaries lived in common, notably St. Francis' Brothers of Penance, and a new form of third order life began to evolve: tertiaries who took vows and lived in common, following a prescribed daily regimen and engaging in the same apostolic endeavors. These communities of tertiaries eventually became known as the third order regular, to distinguish them from the more popular third order secular.

Although there were many lay people in the thirteenth and fourteenth centuries who affiliated themselves to the Carmelite Order in a form of commitment that resembled a Third Order, especially the Company of St. Mary of Carmel, a group of pious women which flourished in Florence from about the year 1300, the actual foundation of a Carmelite Third Order belongs in the fifteenth century at the time of John Soreth. The bull *Cum nulla* of 1452, which established the Second Order, also allowed for the foundation of a Third Order. John Soreth turned his energetic talents toward developing the tertiaries, and in 1455 he composed a rule for them entitled *The Third Rule of the Carmelites*. His efforts with the Third Order seemed to parallel his work with the Second Order, and his rule was apparently not used outside the Lowlands and northern France. His rule attempted to follow the broad outlines of the rule of St. Albert, and there is marked insistence upon his constant theme: continual prayer. He prescribes fast and abstinence for the tertiaries, and obliges them to recite the Little Office of the Blessed Virgin, which could be commuted into a number of Paters and Aves. A unique factor of Soreth's rule, distinguishing it from all other third orders, was the profession of a vow of obedience and a vow of chastity according to one's state of life. Soreth's practice of the two vows for secular tertiaries endured throughout the centuries, and today Carmelite tertiaries are the only Third Order secular members in the Church who pronounce vows.

The Third Order followed the same pattern of national diversification as did the Second Order, and we find a variety of different Third Order rules written in the various national languages. All of these rules, however, seemed to be directed to women, whether married or single, and it is only in the following century that there is explicit mention of male tertiaries, although we do know they existed in the fifteenth century. It was not until the seventeenth century that a general rule was composed for all tertiaries in the world, and it was patterned closely on Soreth's original *Third Rule of the Carmelites*.

During the fifteenth century there were two outstanding members of the Carmelite Third Order: Catherine of Rusaghen, and Louis Morbioli. Catherine entered the Third Order at the Carmelite monastery at Enghien in Belgium as a holy recluse, and lived in a small house near the monastery until her death in 1489. Louis Morbioli (1450–1495) was the son of a rich family in Bologna who squandered his inheritance at an early age in a life of dissipation. After a serious illness, he changed his way of life and entered the Third Order in Bologna. He did public penance for his sins, and preached to misguided souls while holding a crucifix in his hands. He was the cause of many conversions, and after his death he was declared a Blessed by popular acclaim.

The city of Ávila in Old Castile sits at the entrance of a main pass across the Central Sierras, about seventy miles northwest of Madrid. Built on the broad back of a rocky ridge and surrounded by massive granite walls from which rise eighty-six towers, Ávila was a busy political and commercial center in fifteenth-century Spain. Here in this walled Castilian city was enacted the drama which revolutionized the Carmelite Order.

In 1478 Doña Elvira González founded a Beaterio in Ávila dedicated to St. Mary of the Incarnation. She limited the membership to fourteen women, in honor of Christ, the Blessed Virgin, and the twelve apostles. It was a typical Beaterio with all the usual freedom enjoyed in those houses during that era, but near the end of the century Doña González expressed a desire to elevate the house to a regular community of Second Order nuns. Her proposal was not welcomed by all the Beatas, and a split of two factions developed in the community. The group opposing the proposal moved out of the Beaterio and took up residence in Alba de Tormes, but they returned shortly thereafter when Doña González died. In 1513 the Beatas approached the provincial of the Castilian Carmelites with a request that the Incarnation be admitted to the Second Order. The petition seems to have been a compromise between the two factions, because when the provincial received the community into the Second Order in 1515 the Beatas adopted a form of life which contained some elements of a truly spiritual convent while retaining the principal features of the Beaterio. There was a novitiate, and the common recitation of the Divine Office, and a number of religious exercises; but the nuns were still easily able to obtain permission to visit freely outside the convent, and there was a sharp class distinction between nuns from the poorer families and those from more affluent backgrounds—the poorer nuns lived in dormitories, while the others could have a suite of rooms, and a servant to wait on them, if they wished. There was a steady stream of visitors to the convent, and the nuns spent long hours each day chatting and conversing with their families and friends. Despite the profession of religious vows and the accouterments of religious life, the convent of the Incarnation remained basically a Beaterio.

Nevertheless, the Carmelite convent of the Incarnation developed rapidly, and by the year 1535 it had one hundred and forty nuns, and by the year 1550 one hundred and eighty. The convent was moved to a larger building outside the city walls on the north side of Ávila, and the general of the Order finally had to forbid the reception of any more novices for a time. Unfortunately the great majority of these recruits did not possess authentic vocations, but had been placed in the convent by their families. Each family in Ávila seemed to pride itself in having a girl at the Incarnation, and many women were placed there with little enthusiasm for a religious dedication. Furthermore, the early sixteenth century was the era of Spain's great empire, and young men were going abroad in the far-flung and adventuresome areas of the Indies and the Americas, with the result that there were less marriageable males available in Spain at that time. Many young girls in Ávila who could not obtain a husband were thus placed in the convent of the Incarnation by their families, which was hardly the best motivation for a religious vocation.

The Incarnation began to suffer financially under the strain of the large numbers. Despite the dowries the women had to bring with them when they joined, there were not enough donations to care for the outsized community. The nuns from richer families had no difficulty in providing for themselves, but the great majority of the nuns were from poorer families, and they suffered from want of proper food and clothing. This impoverished condition and lack of basic essentials further reduced the spirit of dedication and religious observance at the convent.

That was the strange state of the convent of the Incarnation when on November 2, 1535, an attractive twenty-one-year-old girl by the name of Teresa de Ahumada y Cepeda joined the community. Her entrance into Carmel marked the beginning of a new epoch for the Order.

– V –
THE REFORM

ST. TERESA of Ávila inaugurated the reform of the Carmelite Order. It was the most authentic of all possible reforms because it began with the most valid of origins: a personal reform of her own life. She was not a crusader for reform, nor did she envision herself as a reformer: it was a role that was thrust upon her. But in the process of recasting her own life in the way she felt the Lord was leading her, she returned the Order to its original ideal. "We are of the race of those holy fathers of Mount Carmel," she stated emphatically.

Teresa must also emerge from the sixteenth century as one of the most interesting and intriguing saints the Church has ever produced. A woman of compelling physical beauty, she was a warm, appealing, witty person, outgoing and immensely attractive. She was also profoundly spiritual, a mystic, and a woman of intense prayer. Her writings, hastily composed during odd moments in her busy and energetic life, remain as permanent Christian classics. She had an unbelievable capacity for attracting and influencing people, and has the unique distinction of being the only woman in the history of the Church ever to reform an order of men. And this urgent task of renewal and reform was carried on to its successful conclusion mainly on the strength of her enormous personality.

Born in Ávila on March 28, 1515, she was the third child of Don Alonso Sanchez de Cepeda and Doña Beatriz Davila y Ahumada.[1]

---

[1] The custom in Spanish families is for the child to use the names of both father and mother as the full legal name. Teresa's name, therefore, was Teresa de Ahumada y Cepeda—literally, Teresa of Ahumada and Cepeda. In modern usage, Spaniards place the name of the father first and the name of the mother second, but in Teresa's day either order was acceptable. Thus Teresa listed her mother's name first, while John of the Cross listed his father's name first. Ávila has traditionally been given as Teresa's birthplace, but modern scholarship, particularly the work of Father Ephrem of the Mother of God, has claimed that

Don Alonso had been married previously and fathered three children in that marriage before his wife died; he had nine children by his second wife. He was a moderately wealthy Spanish gentleman of the traditional school: devoted to God and king, pious, somewhat austere, rigorous with his children, but basically a generous man. Teresa's mother lived in his shadow, but she presents a somewhat more appealing picture: a tender woman devoted to her children, a person of deep feelings, a little bit of a romantic, and a devout Catholic. Teresa later wrote of her:

> My mother was also most virtuous. She was subject to very serious illnesses during her life. She bore herself always with the greatest propriety. She was endowed with great beauty, but she was never seen to make anything of it. She was scarcely thirty-three when she died, but her dress was already that of an elderly person. She was meek, but of great intelligence.

Teresa was a spirited and animated child, but she also manifested deep religious feelings early in her life. Her confidante was her brother Rodrigo, four years her senior, and when she was seven years old she persuaded him to accompany her on a journey to the country of the Moors so they could gain martyrdom because she "wanted to see God." The two children slipped out of the house, passed over the bridge on the river Adaja, and were on the Salamanca road a few miles from home when they were apprehended and returned by an uncle.

But Teresa was also the typical Spanish girl of that era, and when she grew into her teens she began to give close attention to her appearance. She dressed carefully and elegantly, preening herself before a mirror and studying her facial expressions and the position of her hands so she could use them to their best advantage. She was a

---

she was actually born in Gotterrendura, a small hamlet about thirteen miles from Ávila. Wealthy Spaniards of Ávila in the sixteenth century usually had a small estate in the country where they spent the winter: these homes were better suited for winter living than the stone buildings in frigid Ávila, and there was a greater abundance of firewood. Don Alonso de Cepeda had such a house at Gotterrendura, and we know definitely that Teresa's mother died there in the winter of 1528. It is entirely reasonable to suppose that Doña Beatriz's third child was born there in the month of March. Avilians have hotly contested this thesis, and it has proved particularly embarrassing to the Discalced Carmelite Fathers in Ávila, who built their church over Don Alonso's town home and now advertise it as the birthplace of St. Teresa.

merry conversationalist, spending long hours with her young cousins, the children of Don Francisco Alvarez, who lived nearby. And she apparently had a youthful romance with one of these cousins, for she writes:

I believe, in fact, that what justified those meetings to me was the possibility that all would end in a good marriage. I also consulted my confessor and various other persons and they all answered me that there was no sin in the many things I had mentioned.

She developed a passion for reading the popular sentimental novels of that age, those contrived romantic stories of chivalry and true love and forbidden love which Cervantes was later to satirize. It was a habit she learned from her mother, who spent a great deal of time reading these flowery books, to the displeasure of Don Alonso, who strongly disapproved. Teresa and her mother had to read their novels secretly: "They annoyed my father so much that we had to be careful lest he should see us reading these books." She and her brother Rodrigo—"he whom I loved best of all"—even collaborated in writing a novel, and when they showed it to their mother she was terrified lest Don Alonso should see it, and it was unfortunately thrown in the fire.[2]

Teresa later castigated herself severely for these years of her life and for the time she wasted in what she called "vanity and frivolity." Her mother died when she was almost fifteen, and the young girl was plunged into deep sorrow. She writes:

When I began to realize what I had lost, I went in distress to an image of Our Lady, and with many tears asked her to be a mother to me. Though I did this in my simplicity, I believe it was of some avail to me, for whenever I have commended myself to this Sovereign Virgin I have been conscious of her aid, and she has eventually brought me back to herself.

Don Alonso sent her to board at the Augustinian convent in Ávila, Our Lady of Grace, a kind of finishing school for girls from the better families. She remained there for a year and a half, and her contact with the Augustinian nuns seems to have prompted her own thinking about a religious vocation. An eighty-year-old nun, Doña Maria Briceno, had the most influence on her.

[2] Rodrigo emigrated to South America in 1535, a year before Teresa entered the convent, and he died two years later fighting the Araucanos Indians on the banks of the Río de la Plata in what is today modern Argentina.

Her good companionship began to reform in me the perverse habits I contracted in bad company, and to revive in my soul the desire for eternal things. The extreme aversion that I had for the life of the cloister subsided little by little, and if I saw a nun shedding tears while she prayed, or practicing some act of virtue, I felt great envy of her, because my heart was then so hard that I would not have shed a single tear if I had read the entire Passion of Our Lord—and this troubled me.

Illness compelled her to leave the school, and when she went to the home of her half-sister in Castellanos de la Canada to recuperate, she mulled over the possibility of her religious vocation. She felt no attraction for the religious life, and fought the idea, but the persistent thought remained that the religious life was the easiest way to save her soul. "I determined to force myself to become a nun," she said; and she rationalized:

I tried to convince myself by using the following argument. The trials and distresses of being a nun could not be greater than those of purgatory and I had fully deserved to be in hell. It would not be a great matter to spend my life as though I were in purgatory if afterward I were to go straight to heaven, which was what I desired. This decision, then, to enter the religious life seems to have been inspired by servile fear more than by love.

She began to visit the convent of the Incarnation to discuss her entrance into the "Order of Our Lady." One of the nuns recalled the charming and attractive nineteen-year-old girl who wore an orange dress trimmed with black velvet and who talked so seriously about becoming a nun. Teresa was a girl of medium height with fair skin and dark, active eyes. Her hair was chestnut color, and she had three small dark moles on her left cheek which gave her a piquant look. She possessed a flashing, contagious smile, and she radiated an air of intense vitality, despite her continual poor health. All her life she remained an extremely neat person, and she was very conscious of the demands of personal hygiene, an attitude which unfortunately was not shared by many nuns and friars of that epoch in Europe. She retained her interest in personal grooming until the end of her life, and after she had viewed her portrait painted by the lay brother John of the Misery when she was sixty years old and then in the highest regions of mystical experience, she exclaimed: "May God forgive you, Brother John. Imagine, after all I have suffered at your hands, you paint me so bleary-eyed and ugly!"

Teresa's decision to become a nun, then, derived from some

rather tortuous thinking. She was an attractive, vivacious girl who felt somewhat unsure of her ability to lead a good Christian life in contemporary Castile, but who nevertheless had a clear concept of the ultimate end of life. The convent seemed the safest course for this high-spirited girl, despite her "extreme aversion" for the cloister. Doing violence to herself, she overcame her natural and temperamental disaffection for the confined life of a nun, and determined to enter the Incarnation, but she encountered one more formidable obstacle: the opposition of her father who wanted her to remain at home and take care of his house until the time came for her to marry. She argued with him, but to no avail. "Not as long as I am alive," he said adamantly. Finally she took matters into her own hands, and accompanied by her younger brother Antonio, she left the house secretly and presented herself as a candidate at the Incarnation. Even this step cost her dearly:

I remember—and I really believe this—that when I left my father's house my distress was so great that I do not think it will be greater when I die. It seemed to me as if since I had no love of God to control my love for my father and relatives, everything was such a strain to me that, if the Lord had not helped me, no reflections of my own would have sufficed to keep me true to my purpose.

The nuns would not, of course, receive this daughter of the prominent Don Alonso without his consent—and without his dowry. They took her in, but sent for Don Alonso immediately. Like many a parent before and after him, he reluctantly conceded to his determined daughter, and gave his permission. He offered a dowry of two hundred gold ducats, provided his daughter with a suitable bed, some clothing, and a number of personal effects. Teresa, on her part, had an unexpected reaction to the convent: her misgivings disappeared almost immediately, and she appeared delighted with her new life:

My entrance into this new life gave me a joy so great that it has never failed me even to this day, and God converted the aridity of my soul into the deepest tenderness. Everything connected with the religious life caused me delight; and it is a fact that sometimes when I was spending time in sweeping floors, which I had previously spent on my own indulgence and adornment, I realized that I was not free from all those things, and there came to me a new joy, which amazed me. . . .

She was an enthusiastic novice, faithful to all of the convent prescriptions, carefully obeying the mother prioress, attending all of the community activities regularly. The nuns of the Incarnation later stated that they felt she was a holy nun, but this was not Teresa's evaluation of herself, as we shall see. At the end of the year's novitiate she made her profession of vows, but a few months later she had a severe breakdown in health, a mélange of headaches, fainting spells, and finally catalepsy, an alarming muscular rigidity. She was given permission to seek a cure and recuperation, and she spent the next eighteen months out of the convent, first in the country village of Becedas, where she employed the services of a woman who had a reputation as a healer, then at her half-sister's home, and finally at her father's house in Ávila. Three important things happened to her during this sojourn. First, she discovered Osuna's book *The Third Spiritual Alphabet* when she paused to visit her uncle's home on the way to the country. This small book was a treatise on prayer, and it gave her new insights into mental prayer which she herself later defined as "nothing else than an intimate friendship, a frequent heart-to-heart conversation with Him by Whom we know ourselves to be loved." The experience of this book and her reflections upon it were to prove the basis of her own life of intense prayer which she began nineteen years later. Then at Becedas she made the acquaintance of the parish priest, Don Fulano, and embarked on a rather hazardous relationship with him. He was an intelligent man, and Teresa liked him immediately and spent long hours in conversation with him. He had "an extreme liking" for her, but Teresa quickly notes in her autobiography that "nothing whatever would induce me to commit any grave offense against God." However, Teresa had some definite uneasiness about the situation: "This man's affection for me was not evil, but there was too much affection, and it came to be not good." Finally he told her that he had a mistress in the village, a woman with whom he had been living for seven years, and the young nun determined to help free him from his problem. "When I knew this, I began to show him more love. My intention was good, but the act was wrong; for to accomplish a good, however great it may be, even a small evil should not be done." She discovered that the priest's mistress had made him wear a small copper idol around his neck, and some people in the village said that the woman was holding him in her power by means of witchcraft. "As for this business of witchcraft, I don't believe it's true," Teresa wrote, but she was insistent that he stop wearing the idol, which she interpreted as a symbol of his servitude to his mistress. Even-

A radical change came over Teresa, and the other nuns noticed it immediately: she no longer spent long hours chatting in the parlor, she became less concerned about her health, and she devoted long hours to prayer. The Lord reciprocated almost immediately: "Scarcely had I begun to flee occasions of sin, and give myself to prayer, than the Lord began to grant me favors, and He made me want to receive them. The Lord gave me quite often the prayer of quiet, and even that of union, which lasted a long time." She explains in greater detail the precise kind of prayer she was experiencing:

I used unexpectedly to experience a consciousness of the presence of God, of such a kind that I could not possibly doubt that He was within me or that I was wholly engulfed in Him. This was in no sense a vision. The soul is suspended in such a way that it seems to be completely outside itself. The will loves; the memory, I think, is almost completely lost; while the understanding, I believe, though it is not lost, does not reason—I mean that it does not work, but is amazed at the extent of all it can understand.

Teresa was concerned that her prayer life be authentic and valid, and not delusionary, or perhaps even hallucinatory, and she consulted the most intelligent guides she could find: first the Jesuits at St. Giles College in Ávila, and subsequently St. Francis Borgia, St. Peter of Alcántara, and the distinguished theologian Peter Ibáñez. They all approved her state and encouraged her to persevere. Soon she began to experience more positive manifestations of the Lord's presence:

I spent the greater part of one whole day in prayer, and then asking the Lord to help me to please Him in everything, I began the *Veni Creator*. While I was reciting it, there came to me a transport so sudden that it almost carried me away. I could make no mistake about this, so clear was it. This was the first time that the Lord had granted me the favor of any kind of rapture. I heard these words: "I will have you converse now, not with men, but with angels."

Thus began a new phase in Teresa's life, lasting until her death, a frequent and entirely unusual religious experience in which she saw the Lord, heard Him speak, and communicated directly with Him. Teresa explained these phenomena as "intellectual visions and locutions," experiences in which the exterior senses, eyes and tactile sensations, were in no way involved, but which were impressed directly on her mind. Teresa was, then, a mystic, living in the most profound regions of religious experience. She had a variety of different manifestations, but the most remarkable of all occurred about the year 1562 when she saw an angel standing by her side holding a long golden spear with a fiery tip. With it he seemed to pierce her heart several times and left her "completely afire with a great love for God."

But Teresa's attractive and dynamic personality was not submerged beneath the intensity of these experiences: she remained the same vivacious personality. In fact, just as she seemed to become considerably more relaxed and peaceful twenty years previously when she finally entered the convent, so now she similarly appeared to discover a new peace and a new joy. Throughout the rest of her life she was the same witty, voluble person, who often perplexed people who met her for the first time and could not imagine that this urbane nun was the same one who was supposed to be receiving visions from the Lord. She was always insistent that her own nuns be cheerful people, and she ruthlessly excluded from her convents any nun who seemed to have a melancholic temperament. "Lord deliver us from sour-faced saints," she said. And the nuns of her convents leave us an unforgettable image of the saint playing the mandolin and dancing for her sisters at recreation. "My chief fear," she wrote, "is that the sisters should lose the spirit of joy by which the Lord leads them, for I know what a discontented nun is."

Cheerful, witty, poking fun at herself and occasionally at other people, she seemed to exert an even greater influence over people with her magnetic personality. "With merely two words and that amazing smile of hers, she enchanted everybody," a Dominican priest said of her. However, she abhorred pretension, and found it difficult to abide in other people. Once, after she had been introduced to a group of pious ladies involved in church work, she confided:

They were saints in their own opinion, but when I got to know them better they frightened me more than all the sinners I had ever met.

Combined with this was her rare common sense. Her letters are filled with practical advice for her various friends to get more sleep, eat better food, consult intelligent counselors. She prays to be delivered from foolish devotions, and she chides superiors who are too rigorous with their charges. On one of her travels she was criticized for eating an expensive partridge when it was served to her, and she looked up, surprised, and said: "There is a time for partridge and a time for penance." To a Carmelite friar who wrote her, urging her to accept a girl into the convent, she answered: "I was very amused at your reverence's assurance that you could evaluate her after meeting her one time; we women cannot be summed up as easily as that."

Teresa presented, in her own life and in her writings, a rare picture of the perfect blend between mysticism and humanism: a thoroughly saintly person, and yet a thoroughly human person. She attained such lofty spiritual heights that commentators often call her "the seraphic virgin," but a more penetrating insight into her temperament might perhaps be gained from a phrase she employed so frequently in her writings—"I just laughed to myself."

Teresa continued to live at the Incarnation for the next seven years after her "conversion," with the exception of the periods of time she was forced to spend at the homes of some wealthy ladies who had asked the prioress if they could have Teresa as a house guest for a while. During that time she became more and more preoccupied with pressing religious problems of the time: the Protestant Reformation in the north, the breakdown in religious and monastic discipline, and the failure of Carmel to maintain its original ideals.

Teresa remarks in her autobiography that she had been thinking for some time about the possibility of establishing a reformed convent of nuns who would follow the original rule without mitigation or deviation, but she first discussed the matter openly in a conversation with a group of friends one day in 1558 at the Incarnation. Maria de Ocampo, an eighteen-year-old boarder at the convent, and the daughter of one of the cousins Teresa had played with as a child, "asked me why we should not become discalced nuns, for it would be quite possible to find a way of establishing a convent." ("Discalced" literally means without shoes, and it was commonly used in religious parlance at that time to indicate an order which had reformed itself and adopted a more dedicated and austere form of life. Members of these orders either went barefooted or wore some form of open sandals. The term "discalced" had particular meaning in Ávila because of the visits of Peter of Alcántara, who had founded his Discalced Franciscans, an order which soon perished, principally because of the brutal austerities and grossly imprudent penances demanded of its members.) Teresa raised some objections to Maria de Ocampo's suggestion, mainly the financial difficulties involved, but the excited girl offered to donate a thousand ducats she had received from her family. At that point in the discussion the group was joined by Doña Guiomar de Ulloa, a wealthy young widow who had become a close friend of Teresa's, and she became enthused with the idea, offering to help substantially from her fortune. They discussed the project for some time, until Teresa finally "agreed to commend the matter very earnestly to God." An answer came quickly:

> One day after Communion, the Lord gave me the most explicit commands to work for this aim with all my might and made me wonderful promises—that the convent would not fail to be established; that great service would be done to Him in it; that it should be called St. Joseph's; that He would watch over us at one door and Our Lady at the other; that Christ would go with us; that the convent would be a star giving out the most brilliant light.

The Lord also commanded her to discuss the matter with her confessor, and thus she explained the plan to Baltasar Álvarez, a Jesuit from the College of St. Giles. She told him that she wanted to found a single convent which followed the rule of Our Lady of Mount Carmel "in its entirety and without mitigation, in the form drawn up by Brother Hugh, Cardinal of Santa Sabina, and given in the year 1248, in the fifth year of the pontificate of Pope Innocent IV." Alvarez, however, saw some formidable difficulties in the plan, but he advised her to discuss it with the Carmelite provincial of Castile, Gregory Fernández. The provincial approved the idea, and together with Teresa agreed that the number of nuns in the convent should be limited to thirteen. Teresa also discussed the matter with Peter Ibáñez, the brilliant Dominican theologian, and he became one of her most enthusiastic supporters.

Teresa was making plans for the reformed convent, and the provincial was drawing up the necessary papers to send to Rome, when a storm of opposition broke out. The nuns at the Incarnation protested against the project, claiming that the new convent was a reflection on them:

> I was now very unpopular in my own convent for having wanted to found a convent more strictly enclosed. The nuns said I was insulting them: that there were others who were better than myself, and so I

could serve God quite well where I was: and that I should have done better by getting money for my own convent rather than for a new foundation.

Even the townspeople began to voice criticisms, and Teresa was publicly denounced from the pulpits in Ávila. On one occasion she was attending Mass at St. Thomas' church with her sister, Juana, when the priest berated "nuns who left their convents to go and found new ones." Juana was extremely indignant, but when she turned to watch Teresa's reaction she saw that she had an amused smile on her face. During all of this she was receiving continued revelations from the Lord about the necessity of the project. "But the Lord appeared and spoke to me about it again and again, and so numerous were the motives and arguments which He put before me that I saw they were valid and the project was His will. He told me that I could now see what those saints who had founded religious Orders had suffered: they had to endure much more persecution than any I could imagine and we must not allow ourselves to be troubled by it." The opposition apparently unsettled the provincial, and he suddenly withdrew his approval for the new convent and refused to write to Rome about it. However Peter Ibáñez remained her loyal supporter and felt that the project should be continued. Nothing was done about the matter for five or six months, until a new rector was appointed at the Jesuit college, Gaspar de Salazar, who approved her ideas and encouraged her to continue working for their accomplishment.

At this point in St. Teresa's story we arrive at some intriguing incidents. The saint knew that God wanted the foundation of the convent, and she had the support of some intelligent and distinguished people, but her own superiors forbade it. She determined to go ahead nevertheless, and she embarked on a series of machinations and maneuvers which cut swiftly through the legal net in which she was caught. "We agreed that the work should be done in all secrecy," she wrote, and it was: she had Peter Ibáñez and Doña Guiomar de Ulloa write directly to the Holy See for permission to establish the convent; and she arranged for her sister, Juana de Ahumada, to purchase a house in her own name and prepare it as a convent. We see the adroit conspirator in Teresa's activities here. Ibáñez undoubtedly composed the petition to Rome, but it was sent over the signature of Doña Guiomar, who presented herself as a benefactor who wished to endow a new convent of reformed

Carmelites and wanted the approval of the Holy See. Thus when the affirmative answer was received from Rome it was addressed to Doña Guiomar and her mother, the wealthy benefactors of the convent. Teresa also obtained a substantial donation from her brother, Lorenzo, who had emigrated to what is today modern Ecuador, and had married the daughter of one of the conquistadors. The house purchased for the future convent was a small two-story building, situated on a narrow street inside the city walls of Ávila, only about fifteen minutes' walk from the Incarnation.

At this juncture the provincial ordered her to Toledo, where she was to live with Doña Luisa de la Cerda, a recent and disconsolate widow who had asked the provincial if she could have some nun stay with her for a while to console her. It was a stroke of good fortune for Teresa because it removed her from Ávila for six months, and allowed her sister to employ workmen to ready the convent without arousing any suspicions. When Teresa returned to Ávila in July of 1562, the brief had arrived from Rome. Dated February 7, 1562, and signed by Pius IV, it permitted the one convent which would follow the original Carmelite rule, and it allowed Teresa to draw up a set of constitutions for the nuns, and as a final guarantee of the project's success, the decree placed the convent under the direct jurisdiction of the bishop of Ávila.

One final difficulty remained. Teresa wanted the convent to live on freewill offerings in conformity with the original thirteenth-century rule, but many of her advisors wanted to see it endowed with a regular income from a trust set up by Doña Guiomar de Ulloa and other benefactors. Teresa was adamant on the point, but she met stern opposition, especially from her friend Peter Ibáñez. He wrote her a memorandum "two sheets long, full of refutations and theology." However, she remained unconvinced. "I replied that I had no wish to make use of theology, and I should not thank him for his learning in this matter if it was going to keep me from following my vocation and being true to the vow of poverty." The matter was finally settled by a direct message from the Lord: "The Lord told me that I must on no account fail to found the convent in poverty, for that was His Father's will, and His own, and He would help me." Ibáñez and the bishop of Ávila, Don Álvaro de Mendoza, relented.

The new convent was officially inaugurated on August 24, 1562, and it was accomplished by stealth, in circumstances which verged on the melodramatic. Teresa had spent the entire day of the twenty-third in the small house, making final preparations, decorating the tiny chapel, even installing a small bell of three pounds which she affixed to the wall near the door. Before daybreak on the morning of the twenty-fourth she stole quietly out of the convent and rendezvoused with a group which included Doña Guiomar de Ulloa, three priests, and the four women who were to become the first nuns in this new convent. These four women had been recommended to Teresa by some of her priest acquaintances, and during the time of waiting for official permission to begin the new enterprise she instructed them in the primitive rule of the Order and prepared them for conventual life. Now, in the dark hour before dawn in Ávila, Teresa led the group furtively through the quiet city, picking her way carefully along the deserted streets. When they arrived at St. Joseph's, one of the priests, Gaspar Daza, the bishop's representative, invested the nuns with a new habit designed by Teresa, and then offered Mass. The small bell was rung vigorously, announcing to the city of Ávila that a new convent was present in their midst. By seven o'clock in the morning the guests had departed, and the nuns were alone in their cloister. Teresa remained on her knees in the chapel until noon, lost in prayer.

But outside a fury was mounting—a "commotion," as Teresa called it. The townspeople, who had already been exercised about the possibility of the convent by the inflammatory oratory from the pulpits, were enraged now that it was accomplished. The mayor and some members of the town council were consulted, and a lawsuit was threatened against Teresa. An angry protest meeting was held in one of the public squares. And over at the Incarnation the nuns were agitated and clamoring against what they felt was deceit on Teresa's part in founding the convent. In the early afternoon a message arrived at St. Joseph's that the prioress of the Incarnation, Mother Maria Cimbron, wanted to see Teresa immediately. Teresa thought that it was more prudent to submit at this stage so she wearily walked back to the Incarnation after appointing the oldest of the sisters to act as superior in her absence. "Lord, this house is not mine," she said to herself, "it has been made for you. Since now there is nobody to watch it, let Your Majesty do it."

She explained the situation to the prioress, who then summoned the provincial, Ángel de Salazar, newly elected to that office and not familiar with Teresa's project. He rebuked her severely for acting without consulting him, and she begged his pardon and asked him to punish her. She later wrote that their criticism of her activities did not cause her "the least trouble or distress," but added, in characteristic fashion, "however, I gave the impression that it did, lest I should appear to be making light of what they were saying." Salazar then made her appear before the entire community of 180 nuns and give an account of her actions. She wrote:

Since I was at peace within myself and the Lord aided me, I gave my account in such a way that neither the provincial nor those who were there found anything to condemn me for, and afterward in private I spoke to him in greater detail, and he seemed quite satisfied.

But he made her remain at the Incarnation until the furor in the city subsided. Due mostly to the enthusiastic support of Peter Ibáñez and his impassioned public pleas for Teresa, the townspeople gradually became reconciled to the idea, but it took six months, and all that time Teresa waited impatiently at the Incarnation. Finally in March of 1563 she was given permission to return to her new convent, and she took with her three nuns from the Incarnation. When she arrived at St. Joseph's she fell on her knees again, and "I all but went into a rapture, and saw Christ, Who seemed to be receiving me with great love, placing a crown on my head and thanking me for what I had done for His mother."

The small house had been adequately prepared for conventual life by Teresa's sister and her brother-in-law according to her directions. The chapel was on the ground floor, with a double grill of latticed wood which separated it from the choir where the nuns heard Mass and recited their office. A number of small "cells" (private rooms) had been prepared for the nuns on the second floor. Two statues, donated by friends, were placed in the positions indicated in Teresa's vision: St. Joseph in a niche by the chapel door, and the Blessed Virgin in a niche by the parlor door. Teresa had written a set of constitutions to implement the rule of 1247, and they emphasized strict cloister, solitude, poverty, and mortification; and they required that each nun make two hours of meditation daily. Teresa directed that the nuns chant the Divine Office on a simple, one-tone note, rather than the elaborate polyphonic melodies that were then in vogue. This was a radical innovation in the recitation of the office by religious, and Teresa stated that her purpose was to make the office more simple and prayerful, and to allow the nuns more time for quiet, contemplative prayer. The habit designed by Teresa was substantially that worn by the nuns at the Incarnation, except that she had ruthlessly trimmed all excesses from it, pleats and folds and great swathes of cloth the nuns had been using, and she allowed no ornamental pleats in the veil. The habit was made from a coarse brown homespun serge, and the nuns wore inexpensive hemp sandals called *alpargatas*. As a symbol of their renunciation of the past and their new allegiance to God, she made the nuns drop the use of their family names and adopt a new religious name. Thus Teresa de Ahumada became Teresa of Jesus.

Teresa remained at St. Joseph's for over four years—"the most restful years of my life," she later wrote. It was her original intention to remain there all her life, for she had achieved the full limit of her plan and ambition. She only wanted to found a single convent which would follow the rule, and she had no intention of founding a series of convents, much less of reforming the Carmelite Order. During those quiet years she began the composition of her *Way of Perfection*, and after outlining some of the Church's problems in Europe, she stated her simple and precise objectives in founding St. Joseph's:

Realizing that I was a woman and a sinner and incapable of doing all that I should like in the Lord's service, and as my whole yearning was, and still is, that since He has so many enemies and so few friends, these friends should be good ones, I determined to do the little that was in me—namely, to follow the evangelical counsels as perfectly as I could, and to see that these few nuns who are here should do the same, confiding in the great goodness of God, Who never fails to help those who resolve to give up everything for His sake.

St. Teresa began writing the first draft of her life while she was still a nun at the Incarnation, and she completed it after she had founded the convent of St. Joseph's. The book was written at the request of Peter Ibáñez, who wanted her to record the principal events of her life and the graces she was receiving in prayer. She apparently wrote a large section of the manuscript during the six months she spent with the widow in Toledo immediately before the foundation of St. Joseph's. Teresa always considered the book her "*libro grande*" (the important book), but it was only the first effort in a literary career which produced a prodigious amount of writing.

She composed all of her major works at the suggestion of her various confessors and directors, and this fact plus the agonized expressions she sometimes used about her writing (she complained of the fatigue entailed, and she said that she would be more useful doing her knitting) have led some commentators to conclude that she was a reluctant writer who only wrote out of duty and obedience. But more perceptive critics have stated that this woman who had composed a novel when she was only in her teens was definitely a born writer who enjoyed the experience of literary communication, despite the agony and tedium of composition. Only someone who really wanted to write could have accomplished so much in the midst of an extremely busy life—four major prose works, a series of shorter works, poems, and numberless letters (there are 445 extant letters, but we have no way of computing exactly how many letters she actually wrote—St. John of the Cross, for example, destroyed all the letters she had written to him). During the crowded years when she was founding her convents of reformed nuns, she stole occasional moments for her literary tasks and often wrote far into the night after the other nuns had retired. Her writing reflects the speed at which she had to write: her very penmanship, a bold, vigorous, almost masculine stroke, races across the page, and the writing is often elliptical, disjointed, and gaily ungrammatical. "I wish I could write with both hands," she said, "so I would not forget one thing while I am saying another." But she was aware of the demands of literary composition, and not careless or indifferent. She writes that her writing "worries me," and when she had completed the *Interior Castle* fourteen years after her autobiography she recognized that her technique had improved: "It is composed of finer enamel and more precious metals; the goldsmith was not so skilled when he fashioned the first work."

The most striking quality about her writing, though, is its highly subjective character: Teresa flashes through on every page. She is not writing textbook material, but rather a vivid, highly personal account of spiritual experience. She is completely natural, uninhibited, and unpretentious. Her lack of affectation and her humanness set her writing in marked contrast to the usual stilted material which comprises the somewhat arch genre known as spiritual writing. Her *Life* is a personal recollection of her career up to and including the foundation of St. Joseph's; and in the text she liberally intersperses comments and directives about religious experience and the life of prayer. The *Foundations* is a long and intriguing narrative about her adventures in founding additional convents of the reform. The *Way of Perfection* is the classic text on prayer, written for her nuns, and explaining encounter with God. The *Interior Mansions*, her masterpiece, was written to give "some insight into the beauty of a soul in grace," and it describes the dimensions of spiritual and mystical growth.

Her writing is prophetic, in the truest sense of that word, because she gives witness to her experience with God. Her message is not formulated with scholarly precision, nor is it phrased in the dispassionate language of the scholar, but it is torn from the very story of her own encounter with God. To the doubting ages which wonder about God and His reality, she can say, with all the fire of her spiritual father, Elijah: "The Lord God lives before whose face I stand." In this she is authentically Elijahan and genuinely Carmelite. In the bull for her canonization, Gregory XV wrote of her:

Almighty God so filled her with the spirit of understanding that she not only bequeathed to the Church the example of her good works, but she enriched it with the heavenly wisdom of her books on mystical theology and other holy writings.

Her statue in the central nave in St. Peter's at Rome is enscribed with the terse phrase *Mater Spiritualium* (Mother of Spirituality), and she is the only woman whose teaching and doctrine is appealed to in the Roman liturgy—this irrepressible nun who wished she could write with both hands, who sat up late at night drafting her imperishable writings by the light of an oil lamp.

In the summer of 1566, a Franciscan, Alonso Maldonado, who had recently returned from missionary work in the Indies, visited the convent of St. Joseph's and described for Teresa the shortage of priests and "the many millions of souls perishing there for lack of teaching." After his visit she went into one of the hermitages in the cloister garden, the huts she had built to give the nuns an occasional period of even greater solitude, and prayed that God would give her "a means for saving some souls for his service." She was distressed at the missionary's account, but she felt powerless to do anything about it. A short while afterward the Lord appeared to her and said "very lovingly, as if He wished to bring me comfort: 'Wait a little while, daughter, and you shall see great things.'" She did not understand this message—until six months later, when the prior general from Rome arrived at the convent.

Nicholas Audet had died in 1562, and Pius IV nominated as the vicar general John Rossi, the son of an aristocratic family of Ravenna who had distinguished himself in the Carmelite Order as a professor of canon law in Rome.[3] Two years later Rossi was elected prior general, and he set himself strenuously to the still unaccomplished task of reform. Leaving Rome in April of 1566, he embarked on an extensive visitation of Spain and Portugal. He was only the third general in the history of the Order to make a visitation to Spain, and the first to ever reach Castile. Rossi immediately presented himself to Philip II, the enigmatic Catholic king who interested himself so closely in the ecclesiastical affairs in Spain that no delegate or legate from Rome could even operate without his approval. The two aristocrats got on well, and the king, who had an almost abnormal interest in the reform of religious orders, seemed to approve of Rossi's work, although he later undermined it completely.

Teresa was apprehensive about the general's visit because she had heard unfriendly things about the man's severity and uncompromising rigor: he was reported to have been such a meticulous visitator that he carefully searched the cell of each friar of the monastery where he visited, confiscating anything he felt to be superfluous; and when he discovered major abuses he sentenced the Carmelite to serve penal time as a galley slave on a ship—all of this, of course, did not accomplish reform, but only further alienated the men.[4] Teresa was fearful that Rossi would become exercised about the furtive manner in which she had founded the convent and perhaps work to suppress it. However, her fears were unfounded: she was able to win him over instantly. "I told him my story quite truthfully

[3] Rossi was commonly called Rubeo in Spain, and that is the way many historians record his name. Rossi means red in the original Italian, and following the Renaissance custom Rossi often signed his name to official documents with the Latin word for red, *Rubeus*; and then the Spaniards Hispanicized *Rubeus* to Rubeo. Thus, Rubeo is the Hispanic form of the Latin form of an Italian name.

[4] The practice of sentencing errant priests to serve a term as a galley slave, pulling oars on a ship, was not an uncommon ecclesiastical punishment in that era. Unfortunately but understandably, these priests became more embittered, and the majority of them escaped and fled as apostate priests to North Africa, or to South America in the New World.

and simply," she wrote, and "he was glad when he saw our way of life; for it gave him a picture, however imperfect, of our Order as it had been in its early days." And Teresa added: "He was able to observe how we were keeping the Primitive Rule in all its strictness —there was not another house in the whole Order where this was observed; the Mitigated Rule is followed everywhere."[5]

When Teresa mentioned to the general that she had many applicants for the Carmel of St. Joseph's but was limited to thirteen nuns in the convent, Rossi gave her permission to make as many foundations as she wished; but shortly afterward he wrote and restricted her foundations to Castile. His only remonstration concerned the fact that she had placed the convent under the jurisdiction of the bishop of Ávila, and thus Teresa placed her subsequent foundations under the jurisdiction of the Carmelite provincial of Castile. Rossi left Ávila, expressing his high regard for this woman about whom he was to write two years later: "She is more profitable to the Order than all the Carmelite friars in Spain."

It is not quite clear how much precise thinking Teresa had been doing about additional convents before Rossi's visit. The multiplication of convents following the primitive rule was beyond her original scope, and yet after his visit, and armed with his permissions, she began to plan other foundations. And something else, too:

> After some days, I began to think how necessary it was, if convents for women were to be founded, that there should be friars following the same rule, and seeing how few there were in this province—it even seemed to me that they were dying out—I commended the matter earnestly to our Lord, and wrote a letter to our Father General, begging him as well as I could to grant this permission.

Teresa's letter, which outlined her reasons for friars who would follow the primitive rule and which concluded by "representing to him what a service it would be to our Lady," reached Rossi in Barcelona. He replied immediately, granting her request and allow-

---

[5] Teresa always made this distinction between primitive and mitigated rule, and she set as her objective the restoration of the primitive rule. She is, of course, referring to the rule with the adaptations of 1247, and purists might object that only the original rule of 1209 could in actuality be called the primitive rule. However, the objection is specious because Teresa's intent was to restore the original tradition of Carmel as it was practiced in the West, the primitive Western tradition.

ing her to establish two monasteries of friars who were to be called "contemplative Carmelites"; and he prudently sent a copy of the permission to the Carmelite provincial. Teresa, however, was preoccupied with making the second convent of reformed nuns, and she had chosen the city of Medina del Campo, fifty miles north of Ávila; she thus put the question of the friars aside for a moment: "Here was a poor Discalced nun, without help from anyone except the Lord, loaded with patents and good wishes but devoid of either courage or hope."

The Jesuits at Medina del Campo made the preliminary arrangements for her foundation, and in the summer of 1567 she set off in three lumbering, creaking carts to establish the second house of the reform. She took six nuns with her, two from St. Joseph's and four from the Incarnation who wanted to join the movement. They spent the night at Arévalo, and in the morning the prior of the Carmelite monastery in Medina, Anthony de Heredia, came out to escort them into the city. The prior offered Mass in the new monastery, but a close inspection afterward showed that the building needed extensive repairs before it would be fit for habitation. A wealthy merchant offered the nuns the upper story of his home while they waited for the repairs to be completed, and Teresa gladly accepted the offer. The nuns remained in these temporary quarters for about two months. During that time Teresa had the opportunity to discuss her reform with the prior and she revealed to him the permission she had from the general to found two houses of reformed friars. She was startled when he volunteered to become the first friar of the new reform. Anthony de Heredia was an esteemed Carmelite from Valencia who had entered the Order at the age of ten, later graduated from Salamanca University, and served as prior in three different monasteries. But he was now fifty-seven years old, and his health was not good. Teresa later wrote about Anthony's offer: "I thought it was a joke, and told him so." But the prior protested, even stating that he had been planning to leave the Carmelites and join the Carthusians so he could find a more dedicated form of life. However, Teresa felt uneasy about him: "Nevertheless I was not very well satisfied, although it made me happy to hear him, and I asked him to let us wait awhile."

The following month Anthony brought another Carmelite to meet Teresa at her temporary dwelling. He was a newly ordained priest, twenty-five years old, and he had confided to the prior that he too wanted to leave the Order and join the Carthusians. Anthony felt that the young man had better speak to Teresa. His name was John de Yepes.

St. John of the Cross, one of the original group of reformed Carmelite friars, occupies a major position in the history of Christian thought—as a doctor of the church, the "mystical doctor"; and as perhaps the Church's most outstanding writer on mystical theology. In association with St. Teresa he was a key figure in the reform movement within the Carmelite Order, although his role was a far different one from hers. Teresa was the organizer, the administrative genius who was able to wrest permissions and donations from the proper people and thus move the work of reform relentlessly forward; John was never considered a major administrative force in the work of reform, although he did for a while occupy a number of important administrative positions: his contribution to reform, rather, was in the area of inspiration, where he stood as a blinding symbol of dedication and fidelity to original Carmelite ideals.

Temperamentally, he presented a striking contrast to the voluble, outgoing Teresa. He was basically a quiet man, deeply reflective, somewhat withdrawn, but nevertheless a friendly, approachable person, who put people immediately at ease. Despite his own personal uncompromising asceticism and austerity, he was extremely kind and sympathetic with others, understanding of their problems and eager to help. But above all, this quiet Carmelite friar, this man of deep prayer and profound mystical experience, presented a vivid image of complete commitment and, if necessary, grim determination.

John was born at Fontiveros, a small town some twenty-five miles northwest of Ávila, about the year 1542, the third child of Gonzalo de Yepes and Catalina Álvarez.[6] Gonzalo de Yepes came from a good family in Toledo, and after both his parents died when he was still quite young he was sponsored by his uncles who were wealthy silk merchants. Gonzalo kept the accounts for his uncles and performed a number of tasks of a general business nature. His work frequently took him to Fontiveros, where he met Catalina Álvarez, an attractive young woman from an impoverished background who

[6] His full legal name, therefore, was Juan de Yepes y Álvarez. The records of his birth have been lost, and the year 1542 is an approximation.

worked as a silk weaver. They fell in love and soon married, but Gonzalo's uncles were so infuriated at him because he had married beneath his station that they discharged him from their employment and banished him from their homes. Suddenly deprived of his position, the young man was forced to learn his wife's trade of silk weaving. But he apparently had little success at it because the family lived in dire poverty. Shortly after John's birth, Gonzalo died, leaving his almost destitute widow with three small children.

Catalina trudged to Toledo, carrying John in her arms, seeking some assistance from her late husband's relatives, but they all refused to help, except a doctor who agreed to take care of one of the three boys, Francis. However, the doctor's wife abused the young boy, and he soon returned to his mother. The second child died about this time, and Catalina desperately began to hunt for the most advantageous place to rear her two other sons. She chose Medina del Campo, where she taught Francis to assist her in silk weaving and sent John, then age nine, to the catechism school, a residential institution for poor boys. John lived at the school for eight years, and he was apprenticed to a number of different artisans, notably a carpenter and a tailor, but he was completely inept at any of these trades. He was a serious and upright boy, however, and he came to the attention of Don Alonso Álvarez, the governor of the plague hospital in Medina, who invited him to live and work at the hospital. John acted as a nurse and a collector of alms, but Álvarez also allowed him to attend the new Jesuit college in the city, where he received an excellent education in the classics for four years.

John expressed a desire to become a priest, and Álvarez volunteered to defray the cost of his education, in the hope that he would one day serve as chaplain in the hospital. But John had become acquainted with the recently founded Carmelite community in Medina, and he was preparing to enter the Order. Álvarez apparently protested this decision so much that when the young man of twenty-one entered the monastery he had to steal away from the hospital secretly at night, and thus both he and his future associate Teresa joined the Order by fleeing furtively from their homes.

After his profession of vows in 1564, he was sent to the Carmelite College of St. Andrew at the University of Salamanca where he attended classes in philosophy and theology at both the university and St. Andrew's. During his years as a student he was carefully evaluating his position as a Carmelite, and he requested permission from his superiors to follow the primitive rule without mitigation, insofar as he could in the framework of the actual situation. This did not seem too practicable, because we soon find him planning to leave the Order and join the Carthusians. In 1567, while he was still pondering all these personal problems, he was ordained, and in September of that year he returned to Medina for the purpose of offering his first Mass. It was then that he met Teresa of Ávila.

The young priest of twenty-five whom Teresa saw was an extremely short man, about five feet in height, thin, with a swarthy complexion and dark eyes. His face was slightly oval, his forehead broad, and his hairline was receding into early baldness. Teresa was then fifty-two, and still attractive in her middle age, despite the fact that she was becoming slightly plump. The nun and the priest presented an interesting study in contrasts—the vivacious middle-aged nun from an affluent family, and the quiet young priest from an impoverished background who had worked his way tenaciously through school.

"When I spoke to the friar I liked him very much," Teresa said, and she explained her project to him, asking him to put off his plan to enter the Carthusians until she had obtained a monastery for reformed friars. She told him that if he wanted to lead a more perfect life "he should lead it within his own Order." Teresa's singular persuasiveness worked again, and John agreed to her proposal, "provided there were no long delay." John had to return to Salamanca for a final year of theology, and Teresa promised to do something about finding a house suitable for a monastery of friars during that time.

Teresa was immediately enthused with John de Yepes. "Although he is small in stature," she later wrote, "I believe he is great in the sight of God." After John and Anthony left her temporary convent that autumn day in 1567, she told the nuns that she now felt she could proceed with the establishment of the friars' monastery, "although I was still not quite satisfied with the prior." She said that she now had "a friar and a half," and that phrase has caused a minor controversy among historians. Some have said that the "half friar" was the diminutive John of the Cross, while others have contended that she was referring to her doubts about Anthony, and that she would certainly not jest about the small stature of the future doctor of the church. Or would she?

After Teresa had established the nuns at Medina del Campo in their regular convent, she departed for Madrid and eventually arrived at Alcalá de Henares in late November. Then in February she was off to Malagón where she founded another convent. This was the pattern of her life for the next fourteen years, and by the time of her death in 1582 she had personally founded fifteen convents of nuns.

In May of 1568 Teresa left Malagón and returned for a visit to St. Joseph's in Ávila. While there, a relative of hers, Raphael Mejía, offered her an abandoned farm house at Duruelo some twenty-five miles away, which she could use as a monastery for the friars. At the end of June, on her way back to Medina del Campo, she visited the site, accompanied by another nun and Julian of Ávila, the chaplain at St. Joseph's. "I always remember the fatigue of that long roundabout journey," Teresa wrote. The sun was scorching, and no one they met had ever heard of the site at Duruelo. They lost their way, wandered in circles for hours, and did not arrive at the property until dusk. And then they found the wooden farm house to be severely disappointing: "It had a fair-sized porch, a room divided into two, with a loft above it, and a little kitchen: that was all there was of the building which was to be our monastery." Teresa's companion said that the building was completely uninhabitable and that no one could endure living there, but the saint began to make plans for using the limited space: she determined that the porch could be used for a small chapel, and the loft as a choir, while the friars could sleep in the downstairs area. The building was so dirty that they were unable to spend the night there, and they had to sleep in a nearby church.

The following morning they made their way to Medina del Campo, where Teresa immediately described the site at Duruelo to Anthony, sparing none of the harsh facts. She told him that if he had the courage to at least begin the foundation the Lord would provide better quarters in due time, but "the important thing was to make a start." Anthony eagerly agreed to begin at Duruelo, adding that "he would be willing to live, not only there, but in a pigsty." John returned to Medina del Campo from his school year at Salamanca in the early summer of that year, 1568, and Teresa took him with her to Valladolid where she was planning yet another convent. He remained with the nuns from August until October, while Teresa instructed John "all about our way of life, so that he might have an exact knowledge of everything." It seems that at this point Teresa had a finer sense of the original Carmelite tradition than John, and she carefully explained to her young protégé the mechanics of the primitive rule. She later wrote that he was such a good man that "I could have learned much more from him than he from me." But she adds, in her typical fashion: "I did not do so, however, but merely showed him the way the nuns lived."

Anthony came to visit Teresa in Valladolid, informing her of the preparations he had made and the articles he had gathered for the foundation at Duruelo. For some odd reason he had collected five clocks, and Teresa commented: "I thought that very amusing. I do not think he even had anything to sleep on." It was arranged that John would go to Duruelo as soon as possible to prepare the building, while Anthony remained in Medina del Campo to conclude his affairs and resign his office of prior. Teresa herself sewed the new habit to be worn by the reformed friars, a Carmelite habit which, like the nuns' habits, was shorn of all excesses—the capuche was shortened, the extra folds of material were eradicated, the mantle reduced in length, and of course, the effete additions of the Renaissance age were removed: the gleaming buckles, the silver buttons on the sleeves, the ruffles and the lace collars. John tried on the habit in Valladolid, but did not wear it regularly until he arrived at Duruelo.

He reached Duruelo sometime in early October, accompanied by a young man who had asked to become a lay brother in the reform. The two men worked on the dilapidated farm house until it was in some semblance of order and ready for community living. On November 27, Anthony arrived at Duruelo in the company of the provincial, Alonso González, and two more recruits: a young Carmelite from Medina del Campo named Joseph who was a deacon; and Luke de Celis, a Carmelite priest who wanted to live in the reformed monastery for a while before deciding whether he should join. On the following day, the first Sunday of Advent, the provincial offered Mass, and then Anthony, John, and the deacon Joseph approached the altar, where they formally renounced the mitigation of Eugene IV and promised to live according to the rule of 1247. After this significant ceremony they signed the deed of foundation:

We, Brother Anthony of Jesus, Brother John of the Cross, and Brother Joseph of Christ, begin this day, 28 November 1568, to live the primitive rule.

They followed Teresa's practice of omitting their family names and adopting a religious title instead, and it is the first time that John used the title "of the Cross." Anthony of Jesus was then appointed prior of the monastery by the provincial, and John of the Cross novice master. The reform of the friars had begun.

Of the original group of five at Duruelo only two persevered through the first year. The lay brother aspirant soon departed; Luke de Celis became ill and returned to Medina del Campo; and Joseph of Christ disappeared from the official records, and is presumed either to have left the reform or to have died. However, other recruits came rapidly from the Carmelite monasteries in Castile, men who wanted to renounce the mitigation and follow the primitive rule, and by the end of the first year there were seven Carmelites at Duruelo. The community followed a brief and simple set of constitutions modeled closely on Teresa's constitutions for the nuns, with strong emphasis on solitude, poverty, two hours of daily meditation, and the simple, one-tone recitation of the Divine Office. Teresa visited the new foundation three months after its inception while she was on her way to establish the nuns in Toledo, and she was deeply impressed with what she saw. "I was amazed to see what spirituality the Lord had inspired there," she wrote. She noted that they had arranged the house according to her plan, and that the small loft which had holes in the roof was used as a choir where the friars chanted the office. They rose at midnight to chant matins, and remained in the choir for some time afterward in deep prayer, and Teresa observed that sometimes "their habits would be covered with snow without their having noticed it." Following the primitive tradition of the prophetic vocation, the friars also preached in the neighboring areas, and Teresa commented on this:

> They used to go out and preach in many places in the district which were without instruction, and for that reason, too, I was glad that the house had been founded there, for they told me that there was no monastery near, nor any means of getting one, which was a great pity. In this short time they had gained such a good reputation that, when I heard of it, it made me extremely happy. . . . When they had preached and heard confessions and had returned to their monastery for a meal it would be very late. But this was very little concern to them, because they were so happy.

She had only one complaint: "severity in matters of penance, in which they were very strict." She cautioned Anthony to exercise prudence in the use of penitential practices, because she was afraid that a lack of moderation might destroy the foundation; and "it had cost me so many desires and prayers to obtain men from the Lord who would make a good beginning." The friars were going barefooted at that initial stage, even on their preaching expeditions, but they later began to wear hemp sandals like the nuns before them.

When Teresa left Duruelo she expressed her "great inward joy" at what had been accomplished. "For I saw quite well that this was a much greater grace than He had given me in enabling me to found houses for nuns." Duruelo represented, as she wrote, "the beginnings of a restoration of the rule of the Virgin, His mother, and our Lady and Patroness."

The second monastery of reformed friars was founded quickly by Teresa in her typically impetuous manner. She was at Toledo in her new convent when she received a message from the Princess of Eboli, stating that she wanted Teresa to come to the little town of Pastrana near Guadalajara and found a convent there. The princess was the wife of Ruy Gómez de Silva, a close friend and advisor to King Philip II, and one of the most influential men in Spain. Teresa did not want to leave Toledo so soon, but she was reluctant to displease the princess because "we were in a very bad way, the reform of the friars having just begun, and from every standpoint it would be useful to have Ruy Gómez on our side, since he had such influence with the king." As she was pondering the matter, the Lord spoke to her and told her to go immediately, "for there was far more afoot than that foundation." She traveled first to Madrid, where she stayed in a Franciscan convent. The morning after her arrival she was introduced to two hermits who had been leading a solitary life by themselves for a number of years. She talked to the elder of the two men, Mariano Azaro, an Italian of extraordinary background: he was a doctor, a mathematician, an engineer, he had attended the Council of Trent as a legal advisor, and he had worked in close collaboration with King Philip II on navigation and irrigation problems in Spain; and when he decided to abandon all of this for a life of complete dedication to God he investigated every Order but found them all "unsuitable for a man of his type"; thus he had been living as a hermit for eight years. He also informed Teresa that Ruy Gómez had given him a good piece of property at Pastrana for use as a hermitage.

Teresa was intrigued with this amazing Italian from Naples, and she tried to convince him that he should join her reform because "in our Order he could keep all his observances with less trouble, for they were the same as our own." She talked to him at great length and concluded by telling him that "he could be of great service to God in this habit of ours." Mariano replied that he wanted to think about it overnight, but Teresa's dazzling persuasiveness had worked again and in the morning he agreed to join the reform, and to bring the other hermit with him, and to deed the property at Pastrana to her. Teresa later wrote that Mariano was "amazed to find that he had so quickly changed his mind, especially —as he occasionally mentions even to this day—at the suggestion of a woman."

Teresa acted quickly. She wrote letters to the Carmelite provincial for permission to establish at Pastrana the second of the two monasteries for which the general had given permission; to Anthony, requesting him to leave for Pastrana immediately, so that he could supervise the beginning of this second monastery; and to Balthasar Nieto, a Carmelite at Medina, a celebrated and eloquent preacher, who had sought admission to the reform, asking him to enter the reform at Pastrana. Teresa and her nuns made habits for the friars from brown frieze given her by the prince, and then they waited for Anthony to arrive. Balthasar arrived first, but Mariano was so impatient to begin the reform in Pastrana that, with Teresa's approval, they had Balthasar invest them in the habit and begin the observance of the primitive rule. The three new friars were known as Balthasar of Jesus, Mariano of St. Benedict, and John of the Misery.[7] Anthony arrived four days later, on July 13, 1569, and re-

---

[7] John of the Misery was born John Narduch in Naples. He was a painter and sculptor by profession, but he had joined Mariano to live with him as a hermit. As a lay brother in the reform he continued to paint occasionally, and he had St. Teresa sit for his famous portrait of her. During the period of persecution against the reform he became frightened and rejoined the mitigation for a time, but he was ultimately accepted back into the reform again. His last years were saddened by paralysis and blindness, and he died in 1616. His name in the original Spanish is Juan de la Miseria. "Miseria" has no precise English counterpart, and "misery" is only an approximation. The word implies humility and abjection, a posture of nothingness before Almighty God. Such terms of self-contempt were frequently used in Spanish religious life at that time: one nun wrote Teresa and signed the letter "Elizabeth of the Dunghill"; and Teresa responded tartly, "I hope you mean that, and they are not just words."

mained to instruct the small community in Carmelite life. He eventually made Balthasar the prior. Mariano and John both entered the Order as lay brothers, but five years later, at the command of his superiors, Mariano was ordained to the priesthood.

The monastery at Pastrana ultimately became the most celebrated and important monastery of the reform in Spain, the house of novitiate where generations of Carmelites were trained in the spirit of the primitive rule. For two centuries most of the general chapters of the reform in Spain were held at Pastrana. St. Teresa had less good fortune with the convent of nuns she established at Pastrana, and her problems were due to the capricious Princess of Eboli. The convent fared well until the death of Ruy Gómez de Silva in 1573 when his young widow descended on the nuns, announcing that in her bereavement she was going to take the habit. The princess, who had given birth to nine children, was still a handsome woman in her thirties, and a black patch worn over her right eye which she had lost in an accident added a touch of the exotic to her bearing. She was reasonably devout but had no vocation to the convent. When Teresa heard that the princess had forced her way into the community, she said: "That will be the end of that house." And it was. The princess brought her retinue and servants with her, and insisted on special privileges and concessions. She received unending streams of visitors, and when she found the cloister grille inconvenient for conversing with outsiders on the other side of the grille she demanded that the prioress admit her visitors directly into the cloister. The prioress, the gifted and saintly Isabel of St. Dominic, finally told her that if she was unable to accommodate herself to the routine of Carmelite life she had better leave the community. The princess retorted that the only person she had ever obeyed in her life was her late husband, adding: "And I will be subject to no one else, and you are a lunatic." She left the convent in great indignation but continued to harass the nuns, even threatening them with a lawsuit. Teresa finally removed the entire community of nuns and relocated the convent in Segovia.

In 1570 the overcrowded community of friars at Duruelo was moved to a new site some four miles away at Mancera de Abajo. Don Luis, the lord of Mancera de Abajo, gave the property to the Carmelites because he felt indebted to Anthony of Jesus. When his wife was in perilous labor at the end of a particularly difficult pregnancy, Don Luis asked Anthony to visit his wife. The prior of

Duruelo laid his scapular on the sick woman, and her child was born quickly and safely. In gratitude, Don Luis gave the Carmelites a new church he had just built, and he constructed a monastery for the friars adjacent to it. Teresa said of the church: "I never saw anything more beautiful in my life." On June 11, the seven friars from Duruelo walked in a silent procession from Duruelo to Mancera de Abajo, with Anthony of Jesus and John of the Cross leading them, to take possession of their new monastery.

Thus by the summer of 1570 a healthy reform movement was flourishing in the Castilian province of Spain. There were two monasteries of friars, Mancera de Abajo and Pastrana, and six convents of nuns, all following the primitive Carmelite rule. The general in Rome, John Rossi, was pleased with the movement, but he was watching it very carefully because he did not want it to get out of hand as had the Albi reform. However, Rossi regarded Teresa's reform as fundamentally a Spanish phenomenon, and not a real solution to his nagging problem: the reform of the entire Order. When Rossi assumed the leadership of the Order in 1562 the prolonged Council of Trent was drawing to a close. The Council had sparked a vigorous reform movement within the entire Church which ultimately eradicated the most grievous abuses of the Renaissance era. Rossi rode on the crest of this cleansing tide in the Church and attempted to reform his own Order. He was able, by dint of his forceful and sometimes ruthless efforts, to stamp out most of the more serious faults, especially the moral ones, but he was unable to effect a fundamental change of spirit. The Order now seemed to be wedded to the fifteenth-century mitigation, rather than to the original thirteenth-century tradition. Until the end of his life Rossi unceasingly urged a return to the original Carmelite ideal.

Teresa's own concept of reform was undergoing an organic development. From her original intention of establishing only one small convent, she had enlarged her plans to include the foundation of additional convents for nuns and then monasteries for reformed friars. As the movement became more popular her plans enlarged even further. But during all the expansion she continued to insist on her fundamental aim: "We observe the rule of our Lady of Carmel, and we keep it without mitigation." Her intention was a "restoration" of the thirteenth-century tradition as embodied in the primitive rule; and she was also keenly aware of the traditional

Marian character of the Order. It was "the rule of the Virgin" she was attempting to restore, and in her wide correspondence, which included king and papal nuncio and friars and nuns, she consistently referred to her reform as "the Order of the Virgin." Her houses were "built for our Lady," and they are "the communities of the Virgin our Lady," and the friars and nuns are "Mary's cavaliers and daughters." They wear "our Lady's habit," and it is the "habit of His glorious mother." Echoing the traditional Carmelite theme of imitation, she writes to the Discalced: "Imitate our Lady and consider how great she must be and what a good thing it is that we have her for our patroness." And, recalling the pristine concept of Mary's ownership and protection, she writes: "The Order is hers, and she is our Lady and patroness."

However, as late as the year 1570 Teresa's plan of restoration was still a limited one restricted to a few houses in the Castilian province of Spain. The "great things" predicted in her vision of 1566 were yet to come.

– VI –
THE STRUGGLE FOR EXISTENCE

F OR nearly a quarter of a century the Carmelite reform movement found itself involved in a bitter and brutal struggle for survival. Before the reform could spread throughout Europe and then to the rest of the world, it had to pass through a period of violent conflict which produced a drama of almost unbearable intensity. Many factors contrived to produce and prolong this fierce struggle, but underlying them all must stand the undeniable fact that seldom in the history of human affairs have so many strong and determined personalities been so passionately involved in the same situation at the same time. Teresa and John of the Cross, Nicholas Doria and Jerome Gratian, the apostolic nuncios Ormaneto and Sega, the Dominicans Fernández and Vargas, King Philip II and the general John Rossi—strong-willed people drawn into a shattering clash of interests and personalities.

The Carmelite reform movement achieved an almost instant popularity in Spain, and from its unpretentious beginnings at St. Joseph's it developed into an expanding network of convents and monasteries which attracted favorable attention from all quarters, even from the royal court at Madrid. In the midst of this sudden and surprising expansion, the first major problem the reform encountered was one of nomenclature. Rossi had been quite insistent that the reformed friars be called "contemplative Carmelites." He was apparently willing to accept the fact that the nuns had been called "Discalced" from the outset, and that when he visited Teresa five years after the foundation of St. Joseph's it would be futile to attempt to change an accomplished situation. But Rossi and the Carmelites of Castile were determined that the reformed friars should not be called "Discalced"—because they interpreted the name as a disparaging and unfriendly reflection on the non-reformed Carmelites. But despite Rossi's insistence, the term "contemplative Carmelites" was never really accepted as popular usage. Teresa had called her nuns "Discalced," and the reform of the friars, which emanated from the reform of the nuns, was almost inevitably called "Discalced" by practically everyone who had any acquaintance with the movement. Teresa herself seems to have been unconcerned about Rossi's strictures, and in her writings we find that she uses the term "Discalced Carmelite friars" from almost the beginning of the reform. Thus in a matter of two or three years after their foundation, the friars were universally and popularly known by the title of "Discalced." This was a source of stinging annoyance to the non-reformed Carmelites, and at the general chapter of Piacenza in 1575 when Rossi lashed out against the Discalced friars, one of the primary objections he raised against them was their name and one of his many ordinances was that they adopt the title he had originally given them. To compound the problem, as the reform increased in numbers and prestige the non-reformed Carmelites found themselves subjected to unflattering nomenclature—at first they were called "mitigated Carmelites," and then "Calced Carmelites," in distinction to the Discalced. This terminology quickly passed from common, popular usage into the official terminology employed by the Holy See, and these unfortunate words have endured until this day. Literally, Calced means "with shoes," and Discalced, "without shoes," and this unimaginative and almost meaningless terminology has been used since the sixteenth century to distinguish between the Carmelite friars who follow the mitigated rule of 1432 and those who follow the primitive rule of 1247.

John Rossi was, at first, an enthusiastic supporter of the reformed friars. He readily gave permission for the two original monasteries in Castile, and within the next few years he gave permission for seven additional monasteries. However, he developed two principal fears about the reform. First, he was afraid that the Discalced friars would become so strong and popular that they would completely overshadow the Calced friars in Spain and thoroughly debilitate the already tottering Spanish provinces. Those fears were realized. Then, on a larger scale, Rossi himself wanted the restoration of the primitive rule throughout the Order, but he justifiably wanted the process to develop from inside the Order and under his direction. He was afraid that his inability to effect a massive restoration throughout the Order, plus the growing popularity of the Discalced, would result in a separatist movement which would terminate in two Carmelite Orders, one following the mitigated, fifteenth-century tradition, and the other following the primitive, thirteenth-century tradition. Those fears were also realized.

The Discalced and the Calced were therefore working from different points of view. The Discalced were convinced that the restoration was necessary and long overdue, and as such it must continue. The Calced were concerned that the Order remain intact and that the Discalced be completely obedient and faithful to the general in Rome. Both sides ruthlessly pursued these objectives with whatever weapons they found available. At times they were both devious, untruthful with each other, and somewhat unscrupulous. The protracted struggle witnessed the worst aspects of the juridicism of the Catholic Church: there were briefs and counter briefs, excommunications, clandestine appeals to different authorities, and legal maneuverings on a bewildering scale. And as the blood ran hotter and passions became more inflamed, it sometimes appeared that the original objectives had been forgotten in the violent clash of personalities.

The fuel for the flame of this struggle was provided by King Philip II. His pan-Hispanic and anti-Roman attitude toward all things Catholic within his kingdom created the two different jurisdictions under which the Calced and Discalced began to operate. This powerful Hapsburg prince ascended the throne at the age of twenty-eight in 1556 at the moment when the Spanish kingdom embraced the Netherlands, the greater part of Italy, Sicily, and large territories in the Americas, the West Indies, and North Africa. He was a powerful ruler and he was quite conscious of his position in European affairs. He has been a controversial figure in history, and evaluations of him have depended largely on the national backgrounds of the various historians. For some he was a tyrannical and bigoted despot, and for others the champion of Christian civilization. During his reign of thirty-nine years he sponsored the decisive naval victory at Lepanto in 1571, he sent the "invincible" Armada to its crushing defeat at the hands of the British in 1588, he involved himself intimately in the internal affairs in the Lowlands and France, and he continued to expand the already far-flung Spanish empire. By the time of his death in 1598 he had depleted the Spanish treasury and the kingdom was on the edge of bankruptcy.

Philip II was in many ways a strange man. Small, slightly built, with the typical Germanic features of blond hair, blue eyes, and fresh complexion, he became more Spanish than the native Spaniards. He was melancholic and moody, and a sickly man during almost his entire reign. But he was unique as a prince of that epoch in that he was irreproachably upright and religious in his personal life, and he lived like a monk during his declining years in his austere apartment in the opulent Escorial. However, his deep feelings for things Catholic was inextricably intertwined with his nationalism, and he remained unmovably anti-Roman all his life. He was a nominal subject of the pope, but he pushed that relationship to its ultimate straining point. No papal decree or appointment was valid nor was it officially promulgated in Spain without his prior approval, and he was not hesitant to contest or disobey any papal decision he pleased. He even invaded Rome and sacked the city during the pontificate of Paul IV. The popes, correspondingly, seemed to live in fear of this Catholic prince who controlled such large regions of the world, and they attempted to placate him at every turn; and this attitude became even more pronounced as he continued to keep Protestantism out of the Iberian peninsula, mostly by means of the horrendous Inquisition. Philip was genuinely interested in the reform of the religious orders, but he was determined that reform would be ultimately controlled by him and not by visiting Italians. The Discalced played on this situation to the fullest, and thus were able to invoke the protection of the king against their own general in Rome. And the Holy See tended to support the temperamental Spanish king rather than John Rossi.

When Rossi made his general visitation in Spain during 1566 and 1567 he encountered violent reactions against his reform measures in the Carmelite province of Andalusia, the vast region south of Madrid, which reaches down to Córdoba and Granada. The Andalusians, people from that southern territory, which contained both lush vegetation and rocky mountains, were a suspicious and truculent race, hostile to outside influences and belligerently defensive of their own ideas. After Rossi departed, the Andalusian Carmelites complained of his visit to King Philip, who had apparently been receiving similar complaints from other religious orders in Spain. Accordingly, the king obtained two different bulls from the Holy See in 1566 and 1567 which placed the religious orders of Spain under the jurisdiction of the local bishops in all things pertaining to reform rather than under the jurisdiction of their various generals in Rome. This arrangement was largely ineffective, principally because the local bishops were mostly neither versed nor interested in the problems of the orders in their dioceses. In 1569 Philip obtained yet another bull from Pius V in Rome which nominated two Spanish priests as general visitors for a number of orders, the Carmelites among them. These two priests, specially nominated by King Philip, were both members of the Dominican Order, and they played a key role in Carmelite history.

Philip always had high regard for the Dominicans of Spain, and he depended upon them a great deal in questions of religious orthodoxy, using them frequently as judges in the Spanish Inquisition. When he was seeking for someone to function as visitator general for the work of reform of the religious orders in Spain, he naturally turned to the Dominicans and selected two men who were then serving as priors in two of their monasteries. Peter Fernández, prior of the monastery at Madrid, was appointed apostolic visitator for the Carmelites of Castile, and Francis Vargas, prior of the monastery at Córdoba, was appointed for Andalusia. They were both sincere and good men, but they made some curious decisions during their years as visitators. Their authority was over both the Calced and Discalced in matters of reform, and their faculties allowed them, among other things, to appoint and dismiss superiors, to found and suppress monasteries, and to contravene the instructions of any Carmelite superior, even the general in Rome. This strange situation, only possible under a ruler like Philip, therefore created a dual jurisdiction within the Carmelite Order: the general in Rome, and the two visitators in Spain. And in the ultimate analysis, the two Dominicans possessed the greater authority, since they were the official representatives of the pope.

The dual jurisdiction created immense confusion, and it provided the Discalced with the opportunity to extend the reform against the wishes of John Rossi. The stage was set for conflict.

Teresa first met the Dominican visitator Peter Fernández in the spring of 1571 at Ávila when she had retired to St. Joseph's after founding her eighth convent at Alba de Tormes. She thought he was "very wise, of saintly life and great learning." Fernández, who was then about forty, a taciturn and thoughtful man, shrewdly evaluated the nun about whom he had heard so much, and he decided that he approved of her. He discussed with Teresa the difficult task he was performing: the visitation of all Carmelite houses in Castile, Calced and Discalced. He then ordered her to Medina del Campo to serve as prioress. After she had departed, Fernández pondered the pressing problem he had unearthed in Ávila: the convent of the Incarnation, Teresa's former home, which was overcrowded, impoverished, and undisciplined. The longer he thought about it, the more he was attracted to a unique and highly unconventional solution—he would send Teresa to act as prioress of the Incarnation for a term of three years. He communicated with her in Medina del Campo, informing her of his decision and commanding her to leave for Ávila at her earliest convenience. Teresa knew the nuns at the Incarnation, and protested to Fernández that they would never accept a Discalced nun as their superior, particularly when she had left that very convent nine years previously because she was dissatisfied with their way of life. But Fernández was convinced it was the right solution, and with the broad powers he possessed as apostolic visitor he insisted she accept the office. A manuscript history discovered at the Incarnation states that Fernández had another reason for the appointment in addition to his concern for the convent's betterment: he had heard some sharp criticisms of Teresa by the Calced Carmelites, and he wanted to avoid any further bitterness by halting her activities for three years while she was serving at the Incarnation. Whatever his reasons, Teresa set out for Ávila in October of 1571, accompanied by the Calced provincial, Ángel de Salazar.

The scene when she arrived at the Incarnation was a wild and bizarre one. The provincial attempted to lead her into the choir to install her in office, but he found the entrance blocked by an angry, hostile group of nuns. He marched to another entrance, and was met by another group of formidable nuns who shouted at them to leave their convent. From somewhere inside the choir a small group of nuns who approved of the appointment started to chant the *Te Deum* in thanksgiving, but their voices were drowned out by the yells and catcalls from the others. Teresa calmly sat down, drawing her mantle about her, while the perplexed Salazar tried to decide what to do next. Finally he summoned the local police, who forced their way into the choir. The provincial installed Teresa, and she turned to address her belligerent community. She told them she had been given the assignment under obedience and was "distressed" by it. "I come here solely to serve and please you in every possible way that I can," she said, "and I hope the Lord will greatly assist me to do this." She said that she had no intention of forcing the primitive rule upon them, but only of helping them to live their own rule and constitutions. "My only desire is that we should all serve the Lord in quietness," she concluded. Then she placed a large statue of the Blessed Virgin in the prioress' place in the choir, and sat at its feet. "Here is our Lady of Mercy," she said. "She is your prioress."

The nuns appeared to have been mollified, and they soon became enthusiastic supporters of their new prioress. A month later Teresa could write: "Glory be to God, there is peace here now—that is something! We are gradually cutting down the nuns' amusements and giving them less freedom, and they are so good about it." And after five months: "Those who were the most obstinate before are now the most contented." Teresa wrote to her wealthy friends, soliciting donations for the impoverished convent, and she begged for food and materials from the people of Ávila. In short time she had the convent in a healthy financial position. She tightened up the discipline of the community, limited the number of visitors, and established an atmosphere of religious life. And into all of this she injected her infectious gaiety, making the Incarnation a happy and contented institution. A remarkable change had come over the unruly convent of the Incarnation.

Teresa realized that she needed an exceptional spiritual director for the nuns to help her cope with the particular difficulties at the Incarnation, and she asked Fernández to appoint John of the Cross to that post. Fernández refused, claiming that John was needed more by the Discalced friars and that there was no Discalced monastery in Ávila where he could live. But Teresa insisted, and continued her pleas to Fernández until he finally relented and appointed John as confessor of the Incarnation.

John, in the meantime, had been serving as the superior of the third monastery of the reform, the college at Alcalá de Henares. From the beginning of the reform, Teresa had encouraged the Discalced friars to locate one of their early foundations near a university so they could both educate their students properly and attract good "men of talent" to the reform from the university population. She discussed the matter with Balthasar of Jesus during the preparations for the foundation at Pastrana, and he suggested they attempt to found a monastery near the University of Alcalá de Henares where he had previously worked as a Calced. Teresa's friend, Ruy Gómez de Silva, helped them make the foundation at Alcalá de Henares: he undoubtedly supplied most of the money for the purchase of a house in the city; and he appealed directly to Rossi in Rome for permission to establish the Discalced friars there. The Alcalá de Henares house was the third foundation of the Discalced friars, one more than the original two authorized by Rossi, and Teresa felt they would have a better chance of an affirmative answer if the petition came directly from the distinguished Spanish nobleman. Rossi promptly gave permission, and Balthasar of Jesus established a community at Alcalá de Henares in 1570, while still serving as the superior of Pastrana. Six months later John of the Cross was sent to Alcalá de Henares to become superior, and he held that office for one year until he received orders from Fernández to proceed to Ávila.

John of the Cross remained as confessor of the Incarnation for five years, living for most of that time in a small house near the convent; the house contained only a desk, and a blanket on the floor, which he used as a bed. He lived alone for a while, but he was later joined by another Discalced friar from Pastrana, Germain of St. Mathias. When Teresa introduced John to the nuns, she said: "Ladies, I am bringing you as a confessor a priest who is a saint." He fulfilled Teresa's expectations, and during his years at the Incarnation he did much to raise the religious standards at the convent by his advice and his example.

John arrived at the Incarnation in 1572, when Teresa's term of office had two years to run. Those two years were the only time in their lives that Teresa and John had any sustained close association, and they both benefited greatly from the experience. In the confessional and in their conversations in the parlor the thirty-year-old priest and the fifty-seven-year-old nun were able to exchange their insights about religion and the mystical life. Teresa explained her unique spiritual phenomenon, and showed her writings to John, and when he later began his literary career he considered them complementary to Teresa's and referred his readers to the writings of "the Blessed Teresa of Jesus, our mother" for the fundamental Christian themes he presupposed in his works. Teresa, on the other hand, benefited from the exposure to his disciplined intellect and his familiarity with the history of Christian mysticism, particularly the works of Plotinus, St. Bernard, St. Gregory, Ruysbroeck, and Pseudo-Dionysius. Teresa accepted him as "the father of my soul," and placed herself under his competent spiritual direction "because our Lord has given him a special grace for this." After they went separate ways, Teresa complained in a letter "that since he went away I have found no one like him in all Castile."

But Teresa was also able to take a bemused view of this serious little friar who preached so earnestly about the life of prayer. Years later, when she was recreating with a group of her nuns, she composed a *vejamen,* a form of pointed Spanish satire, about one of John of the Cross's minor writings: "God deliver me from people who are so spiritual that they want to turn everything into perfect contemplation, no matter what. It would be bad business for us if we could not seek God until we were dead to the world."

The three years at the Incarnation were deeply satisfying spiritually for Teresa. The Lord appeared to her one day while she was at prayer and extended to her His right hand, which was pierced with a nail from the cross. "Behold this nail," He said. "It is a sign that from this day on you shall be My spouse. Until now you have not merited it, but from this day forward you shall look to My honor not only as Creator and King and God, but as My true spouse. My honor is yours, and yours is Mine." Thus Teresa had attained that supreme goal of the mystics, the spiritual espousals, at a time when religious obedience had placed her in the most unpropitious and distracting of circumstances, the guidance of the troublesome community at the Incarnation.

But near the end of her term of office she was chafing to be on her way and continue with the work of the Carmelite reform. She received permission from Fernández to leave Ávila temporarily a few months before the actual expiration of her term in order to establish a convent at Segovia. She made the foundation at Segovia, returned to Ávila to finish her assignment, and then left the Incarnation forever in October of 1574. The following February she founded a convent at Beas, and in May another one at Seville. Teresa was back at work.

John of the Cross, however, continued his duties as confessor at the Incarnation for another three years, until February of 1576, when he was arrested and imprisoned.

During the foundation of the Convent of Beas, Teresa first met Jerome Gratian, a young Discalced Carmelite priest who was to have such a profound and disastrous effect on the lives of Teresa and John and everyone in the reform.

Jerome Gratian was born in Valladolid in 1545, the third son of a large family which had a distinguished reputation for service in public affairs. His father had been secretary to Charles V and Philip II, and two of his brothers served Philip in the same capacity. Another brother was secretary to the queen-regent of Sicily, and his mother was the daughter of the Polish ambassador at the Spanish court. With this background and with his own extraordinary talents he could have had an important career in government, but he chose to enter the priesthood. He studied at the Jesuit college in Madrid, and at the University of Alcalá de Henares, where he distinguished himself as a brilliant student. He was ordained at Alcalá de Henares in 1570 at the age of twenty-five. The following year he made the acquaintance of the Discalced Carmelite nuns at Pastrana when he was arranging for a family friend to enter their convent. He was deeply impressed with the nuns, particularly Isabel of St. Dominic, the capable prioress who later had to deal with the difficult Princess of Eboli. Through the nuns Gratian met the friars at the new monastery in Pastrana, and after debating the matter in his own mind for a year and a half, he took the habit of the reform in 1572, adopting the name Jerome of the Mother of God.

Jerome Gratian was a man of exceptional promise. Deeply spiritual and dedicated to prayer, he was also cultured and polished and well educated. Added to this was his engaging personality and compelling charm. He was an extremely zealous priest, an eloquent orator, and a determined and prolific writer. In addition, he possessed a personality which was amazingly similar to Teresa's: warm, outgoing, captivating. But, unlike Teresa, he had one gigantic flaw in his character: an alarming lack of good judgment which manifested itself at the most unfortunate times. That flaw was to cause his ruination.

Perhaps the most remarkable thing in Gratian's dramatic life was Teresa's instant and astonishing reaction to the young priest when she first met him at Beas in Andalusia in 1575. She was completely captivated by him, and for the remainder of her life she had an overwhelming affection for this gifted Carmelite. She called the three weeks she spent in Gratian's company at Beas "the best days of my life." And about the man himself: "I have not yet fully realized his worth. To me he is perfect and better for our needs than anyone else we could have asked God to send us. I have never seen anyone so perfect and so gentle." And as she recalled her first meeting with him: "I would not have missed seeing him and dealing with him for anything in the world."

During those weeks at Beas Teresa received a vision in which she saw the Lord with Gratian at His right hand and herself at His left. The Lord joined Teresa's and Gratian's hands and told her "that he wished me to take him in place of Himself for my whole life long, and that we were to agree together in everything." Shortly after that she made a personal vow to obey Gratian in whatever command he might give her, providing it was "not against the will of God or the superiors whom I was already bound to obey." Thus we are presented with the amazing spectacle of this sixty-year-old woman, who had already entered the highest regions of the spiritual and mystical life, making a vow to obey a thirty-year-old priest almost as soon as she first met him and before she could possibly know him. The episode clearly demonstrates some impetuosity on Teresa's part, but more strikingly it emphasizes Gratian's unique charm.

Teresa never regretted the vow during the remaining seven years of her life, although she did become more aware of Gratian's defects, principally his alarming lack of good judgment and his stubbornness, and she chided him for them. But her affection for the man increased over the years, and she adopted an attitude toward him which was almost maternal. She wrote him frequently, offering him solicitous advice about almost every detail of his life. "I am worried," she wrote him once, "whether you have remembered to put on more clothes, because the weather is getting cold." And again: "Stop devoting the hours when you ought to be asleep to making plans—however necessary they might be—or to prayer. Please do this out of kindness for me!" She urged him to avoid the city of Seville because a plague was raging there: "For the love of our Lord, do not yield to any temptation to go. It would be the death of us all if you did —or, at any rate, of me. Even if God kept you in good health, it would be the end of mine." And she wrote to the prioress of the convent at Seville, asking her to take good care of him "because he so much needs to be looked after."

Teresa was aware of this extraordinary relationship and the misinterpretations that could be placed on it, and she wrote him a remarkable letter in 1576, a little more than a year after they had first met:

For many reasons it is permissible for me to feel great affection for you and to show it in the dealings we have together. But it is not permissible for the other nuns to do so. When the nuns observe that I say and do things which are allowable for me because of my age and because I know with whom I am dealing they will quite naturally think they can do the same. They must have seen my love for you and the concern I have for your welfare.

Teresa's love for Gratian was one more marked demonstration of her appealing humanness. Gratian in no way approached the stature of the many truly great men Teresa encountered in her life—people like John of the Cross and Anthony of Jesus—but she never responded to any of these men as she did to the attractive and engaging Gratian. She knew his limitations, his faults, and she was exasperated at many of the things he did, but she loved him. In this she was supremely human.

Gratian's role in the Carmelite reform, however, is significant for more important reasons than his relationship with Teresa. When he pronounced his vows at the completion of his year of novitiate in 1573, the reform had made cautious but impressive progress. There were eight convents of nuns and five monasteries of friars. Rossi had given permission for all five monasteries, including the last two at Altomira and Roda, which were again petitioned by Ruy Gómez de Silva. The foundation of these two latter monasteries took place in the years when Teresa was serving as prioress at the Incarnation, and the entire operation was accomplished by the friars themselves without any immediate assistance from Teresa. This marked the beginning of a new relationship between Teresa and the Discalced friars: she was no longer directly involved with their foundations or their business matters, but instead she assumed the position of a parent who had educated her children and was now sending them out into the world on their own. However, she continued to interest herself closely in the work and development of the friars, by advice and encouragement, by vast correspondence, and by her spirited defense when it seemed as if the work might collapse.

The dual jurisdiction which had been erected by the appointment of the two Dominican visitators did not cause any major problems between the friars and Rossi in Rome for the first number of years. In fact, when Rossi learned of the appointment he immediately petitioned the Holy See himself for a revocation of the bull of appointment. In a fine bit of Italianism the Roman Curia sent Rossi a revocation of the original brief, but at the same time sent another brief to Spain re-establishing Fernández and Vargas in their offices, without however informing Rossi of the latter brief. This devious maneuver led Rossi to believe for quite some time that the problem had been solved. Fernández in Castile, though, was conscious of the incendiary nature of the situation and he proceeded with the utmost caution, advising the Discalced friars to consult their general for every major permission they required, particularly the establishment of new monasteries. Vargas in Andalusia was unfortunately not as prudent, nor did he seem to have as much interest in the assignment as did Fernández. He was much more involved in the affairs of his own Order, and he took no action at all in Andalusia for a long time. He did begin a visitation of the Calced monasteries in 1572, but he was soon afterward elected provincial of the Dominicans and he began looking for some way to divest himself of this troublesome task of visiting Carmelite monasteries.

During his visitation Vargas was confronted by the problem of the Calced monastery at San Juan del Puerto, which had only a few friars and was at the point of collapse. Francis Vargas decided upon an unusual solution: he would turn the monastery over to the Discalced and let them staff it with reformed friars. Thus in November of 1572 he established the reform in Andalusia, despite Rossi's specific injunction that the Discalced remain out of that area. Apparently pleased with himself, the Dominican visitator made a second foundation of Discalced in Andalusia a few months later in May of 1573. He obtained property on a hill in Granada near the Alhambra, and brought Discalced friars from Pastrana to staff it—this became the famous monastery of Los Mártires. In the course of this foundation he met the prior of Pastrana, Balthasar of Jesus, and the man seemed to represent for him a solution to the bothersome work with the Carmelites. In April of 1573, Vargas accordingly delegated his full powers as apostolic visitator in Andalusia to Balthasar of Jesus. Then in June of that year Vargas made his last foundation of Discalced in Andalusia: at La Penuela in the Sierra Morena.

In less than a year, therefore, Francis Vargas had managed to complicate matters immeasurably. He had established three foundations of Discalced in Andalusia; and, by an incredible act of bad judgment, he had appointed one of the Discalced friars to take his place as visitator to the Calced. Vargas was to make one more mistake of even greater magnitude.

A few months later, in July of 1573, the Dominican visitator met for the first time the young Jerome Gratian, who had made his profession of vows just three months previously. Gratian had proved himself to be a dedicated and faithful Carmelite during an arduous novitiate year in Pastrana, the novitiate house which had quickly acquired a reputation for penance and austerity—to such a degree that John of the Cross was sent there for a few weeks in 1572 to temper the bizarre penitential practices imposed on the novices by the imprudent novice master, Angel of St. Gabriel. Vargas was immediately fascinated by the charming Gratian, and he peremptorily decided that this was the man who should exercise the office of visitator. He rescinded the faculties he had delegated to Balthasar of Jesus, and sent him back to Castile. Balthasar had only possessed these faculties for four months, and his abrupt dismissal caused him to become bitter about Gratian for years to come, and was undoubtedly the reason behind the charges he later made against the man.

Gratian's appointment as visitator to the Calced and Discalced in Andalusia was an unbelievable mistake on the part of Vargas. He had delegated his already controversial faculties to this young priest only twenty-eight years of age who had completed his novitiate three months previously. Vargas was undoubtedly motivated by his urgency to rid himself of the office in the most expeditious manner, and he was mesmerized by the urbane and articulate and deeply spiritual Gratian, but at this initial meeting it was impossible for him to judge the man adequately or discover his inadequacies. Gratian was initially appalled at the appointment, but he quickly recovered himself and in a matter of weeks he began his visitation of the Andalusian Calced Carmelites. It was a fiasco.

The first thing he did was close the new monastery at San Juan del Puerto, which he decided was inadequate for a Discalced monastery, and he returned the building to the Calced. Then he proceeded to the Calced monastery in Seville, where he received a hostile and abusive reception from the friars—"insolent treatment," Gratian himself called it. He received almost similar treatment from the Calced wherever he went, because they saw in Gratian's appointment what appeared to be the realization of one of their most secret fears: that somehow the Discalced would impose the observance of the primitive rule upon them. That was not Gratian's intention, but he had little opportunity to explain his position in face of the mounting opposition during his visitation. There were murmurings against him and even threats of physical violence. At length, he began to fear for his life, and he would only eat unshelled eggs in the Calced monasteries to protect himself against poisoning.

The event which elevated the crisis to the boiling point was the foundation of the Discalced monastery in Seville. After his hostile reception by the Calced in Seville, Gratian decided, perhaps in anger and in a spirit of retribution, to establish the Discalced in the same city. He contacted the archbishop of Seville, Christopher de Rojas, who was immediately won over by the charming visitator and gave him permission to search for a site in the area. In the course of their discussions about the foundation the archbishop confided to Gratian and his traveling companion, Mariano of St. Benedict, that he was in financial difficulties and that the archepiscopal accounts were in grave disorder. Mariano, the Italian hermit whom Teresa had recruited at Pastrana, offered a solution—there was a friend of his in Seville at the moment, Nicholas Doria, a rather wealthy Genoese banker who was in Spain on business, notably with the king, and who might be able to help the archbishop in his monetary difficulties. Doria did solve the archbishop's problems, and the prelate thus became indebted to the Discalced and remained a staunch supporter and a valuable ally all his life. And Gratian was brought into contact with Nicholas Doria, who was to cause him so much suffering in later years.

The Discalced foundation at Seville was established in January of 1574, and it brought angry cries of protest from the Calced. Here was a foundation of the reform in the capital and largest city of Andalusia, precisely in the key center of the area where the general had forbidden the Discalced to locate. This foundation unleashed much of the latent hostility felt by the Calced all over Spain for the reform movement. The Calced provincials of Castile, Aragon, Catalonia, Andalusia, and Portugal hurriedly assembled for a meeting, at which they drew up a petition to the general attacking Gratian and asking that another brief be obtained from the Holy See revoking his faculties once and for all.

Gratian's most incomprehensible mistake in this whole nightmare of legalisms was his failure to contact Rossi in Rome and inform him of his delegated faculties from Vargas or of his operations in Andalusia. Throughout the whole series of unfortunate events Gratian stubbornly refused to communicate with the general. He possessed legitimate faculties from Vargas, he reasoned, and there was no necessity for dealing with Rossi, particularly when he feared the general might try to block him. When Teresa was later drawn into the conflict she remonstrated with Gratian and pleaded with him to correspond with Rossi, but to her great consternation he adamantly declined to have anything but the most perfunctory contact with Rome.

Vargas, on the other hand, appeared to be delighted with Gratian's activities. The Calced of Andalusia had given the Dominican a difficult time, and he seemed pleased that they were finding Gratian's appointment so oppressive. To throw salt into the wound, Vargas appointed Gratian as provincial of both the Calced and Discalced Carmelites in Andalusia in June of that same year 1574. Even Gratian felt that was excessive and he declined the office, but Vargas imposed it under religious obedience and penalty of excommunication. Thus, Gratian found himself not only the visitator of the Calced in Andalusia, who came into contact with them occasionally during his visitations, but he was now their actual and permanent superior.

Meanwhile Rossi in Rome had not been idle. He apparently had only learned of the continuance of the visitation faculties of the two Dominicans after the Calced in Andalusia protested Gratian's actions. At any rate, he was infuriated when he received the memorandum from the assembly of Calced provincials in 1574, and he protested strongly enough to the Holy See so that all briefs and counter briefs about Vargas and Fernández were officially revoked. This revocation was given at Rome on August 13, 1574, and it should have ended the legal confusion in Spain. But it failed to accomplish that, because there were even further maneuvers in this miasma of juridicism.

Gratian had been presented to Philip II in Madrid, and the king was deeply impressed with the energetic young Carmelite who spoke so convincingly about the need for the reform of the Carmelites. Then Gratian met the apostolic nuncio, Nicholas Ormaneto, the former bishop of Padua in Italy, a good man whom Teresa called "the saintly nuncio." Ormaneto had taken up his duties as nuncio to Spain in 1572, and he was thus the highest and official contact between Philip II and Pope Gregory XIII. He heartily approved of Teresa's reform movement, watching it carefully during his years in Spain, and ultimately becoming Teresa's most powerful ecclesiastical ally. When news arrived in Spain of the comprehensive counter brief that Rossi had obtained from the Holy See, Ormaneto issued another brief in September of that year based on special faculties he had obtained from Gregory XIII before he left Rome which empowered him as a "reformer general" of all religious orders in Spain. Ormaneto, who had undoubtedly consulted with the king, appointed Fernández as "reformer of Castile," and Vargas and Gratian as joint "reformers of Andalusia." Gratian therefore had become more strongly entrenched in his position, and a legal stalemate had been created between Gratian and Rossi.

It was at this juncture in this distressing warfare of legal documents that Gratian first met Teresa. Since she allied herself so closely to Gratian, and since she was now founding convents again after her three years of inactivity at the Incarnation, she began to come under fire too. The Calced of Spain instigated a campaign of vilification and character assassination. Gratian was accused of disobedience to his general, incompetence in administration, and immorality in his private life. And Teresa was charged with being the instigator of the whole problem. She was even denounced to the fearful Spanish Inquisition, and although the charges against her were dismissed after a careful inquiry, she commented about the inquisitional process: "It is abominable how much injustice is rife in this country of ours, how little truth and how much of falsehood." A letter sent to Rome called her an "imposter," and then claimed:

She makes use of the foundation of Discalced convents to justify a freedom of herself which enables her to lead a wicked life. But she has been exposed by God's justice. A day or two ago, she set off on the pretense of founding another convent, but the closed carriage in which she was traveling fell apart in the main square of Medina del Campo, and all the people there could see this nun busy offending God with a certain friar.

These were the kind of libelous reports that Rossi was receiving in Rome as he prepared to convene a general chapter of the Order at Piacenza in Italy in the spring of 1575. Teresa herself said that most of her trouble with Rossi derived from "misinformation."

When Rossi convened the chapter at Piacenza on May 21, 1575, no Discalced friars were present, and the only reports available about the reform were the angry accounts from the Calced friars in Spain and the various libels and calumnies which had been sent to Rome.

Rossi at this point was thoroughly enraged at the Discalced and determined to do everything he could to check the reform, if not suppress it completely. The chapter quickly approved a series of painfully severe edicts against the Discalced friars. The acts of the chapter stated that, whereas "certain disobedience, rebellious and contumacious friars popularly called 'Discalced' were living in houses outside of Castile," and since they had "refused humble obedience to the Father General, they were to leave those houses within three days." In addition to restricting the Discalced to monasteries in Castile, the chapter forbade the use of the word "Discalced," commanding that the members of the reform be called "contemplatives" or "primitives." The Discalced were also forbidden to wear sandals and ordered to wear shoes; they were not to carry staffs, as they had been doing in an attempt to imitate the prophets of Mount Carmel; and they were to "sing Mass and the Office in choir as do the rest of the friars and nuns of the Order."

When Teresa heard of these decrees she immediately stated that they were a calculated effort to destroy her work of restoration, not only because the friars had been restricted to Castile but also because the decrees of the chapter attempted to eradicate the image of a restoration movement—the name, the sandals, the simple recitation of office. In an intriguing letter written to Rossi in June of that year she affirmed her loyalty to him, and her intention to obey him: "It would be a grievous blow to me if I were to offend your Reverence in any way." But she took it upon herself to explain the situation to him "because your Reverence, away there in Italy, does not see what goes on here in Spain, but I see it, and I am telling you all about it." She contends that "the Discalced are most obedient subjects to you and will continue to be so." She attempts to explain the involved legal situation in Spain and the question of the dual jurisdiction, and she honestly admits concerning the Discalced friars that she "cannot altogether acquit them of blame." However, in a wonderfully unrealistic sentence she attempts to shield her favorite Gratian, who was the cause of all their difficulties: "Gratian, on the other hand, behaves like an angel, and if he alone had been concerned, the whole matter would have turned out very differently." After asking him to rescind the decrees of Piacenza, she concludes with an impassioned plea for Rossi to "forget the past, and remember that you are a servant of the Virgin and that she will be offended if you cease to help those who, by the sweat of their brow, seek the increase of her Order." There is no record that Rossi ever answered her letter.

Rossi, indeed, had become disenchanted with Teresa, and after the completion of the chapter proper he issued a further edict that Teresa was to cease her travels and be confined to some convent of her choice in Castile. He did not communicate this decision directly to Teresa, but sent it though the hands of the Spanish Carmelites who were in attendance at the chapter. Teresa knew nothing of Rossi's edict when she wrote the above letter of June, 1575. But when she was informed of it some months later she wrote the general a long and somewhat snappish letter, restating the case for the Discalced again. She complains that Rossi had been misinformed, "but as long as I live I shall do all I can, as I am doing now, to see that the truth is understood by everyone—I mean by everyone who is not swayed by passion." Commenting on his command to retire to some convent, she confesses that "I have been unable to help feeling hurt that I should have been treated like someone who had been very disobedient." Then, in a marvelously feminine statement she indulges in some sarcasm:

I will certainly not hide from your reverence that, so far as I understand my own mind, it would have been a great kindness, and a satisfaction to me, if you yourself had conveyed this order to me in a letter. I should have interpreted it then that you were sorry for the severe trials that I have suffered in making these foundations—I who am not fit for much suffering—and that, as a reward for enduring them, you were ordering me to rest. But even despite the way the order reached me, the possibility of getting some quietness has given me the greatest happiness.

After some delay Teresa finally settled in the convent she had founded at Toledo. She spent only one year there until Gratian liberated her and she resumed her travels, but she thoroughly enjoyed the opportunity to be out of the struggle for a time. "I think I am better than I have been for years," she wrote a short time after her arrival. And she was able to devote more time to her writing, which she accomplished at an amazing speed at Toledo. She was working on her *Foundations*, and she wrote to Gratian about her work: "I think you will be pleased with it when you see it. It makes good reading."

It was unfortunate that this grievous estrangement occurred between the Discalced and the general in Rome. Gratian must certainly bear the major portion of the blame because of his crass and unbelievably stubborn attitude in failing to maintain contact with Rossi. But the general, too, must share part of the blame for the debacle of Piacenza, in that he only listened to one side of the case before issuing his severe and uncompromising edicts. As so often in human affairs, a lack of communication paved the way for further estrangement.

Gratian, however, did not comply so readily with the decrees of the chapter of Piacenza. He approached Ormaneto, and the nuncio issued a decree in August of 1575, just a few days after the edicts from Piacenza arrived in Spain, which appointed Gratian the "provincial superior" of all the Discalced Carmelites and visitator to the Calced in Andalusia "notwithstanding the decrees of the general chapter." Thus a gigantic stalemate had been created, as Ormaneto brought the full weight of his office to protect the Discalced. Looming ominously behind the entire situation, of course, was the slight, black-clad figure of Philip II. His protective attitude toward the orders in Spain was the barrier behind which the Discalced huddled, and without him the Calced would probably have been able to cripple, if not suppress, the reform.

Making a calm survey of the hopeless situation between Calced and Discalced, Teresa arrived at a painful decision shortly after hearing the decrees of Piacenza. She concluded that it would be impossible for the two segments of the Order to live in peace and that some sort of independent status had to be gained for the reform. She determined to appeal to Philip II, with whom she had corresponded previously and whom she called "my friend the king." In a letter of July, 1575, she implored him to help in "the permanent establishment of this edifice we are now constructing." She wrote:

I have lived among Carmelites for forty years, and taking everything into consideration, I am quite convinced that, unless the Discalced are made into a separate province, and that quickly, much harm will be done, and further progress will, I think, be impossible. As this is in your majesty's hands and I see that the Virgin, our Lady, has been pleased to call you to protect and help her Order, I have ventured to write this to beseech your majesty, for the love of our Lord and His glorious mother, to command that this be done.

However, the king, who had been so active behind the scenes in protecting the Discalced, now hesitated for some reason and decided to let the matter stand as it was for the time being. Ormaneto had nullified the force of the Piacenza decrees, and the Discalced were therefore safe in Spain. This sudden and unexpected caution on Philip's part eventually gave the supporters of the Calced reason to believe that he had abandoned the reform. Four years later Philip did intervene directly by petitioning and obtaining from the Holy See independence for the reform. But his hesitant attitude in 1575 was the cause of more suffering and heartache for Teresa in what she called her "great storm of trials."

Gratian attempted to resume his visitations of the Calced, but after he was severely rejected he began to confine his activities to the Discalced. In 1576 he founded another monastery in Andalusia at El Calvario. The Calced, on the other hand, wrote to Rossi and informed him that the Piacenza decrees had been frustrated because of Ormaneto and the king. Realizing that he would receive no support from the Holy See against the king of Spain, Rossi then appointed his own personal representative for implementing the decrees in Spain, a Portuguese Carmelite named Jerome Tostado. Tostado, who had entered the Order in Spain and eventually became provincial of the Catalonian province, was a close associate of the general. He had worked with him in Italy for a number of years, accompanying him on visitations, and serving as a visitator himself for some of the Italian provinces. When he arrived in Spain and presented himself to Ormaneto, the nuncio told him that the king's royal council would not approve of his mission and he had better visit Portugal instead of remaining in Spain. Tostado went to Portugal, but he returned after Ormaneto's death, and Teresa depicts this Portuguese friar in her letters as the villain of the piece.

Gratian, however, was feeling very sure of himself because of the strong stand that Ormaneto had been taking in the defense of the reform. He convoked a meeting of the Discalced at Almodóvar del Campo in August of 1576, and declared his intention of creating a separate province of Discalced Carmelites with its own provincial and its own administration. He advanced the argument that "the powers of apostolic visitors are superior to those of the most reverend general." Gratian was actually on very insecure legal ground in establishing a separate province of Discalced Carmelites, but the assembled friars, who included John of the Cross and Anthony of Jesus, approved the proposal. This action at Almodóvar del Campo, plus the support of Ormaneto, might have led to a final resolution of the embattled situation, but the nuncio fell ill, and he died in the summer of 1577. His successor was Philip Sega, an Italian bishop from Bologna, who had been thoroughly indoctrinated against the Discalced by the information he had received from Rossi's office before he left Rome to take up his duties at the royal court in Spain. Teresa described the new nuncio as "one whom God seemed to have sent to try us by suffering."

Sega was very cautious about the Discalced in the official court circles of Madrid, but behind the scenes he attempted to manipulate against the reform. Teresa wrote about his activities: "He began by showing very marked favor to the Calced friars; and the information which they gave him about us persuaded him that it would be right not to allow our early efforts to proceed any farther." Sega had little use for Teresa, whom he called "a restless gadabout, a disobedient and contumacious woman"; and one of his principal objections to her was that she "taught others against the commands of St. Paul, who had forbidden women to teach." Tostado, now seeing that he had a friend for the Calced in the new nuncio, returned to Spain, and while he could not obtain official permission for his mission, he nevertheless began to act secretly but effectively against the reform.

Gratian reduced his activities radically, and Teresa advised great caution and prudence in that time when Sega was speaking against the reform, and when Tostado was loose in Spain, and the king was apparently doing nothing to help them. Tostado was working to construct a case against Gratian, and he collected a number of signed statements which accused the man of a variety of crimes from abuse of authority to gross immorality. The most damaging of these statements was obtained from a member of the reform, Balthasar of Jesus, who had harbored a grudge against Gratian since the time he had lost his office of visitator to him in 1573. Balthasar's statement was immediately sent to the king, and when Teresa learned of it she wrote an angry protest to Philip: "My attention has been called to a statement against Father Gratian which has been sent to your majesty, and I am appalled at the wiles of the devil and the Calced Fathers." Balthasar, however, wrote a retraction of the indictment before the king had an opportunity to pass judgment on it; and he tried to explain to Teresa and the Discalced that Tostado had wrested the statement from him by force. But Balthasar had forfeited all respect among his confreres, and he spent the remaining years of his life a forgotten man in the reform, and died in the monastery in Lisbon.

To protect herself and her friends at that moment of intrigue, Teresa devised a set of code names that she used in her correspondence. The names are somewhat humorous, but they provide an insight into her sentiments about various groups and people. For example, she called herself in her letters either Angela or Laurencia. John of the Cross was Seneca. Gratian, either Paul or Elisha. Anthony of Jesus, Macario. The nuncio Sega, Mathusalem. The Discalced, either eagles or butterflies. The Calced, either cats or owls. And the Jesuits, ravens.

At length, the full weight of the whole situation came crashing down on one unsuspecting and only slightly involved person: John of the Cross, who in 1577 was still in Ávila serving as confessor for the nuns at the Incarnation.

Jerome Tostado made a visitation to the Incarnation, and finding John of the Cross and his companion Germain of St. Mathias in residence as confessors, he commanded them to leave. John responded that he had been appointed to the position by the Dominican Fernández in virtue of the faculties he possessed as visitator, and that only Fernández could rescind the order. Tostado then returned to the Calced monastery in Toledo, and commissioned the prior, Ferdinand Maldonado, to apprehend the "recalcitrant" John of the Cross and bring him to Toledo for appropriate ecclesiastical punishment. During the night of December 2, Maldonado led a band of Calced friars, soldiers, and laymen to the cottage near the Incarnation. They broke down the door, handcuffed the two friars, and secretly transported Germain to the monastery at Moraleja, where he escaped three months later, and John to the huge stone monastery at Toledo.

Tostado conducted an inquisition inside the monastery in a scene reminiscent of the outrageous autos-da-fé so common in Spain during that epoch. He had the acts of the chapter of Piacenza read to John of the Cross, and then asked him to resign from the reform and join the Calced again, adding that if he refused to do so he would be declared a rebel and punished severely. John refused, and insisted that he could not be called a rebel because he was following the orders of the apostolic visitors. Tostado then changed his tactics, offering him a priorship in one of the Calced monasteries, or, if he did not want that, residence in some comfortable monastery of his own choosing with his own personal library. Finally, in a ges-

ture that demonstrated that Tostado had no appreciation at all of
the caliber of the man he was addressing, he offered him a gold cross
and some pieces of gold. John shook his head sadly at this bribe. "A
man who is seeking Christ in poverty has no need of golden trin-
kets," he said.

The angry Tostado declared him "a rebel and contumacious,"
and had him led to a prison cell in the monastery, a little room
originally intended as a closet, six feet wide and ten feet long, with
only a slit high in the wall to serve as a window. Stripped of his
cowl and scapular, and clothed only in a tattered tunic, John lived
for eight months in that dark cell which was frigid in the winter and
suffocating in the summer. He was fed only bread and sardines and
water. Three nights a week he ate this meager supper kneeling on
the floor in the middle of the refectory, and when the meal was
concluded his tunic was pulled to his waist, exposing his back and
shoulders, and he was submitted to a medieval horror known as the
circular discipline: the Calced friars walked in file behind him, each
one holding a small whip in his hand, and each one gave him a
lash as he passed, some more vigorously than others. The scourging
lasted the length of the psalm *Miserere*, and John bore the scars
from these beatings for the rest of his life. During these appalling
sessions, Tostado, or in his absence the prior Maldonado, denounced
him bitterly before the community and urged him again to renounce
the reform. But the saint remained silent during the tirades and the
beatings, and he was led, bleeding and stumbling, back to his cell.
Historians have been careful to note that the indignities heaped on
John of the Cross were carefully outlined in the penal section of the
current Carmelite constitutions, but it would be difficult to deny
that Tostado applied them with a special viciousness, and that the
Calced placed themselves in a posture of rather glaring inconsistency
since they were not particularly scrupulous about other sections of
the legislation. When Teresa later learned the details of John's torture, she exclaimed: "I do not understand how God can allow such
things!"

As soon as Teresa heard of John's abduction, she immediately
wrote a distraught letter to the king and pleaded for help in rescuing
the saint. She calls John's capture a "public scandal," and notes that
"the Calced fathers have not made it clear by whose authority they
are acting." She pays tribute to John by stating that "people look
upon him as a saint, which in my opinion, he is and has been all

his life," but she says that he "is so weak from all his sufferings that I am afraid for his life." She has some bitter things to say about the abduction of the two Discalced friars by the Calced: "I would rather see them among the Moors, for they might well show them more pity." And about Maldonado, the man who led the abduction party: "It is said he has been made vicar-provincial, and that must be true because he is more capable of making martyrs than anyone else." And she concludes with a poignant and desperate plea for the king's assistance: "Unless your majesty orders all this to be remedied, I do not know where it will all end, for we have no other help on earth."

But the king took no action whatsoever, and Teresa became more agitated. She wrote him additional letters, which demonstrated a growing sense of annoyance with him, and she engaged in a spirited campaign by mail among her friends to elicit help. Her letters are urgent and vivid, and she makes a determined effort to create an emotional appeal for the two abducted friars, noting, for example, that as Germain was led away from Ávila "blood was pouring from his mouth." However, no one seemed willing or able to help, for two reasons: first, John's place of imprisonment had been kept secret, and there was great confusion as to where he was actually being held; and second, the king's unusual silence about this affair created the impression that he had lost interest in the Carmelite reform—and, so people reasoned, if the king's attitude was divorcement from the whole business, then that was the proper attitude for everyone to take.

During the spring and early summer of 1578, John languished in his Toledo prison, emaciated and exhausted, suffering the inner agonies of the abandoned. The thrice-weekly beatings continued until the early summer when his captors seemed to have lost interest in punishing him and the scourgings were administered only once or twice a week. Some younger members of the Calced community later gave statements which related that John "was as immovable as a rock" during the beatings, and that some of the Calced shouted at him: "Insensible block!" One young novice said: "That man is a saint." Six months after his capture, another priest was appointed as his jailer, a young man from Valladolid whose name was also John. This jailer was more compassionate to his charge, giving him an oil lamp and writing materials and also needle and thread to repair his ragged tunic. But of even greater importance, the new jailer was less strict about keeping the door to John's cell locked during the day, and this gave him the opportunity to walk in the corridor and study the floor plan of the monastery.

In August, during the scorching heat, John reached an agonized decision: he must attempt to escape. His health was deteriorating rapidly, and he had no idea when, if ever, his captors intended to set him free. He knew, with a grim certainty, that he was going to die if he remained in his prison at Toledo much longer. His excursions into the corridor had shown him an avenue of escape, and he began to formulate plans. Each day he spent a few minutes working on the screws of the padlock to his door, twisting and loosening them bit by bit to the point where they could be pushed out by a hard blow from behind the locked door. On the night of August 16 he put his plan into action. He slammed his fist against the door, and the padlock fell to the floor with a crash that awakened some of the friars. John remained motionless, and the friars returned to sleep. He stole into the corridor, carrying an improvised rope he had made by tearing his blanket into long strips. He climbed out of a window onto a small balcony, and with the wire from the top of his oil lamp he anchored his rope to the ledge of the balcony. Slowly he let himself down against the side of the wall until he reached the end of the rope and found himself still some ten feet from the ground. He hung there a moment, and then dropped the remaining distance. But he was still behind the cloister wall. He pulled himself laboriously up over the wall and then jumped down into the street. He had escaped.

Some of St. John of the Cross's early biographers have seen something miraculous in his escape from the monastery at Toledo. That a man in such an enfeebled condition could go through the gymnastics of this dramatic escape seemed to them almost impossible, and they had to suppose that John was miraculously supported as he descended from the monastery and was then suddenly wafted into the air by divine power and carried over the wall. But the only comment John of the Cross himself ever made about the spiritual assistance in his escape was a remark that he had prayed to the Blessed Virgin for help. The true drama in the story is this man's fierce determination to get out of his prison and the fantastic exertions to which he drove himself. It is a courageous human story, not a pious miraculous one.

On the other side of the monastery wall that August night in 1578, John was lost in the unfamiliar city of Toledo. He slept the rest of the night in a hallway, and in the early morning asked directions to the convent of Discalced nuns in the city from a startled passerby. Presenting himself at the convent, disheveled, almost collapsing from fatigue, he said to the nun behind the grille: "Daughter, I am Father John of the Cross, and I escaped from prison last night. Tell the mother prioress." Anne of the Angels, the prioress, cleverly contrived to have him admitted into the nun's cloister for the purpose of hearing the confession of a sick nun. A few minutes after she had brought him into the cloister a group of Calced friars arrived at the convent, demanding to know if their escaped prisoner were hiding on the premises. "It would be a miracle if you were to see any friar here," she slyly answered. Nevertheless they searched the church and the parlors, and they apparently mistrusted the prioress, for they commissioned constables to patrol the area all day. In the evening the prioress called upon a friend of hers, Peter Gonzalez de Mendoza, a canon of the cathedral and administrator of the hospital of Holy Cross, who spirited John away from the convent, hiding him in his carriage. He brought the saint, who was now disguised in a black cassock, to his hospital where he secretly took care of him for two months until he was strong enough to travel.

When Teresa learned the sordid details of John's imprisonment she was horrified and angry. "I can tell you I keep thinking of what they did to Father John of the Cross," she wrote in late August. She reviewed the various indignities he suffered, and the fastidious Teresa was particularly appalled at one fact: "And all that time, even though he was at death's door, he never once was allowed to change his tunic." But Teresa was the first to recognize that the tragic episode could ultimately be turned to advantage for the reform:

It is well that this should be known, so that people may be more on guard against these folk. God forgive them! . . . Information should be laid before the Nuncio to show him what those people did with this saint of a Father John, who has committed no fault at all. It is a piteous story. See it is told to Father Germain, and he will do it, for he is furious about it.

What Tostado and Sega had unwittingly done was to provide the reform with a martyr-symbol.

That summer of 1578 marked the turning point in the reform's struggle for life and independence. In July while John was still in prison, the nuncio apparently felt that the time was ripe for taking a firm stand against the Discalced: he officially revoked any faculties that Gratian might have received from his predecessor Ormaneto. But, two weeks later, with unusual celerity, the king's royal council nullified Sega's decree, serving notice that the king was still very much interested in Teresa's reform. Two other events quickly demonstrated that the tide had turned: Tostado was ordered by the king to return to Rome; and the general Rossi died in September. The new general, John Baptist Caffardo, a native of Siena, was more favorably disposed to ending the struggle and he wrote a friendly letter to the Discalced friars.

Teresa meanwhile had been pressing Gratian to legalize the formation of the separate province for the Discalced which he had declared at Almodóvar del Campo two years previously. Still unnerved about John's imprisonment, she wrote to him on August 19: "In every possible way, or however you think best, and on any terms you can get, your reverence must arrange to obtain a separate province; for although even then we shall not be free from trials, it will be a great thing to have at least that security." Accordingly, a second meeting of Discalced friars was held at Almodóvar in October. John of the Cross, still weak and ill, arrived accompanied by Canon de Mendoza's servants, whom he had sent to assist the sick friar. The principal business of this meeting was to appoint a Discalced friar to journey to Rome and represent the reform at the Holy See during the process of seeking independence. The prior of El Calvario, Peter of the Angels, was given the assignment.

There were two amusing consequences of this meeting. First, Sega was enraged when he heard of the meeting, and he formally excommunicated all the Discalced who had taken part in it. Thus we have the unusual situation of a canonized saint and a future doctor of the Church, John of the Cross, excommunicated from the Catholic Church. This legalism had now gone to such ridiculous lengths that none of the Discalced paid any attention to Sega's excommunication. Secondly, Peter of the Angels proved a poor selection for a Roman representative. John of the Cross is purported to have said to him before he departed: "You will go to Italy with your shoes off, but you will come back with them on." Peter never did reach Rome: he arrived as far as Naples where he met some of the Calced who received him cordially and took him to the home of the viceroy of Naples. There he was lavishly entertained for a number of weeks, eating and drinking sumptuously. During the course of his celebrations, he surrendered all the documents from the Discalced which he had been carrying. When he sobered, he returned to Spain in a state of profound chagrin. Ashamed of his disloyalty, he immediately went to the Calced monastery at Granada, where he abandoned the reform and took the habit of the Calced.

Despite these momentary setbacks, the whole struggle was rapidly moving to a close. A friend of Teresa's, the Count of Tendilla, encouraged the king to establish a four-man commission to settle the matter. The commission, headed by the Dominican Fernández, advised the king to seek a formal brief of separation from the Holy See. While waiting for the petition to be processed in Rome, preliminary steps were taken in Spain for unraveling the jurisdictional tangle caused by the spate of briefs and counter briefs issued over the ten-year period. On April 1, 1579, the nuncio Sega, now defeated and reconciled to the inevitable, declared that the Discalced were not subject to the Calced, and with the approval of the king's council, he revoked all the briefs which had been issued during the protracted struggle. As an interim measure, he appointed the Calced provincial of Castile, Ángel de Salazar, as vicar-general of the Discalced until a final disposition was granted by Rome. Both Teresa and Gratian expressed satisfaction with this arrangement.

The Discalced sent another delegation to Rome in May of that same year. After the unhappy experience with Peter of the Angels, the Discalced selected two men noted for their austerity and tenacity of purpose: John of Jesus[1] and Diego of the Trinity. In an unnecessary bit of melodrama these two friars disguised themselves in secular clothes for their trip, and they traveled under their respective family names. At Rome they resumed their proper identity and participated in the discussions about the details of the separate province for the Discalced. The irrepressible John of Jesus was in contact with cardinals, statesmen, and Calced Carmelites, outlining the structure of government the Discalced wanted for themselves. At the last moment the general Caffardo seemed to hesi-

[1] John Roca (1540–1614) was an aggressive, forthright personality, somewhat of a firebrand. After his successful mission to Rome in 1579, he was sent back several times for similar assignments. He occupied a number of important administrative positions in the reform, although Teresa maintained that he had "no talent for government."

tate, and he proposed a compromise whereby all the Carmelites of Spain be ruled in successive administrations by a Calced provincial and then by a Discalced provincial. John of Jesus wrote a memorandum strongly protesting this proposal, and he presented it directly to the Holy See, which ultimately accepted his view. As a result of his persistence, he was able to write to Spain in April of 1580 that the brief was about to be signed.

Pope Gregory XIII issued the decree of separation on June 22, 1580, and the document represented a complete victory for the Discalced. The Discalced were constituted as an independent province within the Carmelite Order under the general supervision of the prior general in Rome. However, the Discalced could draw up their own constitutions, elect all their own superiors, and make foundations wherever they wished. There was to be no fusion at all between the Calced and Discalced, and the Calced were expressly forbidden to molest or interfere with the Discalced in any way. The long struggle was over.

The brief reached Spain in August, and in March of the following year the Discalced assembled at the university city of Alcalá de Henares to execute the brief and elect their superiors. Teresa had been preoccupied for months about this election, and she, predictably, had recommended that Gratian be elected provincial. But the twenty delegates (two from each of the ten monasteries) were not as enthusiastic about Gratian as was Teresa. In a remarkably close election Gratian was elected, but he received only eleven out of the twenty votes cast. His closest rival, Anthony of Jesus, received seven votes. Two other candidates split the remaining two votes: Gabriel of the Assumption, former superior of the college in Alcalá, who was to die suddenly of a heart attack three years later at the age of forty; and Nicholas Doria, the Italian banker who had helped the archbishop of Seville, and who himself had entered the reform only four years previously, but who had already attracted much notice among the Discalced as an administrator of considerable astuteness and ability.

The chapter at Alcalá in 1581, which became known as the "Separation Chapter," established the basic form of administration which the reform has used almost exclusively up to the present day, except for the few years of Doria's administration. The provincial (who later became the general) was assisted by four definitors, a board of advisors which met occasionally to assist him in important decisions. Each region of the reform was in turn governed by a vicar-provincial (later a provincial), and each monastery by a prior. The provincial was to be elected for a four-year term, but the definitors for two-year terms. At the Alcalá chapter the four elected definitors were: Nicholas Doria, Anthony of Jesus, John of the Cross, and Gabriel of the Assumption.

However, the most important item of business at Alcalá was the issuance of a set of constitutions, the first detailed and comprehensive legislation for the Discalced friars. The constitutions of Alcalá occupy a unique place in the history of the reform because they were signed by John of the Cross, Gratian, Anthony, Doria, and all the other important early Carmelites; and this legislation gave articulation to Teresa's basic concepts about the reform movement. The constitutions were presented by Gratian to the chapter fathers at Alcalá, and they received unanimous approval. There is no conclusive evidence about the author of the document, but it is a fair assumption to say that it was written by Gratian in collaboration with Teresa herself. The Alcalá constitutions are entitled: "The constitutions of the religious of the Order of our Lady the Virgin Mary of Mount Carmel, of the primitive observance, who are called Discalced." There are seventeen chapters with numerous subdivisions, and this lengthy legislation reaffirms the practices established by Teresa and Gratian over the years: solitude, mental prayer, simple recitation of office, and poverty. But the theme of the whole document is contained in the first chapter, which addresses itself to the primitive Elijahan tradition and the Marian character of the Order. The Carmelites are successors of those ancient religious who lived "near the fountain of Elijah and practiced celestial prayer and holy penance," and who in turn were followers of "Elijah and his disciple Elisha who dwelled on Mt. Carmel in the vicinity of the city of Acre." There is reference to the scriptural source of the Elijahan tradition in the second book of Kings; and the erroneous legend about the unbroken lines of succession on Mount Carmel from Elijah's time until the twelfth century is recounted. The primitive rule of St. Albert is cited, which the Discalced are to follow. And the Carmelites "were called by the title of the brothers of the Virgin Mary of Mount Carmel" because "they constructed a church for the glory and honor of the Virgin Mary on the side of that mountain where they pledged themselves in a very special way to the Most Blessed Mother of our Savior."

The Alcalá constitutions of 1581, therefore, enunciated Teresa's dream of "a restoration of the rule of the Virgin."

Teresa, now sixty-six and in failing health, was at Palencia near Valladolid where she was founding another convent during the time of the Separation Chapter. But she wrote that it was "one of the most joyful and satisfying experiences that I could ever have in this life." She stated, in a letter written immediately after the close of the chapter: "Now I can say what holy Simeon said, because I have seen happen what I desired in the Order of the Virgin our Lady."

From Palencia, Teresa journeyed to Soria, where she founded another convent during the summer of 1581. In September she returned to Ávila and was promptly elected prioress despite her protestations "that I am not fit for that now, and I would be overtaxing my strength." Nevertheless, in the following January she set out to make a foundation in Burgos in fulfillment of a promise she had made six years previously. It would be her last foundation.[2]

She traveled to Burgos with Anne of St. Bartholomew, who had been her almost constant companion for the past five years. Blessed Anne of St. Bartholomew (García) was the first Discalced lay sister —a position in the community similar to that of the lay brother: they did the manual work of the house, and did not recite office in choir with the other religious. Anne was from a poor family in a

---

[2] At this time Teresa was no longer limited to a maximum number of thirteen nuns for each convent. Her original purpose in so limiting the house was to avoid the overcrowded conditions of convents like the Incarnation where the presence of so many nuns made religious observance extremely difficult. But the number of thirteen proved a little too limited, and in 1576 Gratian allowed her to increase the number to twenty, if necessary; and this number did not include the lay sisters, of whom there could be a maximum of three. The custom of twenty nuns, excluding the lay sisters, was then written into the nuns' constitutions, which were approved at the Separation Chapter at Alcalá de Henares. In the seventeenth century the Carmelite nuns increased the number to twenty-one, the extra one being in honor of St. Teresa herself, whom the nuns said should be present in every convent. This number of twenty-one has endured until the present day. There was never any limitation on the number of friars in each monastery, although Teresa did say that "there should be few religious in each monastery." That statement has always been broadly interpreted in the reform, and some of the larger monasteries have at times contained more than a hundred friars.

rural area near Ávila. She was a shepherdess as a young girl, and when her family tried to arrange a marriage for the attractive girl she declined and stated her intention of becoming a Carmelite nun. Against her family's wishes, she entered St. Joseph's at Ávila in 1570 at the age of twenty-one. She learned to read and write in the convent so that she could serve Teresa as a secretary, and all of Teresa's letters in the last few years of her life were dictated to Anne. When Teresa's health started to deteriorate this kind and gentle and extremely compassionate girl began to accompany her on all her journeys, nursing her in her illnesses, and caring for her as she died. In 1604 she went with a group of nuns to make foundations in France, and was finally elevated to the rank of choir sister. She became prioress of the Paris convent, and founded the Carmels at Tours and at Antwerp, where she died in 1612. Pope Benedict XV beatified the former shepherd girl of Ávila on May 6, 1917.

The Burgos foundation was one of Teresa's most difficult.[8] When she arrived in the city, the archbishop suddenly withdrew the permission he had formerly given for the foundation and told her to go home. But she stayed, living for a time in the attic of a hospital with her nuns until she could obtain the archbishop's permission and find a suitable building for a convent. After three months of interminable discussions and wrangling, she established the nuns in a house next to the river which ran through the middle of the city of Burgos. A few weeks later the river flooded and the convent was filled with water and mud. The nuns cleaned out the convent, and Teresa remained with them until July, during which time she finished the final sections of her *Foundations*.

Teresa at sixty-seven was suffering from a uterine cancer which was rapidly drawing toward its terminal stage. She departed for Ávila, stopping on the way at the convent at Medina where she met Anthony of Jesus, then serving as the vicar-provincial of Cas-

---

[8] In the course of her many foundations Teresa had become an astute businesswoman. She wrote to her brother Lorenzo: "Although I used to detest money and business matters, it is the Lord's pleasure that I should engage in nothing else, and that is no light cross. My experiences with these houses of God and the Order have made me so good at bargains and business deals that I am well up in everything." When Teresa was building the convent at Malagón in 1568 she remained outside all day watching the builders, sitting on a large stone where she had her lunch brought to her for fear the builders would try to cheat her in her absence.

tile. He ordered her to set out the next day for Alba de Tormes because the Duchess of Alba's daughter-in-law was expecting a baby and wanted Teresa to pray at her side. Teresa was appalled: her only thought was to reach Ávila as rapidly as she could so that she could die in her first Discalced convent. Anne of St. Bartholomew related: "I never saw her so sad about anything her superiors had ordered her to do as about this." Wearily, though, she complied with the order and set out for Alba de Tormes in the Duchess' coach. When they arrived they were informed the child had already been born.

Teresa was taken to the Discalced convent in Alba de Tormes where the prioress, seeing her enfeebled condition, put her to bed immediately. "I have not been to bed as early as this for twenty years," Teresa exclaimed. She lingered only two weeks. When she received communion for the last time she said loudly, "It has come at last, the hour I have so often and so much longed for, O my Lord and Spouse. So now it is time for us to see each other at last." On the evening of October 4, 1582, she began to sink rapidly. Anne of St. Bartholomew sat on the bed and slipped an arm under her shoulders, and at about nine o'clock Teresa sighed faintly and died. She was beatified in 1614 and canonized in 1622.

The British historian R. Trevor Davies has called Teresa "one of the greatest women in history, and certainly the greatest woman in Spanish literary history." That is the kind of impact this incomparable woman has had on historians: this mystic, this religious reformer, this unique personality. Shortly before her death Teresa said: "Three things have been said of me, in my youth that I was beautiful, later that I was clever, and now that I am holy. For a short time I believed the first two, and now I have repented of it, but I have never been so deluded as to dream of believing the third." But her protests to the contrary, Teresa did possess the unusual combination of beauty, cleverness, and sanctity.

Her great work, of course, was the restoration of the lost Carmelite tradition. And while her task was to revive a thirteenth-century tradition, she nevertheless put her own indelible stamp on the Carmelite Order for the ages to come, forming it in the unique mold of her own particular act of prophetic witness. Her insights into prayer, union with God, and the Christian life became an inseparable part of the Carmelite tradition to such an extent that the Discalced reform was both Elijahan and Marian and Teresian.

But Teresa is also a saint of the entire Christian world with an imperishable testimony for all ages. Her writings, her fantastic personality, and her example present a compelling portrait of the authentic Christian, truly spiritual and truly human. Pope Paul VI said of her that she is "the light of the universal Church."

During the fifteen years following Teresa's death the reform enjoyed a phenomenal growth in Spain and it took the first steps toward establishing itself outside the Iberian peninsula. By the year 1595 there were fifty-eight monasteries of friars and thirty-four convents of nuns, with a total membership of fourteen hundred Discalced. But this growth was accomplished at the cost of an internal struggle even more bitter than the one with the Calced.

The reform was guided during the first part of that period by Jerome Gratian, who was then at the apex of his career as a Carmelite. He established a monastery at Lisbon in Portugal soon after his election as provincial at the Alcalá de Henares chapter, appointing Mariano of St. Benedict, Teresa's prize recruit from Pastrana, to head the group because he felt an Italian would be more acceptable to the Portuguese than a Spaniard. Then Gratian turned himself to wider horizons: he wanted to follow the thrust of the new exploration and colonization of the late sixteenth century, and move the reform quickly into the new mission territories which were being opened up. After consulting with Philip II, he prepared to dispatch a group to the Portuguese colonies of Africa. In April of 1582 Philip received the five Discalced missionaries in a special audience, and conferred his approval and best wishes on their work. They set out from Lisbon with a Bible and a small catechism for their only tools, as the chronicles relate, bound for Guinea and Ethiopia. But at sea the small boat on which they were sailing collided with a larger boat, and the entire expedition perished. Undaunted, Gratian began to recruit friars for another missionary endeavor.

When the Discalced assembled for a chapter at Almodóvar del Campo in the following year to elect four new definitors in place of those whose offices were then expiring, the question of Gratian's missionary activity was submitted to a heated discussion. Some of the friars suggested that the loss of the first expedition was an evident sign of God's disapproval and that plans for any further expeditions should be abandoned. But more penetrating objections were raised by a group headed by Nicholas Doria, which suggested that missionary work was premature in the young reform: they claimed that the Discalced did not have enough members as yet to insure the establishment of missionary monasteries where the full religious observance could be maintained; and, arguing from a particularly Hispanic point of view, they contended that good vocations could not be expected from the native population because the natives were not culturally advanced to the level where they could embrace the contemplative life. Gratian retorted that Teresa had wanted the Discalced friars to labor in the developing mission lands, and in a dazzling bit of oratory he concluded: "Some think that the welfare of the Order lies in multiplying the number of monasteries in tiny Spanish villages and neglecting everything else. God has not led me by that road, but by the road of saving souls." Gratian's reasoning prevailed, and approval was given by a majority of the fathers for further missionary activities.

At the final session of the Almodóvar del Campo chapter, Doria took the floor to criticize openly Gratian's administration, accusing him of having "ruined the Order" with his bad government. He also denounced Gratian's own personal religious observance, suggesting that the provincial spent far too much time preaching outside the monastery. Then he hinted at the possibility of a special vote to depose the provincial from office, but when he was beginning to gain some adherents he suddenly reversed his position and reminded his listeners that Gratian's office only had two years to run. It was an artful political performance, carefully geared toward the election of a new provincial two years away. Astonishingly, Gratian seemed singularly unperturbed about Doria's attack as the chapter concluded its business.

The second missionary expedition of five friars to Africa set sail from Lisbon in 1583, but it failed to reach its destination. The ship was apprehended by English pirates off the Cape Verde Islands, and the Carmelites were taken as prisoners. This was the epoch in which the British sea captains, notably Raleigh, Drake, and Hawkins, were raiding Spanish shipping in an operation they called "singeing the beard" of Philip II; and it was one of the provoking causes which led Philip to float the Spanish Armada in 1588. The English pirates commandeered the ship on which the Carmelites were sailing and proceeded to harass the five men, beating them, tearing off their habits, and burning their books and religious articles. They eventually deposited them on the island of São Tiago, where one of the Carmelites died, presumably from the wounds he had received from the beatings, while the others proceeded back to Lisbon and then home to Spain. A man of less optimistic disposition than Gratian would have been profoundly discouraged by this second failure, but he immediately began to arrange another expedition, which departed in April of the following year and finally arrived at Angola in the Congo. He also instructed Peter of the Apostles, the leader of the group which had been apprehended by the pirates, to make preparations for a missionary expedition to the Spanish colony of Mexico in the New World.

The most significant and productive foundation made by Gratian during his administration was the monastery in Genoa in Italy. After the Separation Chapter in 1581, Gratian had sent Doria to Rome to report its conclusions to the Carmelite general Caffardo. While stopping in Genoa, Doria's family had offered him some excellent property for a foundation of Discalced friars, and he reported this to Gratian on his return. Doria, incidentally, made such an impression on the Calced friars of Genoa that they offered to elect him prior of their monastery immediately if he would abandon the reform. Gratian presented the offer of the property in Genoa to the chapter fathers at Almodóvar del Campo in 1583 and they unanimously agreed to accept it because it would give them a base of operations close to Rome. In late 1583 Gratian dispatched Doria to lead a group of friars to make the foundation. Some commentators on the Gratian-Doria conflict have suggested that Gratian had sinister motivation in selecting Doria for the Genoa foundation: that he wanted to remove Doria from the scene of operations in Spain. However, that was not the case. Gratian appeared to be too naïve about Doria's machinations to indulge in that kind of political activity. Doria, with his Italian background and his family connections in Genoa, was simply the most qualified man for the assignment, and his immediate success with the Genoa monastery proved that emphatically. Gratian wrote to Doria, commending him for the excellent foundation he had made, and he praised him lavishly back in Spain.

In May of 1585, Gratian convened the provincial chapter at the new monastery in Lisbon. Doria, still at the Genoa foundation, was not present for the elections, but Gratian, with a seeming lack of perception that could have derived only from a profound spirit of religious detachment or from an extreme naïveté, proposed his adversary for the office of provincial. Doria was elected with 26 out of the 28 votes cast. John of the Cross and Gratian were both elected definitors. John of the Cross is purported to have said to Gratian: "You have made the man provincial who will strip you of your habit." The historical authenticity of that statement is extremely doubtful, but knowing the diverse and clashing temperaments of Doria and Gratian, it would not have been difficult to predict some calamity.

The chapter was suspended until Doria could return from Genoa, and the fathers did not reassemble until October at Pastrana in Spain. But during that summer Gratian had the satisfaction of seeing the last of his ambitious projects accomplished, a missionary expedition to Mexico. Arrangements for the Mexican endeavor had been completed by the time of the Lisbon chapter, and the assembled fathers approved of the plan. Accordingly, on July 11, Peter of the Apostles set sail for Mexico with a group of ten friars. Working with the Spanish colonizers, Peter was able to establish the Carmelites in Mexico City without any major problems, and a flourishing province soon developed in the New World. However, the Spaniards, with their persistent and unfortunate disaffection for native vocations, did not recruit or accept any candidates into the monasteries from the native populace, except the children of European stock who were born from the descendants of the colonizers' families. For more than two centuries the Mexican province was mainly staffed by Spaniards who made their profession in Spain and then migrated to the New World generation after generation. But the province collapsed, for all practical purposes, during the nineteenth century when the Mexican people overthrew Spanish rule and expelled the foreigners. During the 1820s hundreds of Spanish Carmelites had to flee, and the province was left with a handful of European-stock Mexicans who somehow kept the scattered remnants of the province alive for a hundred years throughout the various religious persecutions. In 1929, after the more vicious aspects of the Calles persecution had died down, the Mexican province was re-established and reorganized.

Nicholas Doria, the new provincial, took over the reins of government when the chapter reconvened at Pastrana, and he made it immediately evident that his administration was going to be one of high centralization and close supervision of the reform. In a closing speech he enunciated a theme he was to repeat frequently during his nine years in office: an exacting and meticulous observance of the rule and constitutions. But he stressed his theme with such passion and ferocity that it unnerved many of the fathers, who felt that the man must surely be an uncompromising rigorist or perhaps somewhat of a fanatic. "Religious observance is what we need, fathers," Doria said. "If we desire the progress of our reform—then observance! If we want the salvation of souls—observance! I would not feel that I was true to my conscience if I did not repeat these things without ceasing. Even after my death my bones, clashing together in the tomb, will cry out: observance, observance!"

A major new figure had entered on the stage of Carmelite history, and his presence would produce an inner crisis more devastating for the reform than the long struggle with the Calced. And, as before, John of the Cross would be tragically victimized in the process.

Born at Genoa in 1539 of a wealthy and aristocratic family, Nicholas Doria came to Spain as a young man of thirty-one. The Dorias, an established family of Genoese bankers, had maintained financial interests in Spain for many generations, and the brilliant young Nicholas soon distinguished himself in the Iberian Peninsula as an astute financier and businessman. He also composed a treatise on banking and finance which was highly regarded. As we noted, he came to the attention of Philip II, and assisted the king in a number of delicate transactions concerning international finance at a time when the Spanish crown was tottering on the edge of bankruptcy. But in the midst of his spectacular career, Doria suddenly renounced his considerable personal fortune, distributing it to the poor, and began studies for the priesthood in Seville. After his ordination he sought admission to the recently founded monastery of Discalced Carmelites in Seville, and on March 24, 1577, Gratian himself invested Doria with the habit of the reform. Doria adopted the name Nicholas of Jesus and Mary. Teresa was delighted to have the brilliant Italian banker in her reform, and she wrote of him in glowing terms, calling him "a man of great distinction and perfection," and "a man of judgment, very humble, very penitential, who knows how to win people's good will." She observed that Doria lacked "the great graciousness and affability" of Gratian, but she concluded, characteristically, that God "grants to few men so many gifts at one time" as He had to Gratian. Teresa saw Doria as an invaluable ally for Gratian, and she wrote that she was "delighted

to hear that your reverence has such a good companion." Until the
end of her life she encouraged the two men to work in close collaboration, and she wrote to Gratian: "Your reverence must not be
distant with him, for, unless I am mistaken, he will be a great help
in many ways." And she urges Gratian to reach an accommodation
with Doria, "if only to please me." Throughout the few remaining
years of her life, Teresa was able to keep these two men of such
different temperaments on reasonably good terms, but after her
death they had a complete falling out.

After his profession in 1578, Doria was almost immediately made
vicar of the monastery in Seville, and then prior of Pastrana. The
Carmelites recognized his exceptional abilities, and his undeniable
proficiency in getting things done with dispatch. That is the reason
that so many of the Discalced at first preferred Doria's regime to
Gratian's: whereas Gratian was often imprudent, inattentive to detail, vague and unconcerned, Doria was sure-handed, exact, efficient,
and he always proceeded through the proper channels. But these
qualities of a good administrator masked for a time the other side
of Doria's personality. A year before her death Teresa noticed that
Doria "insists that everything should be carried out according to his
own way of looking at things." This propensity continued to develop
as he rose higher in the ranks of ecclesiastical administration, until
he appeared to be, near the end of his life, an unmitigated autocrat.
His regime became an iron-fisted one, and he would broach no
criticism or opposition. The Discalced secretly named him "the Lion
of Carmel."

Doria was a religious man, but his religion was composed of an
extreme legalism and formalism, and it bordered on the fanatical.
When he was visiting a monastery one time, he strenuously disapproved of a book read aloud in the refectory which counseled prudence in matters of penance; but it was pointed out to him that the
book contained excellent material. "How can it be good when it
contains such a chapter as that?" Doria retorted. "Stop reading it.
Souls are being lost through such prudent discretion." He was rigoristic in his own personal life, and rigoristic with the friars, compos-
ing an endless succession of laws and directives. In this he was diametrically opposed to the mentality of Teresa, who wrote: "What
my nuns are afraid of is that we shall get some tiresome superiors
who will lay heavy and excessive burdens on them. That will lead
us nowhere." And when a visitator had written a number of direc-

tives for her nuns, she wrote: "Even reading the regulations made me tired, so what would it be if one had to keep them? Believe me, our rule will not stand additions from tiresome people like that: it is quite hard enough to keep as it is." Doria certainly fell into her category of "tiresome people."

However, Doria did accomplish a number of important things during his administration. He possessed a definite oleaginous and diplomatic charm, and was able to maintain the best of relations for the reform with Philip II, the Holy See, and the general Caffardo. He established thirty-three new monasteries during his tenure of office, and he stabilized the finances so that all the houses were in excellent financial condition. And he was able to lead the Discalced to a position of complete autonomy from the Calced. But the harm that was caused by his own unyielding personality at that critical moment of the reform's history more than outweighed any good he did achieve.

A portrait of Nicholas Doria preserved at Pastrana shows a man of commanding features and aristocratic bearing: his profile is angular and his eyes dark and piercing. But there is no hint of warmth or feeling in the portrait, only a chilling picture of a man determined to succeed.

At the Pastrana chapter of 1585, Doria sponsored the election of Gratian to the newly created office of vicar-provincial of Portugal and John of the Cross to the office of vicar-provincial of Andalusia. At that time Doria seemed to bear no personal animosity to Gratian, and having secured his withdrawal from the office of provincial, he apparently would have been content to allow Gratian to live peacefully in Portugal as long as he remained out of Doria's way. But Gratian was temperamentally unable to do that: he had to protest a number of Doria's policies of which he disapproved. The first of Doria's objectionable policies was his attitude toward the missions: he was firmly set against sending any more Discalced to the mission areas. Doria had to proceed cautiously with the groups already in the Congo and Mexico because of the king's interest in the two missions. He skillfully cut off financial and material help from the Congo group, which was in an advanced mission area, and in a few years the mission collapsed and the friars returned to Spain. But Doria was unable to do anything with the Mexican mission: it was too firmly entrenched in a colonized area and it drew its main support from the Spanish colonists. The Mexican missionaries merely had to endure Doria's regime, without much help from Spain, until further assistance and manpower was sent in subsequent administrations. But despite the Mexican mission, Doria had achieved his objective: he had stopped the missionary endeavor.

The second policy which Gratian found offensive was Doria's attitude toward the Carmelite nuns. Doria was dissatisfied with the organizational structure of the nuns whereby each convent was autonomous, conducting its own elections and arranging its own affairs. Although he was the provincial superior of all the convents, and they were directly responsible to him, the whole system seemed too casual and imprecise to suit him. He wanted a tighter organizational arrangement, something similar to what the friars had, in which he could exercise greater control over the nuns' elections and their internal affairs. It became more apparent as the years passed that his chief motive for wanting greater control of the nuns was his desire to impress on them his own particular brand of religion. Teresa had left her indelible imprint on the nuns, that happy blending of spirituality and humanness, but Doria wanted to replace that with a greater insistence on penitential practices and meticulous adherence to his regulations and directives. However, Doria was never able to achieve his objectives with the nuns, who remained firm adherents to Gratian during the entire struggle, much to Doria's chagrin.

Gratian's third and principal objection to Doria's regime was the new insistence on juridicism and legalism. Gratian contended that the friars were being ruled like children with no respect for the dignity of the human person; and this, he argued, could only produce a juvenile and unproductive mentality in the reform. Shortly after his arrival in Portugal, Gratian composed a monograph entitled, "An argument for charity: Against some who, under the pretext of observance of rules, weaken and disturb it in religious Orders." The document was widely read, and while it did not mention Doria by name it was quite clearly directed against him. This monograph provided Doria with the ammunition he needed when he decided to act against Gratian.

In a meeting with his definitors in August of 1586, Doria began to advance his program. The definitory addressed a petition to the Holy See seeking a complete and absolute separation from the Calced and a new form of government for the Discalced based on Doria's autocratic concept of administration. The petition also contained a request whereby the Discalced could use the Roman liturgy in place of the traditional Carmelite liturgy of the Holy Sepulcher. Doria's avowed intention in seeking the liturgical change was to provide a dramatic symbol of separation between Calced and Discalced. The Holy See granted the liturgical change almost immediately, and also approved the inauguration of negotiations for a definitive separation from the Calced. This process took more than seven years to complete.

The most significant act of the 1586 definitory was its approval of the publication of Teresa's writings. Anne of Jesus, the prioress of the Madrid Carmel, and now the most prestigious Carmelite nun in Spain after Teresa's death, was commissioned to gather the writings and then work in collaboration with the celebrated poet Luis de León in preparing the edition. Prior to that time Teresa's writings had been circulated in manuscript and holograph copies, except for two small printed editions of the *Way of Perfection*. But this edition, the *editio princeps*, published at Salamanca in 1588, was a large, octavo volume of over a thousand pages, containing all the writings except the *Foundations*, which was excluded because too many of the people mentioned in it were still alive. The *Foundations* was first printed in the Brussels edition of 1610.

Gratian intensified his critique of Doria's administration after the 1586 definitory, and it became increasingly evident that the provincial would soon retaliate. At the biennial chapter of April, 1587, Doria arranged for Gratian to be appointed vicar-provincial of the Mexican province, thus removing him completely from Spain. Unfortunately for Doria—and for Gratian, too, as events turned out— there were no sailings for Mexico in that year of 1587, when Drake was pirating on a grand scale and Philip II was preparing the Armada. In July of that year Doria received word from Rome that the Holy See had granted him the first step toward complete autonomy from the Calced: the Discalced were now to be considered a separate congregation within the Carmelite Order, rather than just a province; and Doria's new form of government was approved. This new arrangement was not put into operation for a year, during which time Doria busied himself with preparations—among other things, he presented the brief from Rome to the king for his approval. He also felt he had to prevent any further opposition from Gratian, whom he was regretfully unable to transfer immediately to Mexico. In November he gathered his definitory and passed a severe sentence on Gratian: he was to be deprived of his vote and his right to hold office in the next two chapters. The flimsy pretext on which this penalty was based was Gratian's monograph, plus a reactivation of the same charges the Calced had made against him years before. Gratian at first protested the sentence, then he humbly submitted, offering apologies to Doria, and returned to the monastery in Lisbon. As before, Gratian could now have avoided any further difficulties for himself if he had refrained from criticism of the regime. He was well respected in Portugal; he was busy preaching and writing; and Doria seemed mollified at his compliance and quiet life in Lisbon. However, the whole situation was too much for him to abide silently, and in the following year he returned to the conflict.

In June of 1588 Doria convened a chapter to execute the brief which established the Discalced as a congregation. The principal superior of the reform was now to be called a vicar-general instead of provincial, and he was to be elected for a six-year term. Doria, of course, was the major candidate for that office. He was elected, but to his surprise, he received only thirty-two out of the fifty votes cast. Contrasting this with his almost unanimous election three years previously, it seemed that his hold on the reform was weakening.

Doria then unveiled his new form of highly centralized government, the key part of which was the establishment of a governing body called the Consulta, a group of six officers who lived in the same monastery with Doria and who were his special agents for administering practically all the business of the reform. The Carmelite historian Benedict Zimmerman has written that the Consulta "was more fit for the policing of an unruly Italian republic than for the direction of a religious Order." Practically every detail of administration which was formerly controlled by the various priors in their monasteries, even the appointment of preachers and confessors, was now reserved to the Consulta. It was a police regime of the most intense kind, and it began to cause severe unrest and bitter murmuring among the friars. Segovia was chosen as the seat of the Consulta; and John of the Cross, who had been remarkably docile and quiet about Doria's regime up to that point, was selected as the first member of the Consulta.

Having subjugated the friars to his overpowering regime, Doria then turned his attention to the nuns. He insisted that they refer their business matters to his Consulta, and he began to intervene more in the internal affairs of each convent. But the organizational structure of the nuns still impeded him. He then let it be known that he was going to take juridical action to change the situation by having the nuns' constitutions revised according to his own ideas. These were the cherished constitutions of Teresa, and Doria's proposal of tampering with them brought anguished cries from the convents. At this point, Anne of Jesus stepped into the conflict in order to block Doria. Venerable Anne of Jesus (Lobera) was a truly remarkable woman and a worthy successor to Teresa of Ávila. Born in 1545 from a good family in Medina del Campo, she developed into a striking beauty; and because of her physical endowments she was called "the queen of women" by the people of Medina. She had a host of admirers, and finally she was pursued so insistently by her many suitors that she fled to her uncle's home in Valencia. She came into contact with Teresa through a mutual friend, a Jesuit priest; and the holy mother tried to persuade her to enter the reform. But Anne resisted for some time, despite Teresa's seemingly improbable prediction that the Spanish beauty would eventually become a Carmelite nun. Anne was attending Mass one day when she quite suddenly and surprisingly decided to renounce her active social life and join the Carmelites. At the age of twenty-five she entered the convent of St. Joseph's in Ávila.

Anne of Jesus was a holy and intelligent woman, and a strong-willed person, forthright and outspoken, a fair adversary for Doria in that epoch of strong-willed people. Immediately after her profession of vows, Teresa made her novice mistress at Salamanca, and four years later she was prioress in Beas. She had a long and successful career in administration, and Teresa called her "the captain of the prioresses" and strongly suggested that she be her successor as chief spokesman for the nuns. Anne became a close friend of Gratian; and also of John of the Cross, who wrote the *Spiritual Canticle* expressly for her. In 1604, after the Doria conflict, she led the first group of nuns to France, where she established the original Discalced convent in Paris. She later led the first group of nuns to the Lowlands. She died in Brussels at the age of seventy-five, and in northern Europe she is still called "the second foundress." In 1878 the Holy See approved the heroicity of her virtues, thereby conferring on her the title of Venerable.

When she was prioress of Madrid in 1588, Anne began her campaign to thwart Doria's attempt to change the Teresian constitutions. She had excellent contacts in the capital, and she used them wisely: Princess Maria, the daughter of Philip II, a personal and devoted friend of hers; the nuncio, Caesare Speziano; and the distinguished poet Luis de León. But her two most valuable allies were Gratian and John of the Cross, both of whom worked closely with her, counseling her behind the scenes. Gratian was still in Lisbon and he had to offer all his advice by mail, but John of the Cross in his post of first member of the Consulta was able to visit Anne in Madrid and carefully formulate the plan of attack. Anne first made a direct appeal to the Nuncio, asking him to protect the Teresian constitutions. In October of 1588, the Nuncio issued a decree which "confirmed and approved" the constitutions and declared their "perpetual stability" and pronounced null and void any possible revocation of them. Before the end of the year the Teresian constitutions were republished in Madrid with the Nuncio's letter as a preface. Doria was strangely silent about the Nuncio's approbation, and to all appearances he seemed to acquiesce in the decision. But Anne did not trust him, and she made plans to obtain further protection from the Holy See itself. In 1589 she addressed a petition to the pope requesting him to confirm the constitutions, and also to appoint a commissary general for the nuns who would serve as their superior and liaison with the vicar-general. In her petition she nominated John of the Cross for that office, although John, who had worked with her in preparing the petition, did not seem to be aware of that latter detail. The petition was carried to Rome by a friend of Gratian's. In June of 1590 an affirmative answer was received from Sixtus V: the constitutions were confirmed perpetually; the office of a commissary general was established, who was to be elected in the friars' chapter every three years; but the nomination of John of the Cross was ignored, and no name was mentioned in the papal brief.

Doria was enraged by the brief, and he immediately wrote a violent and condemnatory letter to Anne of Jesus. As a further affront, Gratian had written to Philip II protesting the whole concept of the Consulta. Doria was able to handle that easily enough because the former Italian banker had Philip's complete confidence now, and the day of Gratian's influence with the king had passed. Doria visited the king, and subsequently Philip II reiterated his approval of the Consulta government. But the vexatious problem of the papal brief remained. Doria refused to do anything to implement the brief, and made preparations to seek its revocation from the Holy See.

But first the infuriated Doria had to take care of his adversaries. There was no doubt in his mind now: they had to be eliminated, all three of them—Gratian, Anne of Jesus, and John of the Cross.

In the decade after his escape from the prison of Toledo, John of the Cross's life was busy but relatively calm. He held a number of administrative positions, but until his appointment to the Consulta in 1588 he lived mainly in Andalusia in the south and was therefore removed from the Gratian-Doria excitement in Castile.[4] He had little liking for the office of superior, and he felt that he had no aptitude for government; nevertheless he was a good superior, intelligent, humble, and kind. The highest position he held was the office of vicar-provincial of Andalusia from 1585 to 1587. His most painful act of government during his term as vicar-provincial was the reprimand he had to give two young friars, Francis Chrysostom and Diego Evangelist, who were spending excessive amounts of time outside the monastery. Although John dealt with the friars gently, merely calling the problem to their attention, they accepted the correction with bad grace and became his bitter enemies. In the ensuing years they took the opportunity, as we shall see, to revenge themselves on the saint.

John's principal accomplishment, though, during his decade in Andalusia was the composition of his major literary works. He had composed some poetry while he was jailed in Toledo, and throughout his escape carried with him the few scraps of paper on which he had written the poems. These astonishing poems form the basis of his entire literary production, and they certainly place him in the ranks of the foremost poets of Spanish literature. The poems are

[4] As a true Castilian, John of the Cross did not like the southern country of Andalusia. In 1581 Teresa wrote to Gratian, imploring him to bring John back to Castile in the north: "When I was commiserating sometime ago with Father John of the Cross on his dislike of being in Andalusia—for he cannot endure the people there—I told him that, if God gave us a province of our own, I would try to get him back here. Now he reminds me of my promise and he is afraid they will be re-electing him at Baeza. He tells me that he is begging your reverence not to confirm the election. If that is practicable, it would be only fair to give him this comfort, for he has had his fill of suffering. I certainly hope we shall not found many houses in Andalusia, my father. . . ."

not religious at all, in the accepted sense of the word, but they describe the aspirations of love by a person who seeks and eventually finds his beloved. In the tradition of the Canticle of Canticles, John depicts the psychology and the inner feelings of a man searching for his loved one:

> Where have you hidden,
> beloved, and left me moaning?
> You fled like the stag
> After wounding me;
> I went out calling you, and
> you were gone.

Until he finds her:

> The bride has entered
> The sweet garden of her desire
> And she rests in delight,
> Laying her neck
> On the gentle arms of her beloved.

All of his major prose work is a commentary on his poetry, as he writes: "All the doctrine of which I mean to treat in this *Ascent of Mount Carmel* is included in the following stanzas, and in them is contained the manner of climbing to the summit of the mount, which is the exalted state of perfection we call here the union of the soul with God." While his poetry is free and lyrical, his prose commentary is deeply influenced by his scholastic background, and it demonstrates a determined effort to attain logical precision. Like the writings of Teresa, his material is gathered primarily from personal religious experience; but, unlike her, John reflects in his prose writings some of the major writers in the history of Christian mysticism, particularly Denis the Areopagite, whom medieval Christianity considered to be a disciple of St. Paul but who in actuality was a fifth-century neo-Platonist. Even his handwriting vividly demonstrates the difference of personality and viewpoint between himself and Teresa: his is small, precise, carefully formed; hers is large and scrawling, at times almost illegible.

He began the composition of his *Ascent of Mount Carmel* in 1579, completing it in 1584. He wrote the *Dark Night of the Soul* between 1582 and 1585, and in that same period he also wrote his *Spiritual Canticle*. Thus at one time he was working on three different books. He wrote his *Living Flame of Love* during fifteen days in 1585. He later composed second versions of both the *Canticle* and the *Living Flame.* These works all develop his basic principle that man must search out the transcendent God of history through a program of liberation from all self-interests which drain his love. His goal is union with God through contemplation, which he describes as "a loving knowledge of God." To achieve this state he guides his reader through the "night of the senses" and the "night of the spirit," periods of intense purgation during which man is drawn closer to God in naked faith. The doctrine is clearly existential, as he concerns himself with Man's deepest point of psychological consciousness and his attempt to elevate himself into union with the pure spirit of God.

However, the most striking feature of his work is its almost total lack of reference to the sacraments or any of the traditional features of Catholic piety. While he considered his writing complementary to Teresa's, and refers his reader to her treatment of the more fundamental and traditional themes, he nevertheless decidedly prefers to communicate his own particular vision: the psychology of the inner encounter between man and God. It is remarkable that such works could have been written in the highly orthodox religious climate of Spain with its attraction for ritualistic piety. John of the Cross is closer in doctrine to the religious reformers of the north, like Luther and Calvin, who were trying to express man's pure experience of God without the accretions of medieval piety. And this aspect of his work caused his writings to be suspect for many decades.

Admittedly, John of the Cross's writing is esoteric and specialized —he writes, for example, in the introduction to the *Ascent*: "Nor is it my intention to address all, but rather certain persons of our sacred Order of Mount Carmel of the primitive observance"—but he does offer for all Christians a breath-taking portrait of man's inner self and his potential for union with God. He has remained for four hundred years the Church's mystical theologian par excellence and the ultimate authority in that science. In 1926, Pius XI declared him a doctor of the universal Church, the "Mystical Doctor."

Holographic copies of John's various works were widely circulated in Spain during his lifetime and in the years following his death. After a number of attempts to gather the manuscripts and obtain authorization for their publication, the *editio princeps* was published at Alcalá in 1618. This edition excluded the *Spiritual Canticle*, and presented mutilated and bowdlerized versions of the other books. The changes in the text were obviously made to protect these unconventional writings from the ubiquitous and nefarious Spanish Inquisition, but it proved ineffectual because the edition was denounced to the Inquisition in the very year of publication. Only a spirited defense by the Augustinian Basil Ponce de León protected the edition from confiscation. A full and authentic edition, containing the *Spiritual Canticle*, was published by the Carmelites of Madrid in 1630, and this too was promptly denounced to the Inquisition. The Carmelites defended the edition in a painful examination before the Inquisition, and ultimately they were allowed to continue publication, thus preserving St. John of the Cross in print through that dreary epoch of fear.

Historians have sometimes complained that it is difficult to create an intimate portrayal of John of the Cross because he seems so faceless and opaque. That is certainly the way John of the Cross wanted it, because his chosen path to God was one of humility and abnegation and selflessness. During a vision at Segovia he heard the Lord ask him what favor he wanted from God. "To suffer and to be despised for you," John answered. Nevertheless, the most intimate portrayal which could possibly be fashioned of any man is contained in John of the Cross's writings. The doctrine is an articulation of his own inner life, and he is the perfect incarnation of all the things he wrote about. We are therefore given a picture of the man which is more profound and more searching than any amount of biographical data: we are presented with an astonishing psychological portrait of a soaring mystic who is totally consumed with the reality of God.

One of his contemporaries recalls that John would frequently scrape his knuckles against the wall while he was conversing with others so that he could keep his attention on the matter at hand and not allow himself to become rapt in prayer. His life of union with God, therefore, was his major preoccupation during the decade in Andalusia. He did his work, he faithfully performed the duties required of his various offices, and he spent a good deal of time serving as a spiritual director, for both Carmelites and lay people. But he held himself carefully disengaged from the disturbances in Castile. Doria apparently interpreted this silence on John's part as approval of the regime, and he continued to sponsor the saint for administrative positions of secondary rank.

In 1588, when Doria was engaged in the ticklish matter of establishing his first Consulta, he chose John as its first member, obviously because he felt that this quiet friar was quite maneuverable. It was one of Doria's many mistakes. John of the Cross was anything but maneuverable.

At the beginning of 1591 Nicholas Doria systematically began to eradicate his adversaries. First, Anne of Jesus. He eliminated her easily by deposing her from office and declaring that she must remain in seclusion in one of the convents—this was, interestingly, the same penalty that was imposed on Teresa by the Calced sixteen years previously. Then he announced to the nuns that if the brief concerning the commissary general remained unchanged he would work to have the nuns officially disassociated from the friars and leave them to their own devices. A new pope, Gregory XIV, had been elected in December of 1590, and Doria petitioned him to revoke the brief of Sixtus V; and he requested Philip II to declare the original brief null and void in the kingdom of Spain if it were not withdrawn by the Holy See. In April of 1591, the pope sent a brief which represented a compromise: the office of commissary general was suppressed and the nuns were again placed under the jurisdiction of their various provincials; but the constitutions of Teresa were to remain intact. This seemed to satisfy Doria, who regarded it as the best he could probably do for the time being.

Then, John of the Cross. After the formation of the Consulta, Doria soon discovered that John was not as malleable as he had thought. At the Consulta meetings John had spoken against Doria's various proposals, particularly his attitude toward the nuns. Doria had been able to obtain approval for his projects from the other members of the Consulta, but then John began to absent himself as much as he could from the meetings in a gesture of silent protest. And there was that distressing entente between Gratian and Anne and John which resulted in the brief from Sixtus V. Doria would take care of John at the chapter scheduled for Madrid in June of that year. John could see what was coming, and he confided to the prioress of Segovia, Maria of the Incarnation (to whom he wrote his famous phrase: "Where there is no love, put love, and you will find love."), that he would be "thrown into a corner like an old rag."

Doria passed word to the assembled fathers at the Madrid chapter that John was to receive no office. John sat silently through the elec-

tions while for the first time since his release from prison he was
totally ignored during a votation. What made this even more remarkable was that only three years previously Doria had sponsored him as
the first member of the Consulta. Gratian, of course, was still in
Lisbon, excluded from the chapter by the penalty Doria had imposed
on him. At last, during the business discussions near the conclusion
of the chapter, John raised his hand to speak. It was his shining
hour, his fearless confrontation of Nicholas Doria. He criticized
Doria's whole regime with its excessive legislation, its police tactics,
and its rule by intimidation. He spoke in favor of Anne of Jesus,
and he protested Doria's treatment of the nuns. Finally he defended
Gratian and lamented the sorry treatment the former provincial
was receiving. It was an astonishing performance for a man who
was by temperament reticent and shy; and Doria hastily concluded
that further action would have to be taken against this little friar
who was proving himself so dangerous and troublesome.

After the chapter was officially closed, Doria summoned John of
the Cross and gave him his new assignment—Mexico. It was the
same assignment given to Gratian four years previously, but now
Spanish ships were sailing to the New World again and Doria was
determined that John must leave the country. The port of embarka-
tion was Seville, and John was told to go south and prepare himself
for departure. In late July, John journeyed south to Andalusia and
selected the lonely monastery of La Penuela as a place for a quiet
retreat while awaiting definite arrangements about his passage for
Mexico. He was in good spirits, resigned and not bitter. Before leaving Madrid he had written Anne of Jesus:

If things did not turn out as you desired, you ought to be consoled
and thank God profusely. Since our Lord has so arranged matters, it is
what most suits everyone. All that remains for us is to accept it willingly
so that since we believe He has arranged it this way we may show it by
our actions.

John remained in La Penuela for about two months until he
contracted a fever and needed some kind of medical attention. As
there was no doctor near La Penuela, his companions urged him
to go to one of the monasteries in a more populated area, Baeza
for example. But John had formerly been superior at Baeza, and he
deliberately chose the monastery at Úbeda where Francis Chrysostom was prior, the man who had become his bitter enemy since

John's reprimand to him years ago during his term as vicar-provincial. The saint dismissed his ailment as "a slight bout of fever," but it became apparent when he arrived in Úbeda that he was seriously ill. He was, in fact, dying of osteomyelitis. Francis Chrysostom received him badly, giving him a poor cell and refusing him adequate treatment. John of the Cross's prayer was being answered —"to suffer and to be despised for You."

Meanwhile in Madrid Doria was proceeding against the third member of the entente, Jerome Gratian. In late June he had summoned him to return from Lisbon and report to the monastery in Madrid. He first offered him the post of vicar-general of the Mexican mission, but Gratian's friends advised him to refuse the office since it was so obvious a move to remove from Spain the last major spokesman for the nuns. Gratian declined the office, and Doria promptly had him arrested, holding him incarcerated in the monastery at Madrid. During the long fall of 1591 Gratian was subjected to constant interrogations by Doria's various lieutenants, who questioned him interminably about fictitious improprieties and indiscretions with the nuns in both Spain and Portugal. It was a psychological and inquisitional torture, which police regimes of a later epoch perfected to a finer art, and it served to confuse and exhaust Gratian, who ultimately broke under it. To obtain some substantiation for the bizarre charges Doria sent Diego Evangelist to visit the convents in Spain and procure statements against Gratian. By innuendo and guarded suggestion Diego was able to obtain some vague statements from some of the nuns who apparently did not recognize Diego's purpose. Diego Evangelist, who was the other of John's two enemies from the old days in Andalusia, also took the opportunity to raise questions with the nuns about John's conduct in an obvious attempt to discredit him. The shocked nuns reported Diego's activities to John's friends, some of whom wrote immediately to the dying friar in Úbeda urging him to defend himself with Doria against the charges of impropriety which Diego was stirring up. In November John wrote to one of the friars:

> Son, do not let this disturb you, for they cannot take the habit away from me unless I am incorrigible and disobedient. I am very ready to amend all that I may have done wrong and obey whatever penance they may give me.

But John was beyond the point where Doria or Diego or anybody else could hurt him any longer. He had been submitted to the horrors of the medicine practiced in that primitive era—the cuttings, bleedings, and compresses—but the doctor was unable to stem the ravages of his disease. Some of the friars had written to Anthony of Jesus, now the vicar-provincial of Andalusia, protesting Francis Chrysostom's treatment of John, and the saint's old friend immediately rushed to Úbeda. Anthony arrived on November 27, the twenty-third anniversary of the day he had arrived at Duruelo to join John for the inauguration of the first monastery. The old man—he was now eighty-one—reprimanded the prior for his harsh treatment of the dying friar and had him moved to a more commodious cell. This seemed to bring Francis Chrysostom to his senses, and he begged the saint's forgiveness in a tearful apology which was apparently sincere. John's legs were completely ulcerated, and a large tumor developed on his back. He began to sink on the evening of December 13, and the prayers for the dying were recited over him. However, he interrupted the ritual prayers, and asked that the Canticle of Canticles be read instead. Just after midnight on the morning of December 14, he put a crucifix to his lips and said: "Into your hands, O Lord, I commend my spirit." Then he quietly expired. He was forty-nine years of age. John of the Cross was beatified in 1675, and canonized by Benedict XIII in 1726.

Gratian, however, was still detained at Madrid and weakening badly under the constant interrogations. Finally, completely exhausted and enervated and confused, he signed a paper which was a confession to various unnamed but implied discretions with Carmelite nuns. That was all Doria needed. On February 17 he called a meeting of the Consulta, and had Gratian formally expelled from the Discalced Carmelites. His habit was removed from him and he was told that he could neither preach nor hear confessions until he affiliated himself either with some other order or some diocese. The bewildered man now realized what had happened and what he had signed. "I am innocent of the things they accused me of, and I swear these things on a consecrated altar," he later wrote. He set out for Rome in an attempt to present his case directly to the Holy See, and his subsequent career was both tragic and noble. While sailing between Italian ports his ship was captured by Turkish pirates and he was taken to North Africa where, after being branded on the soles of his feet, he was held captive for two years. He was eventually ransomed by a Jewish friend of his from Lisbon, and he returned to Italy to resume his defense. When he appealed to the pope, Clement VIII listened to his story, and declared: "This man is a saint." It is a lasting tribute to Gratian's nobility and true greatness that he never indulged in any personal criticism against Doria during his defense. He called him "a great servant of God" and stated: "I believe that no hatred or rancor moved them, but the zeal of the Order, and so it must be the devil who is to blame in this case." That unbelievable and astonishing statement could only have been made by a man like Jerome Gratian. The pope, however, was unwilling to reopen the case, but he absolved him of the charges and allowed him to follow the primitive Carmelite rule while living in a Calced monastery. Gratian remained four years in Rome, serving as theologian to Cardinal Deza, and then returned to Spain to assist his dying mother. He spent the remaining years of his life in the Lowlands, where he was of great assistance to Anne of Jesus and Thomas of Jesus in establishing the Discalced Carmelites. He died at Brussels in 1614 at the age of sixty-nine, a truly tragic figure in a tragic episode.[5]

Thus by the spring of 1592 Doria had cleared the field of all his major adversaries. John of the Cross was dead, Anne of Jesus was immured in Madrid, and Gratian was out of the Order. He had everything in complete control. However, there was one thing that even a Nicholas Doria could not control.

Doria's chief preoccupation after Gratian's expulsion from the reform was the acquisition from the Holy See of a definitive statement which would sever the last link holding the Discalced bound to the

---

[5] Jerome Gratian was an energetic writer, producing thirty books in his lifetime, most of which were written in the years following his expulsion from the reform. His writings remained in print throughout the seventeenth and eighteenth centuries, but then passed out of print. Some of his principal works were: *Flores Carmeli*, on the origin of the Carmelites and the Discalced reform; *Josefina*, a treatise on St. Joseph; *The Lighted Lamp*, about mental prayer; *Mystical Theology*; and *Discourses on Mary*. His two most important and popular books have been republished in this century: *Memoir of St. Teresa*, and *Pilgrimage of Anastasius*, an engrossing autobiography written shortly before his death. Gratian's style was lively and interesting, and he wrote in the exquisite pure Castilian of the seventeenth century. Although his writing was uneven, his *Pilgrimage* endures as a significant literary accomplishment. Gratian's brother, Lorenzo Gratian, wrote a book describing the Doria conflict under the intriguing title *Guerra entre Buenos* (War between the Good).

Calced. In 1592 the general, Caffardo, died, and Doria felt that it was now the appropriate time to obtain what he wanted. He attended the general chapter held at Cremona, Italy, in June of 1593, accompanied by a delegation of sixteen of the most brilliant Discalced friars he could find. He included among his companions both John of Jesus (Roca) and John of Jesus and Mary (Aravalles), the saintly novice master who compiled the *Instruction for Novices*, a manual which has been used by Spanish Carmelites since its publication in 1591. The general chapter elected John Chizzola as Caffardo's successor, and the new general appeared to be deeply impressed by Doria's delegation of Discalced friars. He listened sympathetically to Doria's request for the complete and absolute separation of Calced and Discalced, and then suggested to the assembled chapter that it be given immediate approval. The resolution passed easily and was sent to the Holy See for confirmation. In the bull *Pastoralis officii* of December 20, 1593, Clement VIII established the Discalced Carmelites as a separate order, with its own general subject only to the pope.

The pope appointed Doria as the provisional general of the Order until a general chapter of the Discalced, scheduled for Madrid at the end of April, 1594, could officially elect a general. Doria's supporters then petitioned Philip II to obtain from the pope a written statement expressing a desire that Doria be elected general at the forthcoming chapter. (It is more than possible that Doria himself instigated this unusual petition.) Clement VIII's written nomination of Doria as general was in the possession of the papal nuncio in Spain when Doria, on the eve of his greatest triumph, unexpectedly encountered his only unconquerable adversary.

Nicholas Doria had been making a retreat at Bolarque in preparation for the chapter. At the beginning of April he set out for Madrid, stopping first at Pastrana and then proceeding on to Alcalá de Henares. However, he was taken ill during the journey to Alcalá and arrived there in a state of collapse. He was put to bed with a high fever, and after a few days he showed no improvement. The chapter was postponed indefinitely, while doctors worked vigorously to heal him. For a time it seemed as if their labors might be successful, but then Doria began to slip away. As this peculiar man lay dying his conscience was troubled, astonishingly, by only one event of his life—the action he had taken against Jerome Gratian. He died on May 9, 1594, nine days before his fifty-fifth birthday.

And then, suddenly, it was all over. Like the calm that quickly follows a violent tropical storm, peace came to the Carmelite reform after almost a quarter of a century of fierce struggle. Two weeks after Doria's death the chapter assembled at Madrid and elected Elijah of St. Martin as the first Discalced general, a man of irenic and peaceful temperament, a former classmate of Gratian's, and a friar who had served with great kindness and thoughtfulness as the prior of Pastrana and Toledo and then as the provincial of Castile. (Significantly, Teresa's code name for him in her correspondence was *Clemente*—kind one.) He ruled as general for six years and his regime was distinguished by prudence and tact and encouragement of the friars. He dismantled the machinery of the Consulta and eradicated the mood of fear which Doria had generated, substituting instead the true Teresian spirit of joyful adherence to the primitive rule of Carmel. Elijah of St. Martin was that blessed phenomenon of history: the right man at the right time.

The only unhappy footnote at the Madrid chapter of 1594 was the election of Diego Evangelist, John of the Cross and Gratian's antagonist, to the office of provincial of Upper Andalusia. Elijah of St. Martin had reprimanded him at the chapter for past activities, and then Diego set out for Andalusia to assume his new office. But he never arrived there. During his journey south, he was taken ill at Alcalá la Real, and he unexpectedly died a few days later at the early age of thirty-four.

The summer of 1594, then, marked the end of the bitter conflicts which had plagued the beginnings of the reform—the long struggle with the Calced, and the even more grievous inner dissensions caused by the Doria-Gratian feud. Teresa's Carmelite reform had survived its initial period of agonizing birth pangs and was now ready to move into the seventeenth century, a truly golden age of enormous achievement and progress for the Discalced.

The year 1594 was a turning point in the history of the Carmelite Order. From that time forward, there have been, in actuality, two distinct Carmelite Orders, the Calced and the Discalced, each totally independent of the other, and each with its own general, its own administration, and its own legislation; and, of greatest importance, each with its own particular tradition. The Calced Carmelites continued to follow the mitigated rule of 1432, although they did eliminate the abuses of the Renaissance era, both by the post-

Tridentine reform efforts of John Rossi, and later by a French reform movement of the seventeenth century, the reform of Touraine,
which further strengthened conventual discipline and eventually
made an impact on all the Calced monasteries. However, the Calced
tradition remained fundamentally a fifteenth-century tradition, and
as such it was geared to a less austere and retired form of monastic
life and a more active and organized apostolate. In their own deriva-
tive form of Carmelite tradition, the Calced Carmelites have offered
distinguished service to the Church during the past four centuries,
and they have produced a long catalogue of celebrated and saintly
men.

The Discalced tradition, on the other hand, was basically a thirteenth-century one—"a restoration of the rule," in Teresa's words.
And as such, it has since attempted to maintain the ancient prophetic
vocation: the solitary experience of God, coupled with inspirational
and prophetic preaching. But the restoration of this thirteenth-century tradition was accomplished on the strength of Teresa's own
astonishing act of prophetic witness, and the Discalced reform therefore bears the unmistakable imprint of her personality and doctrine
—to the extent that Discalced Carmelites to this day direct their
confessional prayer in the liturgy to "Blessed Elijah and Blessed
Teresa."

This present chronicle will recount exclusively the Discalced
Carmelite story henceforth in the narrative, because our literary
point of focus has been a unique religious tradition in the history
of Christianity: the prophetic vocation—inspired by Elijah, inaugurated by the twelfth-century hermits on Mount Carmel, and revived by the incomparable Teresa of Ávila.

– VII –
EXPANSION

SEVENTEENTH-CENTURY Europe witnessed a bewildering succession of major changes: France had emerged as the strongest Continental power; the Holy Roman Empire proved itself to be, for all practical purposes, defunct; the absolutist prince had taken firm charge of his state; the Thirty Years' War, the last of the great religious wars, solidified religious affiliation in Europe, preventing the free spread of religion and paving the way for the "court religion" theory; Spain fell from its prominence as its age of glory slipped into history; and the success of commercial capitalism was elevating the whole economy. In addition, the epoch of great colonization and exploitation was under way, and European culture was being carried all over the world.

In the midst of this rapidly changing world, the Discalced reform, which until the beginning of the seventeenth century had been almost entirely restricted to Spain, now began to expand throughout Europe and eventually to the new overseas territories. Additional provinces were established all over Europe, and from 1611 until the end of the century at least two new foundations were opened every year. And this impressive expansion of the Discalced Carmelites was accomplished by a glittering array of gifted and intriguing personalities.

It was the second golden age in Carmel's history.

Nicholas Doria had stoutly resisted the expansion of the Discalced Carmelites outside the Iberian Peninsula, but yet, through a strange irony of history, he had unwittingly established a platform in Italy for the world-wide spread of the reform. He himself had carried to Spain the offer of a foundation in Genoa, which Gratian eagerly accepted, sending Doria back to make the foundation. When Doria was elected provincial in 1585, he was succeeded as prior of Genoa by Ferdinand of St. Mary (Martínez), a brilliant young Spaniard twenty-seven years of age, a graduate of the University of Salamanca, who had entered the reform eight years previously and was then only three years ordained. Under Ferdinand's capable direction the community prospered, attracting a number of Italian vocations. However, through the years Doria still sent Spanish Carmelites to help staff the single foundation in Genoa, the most important of whom was Peter of the Mother of God, destined to become the champion of expansion.

In 1590, Doria finally acquiesced to the demands of Marguerite Spinola, a wealthy Genoese widow then traveling in Spain, who had been asking him for a foundation of Discalced nuns in Genoa, promising to subsidize it from her considerable fortune. A group of nuns was sent from the convent of Malagón, arriving at Genoa in December of 1590. After Doria's death, the convent in Genoa became the mother foundation for a succession of other convents in Italy, and at Avignon in France, and at Vienna in Austria.

Peter of the Mother of God (Villagrasa) arrived at Genoa in that same year of 1590. He was born at Daroca in Aragon, entered the reform at Pastrana at the age of seventeen, and was only twenty-five when he reached Italy. He acquired an astonishing facility in the Italian language, and was soon in great demand as a preacher all over Italy, particularly in Rome. He came to the attention of a number of church dignitaries and cardinals, and eventually the pope himself, Clement VIII, the former Cardinal Aldobrandini, a kindly diplomat who was sincerely devoted to maintaining the peace in Europe and spreading the faith abroad. After Peter of the Mother of God had preached an eloquent course of Lenten sermons at the church of La Scala in the Transtevere section of Rome, the pope offered him the church as a foundation for the Carmelites; but the superiors in Spain refused the offer. However, the pope wanted the Carmelites—and particularly Peter of the Mother of God—in Rome, and he was unwilling to forsake the idea, despite the resistance from Spain. In 1597, Clement separated the Genoa monastery from the jurisdiction of the general in Spain, placing it under his immediate protection, and then brought Peter and a few other Carmelites to Rome where he gave them the church of La Scala and built a monastery for them. He also appointed Peter to the office of "apostolic preacher," the preacher at the papal court.

However, the Carmelites in Spain remained unimpressed by the pope's action, and continued to adhere to Doria's policy of non-expansion outside the Iberian Peninsula. Many theories have been offered to explain this curious position of the Spaniards during the 1590s—that, for example, Elijah of St. Martin's sole interest was re-establishing peace after the Doria regime, and he did not want to reopen old conflicts about expansion; that the Spaniards still felt they did not have enough manpower; that they were afraid of being drawn into the foreign missions, which they considered detrimental to the observance of the rule. But the most penetrating analysis, offered by a number of historians, contends that the majority of Spaniards possessed a singularly arrogant and disdainful attitude toward other Europeans, claiming that they were unable to follow the primitive rule as faithfully as the Spaniards. This disaffection for expansion, whatever its cause, was diametrically opposed to the wishes of St. Teresa, who had encouraged Gratian to send the Discalced to other parts of Europe and to the missions. Peter of the Mother of God explained Teresa's objectives to Clement VIII, and in 1600 the pope decided to break the impasse. He divided the Discalced into two distinct congregations, the Spanish and the Italian. The Spanish congregation, which was placed under the patronage of St. Joseph, embraced the territories of Spain, Portugal, and Mexico (which the Spaniards at that time called New Spain). The Italian congregation, placed under the protection of St. Elijah, was permitted to establish itself anyplace in the world except Spain. When someone objected to Clement VIII that there were only thirty Discalced friars in Italy, hardly enough to begin a program of expansion, the pope replied: "Teresa began the reform in Spain with two friars. We have thirty. God will help us." Clement VIII had developed a deep affection for the Discalced friars, and in the brief of 1600 he stated that he had seen from his own observation "how greatly these religious by their prayers, mortification, and austerity, on the one hand, and their preaching, confessing, and administration of the sacraments on the other, were useful to the church and contributed daily to God's glory and the welfare of souls."

This arrangement seemed perfectly agreeable to the Carmelites in Spain, and for more than two centuries they confined themselves to the Iberian Peninsula, except for the Mexican foundations, and the Portuguese missions which were pressed on them by the king of Portugal in the middle of the seventeenth century, and the one group of nuns sent to France in 1604. The Spaniards did not join the Italians until 1875 when the Order was rebuilding after the suppressions of the revolutionary period in Europe; and from that time the Spaniards entered enthusiastically into missionary and expansionary endeavors.

In May of 1605, nine Carmelites assembled at La Scala in Rome to hold the first chapter of the Italian congregation. Ferdinand of St. Mary was elected general, and Peter of the Mother of God was appointed procurator for the missions. All of the chapter fathers then volunteered to go to any mission territory where obedience might send them, a promise which is still taken by all Discalced Carmelites each year when they renew their vows.

The Discalced developed rapidly in Italy. Monasteries were established at Milan, Savona, Parma, Turin, and a second monastery in both Rome and Genoa. In 1607, four Carmelites arrived at the first mission in Persia, and in 1605 four friars were sent to Poland where, beginning with a monastery at Cracow, they founded nine monasteries in a few years. Vocations from all over Europe began to apply to the two novitiates at Rome and Genoa, and many of these friars later returned to their own countries as part of the various expansion groups sent out by the Italian congregation. The writings of St. Teresa, then being circulated for the first time in northern Europe, played a major part in attracting vocations to her Discalced reform. Peter of the Mother of God, however, had devised a more expeditious plan for obtaining additional friars; he encouraged the pope to summon a number of Discalced directly from Spain, men of exceptional talent whom Peter had known before he came to Italy. Thus in the space of a few years some of the most gifted Spanish Carmelites were summarily brought to Rome, the most outstanding of whom were Thomas of Jesus and Dominic of Jesus and Mary. Thomas of Jesus, in fact, received a secret brief from the pope which commanded him to leave Spain immediately without informing his superiors or confreres. He left Spain disguised in secular clothes, and after his departure he was accused of being a fugitive and a canonical process was inaugurated against him, which was later dropped after the facts came to light.

When Peter of the Mother of God first came to Rome he discovered a group of nuns who called themselves Discalced Carmelites living on the Pincian Hill. These nuns, whose only connection with the Order was an acquaintance with the writings of St. Teresa, had been founded by a Spanish Oratorian, Francis de Soto. Peter took the disorganized community in hand, instructed it in the Carmelite traditions, and officially incorporated it into the Order. The convent, which soon became one of the most celebrated in the Eternal City, was expertly guided by Peter, and later by Jerome Gratian during the years he spent in Rome following his release from captivity in North Africa. The Roman convent and the Genoese convent were the nucleus for the expansion of the nuns in Italy and southern Europe. The development of the Carmelite nuns throughout all of Europe was stimulated considerably by the beatification of Teresa in 1614. The friars usually preceded the nuns to the new areas of expansion, except in France and Flanders, and prepared the way for them.

Peter of the Mother of God continued in his role of confidential advisor to the pope under Clement's successor, Paul V, who named him "Superintendent of the Missions" throughout the Catholic world. In 1608 he was elected general of the Italian congregation, but in the same year he died at the premature age of forty-three. He passed away at Nocera in Italy where he had gone to take the baths, apparently as a cure for a severe arthritic condition. When the news of his death was relayed to Paul V, who was at the moment presiding at a consistory, he exclaimed: "A great pillar of the Church has fallen." In addition to his gifts as an orator, Peter was a man of engaging affability and great friendliness, and it is largely due to his personality that the Order was able to develop so rapidly outside Spain. He was also a saintly man, and the historian Cardinal Baronius, a contemporary, wrote of him that "scarcely anyone was considered more holy at that time in Rome."

Dominic of Jesus and Mary succeeded to Peter's position as Superintendent of the Missions, and among his many other interests, he worked indefatigably for a more systematized and organized approach to the missions throughout the world. It is chiefly due to his labors, plus the efforts of Peter of the Mother of God and Thomas of Jesus, that in 1622 Gregory XV founded the *Propaganda Fidei*, the Congregation for the Propagation of the Faith. Ferdinand of St. Mary became the major figure in the government of the Italian congregation after Peter's death. He was occupied in administration during most of his life, and was elected general three separate times. Although he was a more reserved and

austere personality than Peter, he did possess much of Peter's
kindliness and friendliness. He died at Frascati in 1631 at the age
of seventy-three during his last term as general.

The most celebrated Discalced friar in Europe during the seventeenth century was the amazing Thomas of Jesus. A man of wide
interests, he was engaged at one time or another in all the major
enterprises undertaken by the reform in the seventeenth century,
and his life and personality epitomize the Carmelite during the
golden age.

Diego Sánchez Davila was born at Baeza in Andalusia in 1564.
He studied at the University of Baeza, where he received a degree
in the humanities at an unusually early age. He continued his
studies at Salamanca, obtaining doctorates in both law and theology.
After hearing one of his professors extol Teresa of Ávila, he obtained
a copy of her writings, then available only in holographic copies,
and became so impressed with her doctrine that he decided to enter
the reform. He took the habit at Valladolid in 1586, adopting the
name of Thomas of Jesus, and made his profession a year later in
the presence of Jerome Gratian. Thomas was a man of extraordinary
intelligence with an amazing capability for research and synthesis,
but with an even greater gift for original and independent thinking,
freshly and creatively expressed. He was a gentle, friendly person,
and he was apparently quite witty. All his life he suffered from
delicate health, and at various times he was plagued with insomnia.

After his ordination, he was sent to teach at Seville, and while
there he began to study Carmel's now long-abandoned custom of
establishing a few monasteries of complete solitude and contemplation. From his research he conceived the idea of the Carmelite
"desert," a project that was destined to become, as we shall see, an
important part of the Order's development in the seventeenth century. In Thomas' plan, each province would have a desert monastery,
staffed by four permanent members; other friars of the province
could volunteer to live at the desert for a year's time—thus there
would be a permanent community, with perhaps an even larger
group of temporary members. The deserts would be constructed in
the tradition of the original thirteenth-century foundations: solitary
religious living separated from each other and assembling only for
religious services and meals. Absolute silence was to be maintained,
and there would be no apostolate. Thomas showed his plan to

Nicholas Doria, but the general rejected it, mainly because he felt that the desert would attract the best men in the Order and leave the other monasteries sorely depleted.

In 1591, Thomas of Jesus was sent to Alcalá de Henares as a professor of theology, and he explained his desert plan to the superior, John of Jesus and Mary (Aravalles), who became an enthusiastic supporter of the project. With John's help the proposal was submitted to a meeting of Doria's definitory, and the motion passed. In 1592, a remote piece of property was acquired at Bolarque on the Tagus River a few miles from Pastrana, and the first desert community was established. However, Thomas of Jesus, still teaching at Alcalá, was not assigned to the foundation. (It was at Bolarque that Doria made his retreat in 1594, a few weeks before he died.) Thomas was elected provincial of Castile in 1597, and during his administration he founded a desert at Las Batuecas in the rather wild region of Las Hurdes near Salamanca. After his term as provincial he was elected the prior of Las Batuecas, and spent three years there in the eremitical life until he was elected prior of Zaragoza. It was during his term at Zaragoza that he received the brief from the pope in 1607 to leave Spain and join the Italian congregation.

The second phase of Thomas' life began in Rome—his efforts for the work of the foreign missions. He became deeply involved with the missionary spirit that was prevalent in the Italian congregation, and although he volunteered for the missions, especially for the Congo mission, he himself never reached the mission territories. But he did become a close associate of Paul V, and worked with him as an advisor in missionary matters. During his years in Rome, Thomas began a monumental study of missiology, the first major work of that kind attempted in the Church, turning his rare talent and unique genius to this neglected field. He researched deeply through the Vatican libraries and consulted various authorities in Rome, and from his studies and original thinking resulted two books about the missionary apostolate. The first, *Stimulus missionum*, the shorter of the two works, was an appeal for greater interest in the work of the foreign missions, and was published at the command of Paul V in 1610. The other, *De procuranda salute omnium gentium* (On Procuring the Salvation of All Nations), was begun in Rome and published in Antwerp in 1613 while Thomas was working in the northern countries. The *De procuranda*, a massive volume of almost a thousand quarto pages, is a work of genius, a classic study far in advance of its time. Thomas' book discusses the selection and training of future missionaries, with special stress on cultural and linguistic studies of the regions where the future missionary is to work; the method for missionary work; the mentality of the various peoples in mission areas—Moslems, Jews, Greeks, Russians; a system of finance for defraying the cost of the missions; and the establishment of special mission seminaries. He also strongly encouraged the foundation of a "Congregation of Propaganda," a small group of eminent and expert men residing in Rome and meeting on fixed days to study the missionary endeavors in the different regions and then offer help and assistance and direction. He outlined the structure of this Congregation in great detail, noting that the success of the project would depend on obtaining specialists in language and national culture to serve as secretaries for the individual mission areas. Gregory XV used Thomas' work as a master plan for the *Propaganda Fidei* established in 1622, although he unfortunately did not incorporate a number of key ideas. Gregory XV made special mention of the Carmelites' unique missionary contribution in his bull promulgating the foundation of the *Propaganda*.

In 1610, Thomas of Jesus led a group of friars to Brussels, after Anne of Jesus, who had been there since 1606, appealed directly to Rome for the establishment of the Discalced friars in the Lowlands. He founded monasteries at Brussels, Douai, Lille, Liége, and Antwerp, and when these northern houses were erected into a province in 1617 he was made the first provincial. He also led a group to Cologne in 1613 for the first German foundation. In 1619 he founded a desert monastery in the forest of Marlagne near Namur. His crowning work in the north was the establishment of a missionary seminary at Louvain in 1621 where Carmelites were specially trained for work in Holland, England, and Ireland.

During all those busy and active years Thomas continued to write, and by the time of his death he had completed thirty books. In addition to his writings on the missions, he wrote on the history of the Order, the primitive rule, the scapular, and some biographical studies. In the later part of his life he devoted himself to studies on prayer and the mystical life. Two of his first efforts in that field—*Compendium of the Degrees of Mental Prayer* and *Treatise on Mental Prayer*—enjoyed considerable success in his lifetime following their publication in Rome. His *Method of Divine Prayer*, published at Antwerp in 1623, was a major work on mystical theology and has exercised a continuing influence in the field since his time. Thomas of Jesus carefully followed the doctrine of St. Teresa in his writings, and he attempted to correlate it with the teaching of the Scholastics, but his own originality and creativity breaks through at every turn. At the command of Urban VIII his writings were collected and they were later published at Cologne in 1684.

His health began to deteriorate in the Lowlands, and finally in 1623 he retired to the monastery at La Scala in Rome where he was given the office of definitor general. He died a saintly death at the age of sixty-three on May 24, 1627. Thomas of Jesus was a true genius, accomplishing in the span of his sixty-three years what it would take an ordinary man of talent four lifetimes to achieve— the writer, the originator of the deserts, the sponsor of the missions, the founder of the northern monasteries. Men of his caliber are rare in any epoch.

The extension of the Order into France was accomplished in unusual circumstances and involved a group of interesting historical personalities. The first attempt to introduce the reform in France occurred in 1585 as a result of the efforts of an obscure young Frenchman named Jean de Quintanadoine de Brétigny (called by historians M. de Brétigny). This frail youth had been sent to Spain in 1582 by his wealthy family in order to rehabilitate his health. He remained ten years, and during that time he made the acquaintance of Mary of St. Joseph, the prioress of the Carmel at Seville, and decided that he must somehow introduce the Carmelite nuns into France. Brétigny presented his proposal to Jerome Gratian, who was then near the end of his term as provincial. Gratian, in turn, raised the question at the chapter of 1585, and the chapter fathers, including John of the Cross, approved the French foundation. However, Doria became provincial at that chapter, and as we know, he was not interested in expansion outside Spain. In an interview with the young Brétigny, Doria temporized and told him that he would not even consider sending nuns to France unless the friars preceded them there. Brétigny knew that the French, who were extremely hostile to Spain at that epoch because of Philip II's policies on the Continent, would not be likely to admit Spanish priests into France. Nevertheless he made a petition to the French king, Henry III; he did not even receive an answer, and the whole matter died. Brétigny, however, never abandoned hope that the Carmelite nuns would someday come to his homeland, and after he had returned to France and had been ordained a priest he collaborated with Père du Chevre, prior of the Carthusian monastery of Bourgfontaine, in translating the writings of Teresa. In 1601 this translation was read aloud in the famous salon in Paris on the rue des Juifs, the home of Madame Acarie, one of the major figures in French religious history, who herself was to join the Carmelites in her later years and become known as Blessed Mary of the Incarnation.

Barbe Avrillot was born in Paris on February 1, 1566, at the Avrillot residence on the rue Saint-Bon. Her family belonged to the *noblesse de robe* and had considerable wealth. The young Barbe felt an early attraction to the religious life; but after her family strongly opposed the idea, she finally married a rich and attractive young nobleman at the age of sixteen and a half. She was deeply in love with her husband, Pierre Acarie, a charming, urbane, yet quite religious young man who was twenty-two years old when they married. The young couple moved into the Acarie residence on the rue des Juifs, and they eventually had six children. Madame Acarie proved herself a good housewife, educating her children wisely and managing her household and staff with great competence. She and her husband circulated in the most fashionable of social circles, and the young Madame Acarie was an instant success. She was gay, high-spirited, and uncommonly beautiful, a handsome woman with green eyes, chestnut hair, and colorful complexion. The Parisians called her *la belle Acarie* (the beautiful Acarie).

Pierre Acarie was delighted with his attractive and popular wife, and he seemed quite satisfied with the situation until one day he happened to examine some of the books she was reading and he became profoundly disturbed. The book which upset him the most was *Amadis de Gaule*, an amorous novel, rather tame by modern standards, but considered quite scandalous in the France of Acarie's time. Pierre Acarie began to fear that his ebullient wife was becoming too much of the gay *Parisienne*, and after consulting a priest, he threw away her books and substituted some pious and devotional literature in their place. Dutifully, Barbe Acarie began to read the new books, and they effected a change in her that her husband could hardly have expected. A statement from St. Augustine quoted in one of the books seemed to have the greatest impact on the young housewife: "He is indeed a miser for whom God is not enough."

Madame Acarie suddenly decided to make God the ultimate end of all her endeavors, and she embarked on a determined spiritual program which soon led her to the heights of mystic prayer.

The most intriguing element in the conversion of *la belle Acarie* is that it caused little change in her relationship with her family. She devoted more time to prayer, she embarked on a variety of charitable works in the city of Paris, and her salon became the visiting place for the most important religious figures in France. But she remained the loving and devoted wife, the faithful and tender mother of her children, and the careful manager of her household. She had three children at the time of her conversion, and she was to have three more afterward. She continued to heap affection on Pierre Acarie, and she nursed him lovingly during his final illness. She was a rare model of mystic and housewife.

The phenomenon of the Acarie salon on the rue des Juifs was truly extraordinary. Within a few years it became the spiritual center of Paris, the meeting place for the leading figures of the religious revival that was occurring in French Catholic circles after the bellicose years of the Huguenot conflicts. The Acarie home was frequented by people like Francis de Sales, Vincent de Paul, André Duval, Jacques Gallement, and Barbe's young cousin Pierre de Bérulle. The attracting force in all of this was the handsome young housewife, now in her later twenties, who was exerting the same kind of magnetic influence in religious circles that she had previously exercised in the social world. But Barbe was more than just a hostess: she herself was the magnet which drew people from all walks of life—eminent ecclesiastics, doctors from the Sorbonne, religious leaders, and even the poor and the troubled and the forsaken, all of whom came to seek her advice and the insights she had gained from her own inner life of prayer. Francis de Sales, for instance, visited the Acarie salon every day that he was in Paris. Barbe's influence also extended outside the confines of her own home: she maintained a residence for fallen women, she was responsible, by her advice and encouragement, for the reform of a number of religious houses in Paris, and she laid the foundations for the establishment of the Ursuline community. Pierre Acarie bore his wife's activities with amiable good humor, and it is interesting to note that a number of ecclesiastics resented the time and affection she lavished on her husband, regarding it as time lost for more important enterprises. But

Barbe was too good a wife, and too much in love with Pierre, to let herself be drawn away from her family.

M. de Brétigny was one of the habitués of the Acarie salon, and it appears that his purpose in having St. Teresa's works read aloud to Madame Acarie was to stimulate interest in his unfulfilled dream of bringing the Carmelite nuns to France. However, Barbe Acarie, then thirty-five years old, was not impressed with Teresa's writings when she first heard them. But as the reading progressed she began to experience the impact of Teresa's personality and message. Her close friend and first biographer, André Duval, relates what happened next:

> The blessed Teresa appeared to her visibly and informed her of what was God's will for her in these words: "Just as I enriched Spain with this renowned Order so must you, who are bringing piety back to France, endeavor to let the country experience this benefit."

Barbe related the vision to her confessor, the Carthusian Ricard Beaucosin, who regarded it as genuine and then summoned a group of priests to discuss the practicability of introducing the Carmelite nuns into France. They decided against the project because they felt the political tensions between Spain and Henry IV were so great that there seemed to be no hope of obtaining the king's consent to bring Spanish nuns into the country. Barbe put the project out of her mind as best she could, but seven or eight months later she had another vision of Teresa who demanded quite insistently that she start the foundation, promising that all the difficulties would be overcome. Another meeting was summoned at which Barbe herself was present, and the group, which included Francis de Sales and Bérulle, now approved the project. They agreed, however, that in view of the political circumstances the nuns would have to be governed by a group of French diocesan priests rather than by foreign Carmelite friars, and they nominated Gallement, Duval, and Bérulle as the three superiors. Francis de Sales wrote directly to Pope Clement VIII petitioning for approval of the plan, and he cited the convent on the Pincian Hill in Rome as a precedent for a convent of Carmelite nuns established without the assistance and direction of the friars. The pope gave his consent, and to everyone's surprise Henry IV agreed quite readily.

Pierre de Bérulle quickly emerged as the strongest of the triumvirate which was to govern the nuns, and as future events were to prove, he had personal interests in the foundation quite foreign to those of Barbe Acarie. Bérulle, later to become a cardinal and the founder of the French Oratory, has exercised a continuing influence on French Catholic life, but he himself was an enigmatic figure. Born in 1575 in the province of Champagne, he came from a distinguished family of magistrates. He studied at the Sorbonne, was ordained in 1599 at the age of twenty-four, and almost immediately became involved with the group that frequented his cousin's salon. He was small of stature, rather nervous and ill at ease in his mannerisms, but nevertheless a quite determined person. Bremond in his classic A *Literary History of Religious Thought in France* describes him: "Bérulle, at first sight is not impressive, bland, slow, naïve, clumsy even in his diplomatic moves, he has neither the *grand air* nor natural charm." He was a sincerely religious man, and he formed the mentality of the French priesthood for more than two centuries both by his own Oratorians and by the Society of St. Sulpice, founded by one of his disciples, Jean Olier. However, he could be somewhat ruthless in pursuing his goals and quite insensitive to the feelings and ideas of others. Bremond says that "he made straight for his end, looking neither to right nor left, resolute, steadfast, and tense." Bérulle had been formulating plans in his mind for the foundation of an order of women, which he was planning to call "The Order of Jesus and Mary," but when his cousin Barbe started on her Carmelite project he decided that he could perhaps better achieve his objectives with an already established religious order. Barbe apparently knew nothing of this at the time the negotiations for the nuns were going on.

When word was relayed to the general of the Spanish congregation, Francis of the Mother of God (who had succeeded Elijah of St. Martin in 1600), that approval had been granted for a group of nuns to come to Paris, he adamantly refused to grant his consent. He suggested, as an alternative, that Barbe contact the Italian congregation and obtain nuns from them; but at that time there were only two convents in Italy, and the one on the Pincian Hill, which had not as yet been reorganized by Peter of the Mother of God, was less than authentically Carmelite. Furthermore, Barbe wanted nuns in France who had been associated with Teresa during her lifetime. A stalemate developed, and Barbe began to lose hope that she would ever obtain nuns from Spain. She had already begun construction of a convent in the Faubourg Saint-Jacques, and she had seven women waiting to enter the Order. For a while she toyed with the idea of starting the convent with the seven French women, but then she rejected it: she must have women who had been trained as Carmelite nuns for the nucleus of this first foundation.

In 1603, M. de Brétigny was sent to Spain, accompanied by a group of distinguished French ladies who went, ostensibly, to accompany the nuns back to France. It was thought that Brétigny, with his knowledge of Spain and his contacts with the Carmelites, would be able to break the impasse. But he was completely unsuccessful and six months later Bérulle himself journeyed south to settle the matter.[1] Bérulle arrived in Spain carrying a brief from the pope which commanded the Spanish general to release a group of six nuns. For some reason the papal brief stated that the nuns were to be selected from convents in Portugal, but Bérulle was careful to conceal that fact from the Carmelites. The general had to comply with the brief, but he took some petty revenge on Bérulle by assigning a group of particularly untalented and uninspiring nuns. Bérulle, however, stood his ground and insisted that he have nuns who had lived with Teresa. At length, he approached the French ambassador in Madrid, and through him he obtained a decree from the papal nuncio threatening excommunication to the Carmelite general unless he gave Bérulle the nuns he wanted. The general now had to submit completely, and Bérulle, with the help of Brétigny, selected the six best nuns he could find. The group included Anne of Jesus and Anne of St. Bartholomew. The elated Bérulle wrote back to

[1] During his trip to Spain Bérulle met the celebrated lay brother, Francis of the Infant Jesus, at the Carmelite monastery in Alcalá, and expressed his admiration for this modest man who in the space of a few years had become known all over Spain. Francis Sánchez was born near Toledo in 1544, and after working as a sexton in a church he entered the Order at Madrid. A person of great piety and simplicity, he was able to solicit funds for the construction of a hospital at Alcalá and a home for fallen women in Madrid. He was on terms of friendship with King Philip III, whom he addressed as "my elder brother." Francis' reputation even reached Rome, and Pope Clement VIII wrote to him and recommended the Church to his prayers. He died in Madrid in December of 1604. Francis was presented to Bérulle by Joseph of Jesus and Mary, the provincial of Castile, who was to become the humble lay brother's first biographer. This biography, which particularly recounts Francis' deep devotion to the Infant Jesus, was widely read in Spain and France during the seventeenth and eighteenth centuries, and it became one of the favorite books of St. Margaret Mary Alacoque.

Barbe: "Were Teresa alive today she could not give France better Carmelites, unless she should come herself."

The nuns, accompanied by Bérulle, Brétigny, the French ladies, and two Carmelite friars the general had assigned to make the trip, left Ávila on August 29, 1604, and arrived at the outskirts of Paris on October 15. The coach carrying the nuns rumbled over the pont Notre-Dame, and was met by a coach carrying Madame Acarie. They exchanged salutations from the coaches, and then proceeded to Saint-Denise where they all alighted to greet each other. It is a scene to intrigue the most sober of historians, the first meeting of these two women of legendary beauty: *la belle Acarie* and "the queen of women." Unfortunately we have no details of that meeting, nor of their first impressions of each other.

Two days later the nuns were installed in the new convent at the end of the rue Saint-Jacques. Construction had not been completed, and the nuns were only able to use part of the building until the following summer. Yet they began their observance immediately, and a few days later three of the women Barbe had been preparing for the convent were invested in the habit by Michael of St. Firmin, the provincial of Catalonia, one of the friars who had accompanied the nuns to France. Within the next few months the remaining four women were brought into the convent. Anne of Jesus, the prioress, wanted the convent to be dedicated to St. Joseph, but Bérulle, significantly, demanded that it be called the Incarnation, and his view prevailed.

Barbe and Anne of Jesus became close friends, and the prioress found that she had an invaluable ally in the woman who exercised such influence in Paris from her salon and who was able to direct good vocations and donations to the new Carmel. They also found that they had a common antagonist: Pierre de Bérulle. As soon as the nuns were installed in Paris, Bérulle made it quite clear that he alone wanted to govern the nuns and impress his own particular ideas about religion on them. He had been especially annoyed at the two Carmelite friars who had journeyed to France with them, and had written to Barbe from Spain asking her to have the nuncio in France halt the two friars at the French border and make them return. Barbe ignored the letter. Their presence for two weeks in Paris unnerved him, and he became even more agitated when he received a report that Henry IV, then at the castle in Fontainebleau for a short stay, had remarked that the two friars need not hurry back to Spain because he intended to give them a house in Paris shortly. Henry was due to return to Paris the following day, and Bérulle hurriedly arranged transportation for the two friars and spirited them out of the city. Anne of Jesus had been under the impression that the triumvirate rule of the nuns would only be a temporary arrangement until the friars were able to locate in France, but Bérulle assured her that it was permanent. It seemed to Anne that she had been through all this once before, and she immediately extracted a promise from Bérulle that he would not attempt to tamper with the constitutions of Teresa. But he had other plans for inserting his practices of French piety into the nuns' daily schedule. Anne of Jesus, who had withstood and outlasted a Nicholas Doria, was not intimidated by a Pierre de Bérulle, and she resisted him at every turn. However, it was Barbe Acarie who was to carry on the struggle against Bérulle and eventually defeat him.

An astonishing number of women applied to the new Carmel in the rue Saint-Jacques, and in January of 1605 a second foundation was made at Pontoise. Anne of St. Bartholomew was, against her protests, raised to the rank of choir sister, and named the foundress and first prioress of Pontoise. In September of that same year another foundation was made at Dijon, and Anne of Jesus led the group, while Anne of St. Bartholomew was recalled to Paris to take her place as prioress. Thus within a year of their arrival in France the nuns had three convents. Anne of Jesus, however, was not satisfied with the situation in France: she wanted the direction of the Carmelite friars. In December of 1606, after having made arrangements with her friend the Princess Isabel Clara Eugenia, in Flanders, Anne of Jesus led a group to make a foundation in Brussels. She took two of the original Spanish nuns with her, and within five years all but one of the original Spanish nuns had migrated to the Lowlands. Bérulle was not sorry to see them go. He now had only Barbe Acarie to contend with.

Barbe was forty in 1606, and she was witnessing her children grow up and leave the family household on the rue des Juifs. Three of her daughters became Carmelite nuns, and one of her sons was ordained a priest. But her son Nicholas made her a grandmother for the first time in 1608. In that same year she and Pierre found that all their children had departed and they were alone in their home. They seemed to grow even closer in those last years of their marriage as Barbe continued her charitable works and Pierre accompanied her wherever she went. Barbe's health had been poor since a serious illness in 1606, and a broken leg which never healed properly made her more dependent on her husband. However, it was Pierre who died first. He became ill in October of 1613 while they were at their country house at Ivry, and Barbe watched around the clock during the four weeks that he lingered. Her friends pleaded with her to spare herself, but as one witness reported, "her affection for him outweighed every other consideration." As the end approached Duval noted that more than once she broke down completely in the priest's presence. Pierre remained conscious until within an hour of his death, and Barbe sat beside him, talking to him, praying with him. He died on November 16. He and Barbe had been happily married for thirty-one years. The body was taken back to Paris and buried in the family chapel in the Church of Saint-Gervais.

Barbe's major external preoccupation during those latter years of her marriage was the progress of the Carmelite nuns in France. Foundations continued to multiply quickly: after the convents of Pontoise and Dijon, Amiens was established in 1606, Tours in 1608, Rouen in 1609, Bordeaux and Chalon in 1610, and Besançon in 1614. However, Bérulle was becoming more troublesome for the nuns, and after Anne of Jesus' departure Barbe had to carry on the fight against him alone. The basic point of dispute was the Teresian spirit versus the "Bérullian" spirit. In comparing the two, Bremond says that Teresa's spirit was "simpler, more human, more mystical, and more universal." Bérulle believed in a multiplicity of pious practices sprinkled throughout the day and centered chiefly around the Eucharist, and his piety was therefore rather mechanical and contrived. Bérullian spirituality performed a vital service in sustaining the French clergy during difficult times, but it inserted a somewhat artificial and pietistic flavor in French Catholic life throughout the eighteenth and nineteenth centuries. Bérulle wanted the Carmelite nuns, for instance, to maintain perpetual exposition and adoration of the Blessed Sacrament. Barbe opposed him on this and other practices, and she actually had more influence in French religious circles from her prestigious position in her salon than Bérulle had in his office of superior of the nuns. Francis de Sales supported her, and she was able to make her views known to the nuns, who then rejected Bérulle's recommendations.

Bérulle founded his Oratorians in 1611, and from that time he strived even more strenuously to make the Carmelite nuns a female branch of his congregation. However in 1613 Barbe discredited him immeasurably in the case of Madeleine de la Rochepot, a young girl who had entered the convent in Paris. Bérulle was deeply impressed with the girl and thought he discerned in her the signs of an extraordinary vocation. During her novitiate year she had some unusual manifestations which Bérulle promptly diagnosed as a diabolical possession sent to test her vocation. Barbe said the girl was a hysteric and should be dismissed immediately. Since Barbe had convinced the community at Paris of her viewpoint, Bérulle transferred the girl to the Carmel of Pontoise and told the nuns to admit her to profession. Barbe took her fight to the nuns at Pontoise, and they finally decided to dismiss Madeleine de la Rochepot. Subsequent events in Madeleine's career proved that Barbe had been perfectly correct.

After her husband's death in 1613, Barbe was taken ill, exhausted from the long vigils beside Pierre, but as she regained her strength she decided that she would seek admission to one of the Carmels as a lay sister. Her friend André Duval approved of the idea, but he strongly recommended that she become a choir sister. But Barbe remained adamant in her desire to serve God in a low station and in a Carmel far from Paris where she was so well known. She chose Amiens, and in February of 1614, at the age of forty-eight, she entered the convent. The former *grande dame* of Paris society was assigned to the kitchen where she performed her duties humbly and cheerfully. In April she was formally invested with the Carmelite habit, adopting the name Mary of the Incarnation, and after the ceremony she remained in a prayer of ecstasy for two hours. Her biographer Duval then adds, laconically: "When the ecstasy was over, she went off to the kitchen to help prepare the dinner."

Barbe was completely successful as a Carmelite nun, and she demonstrated marked signs of an advanced holiness. Despite her position as a lay sister, she was asked to give spiritual direction to the younger nuns of the community, and she did so, reluctantly but expertly. In the spring of 1616, there was an election for a new prioress of the convent, and notwithstanding her position as a lay sister, she was elected prioress. But she refused the office, saying: "A fine prioress I would make." In her place was elected Anne of the Blessed Sacrament, a friend of Bérulle and a strange woman who almost immediately embarked on a campaign to embarrass and humiliate Barbe. She forbade her to give any further spiritual advice to the nuns, and she made caustic and insulting remarks to her on every possible occasion. Barbe's biographer remarks, however, that "she gave no sign of any discontent." Some commentators have explained this cruel and inexcusable action of the prioress as deriving from her disappointment at being a secondary selection for the office of prioress, while others maintain that it was done at the direct command of Bérulle. News of the harsh treatment reached Paris, and Jacques Gallement, in collaboration with Duval, transferred Barbe to the convent of Pontoise in December of 1616. When she arrived in Pontoise she knelt at the feet of her new prioress and said: "I have come to give you much trouble, for wherever I go I am always the cause of it."

Bérulle, apparently feeling more confident now that Barbe was in the convent away from Paris, began to press his campaign more strongly again. One of his new ideas was that the Carmelite nuns should make a special vow of servitude to Our Lady. It was a typical Bérullian artifice, and when Barbe heard of it she protested against it strongly. Duval and Gallement visited Barbe, and she carefully outlined her reasons against the vow and the steps that should be taken to thwart it. Bérulle's vow was a long, intricate pietism, covering almost three pages of small type, and it was condemned by both the Universities of Louvain and Douai, and by the distinguished Jesuit theologian Lessius, on the grounds that it was obscure, unnecessary, and full of clauses that could cause needless scruples. Francis de Sales also disapproved of it, and Cardinal Bellarmine in Rome later condemned it. The defeat of Bérulle's vow was the blow that marked the disintegration of any hopes he had to control the spirit of the Carmelite nuns in France. Thanks to Barbe's continuing efforts the nuns remained Teresian and not Bérullian. (Bremond has remarked: "If our Carmelites were no more than Bérullians they would interest me little.") The only major and enduring effect that Bérulle was able to accomplish with the nuns in France is that they have remained under the jurisdiction and direction of local clergy rather than the Discalced friars.

In February of 1618, Bérulle called at the Carmel of Pontoise to confront Barbe, the woman who had so successfully blocked his plans. The chronicles of the Pontoise convent relate that "he treated her with asperity and spoke with equal harshness against M. Gallement and M. Duval." Barbe retorted: "They are servants of God as you are, and they uphold what is right for them to uphold." The interview lasted several hours, and the prioress, fearing that Barbe would collapse, entered the parlor to rescue her. She heard some of the reproaches that Bérulle was heaping on Barbe—"among others, that hers was a petty mind, that she was mistaken, and that she has mismanaged everything she had undertaken."

A few days after Bérulle's visit, Barbe was put to bed with an illness which developed into pneumonia. Duval visited her, and she related what Bérulle had said to her. Then she concluded: "And that, Father, is what I am." As Duval was leaving the infirmary, he commented to the prioress about Bérulle's conduct: "God wills suffering for this holy soul, and for me as well. We can only resign ourselves to it. But what words! What violence!"

Barbe's illness was her final one. She lingered from early February until April 18, suffering intensely from cerebral hemorrhages, partial paralysis, and finally violent convulsions. Her last words, spoken to her prioress, were: "À Dieu, ma mère." She was fifty-two when she died, but the witnesses stated that immediately after her death her features relaxed and she seemed to be once again the young beauty who had captivated Paris. In 1791, Pius VI formally beatified la belle Acarie, a woman of uncommon beauty and uncommon life.

Anne of Jesus found conditions much more satisfactory in Flanders. She was received warmly by her old friend Princess Isabel Clara, the daughter of Philip II, who pledged her complete support for any project Anne might undertake. A few days after the nuns' arrival in Brussels, a Mass was offered in their temporary residence by the papal nuncio and attended by the princess and her husband, the regent Archduke Albert; and three years later the nuns moved into a permanent convent which the princess had constructed for them, the famous "royal Carmel" of Brussels. Other foundations followed rapidly: Louvain, Mons, Tournai, Malines, Valenciennes, Gand (Ghent), Douai, Bruges, and Lille.

Anne of St. Bartholomew remained in France during the early years of the Flemish expansion. In 1608 she left Paris to found the convent of Tours, but she was under constant pressure from Anne of Jesus in Belgium to join the Flemish group. She later wrote about her experiences in France: "I remained only seven years in that kingdom, always with the hope of returning to the jurisdiction of the Order; and when I saw no other means of doing so, I made every effort to leave the kingdom." However, she hesitated, fearing that she might be offending God by deserting France, but Bérulle settled her conscience and encouraged her to go. She arrived at Mons in 1611, and in the following year Anne of Jesus sent her to establish the foundation in Antwerp. The new Carmelite prioress soon became celebrated throughout the city of Antwerp because of her sanctity and unfailing kindness, and she was honored as a national heroine before her death. In 1622 the city of Antwerp was imperiled when Maurice Nassau, the Duke of Orange, laid siege to the city with his Dutch fleet. Anne of St. Bartholomew prayed for deliverance with outstretched arms, and a totally unexpected tempest arose which blew the Dutch out to sea and sank most of their ships. Almost the identical episode recurred two years later when the Dutch attacked again, and after Anne had again prayed with extended arms a violent storm destroyed the landing party. The Flemish people attributed their deliverance to Anne and proclaimed her "the liberator of Antwerp." Antwerp still looks to her as a special patron and protectress, and in the dark days of 1940 when an even more sinister evil descended on the city many favors were ascribed to Anne of St. Bartholomew, the former shepherd girl from Castile.

In 1619, Anne of Jesus founded a second convent in Antwerp, a Carmel for English women who were unable to lead the religious life in England because of the discriminatory penal laws. Anne selected five nuns for the original group, two of them Dutch girls and three of them English girls who had already been professed in the Flemish Carmels. She nominated Anne of the Ascension as the first prioress, the former Anne Worsley, the daughter of an aristocratic English family from the Isle of Wight which had been living in religious exile in the Lowlands. Anne had entered the Carmel of Mons in 1608 at the age of seventeen, and she was to prove an exemplary nun and an extremely competent administrator. The English Carmel at Antwerp later founded two daughter houses at Lierre and Hoogstraten, and these three houses remained the only English Carmelite convents during the next two centuries. At the end of the eighteenth century a group set out from Antwerp to make the first foundation of nuns in England, and a group from Hoogstraten departed for the United States, where the first foundation of nuns in the original thirteen colonies was made at Port Tobacco in Maryland.

One of Anne of Jesus' major objectives in coming to Flanders was to obtain the government and direction of the Discalced friars again, and soon after her arrival she began negotiations to bring friars from Spain. But when she found the Spaniards opposed to expansion, she turned to the Italian congregation for help. Archduke Albert petitioned the general in Italy, and Anne herself wrote directly to the pope, requesting that Discalced friars be sent to Flanders. In 1610, Thomas of Jesus set out for Brussels, accompanied by three other Carmelite friars. On their arrival they were given an enthusiastic reception by the people of Brussels, and within a few years they built for themselves a reputation of enormous proportions. Princess Isabel Clara said of them: "Since the arrival of the Discalced Carmelites I cannot recognize the court; I believe it is quite reformed." A second monastery of friars was established at Louvain in 1611, and within a few years more than forty young students from the university joined the Carmelites. Other monasteries were founded in rapid succession at Douai, Lille, Liége, and Anvers; and by the year 1652 there were twenty-four monasteries of friars in the Lowlands. In addition, a successful mission was established at The Hague and Amsterdam in Holland, which had become extremely inimical to Catholics since the arrogant policies of Philip II and his lieutenant, the Duke of Alba. Thomas of Jesus also brought the Flemish Carmelite convents under the jurisdiction of the Order, and he served as their first provincial.

At the same time the friars were establishing themselves in France. A monastery had been founded at Avignon in 1608, but this was in papal territory, not under the jurisdiction of the French king. In 1610 the Carmelites in Rome asked Pope Paul V to intercede for them with Henry IV, and the pope wrote to the king asking him to receive into his kingdom "his dear sons the Discalced Carmelite friars, who in Rome and all over Italy had given such splendid examples of fervor and virtue, by their penance, their preaching and hearing of confessions, and their zeal in so many holy works which accomplish so much good for faithful souls." Henry IV, who had shown himself surprisingly and unexpectedly amenable to all petitions concerning the Discalced Carmelites, acceded to the pope's request and wrote directly to the general in Rome, inviting the friars to Paris. The general wisely selected two Frenchmen for the foundation, Denis of the Mother of God and Bernard of St. Joseph, men who had made their novitiate at La Scala in Rome. Thomas of Jesus included these two Frenchmen in the group he was leading to

Brussels in 1610, and after he had deposited them in Paris he continued his journey to the Lowlands. The decision to select only Frenchmen for this foundation was an extremely prudent one, because the French people, despite the king's invitation, were not particularly cordial to foreign priests.

Denis of the Mother of God (Chevalier de Salagourde) was born at Bordeaux in 1575, and he went to Rome as a young man to study art. However, he did not work very diligently at it and he became somewhat of a bohemian. A chance reading of St. Teresa's writings brought about a radical conversion in his life, and at the age of twenty-five he entered the Carmelite monastery at La Scala. He eventually became the first provincial of the French province. Bernard of St. Joseph (Louis de Genouillac), born near Bordeaux in 1582, was a nobleman, the Count de Vaillac. He became a member of the aristocratic French colony in Rome, and he caused a minor stir in the city because of a well-publicized duel from which he emerged victorious. A serious illness presented him with an opportunity to reflect on his life, and after he regained his health he joined the Carmelites. His profession of vows was a major social event for the French colony, which found it difficult to believe that the dashing young nobleman had embraced the monastic life.

These two young Carmelites laid the foundation for the French province. In 1611 they obtained property on the rue de Vaugirard, and over the years built the famous monastery and church, which is still standing today. French vocations came rapidly, and a second monastery was founded at Nancy. A novitiate was established in 1617 at Charenton, the site of the original thirteenth-century foundation, and the first prior was Clement of St. Mary (Gaspard de Faverge), a convert from Protestantism, and a great-nephew of John Calvin. Other monasteries were started in succeeding years at Lyons, Meaux, Toulouse, Limoges, Bordeaux, and Marseille. There were sixteen new monasteries in the first twenty-five years, and a total of thirty-five by the end of the century.

One of the most celebrated of the French Carmelites during the seventeenth century was Lawrence of the Resurrection, a lay brother at the monastery on rue de Vaugirard in Paris. Nicholas Herman was born in Lorraine around the year 1614, and he became a soldier during the Thirty Years' War. After he was wounded, captured, and then released, this devout man in his forties returned to Paris and entered the Carmelites. For more than thirty years he worked mainly as a cook in the monastery, but he acquired such a reputation for sanctity and spiritual wisdom that he was visited and consulted by the leading ecclesiastics and authorities of his day. A humble and modest man with somewhat of a coarse manner, he was able to articulate with great precision his thinking about the practice of the presence of God. A year after his death in 1691 at the age of seventy-seven, his notes and letters were collected and published in two volumes under the titles *Maximes* and *Lettres*, and they proved an instant success. The theme of his writings is summarized in this statement of his:

The most holy, ordinary, and necessary practice in the spiritual life is the presence of God: that is, to take habitual pleasure in his divine company, speaking humbly and conversing lovingly with him at all seasons, at every minute. One must attempt continually to make all his actions, without exception, a sort of little conversation with God; however, not in a studied way, but just as they happen, with purity and simplicity of heart.

The occasional and unpretentious writings of this modest lay brother—which are known in the English-speaking world by the title *Practice of the Presence of God*—have enjoyed a continuing popularity through the years, and they are appreciated today by Protestants as much as by Catholics.

The Carmelite nuns in France continued their amazing growth throughout the seventeenth century. Two literary events helped the nuns enormously: André Duval published his life of Barbe Acarie in 1621, which went through seven editions in a few years; and St. Teresa was canonized in 1622, and her writings were circulated even more widely in France. By the year 1667 there were sixty-three Carmelite convents in the kingdom of France. Between 1606 and the suppression of 1792, 350 nuns were professed in the one convent on the rue Saint-Jacques in Paris. The last surviving Spanish nun, Isabelle of the Angels, prioress at Bordeaux, made a final attempt to bring the nuns under the jurisdiction of the Order when the friars established a monastery in that city. She petitioned Rome directly, but Bérulle was able to block her efforts and obtain a brief whereby the incumbent superior general of the French Oratory would automatically function as the visitator of the Carmelite nuns in France. He died in 1629, two years after he had been created a cardinal, having at least obtained this single victory over Barbe Acarie who had predeceased him by eleven years.

Of all the French nuns of the seventeenth century, none is more intriguing than Louise of the Mercy, the former Louise de la Vallière, the mistress of Louis XIV. Louise de la Vallière was born at Orléans in 1645, the step-daughter of the Marquis de Saint-Rémy. She was brought to Paris and presented at the court of Louis XIV, the Sun King, that absolute monarch who was driving and goading France to its point of greatest national prominence. Louis XIV was a short, rugged, rather handsome man in a heavy-featured way, and he had a series of mistresses during his long reign. The young girl from Orléans caught his eye, and he immediately installed her as his mistress and court favorite. "Bid me die or leave me," the king said to her. Louise was apparently a woman of rare charm and she enchanted the court. A blonde with sapphire eyes, she walked with a slight limp. The poet La Fontaine wrote of her that she had "grace more beautiful than beauty." And an enemy of hers, commenting on her soft, low-pitched voice, said that "it was so sweet that no one who ever heard it could ever forget it." Louise bore the king three illegitimate children and she seemed to be genuinely in love with him. But she suffered the fate of court mistresses, and after a few years the king replaced her with his then current favorite, Madame Athénaïs de Montespan. Louise, then only twenty-four, was deeply stricken and she retired from court circles, depressed, confused, and anguished. During a five-year period she recovered herself, repented of her past conduct, and embarked on a severe program of penance. At the age of twenty-nine she sought admission to the Carmel on the rue Saint-Jacques. Bossuet preached the sermon at her profession a year later in 1675, and the event was the sensation of Paris. Louise of the Mercy spent the remaining thirty-five years of her life in the convent, and she was an exemplary nun, faithful, cheerful, and extremely penitential. During the period immediately before she entered the convent she had written a treatise about the mercy of God, and in 1680 the prioress published this monograph anonymously under the title *Reflections on the Mercy of God*. However, the authorship of the book published by the Carmel was quite evident, and it became the talk of Paris.

The most delightful scene in the life of Louise de Vallière occurred shortly after she had entered the convent when she was visited by Athénaïs de Montespan, her successor as the king's mistress. It was a scene which could only have transpired between two women. The lady of the court sat on the other side of the convent grille and chatted amiably with the nun who, according to witnesses, seemed to bear the visit with amused indifference. As Mlle. de Montespan rose to leave, she mentioned that she was returning to the palace and would see the king, and then asked: "Is there anything you would like me to say to the king for you?"

Louise bowed her head slightly toward her visitor. "Whatever you like, Madame, whatever you like." Then she turned and walked slowly away.

Athénaïs de Montespan was herself eventually replaced after ten years as the king's mistress, and she returned to visit Louise again at the Carmel, but now to seek comfort and consolation.

Louise of the Mercy died in 1710, and during her final, painful illness, she exclaimed: "Dying in pain is appropriate for a sinner." After her death the Carmel cited her authorship in further editions of her book, adding to it some biographical data, letters, and notes she had written in the convent. The book has gone through numerous editions and remains in print today, these reflections on God's mercy by the former mistress of the Sun King.

The Carmelite reform was carried into Central Europe and southern Germany on the energetic shoulders of Dominic of Jesus and Mary, one of the Spanish Carmelites who had been brought to Rome by papal command. Born at Calatayud in 1559, Dominic Ruzzola entered the Calced Carmelites at an early age, but in 1589 at the age of thirty he transferred to the Discalced Carmelites at Pastrana. He served as the prior of Toledo, and he was living at the desert of Bolarque when he was summoned to Rome. A saintly person and a man of extraordinary organizational ability, Dominic of Jesus and Mary occupied the most important posts in the Order, and he became the favorite of the popes, who employed him on frequent diplomatic missions. He was prior at La Scala, procurator general of the Italian congregation, and finally in 1617 general of the congregation. Pope Paul V sent him on missions to the viceroy of Naples, Archduke Albert of Belgium, and Louis XIII of France, and he delegated him as his personal representative to the Holy Roman Emperor, Ferdinand II, in the early stages of the senseless Thirty Years' War, the last of the great religious wars.

In 1618, Europe was on the verge of a foolish and vicious series of military conflicts which would involve all of the major Continental powers and drag on for thirty devastating years. The Hapsburg prince, Ferdinand II, started the conflict in 1618 when he attempted to depose Frederick, "the Winter King," from the throne of Bohemia, which he regarded as rightfully belonging to the Hapsburgs. Philip III of Spain sent his troops into the Rhineland, while Ferdinand II marched into Bohemia with an army headed by Count Tilly, a renowned Bavarian general. Tilly drove toward Prague, where he hoped to encounter the Bohemian army in a major and decisive battle, and Pope Paul V sent the Carmelite general Dominic of Jesus and Mary to offer his support and encouragement to the Catholic forces. Dominic arrived at the encampment outside Prague, and Ferdinand II immediately asked him to act as chaplain for the troops. He celebrated Mass on the field, administered the sacraments, and is said to have enrolled ten thousand soldiers in the scapular. On November 8, 1620, when Tilly charged forward at the Battle of White Mountain outside Prague, Dominic rode with the troops, garbed in his habit and white mantle and carrying only a cross in his right hand and a picture of the Blessed Virgin suspended from his neck. Tilly routed the Bohemian troops, the Winter King was deposed, and Ferdinand was installed as ruler of Bohemia.

Ferdinand was so grateful for Dominic's assistance that he promised to help him extend the Discalced Carmelites into Central Europe. In 1622 the emperor endowed a monastery in Vienna, situated on a small island in the Danube, and two years later another one, at Prague. These two monasteries, together with the one founded at Cologne in 1613 by Thomas of Jesus, were organized into the first German province in 1626. Maximilian of Bavaria also wanted to demonstrate his gratitude to Dominic, and he introduced the friars to Munich in 1629, and from this foundation other monasteries developed rapidly: Würzburg, Regensburg, Koblenz, and Augsburg. Additional monasteries followed in Austria in rapid succession: Graz, Mannersdorf, Wiener Neustadt, and Linz. Nuns from the Belgian province were brought to Cologne in 1637, and from this initial foundation the Carmelite nuns spread through northern Germany and Bavaria.

The Polish province had developed rapidly since the original foundation at Cracow in 1605, and during the period of expansion in Central Europe they added monasteries at Poznań, Czarna, Vilna, Warsaw, and Przemyśl. Anne of Jesus had sent nuns from the Lowlands to Cracow in 1612, and this became the mother foundation for the Polish convents.

All of these foundations endured severe difficulties during the unsettled period of the Thirty Years' War. The victory at White Mountain proved to be only the first stage of the long conflict as the Protestant powers began to fear that the politico-religious balance of power in Europe had been destroyed at Prague. Christian IV of Denmark invaded Germany in 1625; and Gustavus Adolphus of Sweden, who had already marched into Poland in 1621, joined the German invasion in 1630. The strange Cardinal Richelieu, chief minister of Louis XIII, maneuvered behind the scenes, and finally he marched his French troops against the Spanish forces which were scattered around Europe. The treaty of Westphalia in 1648 brought an end to the hostilities, but by that time great havoc lay over all of Europe. Some of the Carmelite monasteries were in the path of invading armies, some of them were despoiled and plundered, and it is amazing that the new provinces in Germany and Poland were able to survive and expand during that time of senseless ravage.

The monastery at Prague was situated in an area of fierce military combat, but, nevertheless, the now world-famous devotion to the Infant of Prague originated there during those turbulent years. In 1628, a Bohemian noblewoman, Princess Lobkowitz, offered to the monastery a statue which had been brought to Prague by her maternal grandmother when she came from Spain to marry a Bohemian nobleman. The statue, nineteen inches high, a costumed representation of the infant Jesus, made of wax and wood, and depicting the infant holding a small globe in one hand with the other hand raised in blessing, was placed in the friars' choir, and the community felt that their veneration for the statue gained special help from God in their financial difficulties during that time of war. One of the novices was particularly devoted to the statue, Cyril of the Mother of God (Nicholas Schokivilerg), a former Calced Carmelite priest, now in his late thirties, who had recently transferred to the reform. Cyril prayed frequently before the statue, pondering his own personal problem of whether or not he should remain in the reform, and he received the courage to continue in his vocation. In the year 1630 Gustavus Adolphus was sweeping south through Germany and on to Prague, and the Carmelite superiors decided it would be prudential to move the novices to a safer monastery. The novices were transferred to Munich where Cyril made his profession as a Discalced in October of that same year. In 1631, Gustavus Adolphus and his

Saxon allies, eighteen thousand strong, marched against Prague, and the Bohemian garrison of less than a thousand troops quickly fell before the advancing army. The citizens of Prague evacuated the city, and the Carmelites left only two men in their monastery. These two friars were promptly thrown into prison by the invaders, and Saxon soldiers looted the monastery, despoiling and breaking and desecrating as they went.[2] Between the years 1631 and 1637 Prague became a battlefield for the opposing armies. Wallenstein recaptured the city for the Catholic forces, and for years he withheld repeated assaults by the Protestants who hoped to take Prague again. After a devastating plague, some semblance of peace returned to the city in 1637, and the Carmelites returned to their monastery.

Cyril of the Mother of God, who had remained in Munich during the intervening years, was among the first group which returned to Prague, and he immediately searched for his cherished statue. He found it thrown behind an altar, dirty, disfigured, its two hands broken off. He placed it in its former position of honor in the choir, and he later recounted that when he was praying before it he heard the words: "The more you honor me, the more I will bless you." Cyril had the statue repaired, and as the years passed a number of extraordinary blessings were attributed to its influence, the most celebrated of which was the sudden cure of a Countess Kolowrat, who seemed at the point of death in 1639. Upon request of the people, the statue was moved into the public church, and in 1644 a special chapel was constructed for the statue. In 1648, the year of the treaty of Westphalia, the cardinal of Prague solemnly blessed the chapel and encouraged devotion to the statue throughout Bohemia. This devotion soon spread all over Europe, and countless reproductions were made of the original statue during the following centuries. Leo XIII gave his approval to the organization of a confraternity of the infant Jesus of Prague in 1895, stating that he felt this devotion which emphasized Christ's humility was particularly helpful in an age of growing pride. The confraternity was placed under the jurisdiction of the Discalced Carmelites. The statue of the infant Jesus

[2] Catholic historians recount these atrocities of General Arnheim's soldiers in great detail, and while they are inexcusable, it must be remembered that the Protestant campaign through Bohemia was, in part, a retaliation for Catholic atrocities. The Catholic General Tilly, for instance, massacred and looted the city of Magdeburg, killing more than twenty thousand people.

found in so many Catholic churches today is modeled on the original statue which Cyril of the Mother of God repaired in the Carmelite monastery at Prague in 1637.

Dominic of Jesus and Mary returned to Rome in 1621 after his adventures at the Battle of White Mountain, bringing with him the picture he had worn around his neck during the conflict. Pope Gregory XV enshrined it in the Church of St. Paul on the Quirinal, a church which had been given to the Discalced Carmelites in 1608, and he changed the name of the church to Our Lady of Victoires in 1622.[3] In that same year the pope established the *Propaganda Fidei*, appointing to the original congregation thirteen cardinals, two bishops, and Dominic of Jesus and Mary, who had worked closely with the pope on the project. When Urban VIII became pope in 1623 he appointed Dominic his permanent papal legate for diplomatic affairs in Europe.

Dominic's term of office as general expired in 1623, and he was re-elected for another three-year term. He energetically sponsored foundations throughout Europe, and when he completed his term of office in 1626 there were seven flourishing provinces of the Italian congregation: Genoa, Rome, Poland, France, Belgium, Lombardy, and Germany. He was then elected definitor general, an office he held for the remainder of his life. Urban VIII sent him to Vienna to effect a settlement between the court of Austria and the house of Mantua, but he was taken ill and died at the imperial palace in 1630. He was buried at the Carmelite monastery at Unter Dobling near Vienna, where his body remains to this day, partly incorrupt. Urban VIII had named him a cardinal *in petto*, but Dominic died before the nomination could be published. Dominic of Jesus and Mary acquired a wide reputation for holiness all over Europe, and he seemed to have possessed extraordinary spiritual powers because he was popularly called "the thaumaturgus (wonder-worker) of his time."

---

[3] The original picture was destroyed by fire in 1834, and the one now on exhibit in the church of Our Lady of Victoires in Rome is a copy. This picture, however, must not be confused with another Madonna which figured in the life of Dominic, the famous "Lady of the Bowed Head," a painting he exhibited for veneration in Rome in 1610, and which was brought to Munich in 1631, and was finally hung in the Carmelite church in Vienna, where it can be found today.

Thomas of Jesus' plan for the desert foundations, composed while he was a young priest at Seville, became the inspiration for this important movement within the Carmelite reform. He revised and updated his original concept in 1601, in collaboration with Alphonse of Jesus and Mary, the first prior of Bolarque, incorporating the results of a decade of desert experience in Spain, and this plan was used by both the Spanish and Italian congregations. At the time Thomas departed for Rome in 1607 there were four deserts in Spain: those at Bolarque and Las Batuecas, and one in Andalusia, and another one in Catalonia.

Dominic of Jesus, who had lived in the desert at Bolarque, sponsored the movement in the Italian congregation, and deserts began to appear all over Europe: at Varazze near Genoa in 1618; Marlagne near Namur in 1620; Czarna, Poland, in 1629; Vivors, France, in 1641; and Mannersdorf, Austria, in 1644. There were even deserts in the New World: in 1606 one was founded in the Mexican province at Santa Fe near Mexico City, and before the nineteenth-century suppression there were three different Mexican desert sites. At the height of the desert movement, prior to the eighteenth- and nineteenth-century revolutions, there were twenty-two deserts in the Carmelite reform. All of these were systematically suppressed by the modern revolutionaries, with the exception of the desert at Las Palmas near Valencia in Spain, which managed to survive the worst of the political upheavals and thus provide an unbroken link between the deserts of the golden age and the new deserts founded in the late nineteenth and twentieth centuries.

Each desert foundation was constructed according to the pattern devised by Thomas of Jesus. The individual cells were built immediately adjacent to each other and were arranged in the form of a large quadrangle. However, each cell was completely separated from the others, and was composed of a small apartment of four rooms, plus a walled garden behind the hermitage where the Carmelite could work in solitude. One wing of this quadrangle of individual cells contained the chapel, refectory, kitchen, and library—although in some of the early deserts the chapel was placed in the middle of the quadrangle. A fully equipped desert could house about twenty-five men, four of them permanent members and the rest men who stayed for a year or less.

Prayer, silence, and solitude formed the essence of life in the Carmelite desert, and there was no exterior apostolate. Absolute silence was to be maintained and all communication was to be done by signs or writing, although once every fortnight they did assemble for a conference on some spiritual subject followed by an hour's recreation. The monastic day began at midnight with the recitation of matins, and the remainder of the day was consumed in prayer and reading and manual labor. Each desert possessed extensive grounds located in a remote area, and scattered around the desert property were a number of hermitages, sometimes as many as eight or ten of them, where the friar could live in total isolation for an extended period, such as the time of Advent or Lent. When the friar lived in the hermitage he offered Mass in his cell, prepared his own meals there, which usually consisted of a more severe diet of bread, fruit, herbs, and water, and he kept in contact with the main contingent of friars by ringing a small bell at the same liturgical time of the day when the large bell was rung at the church.

Friars were admitted to the desert only after careful scrutiny by the provincial, who determined whether the man had the necessary physical and emotional stamina to endure the rigors of that kind of life. Preachers were frequently allowed to live in the desert for a period of two or three months in order to prepare a course of sermons, provided they follow the desert regulations. In Spain professors were also admitted for a short period to prepare a series of lectures, but in the Italian congregation scholastic study was discouraged. However, the foreign missionaries frequently spent some time in the deserts before departing for overseas in order to prepare themselves for mission life—and in many cases they were preparing themselves for a future martyrdom.

The deserts performed an invaluable service for the Carmelite reform: they provided a permanent place where the friars could temporarily retire to intensify their own encounter with God and their personal religious commitment; they demonstrated throughout Europe the seriousness of the reform; and they kept alive the old desert tradition of the thirteenth-century Carmelites in Palestine.

The Carmelite reform originated in an era which was only a hundred years removed from the invention of metallic movable type. That century had seen the beginnings of the radical and lasting revolution which the printing press was causing in the history of Western culture. A whole new avenue of communication had developed, and ideas could now be easily imprinted on paper and then quickly distributed in unlimited copies. Men of intelligence could exchange ideas more expeditiously, and the common man could now participate more fully in the culture of his time. The presence of the printing press guaranteed that the world would never be the same again and that all future generations would have to cope with the far-reaching implications of that invention.

The Carmelite reform quickly recognized the opportunities and responsibilities inherent in the area of the printed word for those whose vocation it was to be a witness. The prophets of old announced the truths of their message to the people at large through the only means available to them, the spoken word, but the prophets of the sixteenth and seventeenth centuries had at their disposal this new communication system of incalculable magnitude, the printed word. And they used it. During the first century and a half of the reform's history, Discalced Carmelites wrote the amazing total of more than two thousand books, and while many of them were ephemeral and of insignificant value, there were enough good books to create a substantial body of Christian literature and to establish what has become known as the Carmelite school of spiritual theology. Carmelites wrote on a wide variety of different subjects—not always religious subjects—but their forte and their principal contribution lay in the area of explaining man's experience with God, according to the tradition established by the first two writers of the Carmelite reform, Teresa and John of the Cross. The entire Carmelite school, in fact, is deeply rooted in the doctrine of Teresa and John, and it seeks to explain and elucidate it for succeeding generations.

The Carmelite school of spiritual theology has been called a school of mysticism, but that is somewhat of a misnomer. The word "mystical" comes from the Greek word *mystikos* and implies secrets known only to the initiate, and in the Christian tradition it has been used to describe extraordinary spiritual phenomena, such as visions and revelations, experienced by only a chosen few. The Carmelites did, of course, explain these extraordinary phenomena with great clarity and precision, and they coordinated them with principles of sound theology, thus providing a major breakthrough in Christian thought and a truly significant advance over the mystical tradition of the Middle Ages, which tended to be vague, obscure, recondite, and not susceptible to serious study by qualified theologians. But Carmelite writers did more than that: they charted the entire course of man's experience with God, and laid particular em-

phasis on ordinary experience. In the Carmelite school truly mystical experiences are regarded as nonessential, exceptional things
which should lay beyond the range of human desire and are given
only at God's pleasure and for His own good reasons. John of the
Cross's principle of *no admitir* ("do not admit") was frequently
used, which implied that one must resist any apparently extraordinary phenomena until it became overwhelmingly evident, as the result of consultation with a competent director, and long reflection,
that the experience was genuine. However, the Carmelites did try to
encourage a more intense religious experience among Christians,
and they taught that man could and must, by greater fidelity to
prayer and ascetic discipline, attain to a deeper and more rewarding
contact with God. Thomas of Jesus described three stages of prayer:
ordinary meditation, acquired contemplation, and infused contemplation; and he laid particular stress on the middle stage, acquired
contemplation, which he described as a state of prayer in which God
communicates Himself more directly and overpoweringly, but one
in which the person must actively cooperate since there is no question of the infused graces given in mystical contemplation. Thomas
of Jesus' phrase, which he used to describe the experiences recounted
by Teresa and John, is an awkward one, not precise enough, and
other phrases have been substituted over the centuries: the prayer of
simplicity, prayer of recollection, simple view of faith, and active
contemplation. However, Thomas of Jesus' term has had the most
endurance, and it has become a distinctive expression of the Carmelite school.

Five Carmelites of the seventeenth and eighteenth centuries laid
the foundations for the Carmelite school: three Spaniards, one
Frenchman, and one Italian. In addition to Thomas of Jesus, the
two other Spaniards were John of Jesus and Mary (San Pedro), and
Joseph of the Holy Spirit (Velarde). John of Jesus and Mary
(1564–1615) was one of the early Carmelites sent to Genoa by
Nicholas Doria, and he acquired a distinguished reputation as a man
of deep spirituality. He was a novice master at Genoa for almost
twenty years, and during that time he wrote, among other things,
Mystical Theology, The Art of Loving God, and *School of Prayer
and Contemplation.* Like his namesake, John of Jesus and Mary
(Aravalles), he wrote an even more popular *Instruction for Novices.*
Joseph of the Holy Spirit (1667–1736), a kindly man who eventually

became general of the Spanish congregation, wrote a massive study entitled *Course of Mystico-Scholastic Theology*, a work of six volumes of approximately a thousand pages each which correlated the principles of Scholasticism and mystical theology. Joseph of the Holy Spirit served three different terms as the rector of the Carmelite college at Seville, and the chronicles of the house relate that during his regime the monastery was "a truly peaceful Jerusalem where forty students marched with ardor toward the pursuit of wisdom and virtue." The family name of the Italian, Balthasar of St. Catharine (1597-1673), was Machiavelli, and he was a descendant of Niccolò Machiavelli of *The Prince* fame. He entered the monastery at La Scala, and twice served as the provincial of the Lombardy province, and eventually became the procurator general of the Order in Rome where he was the confessor of Pope Clement X. His major literary work was the *Splendori riflessi*, a valuable treatise on spiritual theology. Philip of the Trinity (1603-1671) was, after Thomas of Jesus, the most important writer in the early Carmelite school. Julien Esprit was born at Malaucène in France, and entered the novitiate at Lyons. He studied at Paris and then spent eight years at the Carmelite mission in Goa, India. He was twice the provincial of the French province, and in 1665 he became general of the Italian congregation. His three "Summas" are a work of genius, a masterly attempt to synthesize the full range of Christian theological experience—*Summa philosophiae*, *Summa theologiae* (5 vols), and *Summa theologiae mysticae*. As an intriguing footnote, Philip of the Trinity wrote all his works with the same pen.

The Carmelite writers were working in a difficult field, the shadowy area of man's personal contact with God, but they brought an unusual clarity to the subject because of two distinctive features: they based their teaching on the authentic experience and doctrine of Teresa and John of the Cross; and they made a studied and determined attempt to coordinate their spiritual doctrine with sound theology as expressed in the traditional teaching of the Church and the schools. As a result, the Carmelite tradition has been remarkably free of those perennial hazards of mystical systems—illuminism, quietism, and gross forms of self-deception. The Carmelites have thus been able to preserve through four centuries an authentic and healthy spiritual tradition which illuminated a subject of major consequence, man's encounter with God.

In the field of systematic theology the seventeenth-century Carmelites distinguished themselves by two major works: the *Complutenses*, and the *Salmanticenses*. These two works are a multi-volume course in philosophy and theology produced by a team of Carmelites, most of them Spaniards, over a hundred year period. The *Complutenses* was begun in the Carmelite college at Alcalá de Henares (*Complutum* is the ancient Latin name for Alcalá) by Michael of the Trinity in the early part of the seventeenth century, and it was continued by Anthony of the Mother of God. A Frenchman, Blaise of the Conception, published his metaphysics at Paris in 1640, and his work was added to the series. The completed *Complutenses*, comprising five quarto volumes, was widely used in philosophical circles throughout Europe in the seventeenth and eighteenth centuries, but today it is extremely dated and of merely historical interest. The course actually represented more than the work of the three principal authors and their collaborators, since each chapter was submitted to a careful discussion by the entire Carmelite college at Alcalá, and in the case of difference of opinion the matter was settled by a vote. The same procedure was followed in the publication of the *Salmanticenses*, the theological course produced in the Carmelite college at Salamanca. The first volumes of the series were published by Anthony of the Mother of God in 1630, and subsequent scholars continued the work throughout the century. When completed, there were twenty volumes in the dogmatic theology section and six volumes in the moral theology section. The *Salmanticenses* remains to this day a major and substantial work in the field of Scholastic theology, and the German theologian Mathias Scheeben had called it "the most magnificent and achieved work in the Thomistic School."

The final volume of the *Salmanticenses* was published in 1724, exactly one hundred years after the publication of the first volume of the *Complutenses*. This entire monumental series of thirty-one volumes is structured in the form of a commentary on the doctrine of Thomas Aquinas, and as such is pure Thomism. However, the course attempted to extend the work of Aquinas by deeper penetration into his original questions, by the consideration of new questions, and by the use of later authors and further developments in the field of theology. Perhaps the greatest value of this massive study was that it fortified the more important work being done in the area of spiritual theology by demonstrating that the Carmelite school was grounded in the most authentic principles of sound theology.

The Carmelites of the golden age continued the Marian tradition of the Order, and wrote extensively on the Blessed Virgin. St. Teresa, as we have noted, repeatedly reaffirms in her writings the original Marian traditions of the thirteenth and fourteenth centuries; and St. John of the Cross, who so seldom mentions anything that is specifically Catholic, cites the Blessed Virgin as the model and fulfillment of the spiritual growth he is discussing—in the *Ascent*, in the *Living Flame of Love*, and twice in the *Spiritual Canticle*; and these citations are so extrinsic to his fundamental argument and appear so abruptly in the text that they throw his deep Marian feelings into even sharper relief. Jerome Gratian wrote an exposition on the Carmelite rule in which he revives and extends Baconthorpe's ancient thesis that the rule is patterned on the life of the Blessed Virgin. John of Jesus and Mary (San Pedro) states in his *Instruction for Novices* that the Discalced Carmelite is obliged to honor the Mother of God in virtue of the habit he wears, and he then describes at some length the imitable virtues of Mary—this chapter of his book forms the principal part of the section on the Blessed Virgin contained in the official *Instructions* used in the Order today. Philip of the Trinity, Dominic of Jesus and Mary, and John of Jesus and Mary all wrote complete books on the Blessed Virgin. And two Carmelites wrote books which reasserted the traditional themes: a Frenchman, Gregory Nazianz of St. Basil (1585–1677), authored *The Adoption of the Sons of the Blessed Virgin Mary into the Order of Mount Carmel*; and a Spaniard, Alonso of the Mother of God (1568–1636), who assisted at the death of St. John of the Cross, and later became the procurator of his cause for beatification, wrote *The Scapular of the Blessed Virgin*. However, the most popular Marian book of that era was written by the celebrated first historian of the reform, Joseph of Jesus and Mary Quiroga (1562–1629), *History of the Blessed Virgin*, a factual account of the life of the Blessed Virgin combined with a discussion of the related theological questions—this book has been reprinted a number of times since its original publication in 1655, and the most recent edition was in 1956. The *Salmanticenses* offers a complete course in Mariology interspersed throughout the various sections of that massive work, but the classic combination of traditional Carmelite Marian devotion and the neo-Scholasticism of the age was Philip of the Trinity's thesis that the Blessed Virgin "is the exemplar and final cause of the Order."

The enormous literary output of the seventeenth-century Carmelites, those later-day prophets who accepted the challenge of the printing press, demonstrated that the reform had now committed itself to the task of prophetic expression through the medium of the printed word.

The question of missionary activity outside the European continent had become a thorny one for the young Carmelite reform. Doria had been unalterably opposed to the missions, and the Spanish Carmelites continued his policies, although perhaps not for quite the same reasons. One of the root problems at the base of the issue was the old question raised by Nicholas the Frenchman in the thirteenth century: precisely how much apostolic activity should be undertaken by a man pledged to the prophetic vocation? It had puzzled the Carmelites of the Middle Ages, and it had puzzled some members of the reform—and it will undoubtedly continue to puzzle those who seek for a precise, legal answer to the question, because the apostolate of the prophetic vocation is an inspirational one and therefore something which cannot be fitted into neat categories which cover every need or contingency.

Peter of the Mother of God confronted the mission question directly by asking the respected John of Jesus and Mary (San Pedro) to prepare a study for presentation at the first chapter of the Italian congregation in 1605.[4] The *Assertio missionum* (Statement about the Missions) was the result, and in it John said: "It is clear that the missions are appropriate for our Order. Therefore we should not only approve them, but we should not delay the work any longer." The chapter unanimously approved John's thesis, and all the fathers offered themselves for missionary work. The Carmelites ap-

---

[4] John of Jesus and Mary (San Pedro), the second of the two contemporaries bearing the same name in this chronicle, was born at Calahorra in Spain and for that reason he is frequently called in Spanish chronicles "*El Calagurritano*" —"the Calahorran." During the preparation of his study for the chapter of 1605, he consulted a monograph written in Rome by Jerome Gratian after his release from North Africa in which the former friend of St. Teresa describes her feelings about the Discalced Carmelite missions. Gratian writes: "By my authority as commissary apostolic, I sent Nicholas Doria to Italy, other religious to the West Indies, and others to the Kingdom of the Congo in Ethiopia, and I consulted the *Madre* about all these things and she approved of them."

proached Paul V and asked him to select a mission territory for the Order, and he suggested Persia. Paul of Jesus and Mary (Rivarola), a native of Genoa, was placed in charge of the group, and three priests and a lay brother set out through Germany, Poland, and Russia, following the course of the Volga, sailing across the Caspian Sea, until after a journey of great hardship they reached Ispahan in Persia on December 2, 1607. The mission was soon reinforced with more Carmelites, some of whom proceeded to make a foundation at Ormuz on the Persian Gulf, which at that time was under Portuguese rule. Ormuz was the point of departure for the missions in India, the most rewarding and durable mission in the history of the Carmelite reform. A monastery was established at Tattah in northern India in 1613, and the first mission in the south was established at Goa in 1620. During the course of the centuries, monasteries of the reform multiplied in India, one of the most important of which was Bombay, established in 1717. A successful mission was inaugurated among the "St. Thomas Christians" at Malabar in 1675. From Goa the Carmelites proceeded to Japan and China, where they located at Peking in 1706.

Thomas of Jesus, after his arrival at Rome in 1607, became the chief spokesman for the Carmelite missions. In his writings he asserted that the Discalced Carmelite missions should maintain the primacy of prayer and contemplation, and that regular monasteries of observance should be founded in the mission territories from which the friars could journey to their small mission stations and then return regularly to the main monastery. His plan was followed closely in the early missions, and the chapter of 1632 incorporated it as part of the Carmelite legislation for the mission territories. He was also a constant exponent of the special mission seminary. The chapter of 1605 had decided to found a mission seminary, and one was established at Montecampatri outside Rome: however, Thomas of Jesus envisioned something more elaborate, and he made plans to establish a larger operation at St. Paul's Church in Rome, which had been given to him for this purpose by Pope Paul V. Thomas of Jesus' objective, which received the approval of the pope, was the creation of a distinct missionary congregation within the reform, the congregation of St. Paul, to which would belong all the friars who wanted to serve on the foreign missions. On reflection, the Carmelite superiors felt the plan was unnecessarily divisive and it was rejected, but the Church of St. Paul's was retained and the missionary seminary was transferred there in 1612.[5] It was later transferred again to St. Pancratius outside the walls in 1622. Thomas of Jesus inaugurated the mission seminary at Louvain in 1621, and similar mission seminaries were established at Malta and Goa in 1630. These four Carmelite seminaries provided specialized mission training for Carmelites who had completed their regular studies and who wanted to work on the missions. The friars spent two years at the mission seminary, studying linguistics, dialectics, applied theology, and natural sciences, after which they returned to their home province until the superiors were ready to send a new group of missionaries to some foreign territory. This arrangement guaranteed that there was always a number of friars prepared for missionary work who were ready to depart on short notice.

The Carmelite mission in Mesopotamia has had a curious history. In 1623, Basil of St. Francis, who had been sent from the monastery at Ispahan in Persia, established a foundation at Bassorah (Basra) at the confluence of the Tigris and the Euphrates. The friars made little progress with the Mohammedans, and their principal apostolate was with the Portuguese sailors who used Bassorah as a port of call in their trading operations. There was no further advancement in Mesopotamia until 1638 when a French Carmelite, Bernard of

[5] The Discalced, however, did adopt one feature of the regulations which Thomas of Jesus composed for his abortive missionary congregation: the vow which prohibited the friars from seeking episcopal office. As the new mission territories developed, a number of new bishoprics were created, and Thomas of Jesus wanted to preclude the possibility that any friar would choose the missionary vocation so that he might be quickly elevated to the episcopacy. To prevent this, he prescribed that the missionaries make, in addition to the regular three vows of poverty, chastity, and obedience, a fourth vow by which they pledged themselves not to seek any prelacy, either inside or outside the Order. The vow was adopted by the Italian congregation and prescribed for all the friars, whether missionaries or not, and it was soon made a matter of regulation in the Spanish congregation too. This fourth vow, which is euphemistically called "the vow of humility," is still made today by all Discalced Carmelite friars.

Nevertheless, fifty-one Discalced friars were appointed missionary bishops by the Holy See in the period before the French Revolution, the first of whom was John Thaddeus of St. Elisha (Roldan), who was appointed bishop of Ispahan, Persia, in 1632. The first Discalced appointed to a European diocese was Joseph of St. Mary (Jerome dei Sebastani), bishop of Visignano in the Calabrian region of Italy, in 1667.

St. Teresa (Duval), was appointed the first Latin archbishop of Babylon, the modern Baghdad. Jean Duval had been born at Clamecy in 1597, and after completing his philosophical studies at the Sorbonne, he had entered the Carmelite monastery on the rue de Vaugirard, adopting the name of Bernard of St. Teresa. He was an eloquent preacher, much in demand, and he became extremely popular throughout all of France, acquiring a wide circle of friends. In 1628 he was elected prior of the monastery of Meaux. He was confessor and spiritual director for a wealthy widow, Mme. d'Herouville, who volunteered to endow and support a Latin archbishopric at Baghdad on the condition that the Holy See appoint a Frenchman to that office and allow her to name the first incumbent. The Holy See agreed to her unusual stipulations, and subsequently approved the nomination of her confessor, Bernard of St. Teresa. He was consecrated bishop at Rome in 1638, and he sailed from Marseille for the Near East, reaching Ispahan, but was unable to proceed any farther because of the Persian-Turkish wars. He remained at Ispahan until 1642, when he returned to France in order to seek the king's help in getting his mission at Babylon established. Cardinal Richelieu was deeply impressed with the young missionary bishop, and he ultimately appointed him a counselor of state for ecclesiastical affairs, an office he held for twenty-two years under Louis XIV. Duval was chiefly employed in regulating ecclesiastical matters in Perpignan, the region in southwestern France acquired from Spain in 1642. However, the Holy See was distressed that the bishop of Babylon was now residing in France, and Duval was ordered either to resign his see or admit a coadjutor, and this latter course was followed. During his years in Paris, Duval labored to establish a mission seminary for French priests, and with the assistance of another wealthy widow, Mme. Ricouart, he acquired property on the rue de Babylone, the street which was named for him. The seminary was constructed in 1663, and it became the first house of the famous Paris Foreign Mission Society, of which he is considered one of the founders. Duval lived at the mission seminary on the rue de Babylone until his death in 1669.

It was not until the following century that the Discalced were able to gain admittance to Baghdad. A Greek physician named Testabusa, a friend of the community at Bassorah, presented their case at the palace of the wali in Baghdad, stating that the Carmelites were the heirs of the Khader (literally, "the verdant one," a surname given to the prophet Elijah by the Moslems, who consider him ever living) and that the Khader would be pleased if his descendants were allowed to enter the territory. The Moslems consented, and two French Carmelites from Burgundy established the first foundation at Baghdad in 1731.

The sole missionary endeavor of the Spanish congregation, apart from the Mexican venture, was the operation started by the Portuguese friars in the middle of the seventeenth century. Portugal had declared its independence from Spain in 1640, and it left the Spanish congregation in the awkward position of having its jurisdiction extend over two kingdoms.[6] When Alfonso VI of Portugal began to insist that the Portuguese Discalced work in his colonies in Africa, the Spanish superiors felt it would be more prudent to permit the mission—especially as long as no Spaniard had to be involved. The first Discalced mission in Angola, Southwest Africa, was opened at St. Paul of Luanda in 1659, and in a few years there were eight missions in the territory. In 1665 a foundation was made by the Portuguese friars at Bahia in Brazil. The African and South American missions were in actuality one operation, because during that epoch all Portuguese ships sailing from Lisbon to western Africa proceeded first to South America and then back across the South Atlantic, so they could avoid the North African pirates. The house at Bahia was at first only a resting place for the friars on the tortuous journey to Africa, but it quickly developed into a flourishing mission. Foundations were made at Olinda, Pernambuco, and Rio de Janeiro, and a number of mission stations were opened among the *sertoes* along the rio São Francisco and on the rio Sabuma and Torre.[7] The closeness of the African and South American missions was demonstrated by the fact that one of the friars, Emmanuel of St. Agnes, was appointed bishop of Angola in 1745, and then seventeen years

[6] The relationship between the Portuguese and the Spanish became so strained that in 1773 the Portuguese Discalced were separated from the Spanish and organized into a distinct congregation—thus making three congregations within the reform. However, this arrangement lasted only sixty-one years, because in 1834 the Portuguese were expelled from their monasteries by the government during the period of the exclaustrations, and when the Order began its task of recovery the congregation system was happily abolished.

[7] The Discalced friars in Brazil were called *Teresios* (Teresians), a more felicitous word than Discalced.

later was transferred to the bishopric of Bahia in Brazil. In 1741, the Portuguese friar, John of the Cross, was consecrated bishop of Rio de Janeiro. The first convent of Discalced nuns in Brazil was established at Rio de Janeiro in 1744, and the second at Porto Alegre in 1839.

A number of convents were established in other parts of South America during the seventeenth century, but these were usually founded by the local bishops, who gathered a group of pious women and instructed them in the Carmelite life without any direct foundation from another convent. Thus Bogotá in Colombia was founded in 1606 and Leiva in 1646; and a convent was established at Lima in Peru in 1643. A number of foundations in other countries were made by the Lima convent—Quito in Ecuador in 1653, Sucre in Bolivia in 1665, Guatemala in 1677, and Ayacucho in Peru in 1683. Most of these convents endured, and during the twentieth century they came under a more direct supervision by the Order. On the other hand, the convents in Mexico, beginning with the first one at Pueblo in 1604, were founded by the Carmelite friars, who usually selected the candidates from among the Spanish colonists in New Spain.

A number of the Discalced were martyred in the mission territories during the seventeenth and eighteenth centuries. Among others, Charisius of St. Mary, a lay brother, was killed in 1621 at Ormuz, after having been tied to a tree and cut open alive. In 1672 two Carmelites were murdered by African natives in the village of Aquingengo in the Angola mission; and a group of friars were killed by the Turks at Patras in 1716. But the best-known martyrs of that epoch were the two friars killed at Sumatra in 1638, Blessed Denis and Redemptus.

Pierre Berthelot was born in the French seaport town of Honfleur in 1600. He developed an early fascination for the sea, and became a professional navigator and cartographer. At the age of nineteen he sailed for the Indies as navigator for a French expedition, but his ship was attacked by the Dutch and he was taken prisoner and brought to Java. After his release, he settled in Malacca, where he signed with the Portuguese and was so successful that the king of Portugal named him "Master Navigator and Cosmographer of the Orient." His marine cartography became well known, and his map of the archipelago of Sumatra is still preserved in the British Museum. His contemporaries described him as a handsome, stocky man, blond and fair-skinned, an adventuresome and high-spirited person, with an inquisitive and active mind. His expeditions frequently brought him to Goa, where he became acquainted with the Discalced monastery and its prior, Philip of the Trinity. In 1634, at the age of thirty-four, he abandoned his career and entered the Order, adopting the name Denis of the Nativity. Four years later the Portuguese viceroy of the Indies asked the Carmelites to allow Denis to serve as navigator on an expedition which was carrying a new Portuguese envoy to Sumatra, a trip which appeared to be quite hazardous because of Dutch pirates and hostile natives. Denis' studies were accelerated, and he was quickly ordained to the priesthood so that he could also serve as chaplain on the expedition. A lay brother, Redemptus of the Cross, was assigned as his companion.

Thomas Rodriguez de Cunha was born at Paredes in Portugal in 1598. He became a soldier and traveled to the East Indies as a young man, becoming a member of the governor's guard at Meliapor where he rose to the rank of captain and commander of the guard. He entered the Carmelite monastery at Goa, taking the name Redemptus of the Cross. He was stationed at the Carmelite missions at Tattah and Diu in the kingdom of the Grand Mogul, and then again at Goa where he served as porter and sacristan. Redemptus was an extremely likable person, friendly and jovial, and when he was assigned to the Sumatra expedition he joked with his confreres about having his portrait painted in case he became a martyr.

The expedition arrived safely at Sumatra, where the party disembarked at the port of Achim, but the two friars were unexpectedly seized by natives and imprisoned. Asked to renounce their faith, they refused and were sentenced to death. They were led to a desolate spot on the seashore where Redemptus' throat was slit open, while Denis, a crucifix in his hands, was forced to watch. Then the natives cleaved open Denis' head. Pope Leo XIII beatified Denis and Redemptus in 1900.

None of the exploits of the seventeenth- and eighteenth-century Discalced are more adventuresome or courageous than the activities of the friars in the British Isles. The mission in England was staffed by young Englishmen who traveled to the Continent and entered one of the novitiates in Flanders, France, or Italy, and after taking courses at the missionary colleges at Louvain or Rome, returned as Carmelites to their homeland where they spent a life of apostolic endeavor against a background of intrigue and high adventure. Catholic priests were not allowed to function in England, and if any were apprehended they were imprisoned and deported. The Carmelite mission was always a modest one and the friars worked more as individuals than as a group in a country which had become overwhelmingly Protestant, but the chronicles of the mission offer us a record of men of constant courage and amazing daring. The Irish mission was even more astonishing: the Irishmen who returned to their Catholic but beleaguered homeland were determined to create and sustain a province, despite a persecution of unbelievable bitterness. The Irish friars never surrendered and they kept the province alive during two centuries of adversity, although they were hunted and hounded and killed. The Discalced in Ireland became known as the "Teresian outlaws," and they leave a chronicle of unparalleled heroism and gritty determination.

The first member of the English mission was Thomas Doughty, born at Plombley in Lincolnshire in 1574, a Catholic who fled to the Continent because of the penal laws. He was ordained for the priesthood in 1610 at the English college in Rome, and then joined the Carmelites at La Scala, but he left the novitiate after a few months and went to England. Two years later he returned to the Continent and entered the Carmelites again, this time at the monastery in Brussels. He selected the appropriate name Simon Stock of St. Mary, and was professed in 1613. The following year, the general, Ferdinand of St. Mary, obtained a decree from Paul V establishing the Discalced mission in England, and he sent Simon Stock as the first missioner. Simon Stock, then forty-one years old, arrived in England in April of 1615. He was promptly arrested, but he escaped and was fortunate to make the acquaintance of an Italian merchant who introduced him to the Spanish ambassador in London. The ambassador appointed him chaplain of the embassy, an office which was held by the Carmelites throughout that epoch and which afforded them diplomatic immunity when they could get to the embassy in London. Simon Stock worked in London and in the surrounding areas, but when he was joined by more Carmelites he withdrew to Canterbury, where he was hidden by the Ropers, a

Catholic family related to Thomas More. From Canterbury he made forays to London. He was constantly being sought by the "priest-hunters," and he had many narrow escapes. He writes:

> Often the constables were on my track. One night I was in a house administering the sacraments to some people, while the constables were on the watch outside. The following morning I was sitting in the largest room of the house hearing confessions with the doors wide open. Presently I heard them entering in search of me. I remained where I was while they searched the whole house, and actually looked into the room where I was sitting, but they did not see me, as many can testify. Had I made an attempt to hide myself, or made the least noise, they would have apprehended me.

Simon Stock of St. Mary worked in England for thirty-seven years until his death at Canterbury in 1652 at the age of seventy-eight, and he managed to escape his pursuers during all that time, mostly by means of frequent change of address and the use of many aliases. We know, for example, that at various times he went under the names of Dawson, Hunt, and Simons. He accomplished a great deal, and near the end of his life he wrote:

> As for the fruit of my labors, on an average I reconciled ten or twelve Protestants to the Church every year, and last year seventeen. I have sent fourteen young men into various religious Orders. I have written seven books which have been printed, and some others at the request of private friends which are not published.[8]

Other Carmelites in England were not as fortunate, and a number of them spent considerable time in prison and many of them were deported. However, most of the deportees were able to re-enter England, disguised and under an assumed name. The second Carmelite

---

[8] Simon Stock completed eight books before his death, an amazing feat in a life of adventure and constant moving from place to place. These books were printed at the English presses in the Lowlands, principally at Douai, and were then smuggled back to England. Simon Stock's books were quite well received in England, and enjoyed a wide diffusion in his lifetime and shortly afterward. His first book is titled in the prolix style of that post-Elizabethan era: "The Practice How to Find Ease, Rest, Repose, Content, and Happiness, Containing Directions How to Make Mental and Spiritual Prayer." In the following century another Carmelite with the same name, Simon Stock of the Trinity (Francis Blyth, 1704–1772), wrote twelve books, and also collaborated with Bishop Challoner in the translation of the Rheims Bible.

arrived in England in 1618. This was Elisha of St. Michael (William Pendryck), a Scotsman from Aberdeen, who became a Catholic in Paris while studying philosophy and who entered the monastery on the rue de Vaugirard at the age of twenty-nine. He worked under the protection of Lord Teynham (Christopher Roper) at Linstead Lodge. After Teynham's death he went to Eltham, but thereafter he was pursued more closely and we find him at Exeter, Wells, and Gatton. He was captured in 1641 and imprisoned for a year in London. He died in 1650 at the age of sixty-seven.

In May of 1624, Pope Urban VIII conducted a private departure ceremony for two friars about to embark for England, Bede of the Blessed Sacrament (John Hiccoks) and Elijah of Jesus (Edward Bradshaw), and he told them: "You are bound not for a haven but for perilous shoals. Remember the happiness of suffering continually for the name of Jesus. What a triumph it is to suffer death for the propagation of the faith." Bede, who had been born a Protestant in London and converted to the faith by Simon Stock of St. Mary, was captured and deported twice during his lifetime, and he eventually became superior of the Carmelite mission. Elijah was jailed for a year, and then deported, but he returned secretly to England; he died at Flintshire in 1562.

In October of 1641, Francis of the Saints (Christopher Leigh), a native of Kingston in Sussex, was apprehended by a mounted patrol in the neighborhood of Aylesbury. As he was being questioned, Francis kicked his horse with his spurs and raced off, and he appeared to be making his escape when he ran into another patrol coming from the opposite direction. He was asked to take the oath of supremacy, and when he refused he was brought to London on a horse without saddle, his feet tied under the horse, and his hands bound with iron shackles so tightly that they were skinned and bleeding. He was led through the streets of London while people lined the way jeering and shouting. Thrown into a damp, cold cell at King's Bench Prison, he became seriously ill. Another Carmelite, Anselm of St. Mary (John Hanson), visited him disguised as an official of the Venetian embassy and heard his confession. Francis died after three weeks in prison, at the age of forty-one, and a fellow prisoner later testified that "he bore all his afflictions with a great spiritual joy." His name is included in the list of those defenders of the faith in England whose cause is being considered for beatification.

After the Stuarts returned to the throne in 1658 following Cromwell's dictatorship, the persecution against Catholics relented for a while, but it was renewed with increased fervor at the time of the "Popish Plot" of 1678, that fictitious plan to kill the king which was supposedly uncovered by Titus Oates. Oates, a former Catholic, swore a deposition that implicated the Jesuits, Dominicans, and Discalced Carmelites in the plot, and as a result the Carmelites were hunted with special fury. Some of the older and better-known friars on the English mission had to flee to the Continent for a while, and their places were taken by younger men who were not as easily recognized. Lucian of St. Teresa (George Travers) arrived in England the year of the Oates furor, and by the use of a number of disguises he was able to work with the prisoners in the Tower of London, visiting there at least twice a week and occasionally offering Mass secretly in the Tower. He disguised himself as a steward to Lord Arundell, as a secretary at the Spanish embassy, and as a member of the French embassy staff, his most successful role, for he spoke French fluently since his time at the monastery in Louvain. He was eventually discovered and brought before the Privy Council, but the Spanish ambassador interceded for him, claiming he was a member of his staff, and the case was dismissed. Lucian continued his activities until 1691 when he was arrested again. He died in prison that year while nursing a man with a contagious disease.

The most daring of the friars during that period was Edmund of St. Joseph (George Loop), a native of Hereford who graduated from the missionary college at St. Pancratius in Rome. Edmund arrived in England in 1677 and worked chiefly in his home territory of Hereford, but after the Oates affair he was pursued relentlessly by that expert priest-hunter Captain John Scudamore. Elaborate traps were set for Edmund, but he was able to elude them. He switched his ministry to London, traveling to the city disguised as a farmer's wife with a hamper of vegetables on his head and a basket on his arm. He operated from a small room he had rented, but when Scudamore traced him, he fled over the rooftops and departed for Worcester disguised as a beggar. That disguise was so successful that he used it for years in Worcester, conferring the sacraments at night and during the day passing himself off as a beggar. During the respite from persecution in the reign of James II he opened a public chapel in Worcester. He had a flock of two hundred people there, but the house and chapel were destroyed during the Orange Revolution in 1688, and he had to flee again. Edmund spent the last years of his life working in London, where he was hidden in the home of a Catholic family. He wrote a book on the scapular which was printed in Antwerp in 1709, seven years before his death at the age of sixty-eight.[9] The chronicle of the mission calls him "a very devout and excellent missioner, who has done and suffered great things for the glory of God."

A Flemish Carmelite, Gaspar of the Annunciation (Jean de Donker), born in Brussels in 1656, went to England in 1680 to help the mission during its period of great crisis. He had been trained at the missionary seminary at Louvain and he was an expert linguist. Attaching himself to the staff of the Spanish ambassador in London, he was able to accomplish a fantastic amount of good. The mission records report that he heard as many as ten thousand confessions a year. He assisted the Irish bishop Oliver Plunket imprisoned at Newgate, and he followed him to the scaffold at Tyburn, secretly giving him absolution when he was hung. Gaspar remained in London until his death at the age of sixty-one.

When the persecutions abated during the time of James II, the Carmelites openly established a monastery and public chapel at Bucklersbury in London. Bede of St. Simon Stock (Walter Travers), a former solicitor's clerk in London who had been converted while traveling abroad and who joined the Carmelites at La Scala in Rome, was the superior of the four friars stationed there. They were able to maintain full monastic discipline for a little over a year, until a mob broke in during the Orange Revolution in 1688, destroying the interior and finally setting the whole building on fire. The small community was dispersed, but Bede continued to work secretly in London. Living alone in a rented room, he followed the practices of the Carmelite monasteries, rising at midnight to recite office, making his hours of mental prayer, keeping the fasts of the rule. He worked on the mission for forty years, but when he was an old man his health broke, and he retired to the monastery in Paris where he died at the age of seventy-six.

---

[9] The verbose title of Edmund's book: "The Queen of Heaven, or A Short Treatise on the Institution, Excellency, Privileges, and Indulgences of the Most Famous Confraternity of Our Lady of Mount Carmel, commonly called the Scapular, Together with a Brief Recitation of the Antiquity and Never-Interrupted Succession of the Religious Order of the Carmelites, to Whom the Blessed Virgin Mary Gave This Her Sacred Livery."

Under the Hanoverian rule in the eighteenth century, Catholics fared slightly better; there was little open persecution, but severe penal laws made the practice of Catholicism almost unbearable. No public worship was allowed, and there were fines for attending Mass or educating children as Catholics. The net result of these laws was to reduce the number of Catholics in England to less than one per cent of the population. The Carmelite mission in 1731 numbered twenty-four friars, sixteen of whom were then in England, and eight who were temporarily abroad. Andrew of St. Thomas (Thomas Price) reported the situation in 1731:

> Here in London we are quite numerous, but we cannot live together. We are dispersed through the whole city, and only meet once in three months for the transaction of business and the cultivation of fraternal charity. Neither have we public chapels, but say Mass secretly like the first Christians.

Conditions began to improve in the second half of the century, and the acts of toleration first inaugurated in 1778 made the future seem bright. In 1773, the Order purchased a college at Tongres in Flanders which had belonged to the recently suppressed Society of Jesus. The college was inaugurated in 1774 as a special seminary for the Carmelite missions in England, but twenty years later the college was confiscated and the friars put to rout by the French armies which swept through Flanders during the upheavals of the French Revolution. Throughout the first half of the nineteenth century the Order was brought to the brink of extinction in Europe by the revolutionaries who suppressed the great majority of the monasteries, and there was no place to educate and train Carmelites for England. The mission dwindled and finally collapsed at the death of the last friar in 1849. But in 1862, under the sponsorship of Cardinal Wiseman, the Order was revived in England, and the beginnings of a permanent province were started by the converted Jew, Augustine of the Blessed Sacrament (Hermann Cohen).

The Irish mission was inaugurated in 1625, and for a few years the Carmelites fared much better than their confreres in England. There were a number of Irishmen living in Carmelite monasteries on the Continent during the early part of the seventeenth century, and in 1625 Edward of the Kings (John Sherlock), a native of county Kildare who entered the Carmelites in Brussels and graduated from the missionary college at Louvain and who was then only twenty-nine years of age, petitioned the general for permission to establish the Order in his homeland. The time for such a move was propitious because the grievous penal laws were not being strictly enforced at the moment and there seemed to be a temporary peace in Ireland after decades of struggle with the English. Permission was granted, and in the same year Edward and another friar arrived in Dublin. They obtained a house in Cork Street and in the following year opened a chapel dedicated to Our Lady of Mount Carmel, which soon became immensely popular. Other Carmelites returned from abroad, new vocations were recruited in Ireland, and by the year 1629 the monastery in Dublin numbered twenty-five friars. However, an episode occurred at Christmas of that year which clearly indicated the shape of things to come. The Protestant archbishop of Dublin, Lancelot Bulkeley, a puppet of the occupying British forces, became unnerved at the Carmelites' popularity, and he obtained a warrant and a troop of musketeers to raid the chapel. The archbishop and his soldiers entered the building on Cork Street while Mass was in progress, and ordered his men to arrest the friars and destroy the interior of the chapel. But the people who were in attendance rose up against the soldiers, and pushing, shoving, and shouting, drove them out into the street. They continued their harassment of the troop in the street, gathering clubs and sticks, until the archbishop called off his men and withdrew them to a place of safety and quiet. The incident foreshadowed the principal features of the Irish story for the next two centuries: persecution by the British, and the support of the clergy by the lay people—in fact, the clergy and laity worked so closely together in face of common adversity that the Church in Ireland was able to avoid the abrasive anticlericalism which developed in every other Catholic country.

Edward of the Kings died in that same year of 1629 at the untimely age of thirty-three, and he is called in the chronicles of the Order "the father and founder of the Irish mission." He was succeeded as superior of the mission by James of St. Mary (James Briklane), a native of northern Ireland who had joined the Carmelites in France. Additional foundations were soon made throughout Ireland, and in less than twenty years after their arrival the Carmelites had nine foundations: Dublin, Athboy, Drogheda, Ardee, Galway, Limerick, Kilkenny, Kinsale, and Loughrea. At the general chapter of 1638 in Rome the Irish mission was formally elevated into a province, and it was placed, predictably, under the protection of St. Patrick.

In 1641, a rebellion against the English rule began in the northern counties under the leadership of Sir Phelim O'Neill, and the English retaliated by enforcing the penal laws again and embarking on a cruel and determined program to stamp out Catholicism in Ireland. Churches were destroyed, priests killed, and the practice of the faith forbidden under the strictest penalties. The Carmelite monastery at Cork Street was pillaged and wrecked, and the friars fled for their lives. The monastery at Drogheda was the next to go, and soon all the Irish friars were following the same kind of life as their confreres in England: living in hiding, using disguises, taking assumed names. However, the Irish Carmelites seemed to have been able to remain in groups, and they usually managed to hide somewhere near the area of their plundered monastery. A good many of the friars had to seek exile on the Continent because they were too well known to continue their work, but the majority were able to perform the secret exercise of their ministry. The friars, however, operated under the most oppressive of circumstances. The Puritan troops of Lord Inchiquin were almost fanatical in their efforts to ferret out the clergy, and they frequently tortured lay people, putting them on the rack, to discover the location of priests. It is uncertain exactly how many Carmelites were killed during this persecution because the chronicles were poorly kept in the midst of the confusion and bloodshed. For example, witnesses related that a young Carmelite lay brother was stabbed to death in the street, but there is no record of his identity. And another chronicle of the times speaks of a tree in Langford on which "the Carmelites were hung." However, the three most celebrated Carmelite martyrs of that epoch were a priest, a student, and a lay brother.

Thomas Aquinas of St. Teresa (family name unknown), a young priest, was visiting a woman in Drogheda whose husband and only child were languishing in prison because of their faith when Puritan soldiers surrounded the house to capture him. He hid in a secret closet and they were unable to find him, but when they loudly threatened to burn down the house he surrendered himself. Taken to the prison at Drogheda, he was sentenced to death six days later. His religious habit was smuggled into the jail, and he met the execution party which came to bring him to the scaffold dressed in his habit. The first two attempts to hang him failed as the rope snapped, but on the third try the rope held and he died. The date was June 6, 1642.

Angelus of St. Joseph (George Halley) was an Englishman born at Hereford in 1620 who had been sent to Drogheda to study for the priesthood in preparation for work in the English mission. He was captured after the siege of the city by Viscount Melfont and sentenced to death. He marched to his execution singing the Litany of Our Lady, and after he had been tied to a post he was shot to death. This young man of twenty-two was killed on August 15, 1642. Peter of the Mother of God (family name unknown) was a lay brother stationed in Dublin who remained in the city after the suppression of the Cork Street monastery. He was apprehended on the street while he was collecting food for the hidden community of friars. Imprisoned for many months, he refused either to deny his faith or reveal the location of the Carmelite friars. On August 15, 1643, he was taken to the permanent scaffold which had been erected in the middle of Dublin to intimidate the Irish, and as he approached it he knelt to kiss the ground in a gesture which signified his own feelings of unworthiness in joining the lists of those who had already been martyred there for their faith. Immediately before the rope was sprung some of the soldiers told him he was foolish to forfeit his life, but he replied that there was a wisdom which they could not understand. He was in his early thirties at the time of his execution.

The persecutions intensified with the arrival of Oliver Cromwell in 1649, whose avowed purpose was to break the spirit of the Irish people. He imported Scotch and English planters, Puritans to whom he gave properties he had stolen from the Irish, and great masses of homeless Irish people roamed their island. He declared all priests to be outlaws who could be shot without pretext of trial if they were caught, but sometimes he sold captured priests into slavery for plantations in the West Indies. The Carmelites continued to function during those black days, and some of them, disguised as farmers and peasants, managed to live together in small cabins in groups of two or three. One of the most adventurous friars was Agapitus of the Holy Spirit (Simon Plunket). He was born at Cloweston in the diocese of Meath in 1622 and was sent to La Scala in Rome for his studies. He returned to Ireland in 1648, and he assumed the imaginative disguise of a Puritan soldier. He would frequently slip into a regiment of marching soldiers to travel to the next place he was due to administer the sacraments, and he used that disguise for a great many years and never seems to have been caught at it. On one occasion this irrepressible friar learned that a Puritan preacher who had been scheduled to address a congregation in one of the Cromwellian chapels in Dublin was hindered from reaching the place on time, and Agapitus, dressed in his soldier's uniform, offered to say a few words about Christianity. The people seemed eager to listen to the Puritan soldier, and he preached an impassioned sermon about faith and freedom of conscience.

The Teresian outlaws remained in hiding for the greater part of the last half of the seventeenth century, although they quickly appeared and established a public monastery whenever the persecution seemed to wane. They established themselves openly in Dublin, Drogheda, and Loughrea during the 1680s, but at the time of the Orange Revolution in 1688 they were forced to return to their hiding places in the Irish countryside. During all this time the friars continued to recruit new members, who were sent to the Continental monasteries for their studies and then returned to Ireland to take up the outlaw's life. This surreptitious flow of Carmelites back and forth to the Continent continued almost uninterruptedly, despite the vigilance of the British who had severely prohibited any Irishman going abroad for the purpose of studying for the priesthood. The friars were determined that the province of St. Patrick would endure and ultimately prevail.

During the reigns of William and Mary and Queen Anne, the persecutions against the Irish Catholics were renewed with a finesse that surpassed the savagery of the Cromwell epoch. "Utter extermination" of Catholics was the avowed objective, and even more severe penal laws were enacted in the last part of the seventeenth century and the first part of the eighteenth century. Catholics were not allowed to hold property, to vote, or even to attend school. All priests were ordered to leave Ireland before May 1, 1698, and it was a crime for anyone to harbor a priest. A reward of twenty pounds was placed on the head of every priest. Samuel Johnson decried the laws as "barbarous" and said that the British policy was "the most detestable mode of persecution." The Teresian outlaws continued undaunted: some of them operated in the cities, and we hear of a group living secretly in a tenement in Hammond Lane at Dublin, but most of them were in the countryside with the people. The friars participated in the famous "hedge schools," those secret schools set up in private rural homes to educate the children and preserve literacy. The situation was so bad that the friars dared not carry breviaries or prayer books with them on their missions because the books identified them as priests if they were captured. They did, however, wear small brown scapulars carefully concealed under their clothing. Historical documentation about this period is meager because, understandably, the friars attempted to keep their operations as clandestine as possible and they were loath to record any of their actions in writing. We therefore lack precise dates, locations, and names during that epoch. We only know that the friars were there with the people continuing their work, and that whenever there was a surcease in the persecutions they would suddenly reappear in public and resume public activities. Near the end of Queen Anne's reign the persecution abated, although the penal laws were not rescinded, and the friars established themselves openly in Dublin again. By the year 1720 we find them founding a house at Wormwood Gate in Dublin, and in a small house in Loughrea. James of St. Bernard (family name unknown) was the provincial in 1725 when the province of St. Patrick celebrated its first centenary, a hundred years of unbelievably arduous survival.

In the 1720s we also find the Carmelite nuns in Dublin. The first foundation of nuns had taken place at Loughrea in 1680, but it was a short-lived venture. There had been no direct foundation by another convent; instead the friars had gathered a group of Irish ladies, instructed them in the rule, and then admitted them to profession. Teresa of St. Dominic (Teresa Bourke) was the first prioress. During the Orange Revolution the community was forced to abandon the convent, but the nuns apparently continued to live together, dressed in secular clothing, and following the rule as best they could. The remnants of that group were brought to Arran Quay in Dublin sometime in the 1720s, and the nuns continued to wear secular clothes because of the penal laws, but they did openly profess that they were nuns living the religious life. During the same epoch similar convents were also established at Limerick and Cork. For the remainder of the eighteenth century the nuns in Ireland did not observe a strict cloister, and they engaged in the pressing social work of the moment, particularly teaching school. It was not until the early nineteenth century that the nuns were able to follow the regular life of the Second Order.

In 1743, the penal laws were enforced again, and the friars and nuns again had to relinquish their houses and go into hiding in the countryside. But two years later they resumed living in public, and this time the religious houses were to remain open permanently. The friars in Dublin had moved to another site on Stephen's Street, and a third house was established at Ardbreccan in Meath. During this era of the Hanoverian rule the friars quietly organized a school at Stephen's Street in Dublin, staffed by members of the scapular confraternity especially recruited for that purpose. Young children were still being educated at the "hedge schools" in the country, but the Stephen's Street school trained older students in liberal arts and manual training. The school was directed by Robert of Jesus and Mary (Robert Fitzgerald) and it was maintained until the end of the century, when it became legally possible for Catholics to attend school again.

Conditions ameliorated in Ireland when the acts of toleration were enacted in England. The prior of the Dublin monastery, John of St. Bridget (Patrick Ward), was one of the founders of the United Ireland Society in 1791, a movement which pressed for religious freedom in Ireland. In 1793 the friars purchased property at Clarendon Street in Dublin and began construction of the famous St. Teresa's Church. The building was not completed for twelve years due to shortage of funds, but when it was opened in 1805 it became one of the first restoration churches, and it has remained one of Ireland's most popular churches. During the suppression on the Continent following the French Revolution the Irish friars who were studying abroad returned to Ireland, and a house of studies was established at the monastery in Loughrea. Ireland, unlike England, had remained Catholic throughout the long persecutions, and there was a regular supply of vocations.

Daniel O'Connell, the "liberator of Ireland," was a close friend of the friars on Clarendon Street, and he selected one of them as his spiritual director—Francis of St. Teresa (Francis L'Estrange), a native of Dublin who had recently returned home after studies abroad. This friar was a close associate of O'Connell's, assisting him in the cause of liberty, especially by encouraging support among the people for a peaceful revolution. St. Teresa's on Clarendon Street became a center for the campaign for liberty, and O'Connell held several of the original meetings in the church. On July 8, 1817, a major meeting of delegates from all the counties of Ireland was held in the church proper, and O'Connell took the occasion to give what is recorded as "a long and eloquent speech," thanking the Teresian friars for all they had done for Ireland and for their generous assistance to the cause of human freedom. A similar meeting was held at St. Teresa's in 1827 when the English parliament had rejected a bill favoring Irish liberty. Finally in 1829 the Catholic Relief Bill was passed by parliament, and the first bell rung in Dublin to announce the victory was the one at St. Teresa's on Clarendon Street.

The province of St. Patrick celebrated its second centenary in 1825, completing two hundred years of endurance against overwhelming odds. But a new era had dawned in Ireland, and the Carmelites emerged from the centuries of persecution in a healthy and vital and strong condition. They had remained with the people during the years of trial and oppression, helping them, fighting for their liberty, dying for them if necessary. They were the people's priests, and the people did not forget it when better days came. It was a sober lesson that the Church on the Continent could well have learned.

The most symbolic accomplishment of the Discalced Carmelites during the age of expansion was the retaking of Mount Carmel in Palestine by Prosper of the Holy Spirit in 1631. Martin Garaicaval had been born in French Navarre in 1583 and he entered the Order at La Scala in Rome in 1608, taking the name Prosper of the Holy Spirit. After a year in the desert at Genoa, he departed for the missions in Persia. He was elected prior at Ispahan, and in 1627 he established a foundation at Aleppo in Syria, a commercial center and point of departure for caravans through Persia. But his true goal was Mount Carmel in Palestine, lost to the Order since the massacre of 1291. He petitioned Rome for permission to undertake the foundation in the dangerous territory of the Moslems, but he received a less than enthusiastic reply from the general—a terse note which said, "Climb the Mount Carmel of John of the Cross and forget the Carmel of Palestine." He persisted, and at length he received authorization for the expedition, due principally to the support of the procurator general in Rome, Paul of Jesus and Mary, the friar who had led the first group of missionaries to Persia in 1607. The brief from Rome directed Prosper "to set out for the holy Mount of Carmel, alone or in the company of another, and try to obtain possession of that place, and especially of the fountain of our holy father Elijah." He arrived at Caiffa in the fall of 1631, and presented

his case to the Emir Tarabei, explaining the Carmelites' former
history on Mount Carmel and their Elijahan heritage. For a price
of four hundred piasters the Moslem leader agreed to give him a
deed to the principal Carmelite sites on the mountain. This deed
was signed at Caiffa on November 29, and Prosper immediately
climbed the mountain, erected a temporary altar at *el-chadr*, and
celebrated Mass at this site of Berthold's original twelfth-century
foundation.

Prosper then departed for Rome to present the deed to the general
and obtain money for the purchase. The general chapter of 1632, at
which Paul of Jesus and Mary was elected general, approved the
transaction and ordained that henceforth the superior general would
by virtue of his office be the prior of Mount Carmel, a practice that
is still in force in the Discalced Carmelite Order. Prosper returned
to Mount Carmel that same year as the resident superior of the
community, and he arranged an austere form of monastic life by
using the caves and caverns of the mountain for cells, chapel, and
refectory. Shortly afterward additional foundations were made in
Caiffa and Acre. Prosper himself lived on Mount Carmel until his
death in 1663, and he exhibited great tact and astuteness in dealing
with the difficult Moslem situation. A large monastery in the European style was not constructed on Mount Carmel until 1720.

Philip of St. James, a member of the original community on
Mount Carmel in 1633, wrote in his chronicle that the Order had
returned to Palestine so that "the children of that holy mountain
who for several centuries had mourned their exile from their native
land might again enjoy the possession of the mountain . . . and
follow in the footsteps of their first fathers, Elijah and Elisha."

Carmel had returned to its homeland.

– VIII –
THE DARK NIGHT OF REVOLUTION

CARMEL in Europe during the eighteenth century allowed itself to be drawn into the same regretful condition which afflicted the Church at large: an unhealthy withdrawal from the real world of an evolving society. Eighteenth-century Europe was in the midst of a major revolution, both intellectual and sociopolitical, and the Church did not recognize the phenomenon that was occurring. Over the centuries the Church had so closely identified itself with the old order of things that when the old order fell, the Church, to a large extent, fell with it.

Louis XV of France purportedly said in the early part of the century, "*Après nous le déluge*" (after us the deluge). The waters for this deluge were gathering all over Europe as the age of the absolutist prince was about to come to an abrupt close. The middle class, which had emerged as an identifiable sector of society during the twelfth and thirteenth centuries, was still held subservient to the absolute rule of the autocratic prince, but new and undeniable currents of human liberty and freedom were beginning to rise to the surface in what would become a gigantic storm. However, the Church at large aligned itself with these old and sometimes corrupt monarchies, claiming that the crown was its best ally and protector. Bossuet, for example, taught that the alliance between throne and altar was what he called "natural." The Church was monarchist, committed to the *ancien régime* in an age when democracy was bursting onto the scene of the Western world, and the sad irony of the situation was that these monarchies were not even true protectors of the Church— the "court religion" theory had become so much a part of European life that the state dominated the Church, controlled it, regulated its activities in what had become known as Gallicanism, a word that derived from the French control of the Church in its own territories beginning with the reign of Louis XIV.

The French Revolution was the explosion that set men free and ushered in a whole new epoch in the history of man. Revolutions occurred all over Europe in the following decades as democratic forms of government replaced the iron-fisted monarchies, but even then many churchmen were unwilling to admit that these changes were necessary and inevitable and beneficial. Pope Gregory XVI (1831–1846), for example, still maintained that the first point in ecclesiastical policy was to maintain the alliance between throne and altar, however heretical or intolerant the king might be. The inevitability of democratic forms of government was a hard lesson for many churchmen to learn, and well into the twentieth century there were an alarming number of ecclesiastics who still yearned nostalgically for the *ancien régime*, for an epoch when the Church felt itself to be at once the counselor of kings and an organization which was specially protected and financed by the Catholic crowned heads of Europe. Only in isolated situations, like the Church in Ireland, were priests identified with the common man and with the fresh new breezes of human liberty which were blowing through the Western world.

The Church was even more removed from the intellectual revolution that transpired during the eighteenth century. The amazing scientific advances of Isaac Newton at the end of the seventeenth century had inaugurated a whole new era of respect for intellect, of confidence in the power of reason, of concern for human values. A stunning array of profound thinkers appeared on the European intellectual scene in an epoch which was called the Enlightenment, a term which was so pejorative in the minds of many churchmen that it still frightens some ecclesiastics. Among them were Locke, Montesquieu, Hume, Beccaria, Richardson, Kant, Rousseau, Holbach, and the gifted writer François Arouet, better known by his *nom de plume* Voltaire. These men were artists, social thinkers, humanitarians, liberals, and in the field of religion, either deists or practical atheists. But they were great minds grappling with great ideas—and this terrified the Church in Europe. The only response of Catholic writers to these thinkers was sheer condemnation, artlessly composed in verbose and nearly unreadable scholastic tracts. There was no attempt to study the accomplishments of these men or to communicate with them or to create an avenue of dialogue. Catholics were forbidden to associate with the new thinkers or to read their books or attend their schools. Withdraw, shun, condemn, abhor—those were the orders of the day. And while Catholics were successfully disassociating themselves from this intellectual revolution, the thinkers continued to lacerate the Church in print, by the witty pen of Voltaire or the compelling romanticism of Rousseau. But the distressing fact was that these thinkers were moving society toward a new epoch of enlightened humanitarianism and democracy, and the Church had no part in this movement.

Diderot's *Encyclopedia*, that massive twenty-one-volume work published in the middle of the eighteenth century, became the classic reference text of the Enlightenment, organizing and digesting some of the best thinking of the age. It molded the thinking of the sociopolitical revolutionaries who were soon to create a new order of society in Europe, and it made its impact felt on those residents of the English colonies in the New World who were about to launch the American Revolution. But the *Encyclopedia* was cleverly anti-Catholic and rationalistic, equating the Church with the old monarchical institutions of Europe, presenting it as a political anachronism which must be destroyed with the monarchies. The Church condemned the *Encyclopedia*, placing it on the Roman Index.

Thus when the violent revolutions of the late eighteenth and early nineteenth centuries erupted in Europe, the Church was as much a target as the *ancien régime*. The thefts, the savagery, the brutalities, the ravage, the murder of priests and nuns were all unworthy of and unfaithful to the principles of liberty and humanitarianism enunciated by the thinkers of the Enlightenment. But, to some extent, the Church was partly to blame—it had stood apart, divorced and indifferent, from a major transition in the history of man.

Carmel appeared to be burdened with the ecclesiastical malaise of the age, the spirit of divorcement from the contemporary scene, a sense of comfortable complacency with its own inner accomplishments, an unrealistic attitude that the monarchies were here to stay and the world was never going to change. Throughout Europe the Order leaned heavily on the support and protection of the Catholic thrones—in France, Spain, Germany, the Lowlands, and the Italian states. And the Order continued to grow impressively. Immediately before the French Revolution a census of the Discalced Carmelites showed that there were ten provinces in the Spanish congregation and twenty-four in the Italian congregation. There were 113 convents of nuns in Spain, and 169 in the rest of the world.

But there seemed to be a distressing lack of vitality throughout the

Order in Europe, especially when compared with the dynamism of the preceding century. The Order had committed the egregious mistake so common in the post-Tridentine era of withdrawing from the universities and establishing its own courses of studies within the monastery walls, which was in reality a return to the monastic school tradition of the eleventh century. The result of that one policy was a diminution in the quality of the men who joined the Order: whereas Teresa had wanted the Discalced to establish themselves on the university campus so they could participate in the intellectual movements and attract good vocations, the Discalced of the eighteenth century separated themselves from the university life and found that the new recruits were of inferior quality—good, pious men, but generally lacking the flash and the verve of people like Thomas of Jesus and Dominic of Jesus and Mary in the preceding century.

In that baroque era, the biographies of the Carmelites seem for the most part to be stories of rather insular people, holy enough but totally unaware that their world was about to come crashing down around them. In contrast to the great number of fairly mediocre and uninspiring lives, a few exceptions stand out. In Italy there were Blessed Mary of the Angels at Turin, and St. Teresa Margaret at Florence. Mary of the Angels (1661–1717), a woman of angelic purity, joined the Carmel of Turin at the age of fifteen, ultimately became prioress, and then founded the convent of Mancaglieri. She died at the age of fifty-six after a life of unswerving piety and devotion, and she was beatified by Pope Pius IX in 1865. Teresa Margaret of the Sacred Heart (1747–1770), from the illustrious Redi family of Florence, entered the convent at eighteen and died four years later at the age of twenty-two. She was a sweet young girl who sacrificed herself completely and unstintingly to the service of the nuns in the community, a number of whom were elderly and bedridden; and she endured with astonishing maturity and equanimity the abuse heaped on her by a demented old nun who was under her care. Pope Pius XI canonized St. Teresa Margaret in 1934. The nuns in France received two rather unusual people into Carmel. In 1725 Marie-Jeanne Gauthier, a comedienne from the Comédie Française, and the brightest name in the French theater, abandoned her career and entered the Carmel at Lyons where she led an edifying life for thirty-two years. And in 1770, Louise of France, the daughter of Louis XV, entered the Carmel of Saint-Denis at Paris, dying seventeen years later at the age of fifty-one after a life of heroic penance.

The most distinguished friar of the epoch was John Anthony of St. Bernard, destined to become the first cardinal of the reform. Bernardo Guadagni was born in Florence in 1674, entered the priesthood, and became a canon in the cathedral at Florence. He joined the Carmelite Order at Florence in 1700, and eventually became prior of the monastery in that city and provincial of the Tuscan province. In 1724, he was consecrated bishop of the diocese of Arezzo. When his uncle, Lorenzo Corsini, was elected Pope Clement XII, he was summoned to Rome, created a cardinal, and appointed to the Curia. During three pontificates, Guadagni served as secretary of the consistory, counselor to many other congregations, and vicar of Rome. A man of eminent virtue, despite the apparent nepotism in his elevation to high ecclesiastical office, his cause for beatification was introduced after his death at Rome in 1759. As an interesting historical note, Guadagni's sister, Teresa Maria of Jesus, a nun of the Carmel of Florence, was the novice mistress of the future St. Teresa Margaret of the Sacred Heart.

In that era of close association between altar and throne, no friar was more extraordinary than Emmanual of St. Joseph, the violent critic of the royalty who became known as "the phantom of Madrid." Emmanual Friere de Silva, a member of a distinguished Portuguese family, joined the army and rose to the rank of captain. In 1713, he entered the Discalced Carmelites in the Navarre province in Spain, taking the name Emmanual of St. Joseph. An eloquent preacher, he eventually was stationed at the monastery in Madrid, where he inaugurated a clandestine campaign of critique and satire against the Spanish court. He was a clever writer, and in 1736 he began to compose a series of witty and abrasive satires which parodied the affluence and corruption of the court and particularly of the royal family, Philip V and Isabella. Through his confederates these satirical pieces were secretly printed and circulated in Madrid, and they even found their way into the palace, where they were surreptitiously placed beneath the king's pillow or in his pocket or under the plates in the dining hall. Each Thursday for almost a year these satires appeared regularly, and the infuriated king was unable to discover the author or the system of distribution. As the finger of suspicion began to point toward the friar in the Carmelite monastery, the Spanish general, Joseph of the Holy Spirit, an author in his own right but in a vastly different field, ordered Emmanual to flee Spain for his safety. However, he was apprehended at the Spanish border as he was attempting to cross into Portugal, arrested, and returned to Madrid where he was jailed. Ten months later he escaped, journeyed in disguise to Lisbon, and from there to Florence in Italy. He remained a member of the Italian congregation for the rest of his life, except for a short period in 1746 after the death of Philip V when he returned to Navarre. But he found himself still persona non grata in Spain and had to flee again to Italy. Emmanual of St. Joseph died at the monastery in Prato in Toscana in 1770. He is regarded as the father of political satire in Spain, and his writings were collected and published in 1788 under the title *El Duendo Crítico de la Corte* (The Phantom Critic of the Court).[1]

However, these Carmelites were more the exception than the rule, and the prevailing mood in Europe during the eighteenth century seemed to be one of complacency and self-satisfaction. Only on the missions and in the British Isles was there a spirit of enterprise, a healthy restlessness, and a desire to advance the human condition. In 1761 war broke out in Palestine between the government of Acre and the nomadic sheiks, and in the course of the conflict the monastery on Mount Carmel was destroyed. Funds were collected throughout Europe for a new monastery, which was completed in 1772. Although there was no connection between the trouble in Palestine and the seething discontent which was mounting in Europe, the destruction of Mount Carmel was grimly prophetic of what was about to happen to the Order at large.

The first major indication of the Church's imminent problems was the suppression of the Jesuits throughout Europe between 1759 and 1773. The Church had long regarded the princes of Europe as its main support, but now these princes were showing themselves to be as fickle and as untrustworthy as the later revolutionaries. Voltaire considered the suppression of the Jesuits as the necessary first step toward destroying the effectiveness of the Church, and this Voltairian thesis endured as a key concept of the ensuing revolutions—a bitter

---

[1] *El Duendo Crítico de la Corte* was republished in Madrid in 1788 and again in 1889. It is amusing reading for those who are familiar with the Bourbon court of that epoch. In one satirical piece he imagines a scene in the palace where the court is about to celebrate Christmas by staging a Nativity play —however, the play has to be abandoned because among the ladies-in-waiting there is no one qualified to play the Virgin.

distrust and hatred for the exempt religious orders, those international priests who were not subject to local bishops or easily intimidated by national governments. The revolutions were therefore, in many respects, more antireligious than anticlerical.

The next ominous event was the suppression of the religious orders in Austria by Joseph II in 1781. Joseph II, the son of Maria Theresa of Austria, was an enlightened despot deeply influenced by the writings of the Enlightenment. He tried to construct a new social order in his territories, an attempt which ultimately failed, but he effectively brought the Church under his complete domination. He considered the Church as a department of state, and he regulated such minor details as the number of candles at Mass and the use of incense—and for that he was called, disparagingly, "the Sacristan." In 1781 he commanded the suppression of all religious orders which were not engaged in some kind of social work, and in his decree of suppression he specifically named the mendicants whom he called "parasites and beggars." Thus in one fell blow, all of the Carmelite monasteries and convents were seized by the government in the territories of Austria, which at that time embraced sections of present-day Poland, Italy, and the Lowlands. Most of the friars and nuns emigrated to other provinces of the Order, but some of the friars remained in Austria, serving the people as diocesan priests.

The storm which had been mounting for many decades in Europe finally broke violently at the assembly of the Estates-General at Versailles in May of 1789. Revolutionary theories were passionately announced and the Third Estate proclaimed the establishment of a National Assembly. Louis XVI locked the delegates out of their hall, but they moved to a large building nearby and proclaimed the Tennis Court Oath. The revolution was under way. The Bastille in Paris fell during July of that year, and acts of violence against the nobility and the Church occurred all over France. The National Assembly set about the business of destroying the *ancien régime* and building a new society. In October the Declaration of the Rights of Man was issued, a decree which embodied the ideas of Rousseau and the philosophers of the Enlightenment plus thoughts and phrases from the English Bill of Rights and the American Declaration of Independence.

The Church came under almost immediate attack. During the fall of that year all landed estates held by the Church were confiscated, and on October 19 the National Assembly decreed that all religious vows taken by men and women in France were temporarily suspended. Finally, in February of 1790, religious orders were declared suppressed and abolished and their possessions became the property of the government, the only exception being for orders engaged in education or hospital work. These laws of suppression were not enforced everywhere immediately, but in the course of the next four years they were extended all over France as the frenzy of the Reign of Terror began to mount. The Civil Constitution of the Clergy was passed by the National Assembly in July of 1790, requiring diocesan priests to become salaried functionaries of the state, and only those priests who took an oath to the Constitution (the "juring clergy") were allowed to operate. The Constitution furthermore decreed that all religious—who had already been forbidden to live publicly as religious—could now be freed from their vows by appearing before a civil magistrate and making a declaration to that effect, and in turn they would be given a sum of money.

The Carmelite monastery on the rue de Vaugirard numbered sixty-four friars at the outbreak of the revolution. In comparison with other Parisian communities, the Carmelites did not fare badly during the early days of the new republic because the friars were sympathizers of the revolution, and they were allowed to remain quietly in their monastery, although the church was closed and they were not able to function publicly as priests. Eight friars left the monastery to declare their freedom from vows before a magistrate, but the other fifty-six remained at the rue de Vaugirard until August of 1792 when the Reign of Terror was about to commence. The friars were expelled, and the monastery was converted into a prison.

The September massacres of 1792 ushered in a new phase of the revolution, a fanatical attack of unbelievable venom and irrationality against the Church in France. A religion of reason was established by the government, the Christian calendar was replaced by a new revolutionary calendar which abolished Sundays and holy days, and the Church of Notre Dame was converted into a temple dedicated to the goddess of reason and a prostitute was enthroned on the main altar. The juring clergy continued to function, but they were merely harmless puppets of the state; however, a whole group of priests, religious and diocesan, functioned underground at the risk of death or imprisonment, since only the juring clergy were legally allowed to administer the sacraments, preach, or wear religious garb.

During the Reign of Terror the six Carmelite provinces in France collapsed. Prior to the revolution there had been seventy-nine monasteries of friars and sixty-five convents of nuns, and all of these properties were confiscated by the government. The monastery churches were often turned over to the various dioceses for use by the juring clergy, but the state made use of the monasteries proper and the surrounding land—and this was a usual pattern of the confiscations throughout Europe during the nineteenth century. Many of the Carmelite friars and nuns emigrated to other provinces, mainly those in Italy, the Lowlands, and Spain. Some, like the eight friars at the rue de Vaugirard, defected and renounced their vows. But a great number remained in France, living in secret and attempting to follow their vocation as best they could. The nuns usually disbanded into small groups of three or four women and lived in private homes in the same area, wearing lay dress and attempting to appear as maiden ladies. Within their houses they followed the Carmelite rule, and the prioress would visit the various groups in an effort to maintain conventual discipline despite the circumstances. These furtive convents were frequently discovered, and the nuns either jailed or killed. Madeline of the Cross (Anne Vial), the sixty-two-year-old prioress of the convent at Lyons, was apprehended in one of the secret convents, and together with four of her nuns was guillotined in April of 1794.

It is uncertain how many friars were captured while they were administering the sacraments. Priests who were arrested during the Reign of Terror were either quickly killed, usually within twenty-four hours after their arrest, or deported to the offshore islands of Ré and Oléron or to the infamous penal colony on Devil's Island in the South American colony of French Guiana. Firmin of the Nativity was executed at Amiens, and Dositheus of St. Peter and Theodosius of St. Alexis were guillotined at Arras. Three other Carmelites—Louis, Andrew, and Louis Ambrose—were apprehended in Lyons and were shot before firing squads within a few months of each other. Another friar, Charles (Roland), was hung on a tree near Salon-de-Provence after his right thumb and forefinger had been amputated. The names of the other martyred friars remain buried beneath the bloody seas of that indescribably savage period.

The most celebrated of all the religious executed during the Reign of Terror were the Carmelite nuns of Compiègne, Blessed Thérèse of St. Augustine and the fifteen members of her community.[2] Compiègne is located fifty miles north of Paris on the Oise River, and the Carmelite convent there had been founded in 1641. It had been a successful foundation, and at the outbreak of the Revolution the prioress was Thérèse of St. Augustine (Marie-Madeleine Lidoine), a native of Paris who had entered the convent at the age of twenty-one and had been elected prioress just two years previously, at the age of thirty-five. She was a bright woman, admirably equipped to deal with the crises ahead, and her deep spirituality, particularly as it is manifested in her extant letters, was based on a profound spirit of trust in the goodness of God; and as such it bears a remarkable resemblance to the doctrine of Thérèse of Lisieux a century later. The members of the community were a mixed assortment of personalities, and none of them appears at first inspection to be particularly unusual or outstanding, but they seemed individually to have grown in strength and character as they moved through the drama of their communal martyrdom, thus presenting a striking example of group dynamics in a community setting. In August of 1790, a functionary of the government appeared at the convent and offered the nuns their freedom according to the tenets of the new constitution, but they all refused, stating that the offer was one of a "ridiculous freedom." The nuns were able to remain in their convent two years longer, and shortly before their expulsion the prioress proposed to the community that they offer themselves to God as victims to obtain peace for the Church and the state. All of the nuns agreed immediately, except the two oldest nuns, both octogenarians, who were terrified at the implications of that offering; however, that same evening the two nuns overcame their fear and joined the rest of the community in that heroic act which expressed the spirit and authenticity of their later martyrdom.

[2] The Carmelites of Compiègne have been widely publicized in our time by Gertrud von Le Fort's novel The Song at the Scaffold, from which Georges Bernanos adopted his Dialogues of the Carmelites, a film script completed shortly before his death in 1948. Francis Poulenc in turn based the libretto of his modern opera Dialogues of the Carmelites on the Bernanos script. All three of these works are of outstanding artistic merit, but they take enormous liberties with the historical facts. Blanche de la Force, for example, a principal character in the opera, is purely fictional, a somewhat clumsy artistic device employed to dramatize the terror of the guillotine. Nevertheless the three works convincingly capture the heroism of the sixteen nuns and their growing solidarity as they approach their moment of terrible greatness.

In September of 1792 the nuns of Compiègne were expelled from their convent, and they went into hiding as had other Carmelite nuns, splitting into four groups which took up residence in houses in the area of Compiègne. They continued their clandestine convent life until June of 1794 when they were discovered, arrested, and imprisoned at Compiègne. Since most of the cases at that stage of the revolution were being referred to Paris, the nuns were handcuffed, loaded into open carts and transported to Paris in a two-day journey of heartless discomfort and cruelty. The nuns ranged in age from the two octogenarians, to a group in middle age, to two nuns in their thirties, to the youngest, a novice of twenty-eight. When they arrived at the Paris jail, one of the older nuns was pulled from the cart and dashed to the ground by a soldier. A few days later they were brought to the tribunal of judgment, which was located at a place ironically called the Hall of Liberty. Accused of practicing the religious life against the proscriptions of the constitution and of being "religious fanatics" and sympathizers of the king, they were condemned to death. A witness later testified that as they were led from the hall "their faces were beaming with joy." Back in their prison cell the nuns began to dress themselves in a garb of some similarity to their Carmelite habits. They were already wearing brown dresses, and they fashioned long white mantles for themselves out of pieces of white cloth they had carried with them, and black veils. Thus on July 17, they were carried through the streets of Paris in open carts, dressed as Carmelite nuns, their hands handcuffed behind their backs.

The execution of the nuns of Compiègne was one of the most dramatic scenes in the French Revolution, and it marked a turning point in the Reign of Terror, demonstrating the aberrations to which the Revolution had descended. For could not the doctrine of liberty and humanitarianism enunciated by the thinkers of the Enlightenment even tolerate the presence of sixteen harmless nuns who only wanted to be left alone and say their prayers? As the nuns were transported into the Place du Trône that July 17 of 1794 a deadly hush fell over the crowd. Five thousand people had already been guillotined at Paris during the Reign of Terror, and it had become somewhat of a sport to the crowd, accompanied by cheers and the roll of drums. During the long ride across the city the nuns had been chanting aloud the *Miserere* and the *Salve Regina* and the

Te Deum, and as the carts pulled into the Place the crowd seemed stunned by the sight of these sixteen women standing, swaying, in their creaking carts, chanting their hymns with happy smiles, apparently oblivious to the terror which was only a few moments away. They arrived at the foot of the guillotine, where Thérèse of St. Augustine intoned the *Veni Creator,* and when the nuns had completed the hymn they renewed aloud their baptismal promises and their religious vows in the Order. Thérèse, as prioress, requested to remain until the end so she could guide her community. The young novice, Constance Meunier, was selected first. She knelt at the feet of her prioress, asked for her blessing and permission to die, and then ascended the steps. She refused to allow the executioner even to touch her, and she calmly laid her head on the block. The prioress chanted the *Laudate Dominum,* and the guillotine smacked down, decapitating the novice. The nuns continued the Litany of the Blessed Virgin, as one by one the community ascended the steps and was guillotined. The voices grew fewer and fewer until only Thérèse of St. Augustine remained. She had done her job. She climbed the steps and the guillotine flashed for the last time. Not a sound was heard in the Place during the executions and the drums were not rolled. Pius X beatified the sixteen nuns from Compiègne on May 27, 1906.

The senseless and totally unnecessary execution of these inoffensive women who were guillotined "for the public safety" seemed to have a sobering effect on the mass hysteria which was raging in Paris.[8] The Reign of Terror came to a sudden halt, and ten days later Maximilien Robespierre, the principal leader of this savagery, was himself guillotined on the same spot where the nuns of Compiègne had been killed.

But the damage had been done. The Carmelite provinces of France had been eradicated, and the government intended to keep them that way. The Concordat of 1801 between Napoleon and the pope restored some amount of peace and ostensible harmony between Church and state in France, but there was no mention of religious priests in the Concordat. A report by the French Ministry of Cults in that same year of 1801 states triumphantly that "all the

---

[8] The murder of the nuns of Compiègne was so inexplicable and inhuman that Pius X in his brief for their beatification attributed it to "the infernal powers striving for the destruction of God's kingdom on earth."

monastic institutions have disappeared," and that "ecclesiastical discipline will no longer be disfigured by these disastrous and unjust exemptions and privileges." The French political regimes of the nineteenth century tolerated the re-establishment of the nuns, as we shall see, but the friars were unable to re-establish until 1839, and they remained in a precarious position until after the First World War in this century.

The Carmelite provinces in the Lowlands were almost totally suppressed during the invasion of the revolutionary armies in 1796, except for the friars' monasteries at Bruges, Gand, and Ypres, and the nuns' convent at Liége—all of which were somehow able to subsist during the whole revolutionary and Napoleonic era. During the Napoleonic wars of conquest in the early part of the nineteenth century the ideas of the French Revolution were carried into all the conquered territories and the Carmelite provinces were suppressed wherever the armies marched—Bavaria and Switzerland and the left bank of the Rhine in 1802, the right bank of the Rhine in 1804, Spain in 1806, and the Italian peninsula in 1807. The French employed the same tactics they had learned during the French Revolution; however, the suppressions were mostly peaceful, except for the brutal situation in Spain where the Franco-Spanish War was producing new examples of human savagery.[4]

After the defeat of Napoleon and the re-establishment of the European balance of power by the Congress of Vienna in 1815, the Carmelite provinces in the formerly occupied territories were able to make a partial recuperation. The recovery was only partial, and in most cases short-lived, because the humanitarian ideas of the French Revolution had spread through Europe like a grass fire, independent of the forced imposition of those ideas by Napoleon's armies. The crowned heads who still remained temporarily in power were not unhappy with the suppression of the religious priests in their territories, and the religious were unable to recover all their former properties after Napoleon's withdrawal. The only country

[4] Many of the Carmelite friars, particularly those in the northern section of Navarre, took to the hills and joined the small bands of Spanish soldiers which swept down regularly to harass the French. This type of disorganized military operation was called, for the first time in history, *guerrilla* warfare (literally, little war), and thus a new and distressing word was born into the human language.

where the Carmelites were able to make an almost total recovery was in Spain; after the accession to the throne of Ferdinand VII in 1814 the religious orders were restored to their former position. But the movement for liberty in Europe was under way, and it could not be denied. The royalty had to be abolished, or at least be so legally restricted that it remained only a figurehead, and the Church and the religious had to succumb with it. In addition to the pristine ideas of the French Revolution, the later revolutionaries of the nineteenth century discovered that the state could benefit handsomely by the confiscation of religious properties. Thus much of the eagerness to suppress monasteries and convents was carried along by the desire to steal the properties of religious orders which, in some cases, had been their legal and undisputed possessions for centuries.

Pedro IV of Portugal died in 1834, and his daughter Maria da Gloria was unable to stem the revolutionary tide. The revolutionaries took over the government and suppressed the religious orders, including the Carmelite provinces. In the previous year the inept Ferdinand VII died in Spain, and the Carlist civil war erupted, bringing the new liberals to power. In 1835 the Carmelite Order was suppressed, eight provinces of more than two thousand friars and eighty-three convents of nuns. The same heartless events occurred in Spain as had transpired in France during the time of suppression: legal proscription, furtive conventual life, discovery, death, and imprisonment. There were wholesale massacres of the friars in Madrid, and nine Carmelite friars were murdered in the monastery at Reus in Catalonia when revolutionaries broke into the building. One of the friars at Reus, Andrew of Jesus and Mary, the eighty-five-year-old former general of the Spanish congregation, ill and bedridden, was asphyxiated to death when they pushed a burning torch into his mouth. In 1836 an official statement of the government claimed, suavely: "The religious orders have undoubtedly rendered great services to the Church and state in other times, but since today they are no longer found to be in harmony with the principles of civilization nor the needs of the age, the voice of public opinion demands that they be suppressed." The work of the Spanish revolutionaries was ruthlessly effective, and most of the Carmelite monasteries were converted into military barracks or government office buildings. For more than thirty years the Carmelite Order lay dormant in Spain.

And the revolutions continued throughout Europe. The Carmelite province of Lithuania was suppressed in 1831; Poland, in 1832, and again in 1864. Only the monastery at Czarna remained untouched. In Germany only the monastery at Würzburg in Bavaria endured through the crisis. The Italian provinces made a partial recovery after the Napoleonic wars, but they fell again during the Italian wars of independence and unification under Mazzini and Cavour and Garibaldi—in 1849, and in 1859, and again in 1860. By the year 1866 the Carmelite provinces of Genoa, Lombardy, Naples, Sicily, Piedmont, and Tuscany were destroyed. Only the Roman province remained, and it was suppressed briefly in 1870 when Victor Emmanuel's forces captured Rome. However, that province quickly revived as soon as the hostilities ceased.

The devastation of the Order during the nineteenth century also meant the destruction of most of its far-flung missionary activities. The mission in Brazil collapsed completely when the friars were expelled in 1831 and 1840 during the preliminary struggle for complete independence from Portugal. The Mexican province, as we have seen, was severely crippled by the expulsion of the Spaniards, but it managed to survive multiple persecutions throughout the nineteenth century. The missions in the Near East and the Orient collapsed completely, but the missions in India, which had prudently recruited a steady supply of native vocations, endured and prospered. The Indian missions were also assisted in the nineteenth century by friars from the Irish province, which was now in a healthy state and able to send out its own missionaries. John Francis of St. Teresa (William Whelan), a native of Dublin and a prior of St. Teresa's on Clarendon Street, was consecrated bishop of Bombay in 1843. Another Irish friar, Joseph of the Annunciation (Francis Nicholson), born in Dublin in 1803, was consecrated bishop of Corfu in the Greek islands in 1846.

The British Isles remained largely untouched by the revolutionary upheavals on the Continent following the defeat of Napoleon. Britain had wisely come to grips with the movement for liberty before the storm erupted and had declared a constitutional monarchy. The acts of religious toleration had been decreed at the end of the nineteenth century, but the Carmelite friars were unable to benefit from them because of a lack of vocations and the collapse of the provinces on the Continent. The last friar on the mission was Francis Brewster, a native of Lincolnshire who studied at the new English Carmelite monastery in Tongres, and when that was suppressed, transferred to the monasteries of the Order at Heidelberg and Cologne. He built a church in the town of Market Rasen in Lincolnshire in 1824 and worked there for a quarter of a century. In reply to a government request for information about the Order in England, he wrote: "No superior, no inferior, being the last man." He died in 1849, and the inscription in the parish record notes, *Postremus in Anglia Carmeliticae familiae alumnus* (the last member of the Carmelite family in England). However, the nuns had located themselves in England during the suppressions in the Lowlands. The English convent founded at Antwerp by Anne of Jesus in 1619, and the daughter foundations at Lierre in 1648 and at Hoogstraten in 1678, all came to England in 1794, sailing from Rotterdam and landing in London. The Antwerp group located at Lanherne in Cornwall, the Lierre group at Darlington, and the Hoogstraten group at Canford House in Dorset.

By the middle of the nineteenth century, then, the Carmelite Order was desperately ravaged on the continent of Europe. At one time or another every one of the Continental provinces had been suppressed, and while the Order never ceased to function, it was nevertheless brought to the brink of extinction as its once prosperous provinces were reduced to tattered remnants of their former selves.

The liberal revolutions of the nineteenth century seemed to operate in a chain reaction from country to country, and thus the suppression of the various provinces occurred at different times throughout the century. As the smoke settled in each country and the frenzy abated, the Carmelites were able to begin the labored work of reconstruction, with the result that the suppression and reconstruction of different provinces was sometimes transpiring simultaneously in Europe. Some monasteries, as we have noted, were never suppressed, but this was for individual and local reasons and did not affect the general picture of the Order's ravaged condition. The desert at Las Palmas in Spain, for example, was in a remote, rocky region, and of no value to the land-hungry revolutionaries, and therefore the few desert fathers remained unmolested. The monastery at Loano in Genoa was protected by the powerful Doria family who retained the deed to the property throughout the Italian revolutions and thus safeguarded the friars who were living on what was legally Doria property. And we have seen that the three monasteries in Belgium and those at Czarna[5] and Würzburg were able to survive the upheavals. But despite the early reconstructions and the few surviving monasteries, the Order was in a severely damaged state until 1875 when the major reconstructions were inaugurated and Carmel regrouped itself for the beginning of a new and better epoch.

The monastery at Mount Carmel, while removed from the turbulence of the liberal revolutions in Europe, was nevertheless having its own difficulties during the same epoch. In 1798 the French Directory sent the brilliant young general Napoleon Bonaparte on an expedition to Egypt in order to block the English communications and trade with the Far East. The Egyptian expedition had much publicity but little real success; however, it did bring Napoleon into the spotlight of European politics. On his march down to Egypt, Napoleon encamped outside Acre in Palestine and laid siege to the ancient city. He threw his cannon and his musketeers at Acre, but it held after a fierce struggle, and Napoleon had to proceed south without being able to subdue the defending Turks. He climbed Mount Carmel and commandeered the Carmelite monastery as a hospital for his wounded soldiers. Napoleon left this hospital encampment on Mount Carmel when he departed for Egypt, and thus the Carmelites found their monastery filled with wounded French soldiers and the hilltop covered with the tents of the military guard which remained behind. However, the Carmelites were able to continue their monastic life despite the presence of their uninvited guests—until the Turkish Janissaries learned of the presence of the detested French on Mount Carmel. In 1799, Janissaries of Djezzar rode up the hill, slaughtered all the French soldiers, bombarded the monastery, and drove the friars off the mountain.

In 1804, a small group returned to Mount Carmel led by Julius of the Holy Savior (Raphael Colleja), a Maltese who was a member of the Roman province and who was then thirty-three years old. He cleaned up the debris, buried the remains of the French soldiers who were still uninterred, and re-established conventual life in the

[5] The monastery at Czarna was located in Austrian Galicia and was one of the few monasteries restored after the death of Joseph II in 1790. During that epoch Galicia constituted part of the Austrian Empire, but the Polish settled there in such great numbers that it was eventually incorporated into Poland by the treaties at the end of the First World War.

monastery which was habitable despite the wreckage and devastation of the Turkish bombardment. In 1817, the general in Rome sent to Mount Carmel the talented young lay brother John Baptist of the Blessed Sacrament (Charles Casini), a native of Frascati who had already distinguished himself as a gifted architect.[6] He had started work on the restoration of the ravaged monastery when the Greco-Turkish conflict of 1820 erupted in Palestine. Some of the severest fighting occurred in the area around Mount Carmel, and the friars took refuge in their house in Caiffa. In 1821 the conflict carried to the top of Mount Carmel and the monastery was totally destroyed by cannon fire.

Again the Carmelites climbed their hill and started the process of reconstruction. Casini designed an entirely new monastery, and during the next number of years he toured Europe collecting funds for the construction. The building was started in 1827 and finally completed in 1836. Three years later Pope Gregory XVI declared the new church a basilica and bestowed on it the title *Ordinis Carmelitici caput* (the head of the Carmelite Order). Casini's striking and impressive monastery still remains—except for additions made in 1853 by another lay brother, Charles of All Saints—the building which today stands majestically on top of modern Mount Carmel.

The saga of destruction and reconstruction which transpired on Mount Carmel was appropriately symbolic of the task that lay ahead for the entire Carmelite Order throughout the nineteenth century— the gigantic work of reconstruction.

---

[6] The story of Charles Casini demonstrates the unhappy plight of the exclaustrated religious during the nineteenth-century revolutions. He was born at Frascati in 1778, entered the novitiate at La Scala in Rome in 1801, and then was expelled from the monastery by the invading French troops who closed the religious houses of Rome in 1809. He went to work as an architect, and returned to the monastery when it was reopened in 1814. After his assignment to Mount Carmel in 1817, he remained a member of that community all his life, and died there in 1849.

– IX –
RECONSTRUCTION

THE Carmelite reform made its recovery in a changed world. By the second half of the nineteenth century the liberal concepts of the French Revolution had become a part of European life, and in the year 1867 Karl Marx, an exiled German living in England, published the first volume of his *Das Kapital*, which was the harbinger of a new brand of radical liberalism. Political and military power was moving eastward—it had shifted from France to Germany, and in the twentieth century it would move on to Russia, and perhaps further eastward to China. The working man had emerged as a fully enfranchised and politically empowered person, and he would soon become economically powerful by the establishment of the trade unions. The Church was beginning to find that it had to discover a place for itself in this changed world. The revolutionary upheavals and the blessed loss of the Papal States had made it eloquently clear that the old order had passed, that the baroque age was over, that the Church could no longer triumphantly preside over Christian Europe but instead it must do what it should have been doing all that time—serve the people of God. These lessons were painfully and arduously learned in many cases, and it was not until Vatican Council II in the twentieth century that proper concepts of the Church's role in the world were at length adequately comprehended and articulated.

For the Carmelite Order the sorrow of the nineteenth century was also a time of searching reappraisal and painful but necessary purification. The Order had ridden on the Church's cloud of triumphalism and felt that it had a permanent and uncontested place in Christian Europe. The Order had too much property, too many friars and nuns, and not enough contact with the common man. It had to restudy its ancient prophetic vocation and make it relevant to the real world of a new and modern society. The age of pious divorcement from pressing human problems, of a sacristy mentality in the midst of a societal chaos, had happily passed into history. Again, there were many in the Carmelite Order who found it difficult to learn the lesson of history, who merely wanted to re-establish the old arrangement of things after the smoke of the revolutions had drifted away—and again, there were some who would not be able to comprehend these lessons adequately until the dawn of Vatican II. But on the whole, the Order made an amazing recovery that was truly phenomenal. And it emerged from the bloody era of the revolutions with a dynamism and an enthusiasm it had not seen since the golden age of the seventeenth century. The Carmelite Order, entering into the modern epoch, found itself confronted with staggering problems of reconstruction, but it also discovered itself to be more authentically Elijahan and Teresian.

The few foundations which escaped suppression provided the basis for a large part of the early reconstruction period in the nineteenth century. The province of Belgium, which managed to save three monasteries and one convent from suppression, was reconstructed fairly easily. Melchior of St. Mary (Dessein), prior of the monastery at Ypres when the French revolutionary forces marched through the Lowlands in 1784, was mainly responsible for keeping the four foundations alive during the hard years of the early nineteenth century. The friars had to live quietly and unobtrusively, without religious habits, and they were not allowed to receive novices or educate friars for the priesthood, but Melchior sent young applicants for the Order to Rome for their novitiate and studies. When Belgium obtained its independence from Holland in 1830, the friars in the three monasteries of Bruges, Ghent, and Ypres were immediately able to come out of seclusion: they established a novitiate, recalled their students from Italy, and in the next few years made additional foundations at Ghent and Courtrai. The nuns at Liége were also able to resume open activities after 1830, and they quickly made additional foundations.

In Austria the friars' monastery at Czarna survived the holocaust, and the nuns were able to open a convent at Gmunden in 1828. Two years later another convent was established at Graz; the friars established their second Austrian monastery there in 1844. In Germany the surviving monastery at Würzburg opened another monastery at Regensburg in 1836, and nuns from Gmunden came to

Würzburg to establish the first convent of the reconstruction in Germany. The Austrian and German provinces were on the road to recovery.

In France the nuns made a spectacular and daring recovery, particularly through the efforts of Camille of the Infant Jesus (Camille de Soyecourt), daughter of a wealthy and aristocratic family from Picardy, who had entered the Carmel at the rue de Grenell in Paris in 1784, and who had been imprisoned in 1793 after the convent was suppressed. During the Reign of Terror her mother died in prison and her father was guillotined, but their considerable fortune, which had been saved from the confiscations of the revolutionaries because it was largely invested outside France, passed on to Camille. When peace returned to Paris this exclaustrated nun used part of the money to purchase the former friars' monastery on the rue de Vaugirard from the government. She moved into the large building with a few other exclaustrated Carmelite nuns in 1797, and they resumed a rather clandestine form of religious life, without cloister or religious habits, under the very noses of the revolutionaries in those turbulent days when Napoleon was coming to power. Although the small group on the rue de Vaugirard was not able to establish a true form of Carmelite life until the final defeat of Napoleon almost twenty years later, Camille assisted, by her encouragement and her financial aid, in the restoration of a number of other Carmels outside Paris: Tours was re-established in 1798, Amiens in 1799, Montauban in 1801, Bourges in 1803, and Agen in 1807. However, almost all of these Carmels lived without cloister or habit during the first period of the reconstruction, and they had to resort to numerous subterfuges in order to remain in existence.

When Napoleon was holding Pope Pius VII prisoner at Fontainebleau in 1813, Camille supplied money to the pope and his retinue of "black cardinals." Napoleon's intention had been to thoroughly incapacitate the pope, allowing him no outside contacts nor financial resources, and when Camille's assistance to the pitiable Pius VII was discovered she was promptly arrested, subjected to long and grueling interrogations, and finally exiled from Paris for life. She retired to the small town of Guise where she awaited better days.

After Napoleon was defeated in 1814 and exiled to the island of Elba in the Mediterranean, Camille returned to Paris, and at the same time the friars attempted to establish a monastery in the city.

Bruno of St. Sulpice (Dumesnil) obtained a building in the Faubourg Saint-Marceau and gathered some exclaustrated friars, who resumed a conventual life. However, in the spring of 1815 Napoleon escaped from Elba, landed at Cannes, and marched to Paris where he began his frantic Hundred Days. The old dementia flared up in Paris, and the friars' monastery in the Faubourg Saint-Marceau was suppressed and the friars dispersed. That was the end of this premature experiment to re-establish the friars in France. Bruno returned to work as a diocesan priest, and he died a canon of the cathedral in Versailles.

In the post-Napoleonic era Camille was able to commence a regular conventual life in the building on the rue de Vaugirard, and in 1845 she moved the community to more suitable quarters for a nuns' convent on the avenue de Saxe. She lived until 1849, dying at the age of ninety-one. The process of beatification was inaugurated for this fearless and intelligent woman in 1935.

The Carmelite convents in France had an almost unbelievable development throughout the entire nineteenth century. By the year 1880 there were 113 convents, but only 16 of that number were legally established with the necessary permission of the government. And that statistic tells a great deal about the reconstruction of the Order in France and in other parts of Europe: the antireligious laws were still on the books, but the nuns disregarded them and intrepidly founded their convents, and the government made no effort to impede them or enforce the laws. The friars were not as fortunate: they were regarded with greater suspicion and hostility than the cloistered nuns immured behind their walls, and they had more difficulty in establishing their monasteries and then keeping them open in the face of recurring waves of anticlericalism. Of all the convents founded in France during the nineteenth century, two were particularly significant: in 1865, after many attempts which were blocked because of the political overtones, the convent at Compiègne was re-established, thus providing an enduring monument to the former guillotined community; and in 1838 the Carmel of Poitiers established a convent on the rue de Liverot in the small Norman town of Lisieux, where the brightest star of the Carmelite reconstruction would blaze forth at the end of the century.

The friars were finally reintroduced in France by that major figure of the reconstruction, Dominic of St. Joseph (Arvizu), a Spanish friar from the Navarre province who fled to France in 1839 after the suppression in his native land. Born in 1793 and ordained to the priesthood as a Carmelite in 1824, he became a military chaplain for the Carlist forces during the long civil war, and after the Carlist defeat and the Carmelite suppression he found himself a marked man in Spain. He crossed the Pyrenees with six other Carmelites en route for Bordeaux where they hoped to catch a ship sailing for Mexico so they could work with the Carmelites there. Dominic paid a visit to the nuns' convent in Bordeaux, and the prioress, Bathilde of the Infant Jesus, suggested that the time might now be ripe to make another attempt to re-establish the friars in France. With the approval of Cardinal Donnet of Bordeaux, Dominic publicly opened a monastery in the city, but after a short while the police broke in and dispersed the community. He then obtained a piece of property in the unpopulated mountain region at Le Broussey outside Bordeaux and moved the friars there. This foundation held, and after a time Dominic reopened the monastery in Bordeaux. He obtained more exclaustrated friars from Spain, and then began to receive a number of applications from young Frenchmen, who entered the novitiate at Le Broussey. It appeared as if the friars had a foothold again in France. Dominic was named by the general in Rome as commissary general of the Order in France, and new foundations began to multiply: Besançon, Montigny, Agen, Carcassonne. With the aid of additional friars he acquired from Spain and the new French vocations which were coming in unexpected numbers, he was able to construct a healthy province, and he was named first provincial of the reconstructed French province in 1853. Dominic was summoned to Rome in 1859 in order to work on the general's staff, and in 1865 this remarkable Spaniard was elected general of the Italian congregation. By that year of 1865 the friars in France had fifteen monasteries, and in the preceding year they had managed to return to Paris. Unable to obtain the building on the rue de Vaugirard, which was now a school, they established a monastery on the rue Singer, which a few years later was to be the site of a disastrous scandal felt all over Europe. No small part of the friars' sudden popularity in France was due to the presence of Hermann Cohen, the celebrated pianist and disciple of Liszt, who entered the Carmelites after his conversion and who was destined to lead them back to England.

Hermann Cohen was born of a devout Jewish family at Hamburg, Germany, in 1820. He early demonstrated the beginnings of an extraordinary musical talent, and at the age of eleven his mother brought him to Paris where he became a student of Franz Liszt, who adopted him as a special pupil and sponsored his career. When Cohen was fourteen years old, Liszt arranged for him to give a piano recital, and the young boy was hailed in Paris as a child prodigy and a major talent. He was lionized in the salons of Paris and came under the influence of the eccentric female novelist George Sand, who often brought him to her salon and had him play for her while she composed her novels. Sand called him by the diminutive name of "Puzzi" (a corruption of a German slang word meaning "little darling"), and she mentioned the name frequently in her writings, particularly those that appeared in the *Revue des Deux Mondes,* and thus popularized "Puzzi" all over Europe. As he grew older he began to give concerts in Italy, England, and Germany, and he stayed for a while at the conservatory that Liszt had established at Geneva.

By the time Cohen had grown into his early twenties in Paris he was a complete profligate, indulging freely in all the vices. "My life at that time was wholly given up to following my every fancy and caprice," he later wrote in his memoirs. He became an almost compulsive gambler, losing enormous sums over the years, and he had to give special concerts to pay his gambling debts. At the age of twenty-seven a friend of his asked him to play the organ during a benediction service at the Church of Saint-Valere on the rue de Bourgogne, and the young Jew had an unsettling experience at the very moment of the benediction with the monstrance. "I experienced a strange emotion," he wrote, "as it were, a remorse in sharing in this benediction in which I had no right of any kind." And yet he said that he felt a comfort he had never known before. He returned to the church frequently and continued to experience the same deep emotion. Three months later he was baptized a Catholic, to the chagrin of his family, and he amended his life, moving into a small room by himself on the Left Bank. "I felt," he wrote, "that the God of mercy would pardon me all—that He would turn away His eyes from my crimes—that He would have pity on my sincere contrition and my bitter sorrow." Cohen still owed more than thirty thousand francs in gambling debts, and it required two years of concerts to pay them off. During that time he was considering the possibility of becoming a priest, and when he happened to meet a friar from the monastery in Agen who was preaching in Paris he decided to join the Carmelites. He had become an avid reader of St. Teresa of Ávila, and the recent return of the friars to France seemed providential to him.

He received the habit from Dominic of St. Joseph at Le Broussey, adopting the name Augustine of the Blessed Sacrament, and he was professed in 1850. He wrote: "Now St. Teresa is my mother, the scapular my habit, a cell eight feet square my universe. I am so happy. I feel that I am doing the will of God." After his ordination to the priesthood Augustine became renowned as an eloquent preacher, and he was in demand in all parts of France. When he returned to Paris for the first time, his opening statement from the pulpit of St. Sulpice was: "My first words from this Christian pulpit must be words of repentance for the scandals I once committed in this city." He was also instrumental in founding some of the new monasteries, particularly Lyons and the important one in 1858 at Tarasteix in southern France near the Pyrenees, the first desert monastery founded in France during the reconstruction.

In June of 1862 Augustine was sent to Rome to represent the Order at the canonization ceremonies for the Japanese martyrs which Pius IX was attempting to make as spectacular as possible in an act of defiance and rebuff to the Italian revolutionaries. At Rome he met the Englishman, Cardinal Wiseman, who at that moment was trying to bring the religious orders back to England now that the hierarchy had been restored. The cardinal was especially interested in restoring the Carmelites, who had such a brilliant history during the penal days, and he felt that this famous friar might be exactly the man to lead a group to England. Wiseman broached his suggestion to Elisha of the Immaculate Conception, the Carmelite general, but the general refused, claiming that Augustine was needed in France. Undaunted, the cardinal approached Pope Pius IX directly and asked him to override the general's objections and command that Augustine be sent to England. Pius IX agreed, and when he received Augustine in an audience before leaving Rome he said: "I send you to convert England, as in the fifth century, one of my predecessors also blessed and sent the monk Augustine, the former apostle of that country."

Augustine stopped at Paris, where he arranged for a small group of friars to follow him, and set out immediately for London. He obtained a small house attached to the convent of the Assumptionist Sisters in Kensington Square, and on October 15, the feast of St. Teresa of that same year, 1862, he inaugurated the monastery with the friars who had followed him from France. Wiseman presided at the installation ceremonies, accompanied by the future Cardinal Manning and Father Frederick Faber, and the cardinal in an address recalled that he had been a friend of Francis Brewster, the last friar on the Carmelite mission. "This Order was lost in England," Wiseman said, "with the death of the last of the fathers, but today Teresa finds it here once more. In my imagination, I see Teresa calling the holy virgins about her today and exclaiming, 'Congratulate me, congratulate me, for I have found in England this Order which was lost.'"

The new community in London prospered, English vocations presented themselves, and in 1865 Augustine purchased property on Church Street in Kensington for the construction of a permanent foundation. On July 16 of that year the first stone of a new church designed by Pugin was laid by Cardinal Manning, and the building was completed the following year. The famous Pugin Church stood until the night of February 20, 1944, when it was destroyed by V-bombs during the blitz. A new Carmelite church in Kensington was constructed in 1959. Augustine, then, had laid the foundations for a permanent English province. Additional foundations were eventually made at Wincanton, and at Gerrard's Cross in Buckinghamshire. There was a shortage of vocations after the First World War when the "flower of English manhood" had been decimated in muddy fields of France, and in 1927 the English and Irish provinces were united under one jurisdiction. In 1963 the Discalced Carmelites established a monastery at Oxford, the first Carmelite house at the great university since before the reformation. The nuns in England continued to flourish, too. In addition to the three Carmels which were transplanted from the Lowlands in 1794, Cardinal Manning brought a group of nuns from the Carmel on the rue d'Enfer in Paris to London in 1878. This Carmel at St. Charles' Square on Notting Hill became the point of origin for the great majority of Carmels which were founded in England since that time, and for a number of foundations in Australia and New Guinea. In 1960 there were forty convents of Carmelite nuns in England, Wales, and Scotland.

Augustine himself remained in England until 1868, and became a celebrated figure in London. His English was halting when he arrived, and he was forced to write out sermons completely and read them to his audience, but he soon obtained enough proficiency in the language so that he was as much in demand as he had been in France. He preached widely in England, Scotland, and Ireland. Contemporaries remember him as a short, rather stocky man, with traditional Jewish features. He was an extremely devout person, but yet eager and energetic, and he evidenced such a genuine warmth and sincerity that he attracted a vast circle of friends. He continued to use and develop his musical talents as a Carmelite, frequently giving organ concerts in various churches, and he established a musical tradition of contemporary music in the Kensington church which drew crowds from all over London until the early twentieth century when the liturgical reforms of Pius X interdicted the use of contemporary music in liturgical functions and substituted Gregorian chant.

In 1868 he received permission to return to France and retire to the desert of Tarasteix, but during the next two years he was frequently called from his desert retreat to preach courses of sermons. The curé of Ars, a personal friend of his, had once written to him: "You do well to work at the foundation of a desert, but you yourself will not derive much profit from it." In the year 1870 he was appointed master of novices at Le Broussey, but that same year the Franco-Prussian war broke out and Augustine's presence in the French province made things uncomfortable for his confreres: there were mutterings from people outside the monastery about the German who was living with the Carmelites. To save the Order embarrassment, Augustine volunteered to leave the country until the war was over. On the advice of Cardinal Mermillod, he crossed into Switzerland, and then up to Berlin where he became chaplain to the French soldiers imprisoned at the military prison of Spandau outside the city. While ministering to the prisoners he contracted smallpox and died on January 20, 1871, at the age of fifty-one. The French newspaper L'Univers in its obituary for him recalls his brilliant career as an artist, his accomplishments as a Carmelite, and his labors for the prisoners at the end of his life. The obituary recounts that "he was broken down by excessive fatigue, and that the only repose he could be induced to take was the repose of death," and it concludes: "Being what he had become, by the grace of God, it was fitting that Hermann Cohen should die in this way."

The election of the Spaniard Dominic of St. Joseph as general in 1865 occurred at a propitious moment when the Order was breaking into its second spring. This remarkable man, who had already restored the French province, was an excellent choice for general: Pius IX, referring to his linguistic abilities, called him a "polyglot," and said of him that "he had the energy of a Spaniard, the ardor of a Frenchman, and the diplomacy of an Italian."

In 1868, Dominic began the reconstruction of the Spanish provinces. Journeying to Spain, he gathered some of the exiled Spanish friars who were living in the French province, and took them across the Pyrenees to the town of Marquina in the Basque country where he established the first monastery since the suppression in 1835.[1] But that same year of 1868 another disastrous civil war erupted in Spain and seven years of near anarchy ensued. When peace was restored in 1876 with the installation of Alfonso XII and his primitive constitutional monarchy, the Carmelites were able to resume the work

---

[1] An interesting case history of an exclaustrated Spanish friar during the period of the suppression is supplied by Francis of Jesus Mary Joseph (Palau), who was born in Aytona in 1811, professed in the monastery at Barcelona in 1833, and was a student in 1835 when the provinces were suppressed. Ordained in Spain a few years later, he became, like Dominic of St. Joseph, associated with the Carlist forces during the revolution, and had to flee across the Pyrenees in 1838. However, a few years later he stole back into Spain and quietly established a catechetical school in Barcelona. As conditions became more settled in Spain, he began to wear the Carmelite habit openly, and in 1854 he was arrested and deported to Iviza in the Balearic Islands. But three years later this intrepid man was back in Spain again. In 1860 he founded a Third Order community for women called the Discalced Carmelite Missionaries, which engaged in educational and social work. This community flourished during his lifetime, and after his death it was divided into two separate communities, both of which were engaged in the operation of schools, hospitals, and various works of charity. These two communities continued to develop and spread throughout the world, and today they number over five thousand tertiary sisters. Francis traveled to Rome in 1870 for the Vatican Council, at which he was to appear as an expert in a discussion about reactivating the ancient rite of exorcism, but when the Council was dispersed he returned to Spain. He died at Taragona in 1872.

of reconstruction. In 1876, the monastery at Larrea in Navarre was re-established, and in the same year the one at Ávila; the following year saw the re-establishment of monasteries at Burgos, Segovia, and Alba de Tormes. And then an astounding whirlwind of foundations ensued. By the end of the century there were four flourishing provinces of Discalced Carmelites in Spain. And by the beginning of the First World War there were five provinces with thirty-eight monasteries. The nuns enjoyed an even more astonishing reconstruction. All but three of the convents in existence at the time of the suppression in 1835 were restored during the period of the reconstruction, and in addition a number of new convents were founded so that by 1914 there were a total of 106 convents of the reform in Spain. The Order in Spain had been magnificently reconstructed.

Dominic of St. Joseph, as general of the Order, was one of the fathers at Vatican Council I when it opened in 1869, but he died in July of 1870 while the council was in session. On July 15 of that year, just three days before the definition of papal infallibility, Napoleon III declared war on Prussia and the Franco-German war was under way. French troops which had been garrisoned in Rome protecting the pope began to leave for the combat areas in the north, and the city was now unprotected from the Italian revolutionaries. By August a large number of the conciliar bishops had left Rome, and on September 30 Garibaldi marched on the city with his Redshirts. On October 2, a Roman plebiscite returned a large majority vote in favor of annexing Rome to Italy; and on October 20, Pius IX, now a self-imposed "prisoner of the Vatican," prorogued the council, which was not formally closed until 1962. In the turmoil of the capture of Rome and the suppression of religious houses, the Carmelites could not hold elections to determine the successor to Dominic of St. Joseph. It was not until 1872, when conditions settled and the Order had re-established itself in Rome, that the next elections were held; an Italian, Luke of St. John of the Cross, was made general. During the next three decades the friars and nuns set themselves to the task of permanent reconstruction of the Order after the upheavals of the century, which dated back to the invasion by Napoleon in 1807. Jerome of the Immaculate Conception (Gotti), from the Genoa province was elected general in 1881, and during his eleven-year administration the Italian province made significant advances. By the year 1914 there were five provinces in Italy, with thirty-two monasteries of friars.

The Polish province had started on the road to recovery in the middle of the century, but a major part of its development must be attributed to Joseph Kalinowski, who entered the monastery at Linz in 1877. Kalinowski, born in Vilna in 1835, had attended the University of Vilna, and then joined the army to fight in the Polish uprising against Russia in 1863. He was captured by the Russians in 1864 and spent ten years in a Siberian prison camp. During that wretched decade in his life he proved himself to be a person of extraordinary compassion and charity for his fellow prisoners, assisting them in every way possible, giving them his precious and meager food, caring for them when they were sick. Witnesses later related that a frequent prayer among the Poles jailed in Siberia was: "Through the prayers of Kalinowski, have mercy on us!" This represented a marked change for Joseph Kalinowski, who wrote in his memoirs that he had fallen away from the practice of his religion while he was at the university during a period he called his "apostasy." He was transported to Smolensk in 1874, and then was released from imprisonment, at the age of thirty-nine. He taught school in Vilna, traveled to Paris where he worked as a tutor, and then returned to Linz, where he entered the Carmelite monastery at the age of forty-two, taking the name Raphael of St. Joseph. He was ordained a priest five years later, and shortly afterward was elected prior of Czarna. During twenty-five years as a priest he worked indefatigably as a preacher, a religious counselor, and an administrator in the Order. His special apostolate was with the schismatic Russians along the Polish border and inside territorial Russia. "It is the providential mission of Poland," he wrote, "to render to Russia good for evil, and to bring at the price of heroic effort, the light of the true faith." Because of Raphael of St. Joseph's personal sanctity and his particular status in Poland as a political hero since his days in Siberia, he greatly popularized the Order and is regarded as the main force in the reconstruction of the Polish province. He died at Wadowice in 1907 at the age of seventy-two, and his process for beatification, introduced shortly after his death, had reached the apostolic stage by 1962.

A major advance in the process of reconstruction was accomplished by the union of the Spanish and Italian congregations in

1875. By a decree of Pius IX in February of that year, the entire Order was reunited under one general and the futile and divisive system of the dual congregations was abolished. The Spanish Carmelites of the reconstruction period were submitting themselves to a searching re-evaluation as they gathered together the tattered remnants of their provinces, and the most important and heartening result of their reflections was the decision to embark on the work of the foreign missions. Spanish Carmelites went to Cuba in 1880, Chile and Argentina in 1899, Bolivia in 1903, and Colombia, Brazil, and Peru in 1911. And throughout the twentieth century Spanish Carmelites spread to almost every country in South and Central America. There was also an interesting crossover of traditional mission territories: Spanish Carmelites went to India, and Italian and Flemish Carmelites went to Brazil. In 1858 French Carmelites went to Iraq and Persia, and by the time of the First World War there was a string of monasteries along the Persian Gulf and the Gulf of Oman, plus houses in Syria and Lebanon. The vigorous missionary effort of this epoch was one of the healthiest signs of an authentic reconstruction as Carmel moved into the modern era.

There were, however, major reverses during the process of reconstruction, and one of the most disastrous events was the sad case of Hyacinth of the Immaculate Conception at the monastery on the rue Singer in Paris. Charles Loyson was born in Orléans in 1827, and studied at the Sulpician seminary in Paris, where he was ordained as a Sulpician in 1851. He left the Sulpicians in 1858 and entered the Dominican novitiate, but four months later he transferred to the Carmelite novitiate at Le Broussey, where he made his profession in 1860, taking the name Hyacinth of the Immaculate Conception. He was an exceptionally gifted preacher and within a few years he acquired a reputation as the greatest Catholic orator in France, superior even to his contemporary Lacordaire. Hyacinth was the preacher for the Lent at the important pulpit of Notre Dame in Paris for the years 1864 to 1868. He was also the prior of the new monastery on the rue Singer. He became involved in the bitter debate that was raging in Europe about papal infallibility as the Vatican Council approached, and he aligned himself with those outspoken anti-infallibilists, Dupanloup in France and Dollinger in Germany. When it appeared that the doctrine would carry in the council, Hyacinth openly rebelled in September of 1869, renounced the Order and the Church, and declared he was about to found his own reformed church.[2] Dollinger later bolted and founded the "Old Catholics" in Germany, but Dupanloup discreetly left the council sessions in Rome before the matter came to a vote. But there was apparently more to Hyacinth's case than his intellectual problems about infallibility, for in 1872 he married an American lady he had known for a few years, Emile Jane Merriman (nee Butterfield), a native of Oswego, New York, a wealthy thirty-nine-year-old widow, and the mother of two children. This woman had been traveling in Europe when she was introduced to the preacher of Notre Dame in 1868 by a mutual friend, and in July of that year he received her into the Church. (She wrote in a letter of May, 1869, addressed to Isaac Hecker in New York that while she loved Pius IX as chief pastor and head of the Church, she did not believe in his infallibility and never would.) Loyson married her in London, and they had one son, Paul, born in Switzerland in 1873.

The Loyson case was a *cause célèbre* in France and reverberated all over Europe. His preaching alone had brought him to a position of national prominence, and the burning question of papal infallibility served to carry it throughout Europe. When Pius IX was asked by a naïve questioner what punishment he thought God would give to Loyson for his defection, the pope answered: "He has already received his punishment—he has married an American."

---

[2] Hermann Cohen, who was then at the desert at Tarasteix, wrote a touching letter to Hyacinth on September 27, 1869, a few days after the news of his defection:

My dear Father Hyacinth,
    Give ear to a friendly voice pleading with you to return to your Carmel and to holy mother the Church of God which you must serve as a faithful minister. Please, reconsider your decision and come. Would you not sing again with us of how good and joyful it is for brothers to live in harmony. Think of those you have left sorrowing behind you, and remember the joys of the Carmelite life. . . . You cannot imagine how dear you are to me now. Come, make haste, you are still in time. We shall welcome you most tenderly; we shall cure your wounds with the oil and wine of the good Samaritan. . . . You may disregard my solicitude for you, if among your new friends of the world, you find an affection as pure, disinterested, and firm as mine.

Yours in Jesus and Mary,
Augustine of the Blessed Sacrament
Discalced Carmelite

Loyson abandoned the idea of founding his own church, became a freethinker, associating himself with no particular sect, although he lectured widely in Protestant churches. He lectured in the United States in 1883 and 1884. St. Thérèse of Lisieux, who entered the Order in 1888, was profoundly disturbed by the Loyson case, and she prayed for him all her life, offering up her last communion for him before she died. Loyson outlived his wife, and died in Paris in 1912. During his last moments he held a crucifix in his hands, pronouncing an ejaculation of his childhood, "My sweet Jesus," and this has led some admirers of St. Thérèse to believe that her prayers for him were ultimately efficacious. However, his biographer claims that he did not show any signs of regret for the past. During the last quarter of the nineteenth century, Loyson, lecturing through Europe, remained a nagging scandal for the Church, and he seriously tarnished the reputation of his Order in France during its difficult period of recovery.

After Bismarck completed the unification of Germany in 1871, he inaugurated his *Kulturkampf* (battle for culture), an attempt to create greater state absolutism, particularly by destroying allegiance of his Teutonic people to a pope in Italy. In the course of this purge, which began in Prussia but soon spread to the other Germanic states, Bismarck started to expel the religious orders, beginning with the Jesuits. The Carmelites were near the end of his list, and by the time the *Kulturkampf* began to prove ineffective in the 1880s, due chiefly to the efforts of Windhorst and his Center Party, only a few Carmelite houses had been suppressed. However, the friars and nuns prepared themselves for the purge and arranged for the transfer of their houses to Belgium and Holland. The few houses that did take refuge in the Lowlands returned to Germany after Bismarck revoked the *Kulturkampf* laws in 1887.

A similar situation occurred in France during the early part of the twentieth century with the enactment of the *Lois laïques*, a more bitter and successful French version of the *Kulturkampf*. In 1901 the Third Republic inaugurated a series of antireligious laws which again saw the suppression of all the friars' monasteries. However, only a few of the nuns' convents were suppressed. The *Lois laïques* were rigidly enforced until the end of the First World War, when they fell into obsolescence, but during that time the various monasteries were relocated in other European provinces—there was one monastery of French Carmelites in Spain, one in Italy, one in

Belgium, and one in Monaco. All of these monasteries returned
to France after 1919. But the most heartening factor about the
later-day suppressions in Germany and France was that the Order
had learned how to cope with governmental suppression of monasteries and convents by transferring the entire community to a free
area until the particular purge had passed.

Carmel produced a number of unusual and saintly women during
the period of reconstruction in the second half of the nineteenth
century. Among others, there was Mary of Jesus Crucified (1846–
1878), the Arab girl born at Abeldin near Nazareth who entered the
Carmel of Pau in southern France close to the Pyrenees. She became a lay sister, and she was sent with a group of nuns to Bethlehem when Pau made a foundation there in 1875. This simple nun
was an ecstatic and has left some remarkable notes describing the
working of the Holy Spirit in the souls of the just. She died at the
age of thirty-two, and when her body was exhumed in 1929 during
the process for her possible beatification her heart was found to be
incorrupt and was transferred to the convent at Pau. The heroicity
of her virtues was declared in 1936, and she now possesses the
canonical title of Venerable Mary of Jesus Crucified.
   A French nun at the Carmel of Dijon, Elizabeth of the Trinity
(1880–1906), has had a considerable amount of popularity in the
twentieth century because of her posthumously published writings
about the indwelling of the Blessed Trinity. Elizabeth Catez was
born at Dijon, the daughter of a military officer, and she was given
a very careful and cultivated education. She demonstrated a definite
musical talent and was sent to the conservatory at Dijon, where she
became one of its most gifted students. At the age of fourteen she
decided to become a nun, but her mother insisted that she wait until she was twenty-one. Her confessor, the Dominican Father Valle,
instructed her in the doctrine of the indwelling of the Trinity, and
it became the fundamental theme of her religious thinking during
those years of her late teens when she was waiting to enter the convent. Her mother, who had assumed complete charge of her education after her father's death, dressed her in the best of fashion and
insisted that she participate in dances and other social events—all of
which Elizabeth did, while still developing a more profound spirit
of religious recollection. She entered the Carmel of Dijon a few
weeks after her twenty-first birthday, and proved herself to be an

exemplary nun. During her short five years in the convent she gained a deeper understanding of Trinitarian theology and the Pauline Epistles; and taking a phrase from the Epistle to the Ephesians, she articulated her whole life as a "praise of [God's] glory." Elizabeth of the Trinity died of a stomach ailment at the age of twenty-six, and a few years after her death the convent published a short collection of her occasional writings, notes, letters, poems, and particularly her reflections during her last retreat. These were given wide diffusion by Michel Philipon's masterly commentary on her doctrine, which was published in 1939. Her cause for beatification has been introduced at Rome.

Quite different from these two unpretentious young nuns who died pious deaths at an early age is the story of Alessandra Rudini, who became a celebrated Carmelite nun after a tempestuous life. She was the daughter of a noble and wealthy Sicilian family, but she was born at Naples when the ship on which her pregnant mother was sailing had to make an emergency landing because of the impending birth. Commenting on the circumstances of her birth, her father said that "she seems to have the sea's restlessness in her." Alessandra was brought up in the whirl of Sicilian society, and after her mother died her father took her into the circles of international society—in Paris, London, Vienna, and St. Petersburg. She grew into a tall, blond girl, a little less than six feet in height, with handsome, sultry features. After tarrying with many suitors, she married the Marchese Carlotti and moved with him to Verona. The young Contessa Carlotti had two sons, but her husband soon died and she was a widow at the age of twenty-four. Moving to Rome, she embarked on a wild round of social life, and met the poet Gabriele D'Annunzio, whose mistress she became for four years. During those years she disassembled completely, and she began to take morphine until she had developed an addiction for it. D'Annunzio, who called her his *Nike*, finally tired of her, and broke off the relationship. Alessandra then tried to pull herself out of her descent, and a few years later she took a trip to Lourdes which suddenly gave her the strength to break with the past. D'Annunzio, in the meantime, wanted to resume his affair with her, but she writes in a letter to a friend: "I have not gone to Rome this winter, and I will not go because G. D'Annunzio has established himself there waiting for my arrival. I have received many letters and telegrams from him recently. But I have loved him so very sincerely and profoundly (and may God pardon me that it was not pure) that it would be too painful and sorrowful for me to meet him again."

In 1911, at the age of thirty-five, Alessandra entered the Carmel at Paray-le-Monial in France, taking the name Mary of Jesus. "Lord God, we are home," she said when she entered. She became novice mistress, and eventually prioress of the convent, and then founded three important convents: Valenciennes, Reposoir, and the prestigious Carmel on Montmartre in Paris. Mary of Jesus became a celebrated figure in France during her lifetime, distinguishing herself as a saintly nun and a prudent administrator, and she died at her convent of Reposoir in the French Alps at the age of fifty-four in 1931. Two years after her death Gabriele D'Annunzio was asked to give a statement about her for a forthcoming biography, and he said: "Write, write! She was a woman descended from heaven in order to manifest a miracle on the earth."

St. Thérèse of Lisieux stands in marked contrast to many other figures described in this chronicle of the Carmelite Order: she was not, in the broad sweep of history, a major historical figure, nor was she involved in any great moments or grand passions or intriguing situations; she did not mold history or have any significant impact on the times in which she lived; and when she died of a tubercular condition at the age of twenty-four in the quiet Norman town of Lisieux her death went virtually unnoticed, except by the nuns in her convent and a few family friends. And yet Pope Pius XI, a scholar of no mean ability, has called her "the greatest saint of modern times." The solution to this apparent enigma lies in an understanding of Thérèse's mission in the modern world—her eloquent act of witness to God's reality in her uneventful life, particularly through the pages of her autobiography published shortly after her death. For a doubting, fearful world she points out the way to dialogue and union with a real and loving God.

Thérèse Martin was born in Alençon on January 2, 1873, the youngest of five daughters born to Louis and Zelie Martin. Louis Martin was a highly successful watchmaker and jeweler who was able to retire from his profession at the age of forty-seven, and he lived in an upper bourgeois class of society, owned his very comfortable home, and had his money invested in real estate. His last child, Thérèse, was a sickly infant and had to be boarded with a wet nurse for the first year of her life. A warm and affectionate child, she was deeply devoted to her family, and the death of her mother when Thérèse was three and a half was a traumatic experience, plunging her into a state of sadness and sensitivity which she suffered for eight years. In her autobiography she divided her early life into three distinct periods: the first, the happy and untrammeled period before her mother died; the second, the nine years from 1877 to 1886, her "winter of trial," as she called it, a time of sensitivity and weariness and occasional religious scruples; and the third, the period between 1886 and 1888, beginning with her sudden "conversion," a moment when she seemed to gain the maturity she had been struggling for all those years, and terminating with her entrance into the convent.

The only extraordinary event during that period was her illness in 1883, six years after the family had moved from Alençon to the small Norman town of Lisieux. For three months she suffered a strange mélange of convulsions, hallucinations, and comas, and it was feared that the ten-year-old child would die. However, she was cured almost instantly after the family prayed to the Blessed Virgin for her, and Thérèse always maintained that she actually saw a small statue of the Virgin in her room smile at her. She was a deeply religious child, and she stated near the end of her life: "From the age of three I have never refused anything to the good God." Her religious concepts matured in her early teens, and she developed an intense interest in the apostolate, and for that reason decided to enter the Carmelite convent so she could pray for souls and priests. She was fourteen when she applied to the Carmel of Lisieux where her two sisters, Pauline and Marie, had preceded her, but there was some hesitancy on the part of the ecclesiastical superiors about accepting such a young girl. During the period when the matter was under consideration, she made a pilgrimage to Rome with her father, and in the course of a general audience with Pope Leo XIII, she hurriedly asked him to permit her entrance into Carmel, despite a prohibition against speaking directly to the pope. He gently assured her that she would enter if it were God's will, and when she continued to plead her case the papal guards lifted her away. Leo placed his fingers on her lips and then blessed her, his eyes following her kindly as she left the chamber.

On April 9, 1888, Thérèse entered the red brick convent on the rue de Liverot where she spent the remaining nine and one-half years of her life. She took the name Thérèse of the Infant Jesus. She was a relatively tall girl, about five feet six inches, and she had blonde hair, and her eyes were what the French call *pers*, something approaching blue-gray. Her features were even and pretty, and she had a pleasant smile which gave her the appearance of a charming, pleasant girl from the provinces. She was somewhat quiet and reserved, but on occasion she could be quite spirited and frolicsome, and she intrigued the nuns in the convent with her gift for mimicry. What was not immediately evident, however, was her sheer will power and her rugged determination.

The prioress at the Lisieux Carmel was Marie de Gonzague, a strange woman of mercurial temperament who craved attention and flattery and stood on petty ceremonies. There was a split of two factions in the community about the prioress' qualities for office, and some biographers have eagerly grasped at this situation in an attempt to inject some drama in Thérèse's life. However, Thérèse seemed to abstain from the inner politics of the community, remaining aloof from the petty discussions which took place particularly around the time of elections. She quietly went her way, performed her duties, and remained unerringly faithful to the rule—but in such an undemonstrative way that many of the nuns had no comprehension of the profound nature of her sanctity until her memoirs were posthumously published.

Thérèse was appointed acting novice mistress in 1893, and during that time she had the opportunity to articulate some of her own religious insights, especially the doctrine she called her "little way," a somewhat coy phrase which expressed the nature of her relationship with God. She explained her "little way":

It is to recognize one's own nothingness, to expect everything from the good God as a child expects everything from its father. It is to be concerned about nothing, not even about making one's fortune. . . . I remain a child with no other occupation than gathering flowers, the flowers of love and sacrifice, and offering them to the good God for his pleasure. . . . Finally it means never being discouraged by your faults, because children fall frequently but are too small to hurt themselves.

Beneath the fulsome and slightly saccharine language of that *fin de siècle* style of writing, Thérèse's thought stands out, bright and challenging: an invitation to a daring love. She said: "My way is a way of love and confidence." Pope Benedict XV said it "contained the secret of sanctity for the entire world," and Pius XI, who stated that "if this way of spiritual childhood were practiced everywhere, it would bring about the reform of human society," concluded that the essence of her program "consists in feeling and acting under the discipline of virtue as a child feels and acts by nature."

In March of 1896 Thérèse experienced the first manifestations of the tubercular condition which would take her life in eighteen months. She continued the conventual observance as well as she could for over a year until she was finally placed in the convent infirmary. During her final illness she was plagued with fatigue, racked with pain, and cast in a bitter temptation against faith, but she remained bright and cheerful until the end. She died on the evening of September 30, 1897, at the age of twenty-four. Her final words were: "My God, I love you."

She had written her memoirs in three sections during the last few years of her life, all at the command of her superiors. These manuscripts were collated after her death, corrected, and published exactly one year from the date of her death. Then there occurred what Pius XI called "a hurricane of glory": additional copies were requested, new editions published, and in the next fifteen years more than a million copies were distributed. *The Story of a Soul* has enjoyed an amazing and a continuing popularity: it is an astonishingly candid human document, and it describes, despite the difficulties of the Victorian style, Thérèse's own religious experience. In the last few lines of the book, composed in pencil shortly before her death because she could hold a pen no longer, and written in a shaky hand, she states: "I am certain that if my conscience were burdened with every possible sin, I would still cast myself into Jesus' arms, my heart bursting with repentance, for I know how He cherishes the prodigal child who returns to Him." And then in the final sentence of the book she says: "I fly to him on wings of confidence and love." It is this deep experience of the reality of God and her audacious trust in Him that has made her so popular and important in the modern world.   .

Thérèse of Lisieux was beatified in 1923, canonized in 1925, and declared copatroness of the missions in 1927. In the bull of canonization, Pius XI placed her firmly in a historical perspective when he stated that she fulfilled her vocation and achieved sanctity "without going beyond the common order of things." And that has been her genius—to show that even persons like her, unknown, unimportant, removed from the large dramas of life, can achieve sanctity and union with the living God. In the full stream of the Carmelite tradition, she was a witness par excellence.

Thérèse's star blazed on the horizon of the Catholic world at the beginning of the twentieth century, and it brought new prestige and distinction to her Order. She was the crowning glory of the arduous work of reconstruction.

– X –
CARMEL IN AMERICA

THE Discalced Carmelites reached what is today the continental
United States in both the seventeenth and eighteenth centuries,
and while most of these efforts did not produce lasting foundations,
some of them were nevertheless an important part of early American
ecclesiastical history.

The first Discalced to reach the American shore were the three
Spanish friars who sailed with the Vizcaino expedition to California
in 1602: Andrew of the Assumption, the superior of the group;
Thomas of Aquinas; and Anthony of the Ascension, the most renowned member of the expedition, a graduate in cartography from
the University of Salamanca, who is today honored and depicted in
a mosaic dedicated to him on the exterior façade of the National
Shrine of the Immaculate Conception in Washington, D.C. The
three Carmelites were assigned as chaplains to the expedition, but
Don Sebastian Vizcaino appointed Anthony as his personal cartographer. Three ships set sail from the port of Acapulco in Mexico
on May 5, 1602, and on November 11 they disembarked on what
is today San Diego. Proceeding up the coast line they stopped at
Catalina Island and Monterey and then sailed almost as far as San
Francisco, the northernmost point any priests had penetrated in the
new California territory. At Monterey the friars named the promontory guarding the approach to the area "Carmelo" because of its
resemblance to Mount Carmel in Palestine, and they called the
river which flowed into the bay "río Carmelo"—and anglicized versions of these names are still used today. The friars did some apostolic work with the Indians, and Anthony charted the previously
unexplored area. His cartography is today preserved in the British
Museum in London. Returning down the coast line, the expedition
arrived back at Acapulco on February 21, 1603.

Philip III granted the entire area of what is the present-day state
of California, which at that time belonged to Spain, to the Dis-

calced Carmelites as their exclusive mission territory. Unfortunately, the Carmelites did nothing further in the California mission, because the Spanish explorers lost interest in the area, but a century and a half later Junípero Serra evangelized the territory and he named his *Carmelo* mission in honor of the Carmelite friars who had reached there in the early seventeenth century.

In England, the first friar of the mission, the energetic Simon Stock of St. Mary (Doughty), was extremely interested in the new colonies in the northeastern part of America, and while the English Carmelites were unable to attempt an American mission because they were barely able to hold their own at home, Simon Stock did petition the Holy See for something to be done about it. As the result of his promptings the Holy See created the Prefecture Apostolic of New England in 1630; however, peace was restored between England and France in March of 1632 and the plan was discarded. In September of that year the New England territory was placed under the jurisdiction of the prefecture of Acadia in Canada. While the New England prefecture existed only on paper, it was nevertheless the first action of that kind taken by the Holy See in regard to a region which later became part of the United States.

The first formal mission of the Discalced Carmelites in America was founded in the Louisiana territory in 1720. The Company of the Indies, the French trading company which had been given the charter to the territory by the Duke of Orléans, was legally responsible for providing religious services for the inhabitants; and in 1719 Captain Poyer, acting in the name of the directors of the company, invited the French Carmelites from the Normandy province to accept the mission. The definitory general in Rome approved the project, and then secured from the *Propaganda* a prefecture apostolic for the Order in Louisiana. James of St. Martin (Robert Avise), a native of Rouen, was appointed prefect by the Holy See, and he led a group of four friars to the city of Mobile in the present-day state of Alabama, arriving in August of 1720. He died unexpectedly in October of that year at the age of fifty-one, and his office was given to another Carmelite, John Matthew of St. Anne, who had the distinction of winning the first converts recorded in the region when he received two Calvinists into the Church.

However, the mission lasted only about two years because the Carmelites became unwittingly involved in one of the many muddled ecclesiastical situations in the New World. In 1722 the Company of the Indies invited the French Capuchins to New Orleans, and then sought a reapportionment of the mission territories from the bishop who had jurisdiction over Louisiana, Louis de Mornay in Quebec. In May of 1722 the bishop divided the territory so that everything east of the Mississippi and as far north as the Ohio River was given to the Carmelites, whose superior would reside at Mobile, while everything west of the Mississippi went to the Capuchins, whose superior would reside at New Orleans. The Carmelites agreed to the arrangement, and everything seemed satisfactory for six months until de Mornay, who had been traveling in Spain when the Carmelites first came to Mobile, was informed of the prefecture that had been obtained by the general in Rome in 1720. De Mornay typified some of the serious problems the Church was having in the New World: he resided in Quebec, but never once set foot in the Louisiana territory during all the years he administered the area up to his retirement in 1733, and he was an unmitigated Gallican who would deal only with the French crown or the trading companies, refusing to carry on any negotiations with the Holy See. His Gallican sensibilities were irritated by the fact that the Carmelites possessed Roman jurisdiction, and he summarily dismissed them from the Louisiana territory only six months after he had reapportioned the area. He then gave the Carmelite territory to the Capuchins, who had not bothered to obtain permission of the Holy See before coming to America. Although the Carmelites had an excellent case in Rome, they were unwilling to exacerbate the confused situation, and they returned to France in the spring of 1723.

French Carmelites came to America again during the American Revolution, serving as chaplains to the French troops. They all returned home with the French after the final surrender of the British, except the amazing Paul of St. Peter who was to stay in America for the remainder of his life and carve for himself a permanent niche in American ecclesiastical history. Paul of St. Peter (Michael Plattner) was a German, born at Dettelbach in the diocese of Würzburg in 1746. He joined the Cologne province of the Carmelites and was ordained in 1769. Historical documents offer no reason for his transfer to the French province, but we find him there when France decided to harass England by coming to the assistance of the rebelling colonists in America. Paul was assigned as chaplain to the *Régiment de Royal Deux-Pont,* and his immediate superior was the celebrated Rochambeau. After the Treaty of Paris in 1783, which formally ended the war and recognized American independence, the French envoy in Philadelphia requested Paul to remain in America so that he could minister to French-speaking Catholics on the banks of the Mississippi.

Paul of St. Peter was a man of genuine zeal and boundless energies, an assertive and forthright person who was always prepared to correct abuses with strong language. His protests about injustices perpetrated against his people sometimes got him into trouble, and once he was sued for his violent words, although the charges were later dropped. His apostolic work took him to the Illinois territory, St. Louis, and Louisiana. He first journeyed to Vincennes, where he cared for a parish as well as a mission at Kaskaskia. During that time he was involved in a heated dispute with a land firm which Paul felt was trying to exploit the settlers. In 1786, Father Gibault asked him to assume charge of an Indian mission at Cahokia directly across the Mississippi from the city of St. Louis, and Paul ministered to the Indians, rebuilding the ruined mission, until 1789 when he requested permission of the bishop of Louisiana to follow the Creoles who were migrating to the Spanish side of the Mississippi River. He moved into the Baton Rouge area in 1789, thus completing his service in the Illinois territory. The history of the archdiocese of St. Louis says of him that "the coming of the Carmelite Father to the Illinois country was a real God-send, a boon that enabled hundreds and hundreds to save their souls, and greatly helped to tide over the Church during its stormiest period, unto a more gracious time."[1]

Paul remained in the Louisiana territory for the rest of his life. He worked in a number of locations until his appointment as pastor of St. Gabriel's in Iberville in 1804, a position he held for the next twenty-two years, the longest pastorate in the long annals of that historic parish. He continued to work with great vigor and success

---

[1] In March of 1785, John Carroll supplied the *Propaganda* in Rome with the first detailed report on Catholicism in America, and after outlining conditions in the thirteen colonies, he stated that he had received reports that there were many Catholics in the vast area between the Appalachians and the Mississippi—most of them French-speaking—but he knew of only one priest working among them, "a German Carmelite who had come to this country by way of France." It must be noted, however, that Carroll's hearsay information was incorrect: there was more than one priest working in the territory, but Paul of St. Peter was the only one known back in Baltimore.

almost up to the time of his death at the age of eighty-one. His last handwritten entry in the record of the parish is a baptism on August 9, 1826. He died in October of that year. The American historian Rothensteiner wrote about Paul of St. Peter that "his memory still lives as one of the most remarkable men of our early western days."

There was another lone Carmelite missionary in the United States at approximately the same time, the Irishman Paul of St. Patrick (Ralph Fitzpatrick), who had been born in Dublin in 1750. He was sent to the novitiate at Genoa in Italy in 1722, and after his ordination he returned to Ireland where he worked on the mission for a number of years. In the late 1780s he received permission to help the Catholics in the United States at the time when an appeal was being broadcast in Europe for English-speaking priests. He labored in the state of Pennsylvania until his death in Philadelphia at an unknown date.

The next formal mission of the Order in the United States was in New Jersey in 1875. During the *Kulturkampf* in Germany, the friars were beginning to relocate their monasteries in preparation for an expulsion by Bismarck. One group from the province of Bavaria, headed by Augustine of St. Joseph, was sent to the state of New Jersey, where the friars obtained property in the city of Paterson. They constructed a red-brick monastery and church, and the foundation seemed to be prospering when in 1879 the provincial in Bavaria suddenly decided to withdraw the friars and send them to what he considered a more urgent foundation at Geleen in Holland, another refuge monastery from the *Kulturkampf*. The Geleen foundation was successful and it remained a permanent foundation after the *Kulturkampf* laws were rescinded, while the new monastery in Paterson was sold to the Franciscans, who used it as their novitiate. It was not until the twentieth century that the friars were able to establish permanent foundations and begin the construction of the American provinces.

The first convent of Carmelite nuns in the United States was founded in Maryland in the year 1790. It was the first convent of any kind in the original thirteen colonies, and since it was founded seven years after the Treaty of Paris it was, of course, the first convent of religious women in the United States of America. (The first convent in territory which was later to become part of the

United States was the Ursuline community at New Orleans, founded by French Ursulines from Rouen in 1727.)

The convent in Maryland was established by four nuns from the convent at Hoogstraten, three of whom were Americans who had traveled to Europe expressly to join the Order. Throughout the period of the penal laws in Maryland during the eighteenth century, no convents were allowed in the state, and a number of ladies from Catholic families had gone to the Lowlands in order to enter one of the three English-speaking Carmels at Antwerp, Liége, and Hoogstraten. At the time of the American Revolution two of these women occupied important positions: Bernadina of St. Joseph (Ann Matthews) was prioress at Hoogstraten, and Margaret of the Angels (Mary Brent) was prioress at Antwerp. The two American nuns had corresponded frequently over the years concerning the possibility of a Carmelite convent in their native land, and after the abolition of the penal laws they began to formulate specific plans. The bishop of Antwerp contacted John Carroll in Baltimore, who had been appointed prefect apostolic of the American prefecture erected in 1784, and he willingly gave his permission, stating that he was eager to have the Carmelite nuns in America so they could offer their prayers "that the faithful may increase in numbers and piety, and the pastors in zeal, useful knowledge and truly Christian prudence." Carroll had a genuine need of their prayers, for in his report of 1785 he estimated that there were only about 25,000 Catholics in the thirteen states—15,000 of whom were in Maryland, and 7000 in Pennsylvania—and only about thirty priests.

Bernadina was named first prioress of the American Carmel, and she selected for the initial group her two nieces who had entered Hoogstraten in 1883: Aloysia of the Blessed Trinity (Ann Teresa Matthews) and Eleanor of St. Francis Xavier (Susana Matthews). An Englishwoman, Clare Joseph of the Sacred Heart (Frances Dickenson), was named subprioress. On May 1, 1790, the group of four nuns embarked from the small island of Texel off the coast of Holland, arriving at New York on July 2, where the ship docked for two days, and then proceeded to Norfolk, Virginia. A small vessel took the nuns through Chesapeake Bay and up the Potomac River to Pope's Creek in Charles County, Maryland, arriving there on July 10, 1790. Four years later the nuns in the convent back in Hoogstraten had to flee from the revolutionary French troops, and they relocated, as we have noted, in Dorset, England.

The nuns were accompanied on their voyage to America by Father Charles Neale, a native of Maryland who had for ten years been serving as the confessor of the convent in Antwerp. Neale is an interesting figure: he entered the Society of Jesus at Watten, Belgium, in 1771, and he was still a novice when the Jesuits were suppressed in 1773. He nevertheless continued his studies for the priesthood, was ordained a diocesan priest, and remained in the Lowlands. He enthusiastically encouraged the establishment of nuns in America, and escorted them to Maryland where he remained as their first chaplain. Through correspondence he affiliated himself with the Jesuits in White Russia, the only place in the world where the Society existed during the suppression, and in 1805 he made his vows in the Society of Jesus. He later became superior of the American Jesuits after the restoration of the Society.

The nuns at first occupied property owned by the Neale family at Chandler's Hope, but it proved unsuitable and some weeks later Father Neale obtained another site at Port Tobacco, an extensive tract of eight hundred acres. On October 15, 1790, the feast of St. Teresa, the community was canonically established, and the Carmelite nuns began their official existence in the United States. Bernadina continued in office until her death in 1800, when she was succeeded by the subprioress, Clare Joseph. In 1831, the convent at Port Tobacco was transferred to the city of Baltimore because the area in southern Maryland had suffered a sharp economic decline and also because the nuns were being harassed by lawsuits filed against them by unfriendly neighbors. They were defended in one of these suits by Roger Taney, who was later to become a celebrated chief justice of the Supreme Court. The prioress at the time of the transfer to Baltimore was Angela of St. Teresa (Mary Mudd), a member of the famous Maryland family which was to figure so tragically in the Lincoln assassination some years later. When the nuns arrived in Baltimore, Archbishop Whitfield requested their temporary help in the work of education because of the critical shortage of nuns and religious in the United States. He obtained an indult from the Holy See, and for the next twenty years the nuns conducted a girls' academy outside the cloister, despite the fact that this type of work was foreign to the Teresian tradition of solitude and retirement. The prioress assigned four nuns to staff the small academy, and each morning they left the cloister to teach classes in the building adjacent to the convent. The school was abandoned in 1851 when the presence of teaching sisters in the archdiocese made this unusual situation no longer necessary.

The great majority of the subsequent Carmelite convents in America can trace their lineage back to the Baltimore Carmel. In 1863, five nuns from the Baltimore convent made a foundation in St. Louis, and then in 1877 a group of nuns from St. Louis made a further foundation in New Orleans. And in 1890 Baltimore established another convent in Boston. In the early part of the twentieth century Baltimore sent out groups of nuns to Brooklyn, Seattle, Wheeling, New York City, and Bettendorf in Iowa; and these convents, in turn, made a number of foundations themselves. By the year 1960 more than forty convents had descended from that first group of four nuns which Bernadina of St. Joseph led to Port Tobacco in 1790.

In 1915, nuns from the convent at Quaeretaro in Mexico established a convent at Grand Rapids, Michigan, and that convent was the point of origin for a number of other foundations, including ones at Buffalo, Detroit, and Kansas City. Three other Mexican convents made foundations in the United States: Guadalajara at San Francisco, Tulancingo at Dallas, and Durango at San Antonio. And still another group of American convents originated from the Carmel at Montreal in Canada which had been founded by French nuns from Rheims in 1875—Loretto, Columbus, Little Rock, and Mount Carmel.

The growth of the Carmelite nuns in the United States was truly astonishing, particularly in a country which had been characterized as activistic, shallow, and hardly suited for the development of the contemplative life. By the year 1966 there were 68 Carmelite convents in America, the third largest national group in the world, surpassed only by Spain with 149 convents and France with 122 convents.

The American Carmelite provinces were established in different parts of the country by German, Spanish, and Irish friars. The Germans were first when, after their abortive attempt in New Jersey during the 1870s, they returned to America again and located in Wisconsin in 1906. Two friars from the monastery at Regensburg in the Bavarian province, Eliseus of the Sacred Heart (John Mekina) and Kilian of the Mother of God (Francis Gutmann), traveled through the midwestern and northwestern parts of the United States in 1905 seeking a suitable site for a foundation, particularly in the areas settled by German immigrants. Archbishop Messmer of Milwaukee offered them a property called Holy Hill, a well-known Marian pilgrimage site about thirty miles northwest of Milwaukee. Holy Hill had an interesting history even before the arrival of the Carmelites: it was originally Indian property owned by the Menominees, who lost their property rights in Wisconsin after the Black Hawk War and were cruelly expelled from the state in 1838 and forced to seek new homes beyond the Mississippi. European immigration into the area was rapid, and the new Catholic population of southern Wisconsin was composed largely of people from the Rhineland and Bavaria. In 1855, twelve years after the establishment of a bishopric in Wisconsin, Father Francis Paulhuber purchased the property at Holy Hill from the government and erected a large white oak cross on the summit of the hill, the highest elevation in southern Wisconsin. A log cabin chapel was built on the hill in 1862, and Holy Hill became a pilgrimage site over the years, especially after a wooden, hand-carved statue, made in Germany and exhibited at the Philadelphia Exposition of 1875, was carried to the hill and installed there in 1878.

The Carmelites took formal possession of Holy Hill in 1906 with a small community of four friars: Eliseus, who was appointed first superior, Kilian, and two lay brothers who had been sent from Bavaria. They used a renovated farm house as the first monastery. Eliseus, a native of Holland who had joined the Bavarian province, had previously spent fourteen years on the Carmelite missions in India, where he wrote five books in English about Christianity and language on the Malabar Coast. He eventually returned to Europe, dying in the monastery at Geleen in 1941 at the age of seventy-eight. Kilian, also a Hollander, succeeded him as superior at Holy Hill, and remained for the rest of his life in America, where he acquired a reputation as an astute moral theologian. He died in Milwaukee in 1942 at the age of seventy-nine. Other friars were sent from Germany to staff Holy Hill, and in 1912 they also accepted a parish for German-speaking people in the city of Milwaukee, where they built a church and monastery dedicated to St. Florian. A brick monastery was constructed on Holy Hill in 1920, and in the following year a novitiate was established and American vocations began to apply for admission to the Order. A large shrine church was built on Holy Hill and it was formally dedicated by Archbishop

Stritch of Milwaukee in 1931; and in 1938 a massive, six-story monastery was constructed adjacent to the church. Finally, in 1956 a new wing was added to the church to serve as a shrine for the original statue of Our Lady of Holy Hill, which had been brought to Wisconsin in 1878. Each year hundreds of thousands of pilgrims and tourists visit the shrine on Holy Hill, which celebrated its first centenary in 1962.

Another group of friars located in the state of Arizona in 1912: Spaniards from the Catalonia province founded houses at Tucson, Phoenix, Sonora, and a number of mission stations to care for the Spanish-speaking residents of the state. In 1916 the friars from Arizona established a monastery in Washington, D.C. Joseph Mary of Jesus (Isasi), a former missionary in Cuba, led a group of friars from Tucson to the nation's capital, and on October 15, 1916, a monastery was formally established in the area near the Catholic University. In his letter welcoming the friars to the archdiocese of Baltimore, Cardinal Gibbons wrote: "I pray the blessing of Almighty God may rest upon your works, and I hope and am sure that you will have a great and deserved success."

During the same period other Spanish friars from Mexico established themselves in the southern part of the United States. Friars from the Valencia province of Spain had returned to Mexico in 1913, almost a century after their expulsion, in an attempt to revive the Mexican province and assist the few Mexican friars who had managed to survive the persecutions. But a year later a new persecution erupted under President Carranza, and the Spaniards had to flee again, some to America and some to Cuba. As before, the Mexican friars remained, went into hiding, and continued their work surreptitiously for another fifteen years until conditions settled again. The Spaniards who fled across the Rio Grande first came to Holy Hill in Wisconsin for a refuge, and then they were instructed by their superiors in Spain to establish houses in America. They journeyed south, looking for Spanish-speaking people, and finally settled in the diocese of Oklahoma City, first at a small mining village named Pittsburg. They were joined by the friars from Cuba and by other friars directly from Spain, and by the year 1926 the Carmelites had seven foundations in the area, including Hartshorne and Oklahoma City. American vocations were recruited, and the province eventually spread to Texas and Arkansas.

Friars from Ireland came to the state of California in 1924, establishing their first monastery at Alhambra. Over the years they founded other houses at Encino, Redlands, Oakville, and San Jose. These California houses were staffed almost exclusively by Irish friars for almost a quarter of a century, but in 1955 a novitiate was opened at Oakville and Americans were recruited for the province.

As vocations became more numerous for the Carmelites in America, the various monasteries were grouped into territorial provinces. In 1940 the monasteries in Wisconsin and Washington, D.C., were detached from their mother provinces in Europe and joined in an American union. After the war in 1947, this union was canonically elevated to the status of a province under the title of the Immaculate Heart of Mary, and further foundations were made in the states of Massachusetts, New Hampshire, Ohio, and New York. In the same year, the monasteries of Oklahoma and Texas were formally elevated to province status under the title of St. Thérèse. And in 1964, the monasteries in California and Arizona were grouped in an American province.[2]

The American Carmelites made their own contribution to overseas expansion when in 1947 six friars from the Immaculate Heart Province established a mission in the diocese of Lipa in the Philippine Islands. Other friars from the province followed, and three years later the mission territory was separated from the diocese of Lipa and established as the prelature of Infanta, a three-hundred-mile strip along the east coast of Luzon and the entire island of Polillo. On April 25, 1950, the Holy See entrusted the prelature of Infanta and its almost seventy thousand inhabitants to the American province of the Immaculate Heart. Patrick of St. Cecilia (Harman Shanley), one of the original friars who went to the Philippines in 1947, was consecrated the first bishop of Infanta in 1953.

The story of the Carmelites in the United States is one more episode in the Order's continuing commitment to expansion and progress and communication of the Teresian message throughout the world. However, there was something uniquely American in the development of the friars, something which has been an integral part of the history of the United States—the amazing and totally unex-

[2] Friars from Poland opened a monastery at Munster, Indiana, in 1949. This house serves as a refuge house during the Communist regime in Poland, and the friars there minister to Polish-speaking people in the greater Chicago area.

pected ability of peoples from different national backgrounds to live together in relative peace and to produce a new breed upon the earth: the American. The European has been traditionally unable to establish a relationship of trust and cooperation with people of other European nations, and many times with different cultural segments of his own nation. But yet this historical divisiveness was, on the whole, overcome in the growth and development of the United States. And the Carmelite friars participated in and benefited from this unique trait of the American personality. Friars from Germany, Ireland, and the two provinces of Spain dedicated their lives and talents to producing a new entity in the Carmelite Order: the American friar. In 1966, for instance, only sixty years after the initial foundation at Holy Hill, the province of the Immaculate Heart had 130 professed friars, and of that number 121 had been born in the United States. The American Carmelite had emerged and entered into the chronicle of Carmel's history, demonstrating once again that the Carmelite tradition is a universal ideal which is adaptable to individual cultural and national situations.

- XI -

CARMEL IN THE TWENTIETH CENTURY

THE distinguished Carmelite historian Silverio of St. Teresa has stated that Carmel in the twentieth century entered into another golden age—indeed, the best epoch to date in the Order's long history. It is too early to evaluate those claims adequately because the Order is still involved in the epoch, and the historian accordingly does not possess the necessary vantage point to formulate an objective and dispassionate conclusion. Nevertheless, Carmel in the twentieth century is demonstrating remarkable signs of vitality which seem to suggest that Silverio's assertions may not be too far from the truth.

At the beginning of the century, the Carmelites were completing the mammoth task of recovery from the nineteenth-century suppressions, and they were also expanding into new territories. Numerically, there were fewer friars after the reconstruction than there were immediately prior to the French Revolution, while conversely there were more nuns. This, however, seemed to be a more satisfactory and proper balance. The First World War, that long conflict which sought to maintain the balance of power in the West and which naïvely presented itself as the war to end all wars, did not appreciably retard the work of expansion. A number of friars were drafted to serve in the respective armies as chaplains or soldiers, and the monasteries and convents which lay in the battle areas in France and Germany and Italy were forced to relocate themselves temporarily until the fighting ceased. However, as we shall see, the Order did not fare as well during the later conflicts of the century.

Mankind was presented with a curious paradox as the history of the human race moved into the third quarter of the century—the world had achieved astonishing scientific and technological and sociological progress, but it had not solved the dilemma of a peaceful and fraternal cohabitation of nations on this earth. The emergence of nuclear weapons had convinced some people that the ultimate deterrent for war had been discovered, while many others felt that the means for ultimate chaos was now present on the earth. In the 1960s the Church undertook an extensive and searching reappraisal during its conciliar age of renewal as it sought to serve this paradoxical world more honestly and more efficaciously. And Carmel embarked on its own program of reappraisal and renewal, assessing the accomplishments of the century, admitting the mistakes of the past, and pledging itself to make its traditional prophetic vocation more relevant and timely in the modern era.

The European provinces of the Order, now firmly re-established after the suppressions, provided the personnel for a continuing expansion. The Spaniards, as we have noted, began to lend themselves eagerly to the overseas missions, particularly to the South American and Central American countries, but they also joined the Flemish friars in the historic missions along the Malabar coast of India. During more than three centuries in India the Carmelites continued to foster native vocations to the Order and to the developing dioceses. In the course of history, the Order has elevated three mission regions to the status of dioceses and then turned them over to the native clergy; and in the twentieth century the Order has charge of the dioceses of Vijayapuram and Trivandrum. In 1831, the Carmelites established a Third Order regular congregation of priests in the Syro-Malabar rite, which today numbers almost five hundred religious, the largest congregation of religious in India. The Carmelites also founded and staffed a seminary for native clergy at Verapoly in 1682, and transferred it to Alwaye in 1932, where it numbered almost 350 Indian seminarians by the middle of the century, the largest seminary on the Catholic missions.

The Order continued its traditional missions in Lebanon, Turkey, Arabia, Iraq, and Palestine. French friars returned to Iraq as early as 1858. An interesting apostolate has been undertaken by the friars who established a monastery at Cairo, Egypt, in 1926, and who constructed an impressive church, dedicated to St. Thérèse in 1932, which attracts large crowds of Mohammedans and schismatic Christians. Another unusual mission was established by the friars at Kuwait in Arabia, where they serve the international community which migrated there with the development of the oil industry. The friars also established houses in the Belgian Congo and Nigeria during the century.

The friars returned to China in 1948 when men from the province of Venice established a mission at Hwangchow and another one later at Peking. These friars were all arrested by Chinese Communists in 1951, brought before a kangaroo court, and then expelled from the country. They traveled to Japan, where they established the mission of Ishikawa-Nogoya. Other friars from the province of Lombardy came to Tokyo in 1952, where they founded a Carmelite monastery in a former Shinto temple.

The North American continent witnessed the development of the provinces in the United States during the twentieth century, as well as the emergence of the Mexican province after a century of secretive and clandestine existence. A handful of native Mexican Carmelites managed to remain in hiding and survive during the Carranza and Calles regimes, and by 1921 there were only sixteen friars in all Mexico, living in disguise and secretly administering the sacraments. When the Calles persecution abated in 1929, the friars emerged from hiding, resumed their monastic life, and laid the foundation for a flourishing province which numbered ten monasteries by the middle of the century. The first Canadian monastery was established at Nicolet, Quebec, in 1955 by friars from the Avignon province of southern France. The Spanish friars founded five monasteries in Cuba, dating back to the first foundation at Havana in 1880, but they were all expelled at the beginning of the Castro regime. However, they were allowed to return in 1962, and they regained possession of four of their monasteries.

The Irish province, now enjoying the reward of its centuries of persecution, was the most enterprising missionary province during the twentieth century. In the 1920s the Irish went to the assistance of the English province, which was suffering a shortage of vocations. In 1924 they established the first monastery in California and subsequently laid the foundation of the western American province. In 1948, the Irish friars established a monastery at Brisbane, Australia, and soon afterward another one at Perth. In 1954, they followed the Americans to the Philippines, opening a mission some distance from them in the southern island of Jaro; and in addition they constructed a church and monastery dedicated to Our Lady of Mount Carmel in the city of Manila. During more than four centuries the doughty Irish friars have exhibited a rare spirit of courage and resiliency and enterprise, and their story must surely be one of the most impressive and inspiring in the whole narrative of Carmelite history.

The Carmelite nuns also participated in the world-wide expansion of the post-construction era.[1] In 1861, the convent of Lisieux founded a monastery at Saigon, the first Carmel in Indochina and the origin of a number of other convents in that part of the world. The convent at Hanoi was founded in 1895, and it was for this Carmel that St. Thérèse of Lisieux unsuccessfully volunteered near the end of her life. The first convent in China was established at Shanghai in 1869, the first one in India at Mangalore in 1870, and the first one in the Philippines at Iloilo in 1923. Two events of the middle 1920s gave an even further impetus to the foundation of these contemplative convents in the foreign mission territories: in 1926, Pius XI published his encyclical *Rerum ecclesiae*, which underscored the importance of the contemplative life for the mission apostolate; and in 1927, the same pope named St. Thérèse, a contemplative nun, the copatroness of the foreign missions. Throughout the second quarter of the century a series of convents was established in Asia, Africa, and Oceania, so that by the time of Vatican Council II there were more than seventy convents in these three underdeveloped areas of the world.

Another sign of the new vitality of the twentieth century was the re-establishment of the desert monasteries by the friars. The desert of Las Palmas in Spain survived the suppressions, as we have noted, but in 1888 extra space was needed for the surprising number of new candidates, and the monastery was converted into a novitiate. In 1897, a new desert was founded at Herrera near Burgos by John Vincent of Jesus and Mary, who was later to distinguish himself for his sanctity and apostolic endeavors on the missions in India. This desert at Herrera was transferred to La Reigada in Navarre in 1905, where it remains to this day. The old desert property at Las Batuecas was repurchased by the Order in 1919, and after some unsuccessful preliminary attempts, desert life was re-established there in 1941. The French desert founded at Tarasteix by Hermann Cohen was con-

---

[1] During the period of the reconstruction the nuns were frequently placed under the immediate jurisdiction of the local bishop rather than the friars, who were having their own problems of recovery. And in the twentieth century the majority of the Carmelite nuns remain in this jurisdictional position. The superior general in Rome exercises what is euphemistically called a "paternal jurisdiction" over those convents by virtue of the fact that he controls the nuns' constitutions, legislates questions of Carmelite customs for them, and serves as liaison with the Holy See.

fiscated by the government of the Third Republic during the partial suppressions of 1880, but another desert was founded by the French-speaking provinces at Roquebrune near Nice in 1948. The latest Carmelite desert is an Italian one founded at Torre di Campiglioni near Florence in 1963.

Carmel in the twentieth century, then, was manifesting dramatic indications of a full recovery from the suppressions of the nineteenth century and the malaise of the eighteenth century, and a new dynamism seemed to be present in the Order, which recalled the golden days of the seventeenth century. Statistically, at the opening of Vatican Council II in 1962, the Discalced Carmelites numbered more than four thousand professed friars who were grouped in twenty-eight provinces. (At that time, the province of Poland was in a flourishing state, despite the Communist regime, while the province of Hungary was sorely oppressed.) In addition, the Carmelite missions were spread throughout the world and were committed to the care and jurisdiction of one or another of the established provinces. The Carmelite nuns numbered about fifteen thousand women who lived in more than seven hundred convents located on the five continents of the world.[2]

Almost two hundred friars have been consecrated to the episcopacy during the four hundred years of the Carmelite reform's history, and some of the most celebrated of these men have lived in the present

[2] There are also sixty-three congregations of religious aggregated to the Discalced Carmelite Order. These congregations often follow an adapted form of the Carmelite rule, wear a modified version of the habit, and enjoy official status conferred by the Holy See as affiliates to the Order. In addition to the Discalced Carmelite Missionaries of Francis Palau mentioned in a previous note, the largest congregations are the Carmelites of Charity, a Spanish group of sisters numbering more than three thousand members who engage in educational and social work; the Carmelite Sisters of the Divine Heart, a community founded in Germany in the last century, which has had a rapid growth in the United States; and the Carmelite Sisters of St. Thérèse, founded in Oklahoma in 1917 by a friar from the American province of St. Thérèse. In India there are six affiliated congregations of sisters in the Syrian rite, the largest of which is the Carmelite Tertiaries of Ernakulam, numbering more than four hundred members; and there are four congregations in the Latin rite, the largest of which are the Apostolic Tertiaries of Our Lady of Mount Carmel, with more than six hundred members. As mentioned previously, the tertiary priests of the Syro-Malabar rite have around five hundred members. The most interesting of all the affiliated congregations of men is the Servants of the Paraclete, the American community founded to assist in the rehabilitation of errant priests.

century. The Indian missions were distinguished by Aloysius of St. Mary (Aldracius Benziger), a native of Switzerland, and scion of the famous European publishing house, who entered the Flemish province at Bruges in 1884. He went to the mission of Trivandrum in India in 1890, and ten years later he was nominated bishop of Quinlon in southwest India, where he served for thirty-one years. The *Osservatore Romano* in 1931 called Archbishop Benziger "one of the greatest apostles of our time in India." The mission in Cuba was distinguished by Valentine of the Assumption (Emmanuel Zubizaretta), who arrived in this hemisphere by a rather tortuous route. He was a native of the Navarre province in Spain and a professor of theology, and in 1906 he was elected prior of the monastery at Burgos. In 1907, the Spaniard Ezechiel of the Sacred Hearts was elected general of the Order, and he took the prior of Burgos to Rome with him as his secretary. The gifted Valentine came to the attention of Pius X, who sent him to Cuba as apostolic visitator of that island, and he was so pleased with the Carmelite's report that he appointed him bishop of Cienfuegos in 1914. Eleven years later he was made archbishop of Santiago in Cuba, and he stayed there until his death in 1948. Archbishop Zubizaretta has perhaps an even greater claim to fame by his textbook in dogmatic theology, first published in a three-volume edition when he was a professor in Spain, and later augmented to a four-volume treatise for subsequent editions while he was in Cuba. His short abstract of the entire treatise, the *Medulla theologiae dogmaticae*, was published in 1933 and became a handbook for seminarians all over Europe until after the Second World War.

However, the most illustrious of the Carmelite churchmen of this century were the three cardinals: Gotti, Rossi, and Piazza. Jerome of the Immaculate Conception (Anthony Gotti) had been elected general in 1881, after attracting considerable attention as the official theologian of the Order at Vatican Council I. He was re-elected general in 1889, but three years later Leo XIII consecrated him bishop and sent him as apostolic internuncio to Brazil. Archbishop Gotti remained in Brazil until the consistory of 1895 when Leo XIII named him cardinal and brought him back to Rome. In 1902 Cardinal Gotti was appointed to the important post of prefect of the congregation of *Propaganda*. Gotti figured dramatically in the turbulent conclave of 1904 after the death of Leo XIII. He and Cardinal Rampolla, the Secretary of State under Leo XIII, were the leading candidates for the papacy on the first two ballots in the conclave when immediately before the third ballot Cardinal Puzyna rose to announce that he had been instructed by Emperor Franz Josef to exercise the Hapsburg's ancient privilege by vetoing Rampolla. The conclave was thrown into turmoil, and while the cardinals officially refused to honor the veto, nevertheless both Gotti and Rampolla lost ground on the succeeding ballots and the cardinals shifted their votes to the relatively obscure Cardinal Giuseppe Sarto, who became Pius X. Cardinal Gotti continued in his office of prefect of *Propaganda* until his death in 1916.

Cardinals Rossi and Piazza both received the red hat in the 1930s, and one succeeded the other in the prestigious office of secretary to the Sacred Consistory, the congregation which is charged with the appointment of bishops throughout the world. Raphael of St. Joseph (Charles Rossi), who was born in Pisa in 1876, entered the Tuscany province of the Order. He was brought to Rome as an assistant to another Carmelite bishop, Denis of St. Teresa (Alphonso Steyaert), a Flemish friar who spent twenty years working in the Roman Curia. Raphael himself was nominated bishop of Volterra in Italy in 1920, but three years later Pius XI brought him back to Rome again to serve as secretary to the consistory. Rossi, although a violent anti-Fascist, was one of the chief engineers of the Lateran Treaty with Mussolini in 1929, and the following year he was created a cardinal. He died in 1948, and was succeeded in the consistory by Adeodatus of St. Joseph (John Piazza), who had been born in Venice in 1884. After serving as a military chaplain in the First World War, then as prior of Brescia, and finally as procurator general of the Order, he was made bishop of Venevento in 1930, and then patriarch and cardinal of Venice in 1937. Cardinal Piazza remained in his important office in the consistory until his death in 1957. These two Carmelite cardinals who had somewhat similar ecclesiastical careers were men of vastly different temperament: Rossi, short and slight of stature, was a reserved, austere man, precise and meticulous in his work; while Piazza, large and overpowering in his physical presence, was very much the extrovert, warm, friendly, and enormously appealing, a dynamic preacher who wrote fairly good poetry in his spare time. Contemporaries of the two cardinals frequently remarked on the striking resemblance these two men bore to the two diverse personalities of John of the Cross and Teresa of Ávila.

Carmel in the twentieth century manifested a dedication to the act of literary witness similar to that of the seventeenth century, and among the many gifted authors of the epoch a few have accomplished work which gives every indication of having permanent value. Bruno of Jesus and Mary (Jacques Froissart, 1892–1962), a friar of the Paris province, was a pioneer in the field of religious psychology. This graduate of the University of Lille was in 1930 appointed editor of *Études Carmélitaines,* a rather pedestrian magazine which he converted into a distinguished journal of religious psychology, at that time an unexplored field of intellectual endeavor. Bruno stated that his object was to explore in depth the spirituality of Teresa and John of the Cross and then to "compare the results of their high experience with the findings of the psychological and psychiatric sciences." His journal attracted world-wide attention, and in 1935 he organized the first Congress of Religious Psychology, which convened in the Carmelite monastery at Avon-Fontainebleau and gathered together from all over the world theologians, philosophers, physicians, and psychiatrists. The Congress continued to meet every year, except for the war years of 1940 to 1945. Bruno also wrote highly praised biographies of St. John of the Cross, Madame Acarie, the martyrs of Compiègne, and the Spanish mystics. In 1948 he was elected president of the *Académie Septentrional,* and in 1957 he was awarded the order of the Rose d'Or. Another member of the Paris province, François of St. Mary (Francis Liffort, 1910–1961), founded the *Vigne du Carmel* in 1945, an excellent collection of books which deal with spirituality and Carmelite history. François was the author of a number of books himself, but his most masterful achievement was the preparation in 1956 of the critical edition of St. Thérèse's autobiography, which he published in a photographic facsimile edition, accompanied by careful notes which satisfied the most exacting demands of scientific history. Shortly before his death he carefully collected and published the forty-seven extant photographs of St. Thérèse in a single volume.

Gabriel of St. Mary Magdalen (Adrian Devos, 1893–1953), a friar from the province of Belgium, was summoned to Rome in 1926 to serve on the faculty of the international Carmelite college of theology; he remained there for the rest of his life. A graduate of the University of Lille and the Angelicum, he acquired in Rome a distinguished reputation for his books on spirituality, most of which were composed in Italian. He wrote on John of the Cross, Teresa, and the theory of acquired contemplation, but his most celebrated work was the posthumously published *Divine Intimacy*, a six-volume series of meditations and reflections, which was specially recommended to all Christians by Pope John XXIII and which has gone through multiple editions in almost all the major languages of the world. In 1941, Gabriel founded the magazine which was eventually called the *Rivista di Vita Spirituale*, a distinguished journal of studies on spirituality.

The Spanish friar Crisogono of the Blessed Sacrament (Lawrence Garrachon, 1904–1945) founded a similar scientific journal of spiritual studies in Spain in 1941, the *Revista de Espiritualidad*, and he himself acquired a wide literary reputation for his books on ascetical and mystical theology, but his promising career was abruptly terminated by an untimely death at the age of forty-one. The most famous of all the Spanish writers was Silverio of St. Teresa (Julian Gómez, 1878–1954), who combined a long career in ecclesiastical administration with an enormous literary output of great importance. The author of more than fifty books, he was both prior and provincial in his own province of Burgos, and at the time of his death he occupied the office of superior general of the Order. Silverio edited critical editions of the writings of Teresa and John of the Cross and Jerome Gratian, and he wrote a twenty-volume study of Carmelite mysticism plus a three-volume study of the inner life of the Carmelite nun. But his monumental work was the *Historia del Carmen Descalzo en España, Portugal y America*, a major study of the Carmelite reform in the Spanish-speaking world.

The international college of the Order in Rome, a pontifical university called the *Teresianum*, was founded in 1926 for the education of friars from all the provinces; and since 1947 the faculty of the college has published the *Ephemerides Carmeliticae*, a multilingual journal of historical and spiritual studies. The international Institute of Spirituality, founded in 1957 as a separate department of the college, has since 1964 admitted students who are not members of the Order, and it is the only college in the world authorized by the Holy See to grant degrees in spiritual theology.

A macabre dress rehearsal for World War II took place in Spain during the vicious civil war of 1936–1939. The same conditions existed in Spain during the 1920s as had been present in France prior to the French Revolution—social injustice, oppression of the poor, and denial of civil liberties. During the reign of Alfonso XIII there was a retrogression from the liberal wave which had swept over Europe during the previous century, and Spain in the early twentieth century began to resemble the old iron-fisted monarchies of the pre-French Revolution era. The Church in Spain was again identified with the monarchy and little attention was paid to the social doctrine of Pope Leo XIII. And there was a new factor operative in Spain: a small but effective and dedicated Communist party which was carefully directed and assisted by the Communist International in Moscow. In 1920, Lenin had predicted that the next successful Communist revolution would occur in Spain.

To suppress the liberal movements in his country, Alfonso XIII established a dictatorship in 1923 under Primo de Rivera, but despite the strong measures of the Rivera regime the tide could not be stopped. In 1930 Rivera resigned, and in April of the following year the parties of the Left declared Spain a republic. There was an initial reaction against the Church; for instance, the large Carmelite monastery at the *Plaza de España* in downtown Madrid was set on fire but no extensive damage was done. In the election of 1933 a confederation of Catholic Rightist parties, the CEDA, obtained the most votes, but not enough for an absolute majority, and thus a coalition government was formed between the CEDA and the socialists. During the next two years Spain was brought to a state of near anarchy as this shaky government tried to maintain its authority and the two factions fought for supremacy. A number of Leftist revolutions and strikes broke out through Spain, and in October of 1934 the Carmelite monastery at Oviedo near Burgos found itself in the area of a Socialist uprising. The prior of the monastery, Euphrasio of the Infant Jesus, disbanded the community and ordered the friars to flee in secular clothes. Each one of the friars was apprehended and arrested someplace in the city before being able to make an escape, but they were all released two weeks later when the uprising had run its course. The only fatality was the prior himself, who was shot by a firing squad while uttering words of forgiveness for his executioners. Euphrasio is regarded as the protomartyr of the many Carmelites killed during the next few years in Spain.

In the February elections of 1936 the liberals won a decisive victory at the polls, and the new government, now strongly controlled by the Reds, began a major purge against what they considered the dissident elements in Spain—principally aristocrats, the military, and the clergy. During the next few months a revolution was plotted by the military, chiefly the military in exile—Franco in the Canary Islands, and the Spanish Foreign Legion in Morocco. The revolution was declared on July 18 of that year, and Franco was flown back to Spain while the Foreign Legion invaded from the south. For the next three years Spain was torn apart by a brutal civil war, and during the major part of the war, Franco's forces, which were called the Nationalists, occupied the south of Spain and Navarre in the north, while the Communist-dominated government forces, which were called the Loyalists, occupied the rest of the north and practically all the major cities. Hitler sent his Nazi troops to help Franco, and the Russians supported the Loyalists. In the midst of this conflict of ideologies and armies, the Church was severely persecuted wherever the Reds gained control. All priests were declared enemies of the Communist state and were shot on sight without trial.

Carmelite monasteries and convents were confiscated in the Loyalist territories, and the friars and nuns fled, some to live in hiding, others to take refuge in either the Nationalist territories or across the border in France, Belgium, and Italy. During the course of the war, 103 Carmelite friars and 5 Carmelite nuns were executed. In the early stages of the conflict, entire communities of friars were slaughtered en masse, but in the following years they were killed individually as they were apprehended. The community of friars at Toledo, for instance, was marched outside the monastery and gunned down against the church wall. On the other hand, the community at Burriana disbanded before the Reds reached the monastery, but most of the friars were captured within a few days and shot. The procurator of the monastery, Angel of the Holy Family, typified the spirit of the Spanish priest when he cried out *Viva Cristo Rey!* at the moment he was being shot.

There were many poignant stories during the sad days of the war. Athanasio of the Sacred Heart, a saintly former novice master sixty-seven years of age, was traveling on a train to Santander, unaware that the city had been taken by the Reds. When he stepped off the train in the Santander station, he was immediately seized by soldiers, dragged out into the street, and shot. Paulino of the Blessed Sacrament, a professor of history at the *Teresianum* in Rome, was visiting his native Spain when the revolution broke out in 1936: he had been staying at the monastery in the *Plaza de España* in

Madrid where his own father was stationed as a lay brother, having entered the Order after his wife's death. Paulino and his father, John Joseph of the Virgin of Carmel, left the monastery with the rest of the community when the violence erupted, and hid in a nearby home. But they were discovered and taken to one of the parks of Madrid where they were shot. As the two Carmelites, father and son, were waiting for their execution, they turned to embrace each other, and in the moment of their embrace they were gunned down.

The monastery at Barcelona was surrounded by soldiers before the friars could escape, and they were ordered to come out of the building with their hands raised in the air. The provincial of Catalonia, Luke of St. Joseph, led the friars out of the monastery, and as they emerged through the front door they were shot. In the confusion of the massacre, seven of the friars escaped, but they were quickly hunted down and executed. Luke of St. Joseph (Joseph Tristany) had spent a number of years on the missions in Arizona and was a former prior of the monastery at Tucson. In 1919 and 1920 he resided at the monastery in Washington, D.C., where he wrote his well-known book *Holiness in the Cloister*. After serving as a definitor general in Rome he returned to his native Spain. He had been elected provincial only a few months before his violent death at the age of sixty-four. Another former resident of the United States was killed during the hostilities: Edward of the Infant Jesus (Richard Farré), a native of the town of Torms who came to the monastery of Washington, D.C., in 1923 as a young man of twenty-six. After obtaining a degree in theology from Catholic University of America, he was elected prior of the monastery for the years 1927–1930. He was thirty-nine years of age and prior of the monastery of Tarragona in his native Spain in 1936, but he was preaching a novena at the nuns' convent at Tiana near Barcelona when the revolution broke out in July. Edward removed his religious habit and hid in a private home at Tiana along with another friar whom he had met at the convent, Gabriel of the Annunciation. However, soldiers who were searching the area discovered the two men, and after they freely admitted that they were priests, they were taken out on the highway and shot.[3] Both of the priests who had been superiors of American

[3] Gabriel of the Annunciation (Joseph Balcells) was the librarian of the *Teresianum* at Rome, but he had returned temporarily to his native Spain for the ironic purpose of lecturing on social reform. His brother, Albert of the

monasteries, Luke of St. Joseph and Edward of the Infant Jesus, are included among those Spanish religious being considered by the Holy See for possible beatification as martyrs.

The nuns were usually unmolested after they had been ejected from their convents, and as we have noted, only five of them were killed. Three nuns were shot down in the street as they attempted to flee from their convent in Guadalajara, and another nun was killed in Albal near Valencia. Maria Sagrario of St. Aloysius Gonzaga, the prioress of the convent in Madrid, a brilliant nun who had been the first woman to gain a doctorate in pharmacology from the University of Madrid, was thrown into jail, and in August of 1936 she was shot in the *Pradera de San Isidoro*, the small park in Madrid which was the scene of many of the executions.

An intriguing episode transpired at the convent at Cerro de los Ángeles, a few miles from Madrid. The community was marked for execution, and the nuns were herded out of their convent and loaded into a truck which would take them to Madrid where they were to be shot before a firing squad. As the truck lumbered toward Madrid, the prioress reminded the nuns of the example of the community at Compiègne over a century before, and she led them in the singing of the *Te Deum* and the *Salve Regina*. The sound of these defenseless women singing their hymns while they were being ferried to their deaths began to unnerve and unsettle their captors, and when the truck reached the outskirts of Madrid the nuns were set free.

With the surrender of Madrid in March of 1939 the war came to an end, and Franco established a national government with his Falange party. The Carmelites took possession again of their monasteries and convents, and the Order in Spain resumed its normal activities after three years of holocaust. But 108 new martyrs had been added to the Carmelite family.

In September of that same year Adolf Hitler ordered his Panzer divisions into Poland, and another and vastly more devastating war had begun. During the Second World War the Order suffered the same upheavals which were transpiring all over Europe. Monasteries

---

Sacred Heart, was a lay brother in the monastery of Washington, D.C., at the time of his execution, and after the civil war Albert was promoted to the priesthood so that he could take his brother's place in the ranks of the slain clergy.

and convents were evacuated in the areas of military conflicts, and some houses were totally destroyed; the monasteries at Kensington in London and at Würzburg in Bavaria, for instance, were both demolished by aerial bombardment. Some Carmelites were killed as part of the civilian population which was victimized by the sudden death which rained from the sky in that war of highly developed air power, while other Carmelites were executed because of their opposition to the *Ubermensch* philosophy of the Nazi menace. And many Carmelites were drafted to fight in the six-year struggle which raged on three fronts.

The most publicized of the drafted friars was the provincial of the Paris province, Louis of the Trinity, who became an admiral in the navy, an international figure, and one of the chief architects in the construction of the Free French forces after the fall of France. Georges Thierry d'Argenlieu was born in 1889 of a Breton and Picard family which had a distinguished history of military service, and he followed the family tradition by entering the *École Navale*, graduating at the age of seventeen. During the First World War he received the Legion of Honor for his efforts in the Moroccan campaign, and at the time of the armistice he was a lieutenant commander in charge of patrol craft engaged in antisubmarine warfare. He abandoned his promising naval career in 1920 at the age of thirty-one, and entered the Discalced Carmelites, taking the name Louis of the Trinity. He acquired a wide reputation as a preacher and retreat master and a frequent contributor to the *Études Carmélitaines*, and at the time of the French mobilization in the summer of 1939 he was the provincial of the Paris province. In his final address to the friars he stated: "This storm will pass just as other storms have passed. One day, in God's good time, we shall be back here again sheltered by the rule of our Order. For those who do not return, God will receive them." Then he took off his habit and donned the uniform of a commander in the navy.

D'Argenlieu was appointed to the general staff and stationed at the Cherbourg Arsenal, but he was captured by the Germans in June of 1940 when Cherbourg fell before the blitzkrieg in a fierce battle in which he was cited for his gallantry. Three days after his capture he leaped from a moving convoy train which was taking prisoners back to Germany, and disguising himself as a Norman peasant he made his way to the coast where he commandeered a fishing boat and sailed to the channel island of Jersey. A few days later he reached England and immediately presented himself at the Carmelite monastery, but the English friars were unwilling to believe that this poor peasant in the blue cotton shirt and wooden shoes was the provincial of the Paris province. However, his identity was confirmed by the French who were gathering in London after the evacuation from Dunkirk. Almost a hundred thousand French military had escaped to England in the amazing operation at Dunkirk, and General Charles de Gaulle was organizing them into a Free French force. The greater part of the French navy had sailed to Africa as a result of what the Free French called "Pétain's bargain with the devil," and d'Argenlieu was commissioned by de Gaulle to gather what remnants he could and, most importantly, regain French Africa for the allies' cause. Late in 1940 the British ferried de Gaulle and d'Argenlieu on the H.M.S. *Devonshire* to the African port of Dakar for the purpose of convincing the colonists to abandon the Vichy regime. De Gaulle remained on the ship's bridge while d'Argenlieu headed for shore, standing in the bow of an open boat beside the tricolor of France and holding a white flag in his hand. Although the party had been assured of a safe landing, he suspected a trap as the boat neared shore, and he had just ordered the landing craft to halt when guns from the shore opened fire. He was seriously wounded, but he managed to return his craft to the ship, and six weeks later he was back on the bridge of a destroyer, standing on crutches while he directed assaults against Gabon, Port Gentil, and Libreville, winning those equatorial ports for the Free French and thus providing the avenue for General Leclerc's important drive to the north.

In the following year Admiral d'Argenlieu was appointed by de Gaulle as high commissioner for the French territories of the Pacific and the Far East, and again he won the French colonists over to the Allies' cause. Under his command New Caledonia was used as a jumping-off point for the allied naval sweep of the Pacific. During those years he was also sent on diplomatic missions to Canada; to the United States, where he conferred with the Secretary of State, Cordell Hull; and to Casablanca, where he met with Roosevelt. Admiral d'Argenlieu was small of stature but he had fine features and aristocratic bearing, and he was possessed of a great quantity of Gallic charm and personality. He was always impeccably groomed, and his manners were flawless. However, he was a quite determined person, and his own deserved reputation for boundless bravery and courage made him a formidable figure.

He returned to London in 1943, where he was appointed commander of the French naval forces in Britain, and he played a key role in planning the invasion of Normandy. On June 14, 1944, he boarded his flagship, the destroyer *La Combattante*, and sailed for France with de Gaulle standing beside him on the bridge. And, in what surely must rank as one of the truly great moments in French history, Admiral d'Argenlieu walked side by side with General de Gaulle down the Champs Élysées following the liberation of Paris. Hundreds of thousands of Frenchmen applauded and screamed and cried in that scene of overpowering emotion while the two comrades-in-arms marched through the city to the cathedral of *Notre Dame*, where a solemn *Te Deum* was chanted in thanksgiving.

After the defeat of the Japanese, d'Argenlieu was appointed governor general of Indochina and commander-in-chief of all French forces in the area. He spent twenty months attempting to stabilize the situation in that difficult French colony, but finally in 1947 he requested permission to return to his monastery. Before his retirement he was given a number of awards in Paris, including the Grand Cross of the Legion of Honor and the *Médaille Militaire*. On September 2, 1947, the British ambassador invested him as a Knight Commander of the Order of the Bath, one of England's highest awards to distinguished foreigners. Then he removed his admiral's uniform and clothed himself again in the brown habit of a Carmelite friar.

Louis of the Trinity lived for seventeen years after his return to the monastery, and he spent those years as quietly as he could. He attempted to remain out of the public eye, seldom preaching in public because he was commonly regarded as "the voice of de Gaulle" and he wanted to avoid the possibility of having political overtones read into his statements. His principal apostolic activity during those later years was preaching retreats to closed groups, such as priests and nuns. He died at the age of seventy-six in 1964, and he was buried at Avrechy-Argenlieu in the presence of de Gaulle and other civic and military officials. The *New York Times* in its obituary for Louis of the Trinity stated: "For generations the men of the d'Argenlieu family had gone into the Church or the navy in France, but Georges Thierry was the first to do both."

A more tragic figure during the Second World War was the renowned Jewish convert Edith Stein, who became a Carmelite nun and who was arrested by the Gestapo and killed in the gas chambers at Auschwitz. Edith Stein was born at Breslau in Germany in 1891 of an orthodox Jewish family. An exceptionally intelligent girl, she entered the University of Breslau at the age of nineteen, where she majored in philosophy. She became intrigued with the phenomenology of Edmund Husserl, which is regarded as the forerunner of modern existentialism, and she obtained permission to continue her studies with Husserl himself in the city of Göttingen. In 1916 she followed Husserl to the University of Freiburg, where she obtained her doctorate *summa cum laude*, writing a dissertation "On the Problem of Empathy." She then became Husserl's personal assistant, proving herself a brilliant existentialist thinker and dedicating her energies to what she called "her only passion, the search for knowledge."

Edith Stein stated that during her university career she could be considered an atheist because she was unable to believe in the existence of God, but she was nevertheless profoundly impressed by some close Catholic friends. Then in 1921 she spent the summer with some Protestant friends at their home in the Palatinate, and when she was looking for something to read one evening she discovered a copy of St. Teresa of Ávila's autobiography in their library. She began to read the book and became increasingly more fascinated, remaining up the entire night to finish the life of the sixteenth-century mystic. She completed it in the early morning, and exclaimed: "There, that is Truth!" She embarked on a study of Catholicism, and on January 1, 1922, she was baptized in the Church.

After her conversion she obtained a position teaching German literature at the Dominican convent school at Speyer, and she started on the great philosophical work of her life, which she called "a search for the sense of Being and an attempt to make a correlation between medieval thought and the vital thought of our time." Her book entitled *Husserl's Phenomenology and the Philosophy of St. Thomas Aquinas* was the product of that endeavor. During the nine years she remained at Speyer she also published a number of other books, including *Psychic Causality, Individual and Community, The State,* and translations of Newman and Aquinas. In addition, she lectured widely in Germany, Austria, Switzerland, and France. Her lecture on "The Ethos of Woman's Vocation," given at Salzburg in 1930, brought her to national prominence. She presented a striking image on the lecture platform, this quiet, dignified woman with the strong, handsome face and dark features, who enfolded the brilliance of her mind with stunning clarity and precision.

In 1932 Edith Stein became a lecturer at the Institute of Scientific Pedagogy at Münster in Westjalen, where she remained for two years. She had cherished a desire for many years of entering a Carmelite convent, but her spiritual directors advised against it, protesting that she had a great intellectual mission to perform in the world. But in 1933 Hitler forbade non-Aryans from holding teaching positions, and she was forced to resign from the Institute. Her director then gave his assent to her long-time desire, and in October of that year she entered the Carmel of Cologne, adopting the name Teresa Benedicta of the Cross. She was an excellent nun, a deeply contemplative soul who was at last enjoying the full opportunity of penetrating to the core of existence by her life of close, personal union with the living God. But this towering intellectual who had been lionized in Europe for years found herself almost completely inept at the housekeeping and menial chores of the convent. "It is a good school of humility," she wrote, "to have to do things constantly which, despite a great effort, I accomplish only very imperfectly." However, she was deeply contented in her new life. Gertrud von Le Fort, an old friend, remarked on Edith's "radiant, almost transfigured countenance" after a visit, and a friend from the university said, "Her happiness overwhelmed me."

The provincial of the Carmelite friars ordered her to continue her writing in the convent, and during the remaining nine years of her life she wrote a number of minor works and two major books: *Eternal and Infinite Being*, a further discussion of Christian existentialism; and *The Science of the Cross*, a modern presentation of the doctrine of St. John of the Cross with particular emphasis on the relationship of suffering and death to the paschal mystery. But Edith was also preoccupied with the sufferings caused to her people (she wrote of the Jews as "we") by the Nazi pogroms and terrorisms. "I spoke to the Lord," she wrote, "and told Him that I knew it was His Cross that was being laid on the Jewish people. Most of them did not know that; but those who did, ought to embrace it willingly in the name of all. This I desired to do. He only needed to show me the way."

The way was becoming clearer as Hitler intensified his "final solution" to the Jewish question. By 1938 her situation in the convent was precarious and her presence dangerous to the rest of the community, and thus in that same year she was secretly taken across the border to the Dutch Carmel at Echt, which had originally been founded by the convent of Cologne as a house of refuge during Bismarck's *Kulturkampf*. On Passion Sunday of 1939 she wrote to the prioress in Cologne: "I ask your reverence's permission to offer myself as a victim of expiation for a true peace." After Hitler's occupation of Holland she again found herself in danger, and preparations were under way to send her to a convent in Switzerland when Gestapo officers marched into the convent and arrested her on August 2, 1942. In July of that year the Dutch hierarchy, under the direction of the primate Archbishop De Jong, had issued a pastoral letter condemning the persecution of Jews, and a few weeks later the Germans took reprisal by arresting all converted Jews in Holland. The German general-kommissar stated in a newspaper interview that the arrests were a direct reprisal for the bishop's statement, and the German authorities must now "consider Jewish Catholics as their worst enemies" and "see to it that they are deported with all dispatch to the East."[4]

Edith Stein was loaded into a police van, and the Gestapo took her to the internment camp at Westerbork. She walked into that scene of terror and fear calmly and confidently, and she became a source of strength to the other prisoners. One witness, a Jewish businessman, later related: "Sister Benedicta stood out from among those brought to the prison camp because of her great calmness and recollection. The cries, distress and confused state of the new arrivals was indescribable. Sister Benedicta went among the women as an angel of mercy, calming and helping them. Many of the mothers were on the verge of madness, succumbing to a black and brooding melancholia. They neglected their children and could only weep in dumb despair. Sister Benedicta took care of the little children, washing them and combing their hair, and bringing them food and looking after their other basic needs."

[4] The execution of Edith Stein is a graphic example of the dilemma that European churchmen were confronting concerning public statements about the Nazi persecution of the Jews. Public statements were met with grim reprisals— not against the author of the statement, but against innocent victims. Thus the churchman who made a statement found that the situation remained unchanged while more people were killed, and he was left with the frightening knowledge that he had caused their deaths.

On August 7, Edith Stein was put on a prison train bound for the East, but before her departure she managed to smuggle a note to the prioress of the convent: "I am quite content now. One can only learn the science of the cross if one truly suffers under the weight of the cross. I was entirely convinced of this from the very first, and I have said with all my heart: *Ave Crux, Spes Unica*." She was brought to Auschwitz and executed on August 9, 1942. At her death she had reached not only the fullness of Christian maturity, but also the deepest point of intellectual penetration of the existentialist philosophy, for her act of certitude on the way to Auschwitz—"I am quite content now"—is the final affirmation and the only true response to the existential anxiety of our age. Cardinal Frings, the archbishop of Cologne, introduced the cause of beatification for Edith Stein in 1962.

Another victim of Hitler's "final solution" was the French friar who has become known in the English-speaking world as Père Jacques, a man of unyielding principle and heroic courage who died after imprisonment in the concentration camp of Mauthausen. Lucien Bunel was born in 1900 of poor parents in the region near Rouen, and as a youth he entered the minor seminary and was eventually ordained for the diocese of Rouen. For five years he served as a teacher at a Catholic school for boys in Le Havre where he exhibited a rare talent for directing and inspiring youth; and he also applied his indefatigable energies in working with the people in the dock area. Bunel was a man of deep prayer and mortified life, but he was also a completely individualistic person, high-spirited, irrepressible, with an original mind which applied itself vigorously to experimentation and new forms of pedagogy. He was regarded as an excellent teacher, but he was a source of exasperation to many of the faculty members. Bunel had nourished an aspiration for many years of entering a religious order, and after making a retreat in the Carmelite monastery at Avon-Fontainebleau he decided to enter the Order. He was invested with the Carmelite habit at the monastery of Lille in 1931, taking the name Jacques of Jesus, and his novice master was the future provincial and hero of World War II, Louis of the Trinity. "The more I study the life and works of our saints," he wrote from the novitiate, "the more I love them with greater attachment, like parents or older brothers and sisters, and I appeal to them with complete assurance that my prayers will be answered."

After his novitiate Père Jacques was sent to the monastery at

Avon-Fontainebleau, and he became involved in a new project the Paris province was undertaking, the establishment of a juniorate attached to the monastery which would serve as a source of new vocations for the Order in France, which was still rebuilding after the years of exile in the first part of the century. The original plan provided for a school which would be exclusively for young men desiring to enter the Carmelite Order, but as the result of Père Jacques's prodding the school was opened to all qualified students. The entire project was abandoned after the Second World War, but during the years that Père Jacques served as headmaster the school functioned as a model of progressive education. The *juvenat*, which was dedicated to St. Thérèse of Lisieux, had at its moment of highest enrollment ninety students, and the boys responded to their headmaster with an overwhelming devotion, this vigorous Carmelite friar with the ascetic face and deep-set piercing eyes and almost constant smile who prodded and cajoled and sympathized with his young charges.

Père Jacques was drafted in the mobilization of 1939, and the school was converted into a Red Cross hospital. He became a sergeant-major in an artillery battery at Bazilles, and then at Remenoncourt, and he was taken prisoner in June of 1940 in the roundup of French troops after the debacle of France's collapse before the blitzkrieg. Released in November of 1940, he returned to Avon-Fontainebleau, and he reopened the school in January of the following year. He suffered great agonies of spirit at the persecution of the Jews during the German occupation, and with the permission of Philip of the Trinity, the provincial, he secretly enrolled three young Jewish boys in the school under assumed names in the fall of 1942. He realized the personal danger to himself in this action, and he wrote to his brother: "It is very possible that before long something will happen to me. If I am shot, rejoice, for I shall have realized my ideal—to give up my life for those who suffer." On the morning of January 15, 1944, the Gestapo marched into Père Jacques's classroom and arrested him for harboring Jews. He was taken out to the courtyard, and the entire student body was assembled. The three Jewish boys were arrested, and the Gestapo leader shouted to the students: "Are there still any Jews among you?"

"No," the boys answered. (There was one other Jew in the school, a young man Père Jacques had employed as a worker, but he was not discovered.)

"They are our comrades like the others," one of the students cried out.

"You cannot be comrades with a Negro, you cannot be comrades with a Jew," the Nazi shouted back.

Then Père Jacques was led from the courtyard by two members of the Gestapo, and the students cried out, "Au revoir, Père Jacques," and began to applaud frantically. "Shut up," the Gestapo leader shouted. "Shut up! Silence!" At the gate Père Jacques paused, turned toward his boys, and waved a great gesture of farewell. He would never see the monastery again.

Père Jacques was held prisoner by the Nazis for over a year in four different prison camps, each one progressively worse, and during that time he performed an extraordinary and astonishing act of Christian witness, almost as if the entire forty-four years of his life had been a preparation for that time of greatness. He was first incarcerated for two months at the Fontainebleau prison on the rue Damesme in a period of questioning and interrogation. When told that he had disobeyed the laws of the Third Reich, he responded: "I know nothing about them. I know only one law—that of the Gospel and of charity. Shoot me, if you wish. You do not frighten me, and death was not created to frighten me." After intensive grilling sessions, the Gestapo chief stated in the presence of witnesses: "What a man! He has only one fault, that of not being a Nazi." The provincial, Philip of the Trinity, presented himself at Gestapo headquarters and said that it was he who had given the order for Père Jacques to shelter the Jewish boys and that accordingly he should exchange places with the prisoner, but the Gestapo ignored this heroic offer. When Philip was allowed to visit Jacques he told him that he was working to have him released, but Jacques entreated him to make no further effort to obtain his freedom. "Priests are needed in the prisons—if you only knew . . ."

He was taken to the prison camp at Compiègne, a fairly civilized compound which resembled a prisoner-of-war camp. There was an improvised chapel in the camp and facilities for offering Mass, but when Père Jacques arrived only three or four prisoners were attending daily Mass. However, within a few days the dynamic friar had attracted a congregation of two hundred prisoners, and he had organized a catechism school in the camp. One prisoner recalled after the war: "I can still see Père Jacques kneeling on the floor of this wretched barracks, without a *prie-dieu*, without any support, his whole soul concentrated and united with God. Nothing comforted me so much as this sight of Père Jacques." He also made friends with the Communists interred in the camp, and long after the war they remembered him with respect and affection. "Père Jacques was a believer," the Communist Émile Valley reported, "a Christian as Christ wanted one to be." The Nazis became alarmed at his efforts to Christianize the camp and after two months he was deported in handcuffs to Saarbrücken in Germany, a camp of terrors inhabited by living skeletons. The prisoners were fed starvation rations of hot water and a few spoonfuls of dehydrated vegetables, and they were subjected to beatings, humiliations, and the constant threat of death. After Père Jacques had been in the camp two weeks all the prisoners were assembled to witness a spectacle performed for the camp commander, Lieutenant Schmool. The lieutenant had brought his wife and two teen-age children to the camp for a visit, and seated on comfortable chairs and surrounded by Nazi officers who were smoking cigars, they talked and laughed while they watched two prisoners torn to death by four savage dogs. Père Jacques attempted to maintain the prisoners' morale and he shared his precious food with them, but by the time the group was transported at the end of April, a month after their arrival, only seven men of the original group of fifty that had been brought from Compiègne were still alive.

In April of 1944 he was transferred to the infamous camp at Mauthausen near Linz in Austria. Mauthausen, which overlooked the romantic Danube River, was a place of unbelievable depravity and brutal inhumanity where more than 120,000 men were killed in a three-year period. Père Jacques was actually imprisoned at a satellite camp called Gusen located in a valley three or four miles from the main camp, and he was first assigned to a construction crew which was building a reservoir and then to a small munitions factory. The prisoners worked twelve hours a day, ate pitiful rations, and were quartered in blockhouses of incredible squalor and confinement. Prodded and beaten by the SS guards, the men wore tattered rags and were treated like dumb beasts. And that was the most grievous torture of the camp—the Nazis' attempt to debase the prisoners and dehumanize them to the level of savages who groveled for food and fought among themselves. Père Jacques walked into this horror calmly and majestically, and he quickly manifested to his fellow prisoners his mastery of the situation. He encouraged the men, he comforted them, he gave away his food and clothing, and he became their priest, talking about God, hearing confessions, and after a while he even offered Mass secretly, using a glass for a chalice, and thereby bringing the Lord into that living hell. He was nicknamed "the Curé of Gusen" by the prisoners, and as before he won the respect of all the men, even the Communists. He combated the Nazis' program of dehumanization by cleverly maintaining a constant discussion of matters geared to make the men keep using their minds—art, literature, the theater, politics. One survivor of the camp recalled: "He would say to me, 'Do you know the Fontainebleau forest?' or 'What do you think of secondary education in France?' He was surprised to learn that I did not know Gide—'a mystic seeking his proper course,' he called him. . . . Another day we would talk about all the great classical and romantic writers; he characterized them in concise, exact words, often in the form of a paradox." Another prisoner stated: "On one occasion, after one of those demoralizing, cruel, ignoble scenes which occurred daily in the camp, we were talking about paradise, and I said: 'These SS, I think we at least will not find them up there.' He answered, 'You know nothing about it. Possibly they are sick and not responsible.' To be capable of such a view in Gusen was proof of an astonishing control in judgment."

Through the spring of 1945 there were continual rumors in the camp that the American forces were driving on Gusen, and near the end of April the sound of the guns of the liberating army could be plainly heard. On April 28 the prisoners from Gusen were assembled and lined up for a march back to the main camp at Mauthausen, and one of the prisoners later recalled Père Jacques standing in the ranks of tattered men: "My last vision of Gusen, and the assembly area where so many men had perished, is for me inseparable from the memory of this man, the priest who dominated in this misery and overcame a disaster and who in the end gave us victory, the victory of Man over a system born of power and the lower instincts." At Mauthausen the Nazis were preparing a mass extermination of the prisoners by gas before the American forces reached the camp, but they were unable to complete their plans because on May 5 two American machine-gun units set themselves up outside the camp and began firing at the gates. The SS guards were thrown into a panic, believing that the entire contingent was outside the gate, and they surrendered the camp to the handful of American soldiers.

The prisoners shouted with joy, and ran around in a frenzy, destroying the crematories, exulting in their new freedom. But there was chaos in the camp, and Père Jacques was unanimously elected to the presidency of the French committee for restoring order and arranging for the transfer of the former prisoners. From May 5 to 9 he worked eighteen hours a day, despite the fact that his health was broken from the year of malnutrition and his ceaseless efforts for his fellow prisoners. He was a gaunt shadow of his former self, and his eyes appeared to have been smudged into his head with pieces of charcoal, and he was racked with a persistent hacking cough. On May 10 he was taken to an infirmary in Linz, where his ailment was diagnosed as bronchial pneumonia, and he was placed in the hospital of the Sisters of St. Elizabeth. He received communion for the final time on June 2, and that evening he died. The priest who attended him said: "Père Jacques died very quietly, without a gesture, without a cry, without a lament."

His body was later taken back to the small cemetery at the Carmelite monastery in Avon-Fontainebleau, and it remains there, topped by an austere white cross. His memory has endured in France and it has spread around the world, a testimony to his unconquerable belief in the Christian message and the indomitable spirit of man. A survivor of Gusen said of him, in eulogy: "We lived because we veiled our eyes. Père Jacques could not continue to live because he did not veil his eyes. When one saw that human mass reduced to such a state, one said to oneself: these are no longer men. Père Jacques did not see them as a crowd, but he saw each individual there as a man." His cause for beatification has been introduced in Rome, and there is ample testimony to the heroicity of his virtue given by those for whom he sacrificed his life.

During the dark days of World War II the Order was guided by Peter Thomas of the Virgin of Carmel, the saintly friar from the province of Genoa (the small Italian province which has given fourteen generals to the Carmelite reform) who was elected superior general in 1937 and who was continued in that office by Pius XII when conditions in Europe made it impossible to assemble for the regular elections held every six years. In the midst of the war he encouraged the friars and nuns to maintain their Carmelite ideals while the world exploded around them, and in a pastoral letter he restated Carmel's traditional devotion to Mary: "Our Carmelite vocation is to know, love, and imitate Mary, and to lead others to the knowledge, love, and imitation of the Blessed Mother of God."

Peter Thomas was killed in an automobile accident on a lonely highway near Shamrock, Texas, in 1946 while making a visitation to the American provinces, and he was succeeded by the celebrated Spanish writer Silverio of St. Teresa who, ironically, also died during a visitation to the North American continent when he suffered a heart attack and expired at Mazatlán, Mexico, in 1954. As the world struggled to recover from the six years of holocaust, Silverio of St. Teresa spoke to the Order of its continuing commitment to its historic traditions, and in a pastoral letter of 1952 he recalled the Elijahan heritage and the double spirit which was transmitted "to Elisha and to those who lived with him on Carmel . . . and to those who continued that life under the New Law, with only the differences which the New Law imposed on them." Interpreting the scriptural "double spirit" as a symbol of the prophetic vocation of prayer and apostolate, Silverio wrote:

The Order's most highly endowed members who have become distinguished for the sanctity and learning have accordingly adopted the double spirit which Elijah left as an example to the Order, and in their lives of contemplation and apostolate they have looked to him as their sure guide.

The great prophet Elijah, therefore, remains as real an inspiration to the twentieth-century Carmelites as he was to the original twelfth-century hermits on Mount Carmel.

This chronicle must end where it began—on the mountain of Carmel in Palestine.

In May of 1965, the superior general of the Order, Anastasio of the Holy Rosary, summoned the provincials of the various provinces throughout the world to a meeting on Mount Carmel for the purpose of discussing the state of the Order at the time of Vatican II in the age of renewal. Late in the afternoon of May 7 the group gathered in the recently excavated ruins of Brocard's original chapel near the fountain of Elijah at *wadi 'ain es-sich* where the general offered Mass in the open air. And that Palestinian mountain which had witnessed massacre and bombardment and hostile armies was again the scene of Carmelites at prayer as these representatives from the far-flung provinces joined their voices in testimony of Carmel's enduring and invincible commitment to its historical vocation. Friars from Poland, Ireland, America, and the other provinces knelt on

CARMEL IN THE TWENTIETH CENTURY 365

the same spot where Brocard had assembled his community—modern descendants of those original Carmelites.

Pope Paul VI sent a special letter, *Carmeli Montis*, to the assembled superiors, dated May 3, 1965, in which he stated that Mount Carmel "perpetually recalls the name and mighty deeds of your father Elijah" and is "the birthplace of your Order." He reminded them that the Order is "singularly devoted to the Virgin Mother of God," and that St. Teresa and St. John of the Cross "laid new foundations for the Order" and "restored the ancient observance." Then the pope outlined his hopes for Carmel in the twentieth century: "Let the norms of contemplation and the apostolate of St. Teresa and St. John be faithfully and sincerely observed . . . so that the members of your Order may be witnesses of the true values which never fail." And: "Another matter we have greatly at heart is that the Discalced friars dedicate themselves with all possible diligence to the work of expounding, in a truly scientific manner, the fundamental norms of the spiritual life, and the laws and principles which govern ascetical and mystical theology, as it is called, especially that which is concerned with leading souls to a deeper life of prayer and contemplation." And: "We very much desire that they assist the nuns of the Order of the Blessed Virgin Mary of Mount Carmel in a spirit of fraternal charity, so that they may reach the summit of their vocation, following the way which in the course of the centuries has seen many shining examples of holiness." And finally Pope Paul VI bestowed his blessing "on the assembled superiors and on all the members, both men and women, of your religious family."

Religious family. That is the phrase used so frequently by Vatican II in its *Constitution on the Church* when it discusses religious orders. It is a fitting phrase because it explains the history of any religious order in its most profound aspect—people who live together in fraternal union with a strong bond of comradeship in their historical origins and traditions. A religious order, therefore, is an appealingly human organization, and it confers on the Church not only supernatural benefits and apostolic accomplishments but also a tangible and enduring witness to fundamental human values. This chronicle has recounted the story of Carmel, and as such it is a long narrative of men and women who were willing to work and suffer and, if necessary, give their lives for their religious family. And this human story has ennobled and dignified the harsh world in which we live.

When the friars from around the world assembled at the *wadi 'ain es-sich* in 1965, the Order had completed more than eight centuries of history, and it had been peopled by persons of varying temperament and background and personality. There are no stereotypes in this narrative, only the story of authentic men and women, unique and individual. But that is true of the people in any family. Berthold, Brocard, Simon Stock, Peter Thomas, John Soreth, Frances d'Amboise, Teresa, John of the Cross, Thomas of Jesus, Madame Acarie, Denis and Redemptus, the nuns of Compiègne, Hermann Cohen, Thérèse, Edith Stein, Père Jacques.

And the chronicle continues. . . .

BIBLIOGRAPHICAL NOTE

BIBLIOGRAPHICAL NOTE

The facts in this chronicle of more than eight centuries have been gathered from a vast number of sources, and I would like to cite a few of the more significant and valuable ones. The *Monumenta historica Carmelitana* (Lerins, 1907) by Benedict of the Cross (Zimmerman), O.C.D., is an excellent critical appraisal of the Order in the medieval period. Zimmerman (1859–1932), a native of Switzerland who joined the English province, is undoubtedly the finest historian the Carmelite reform has produced; he brings his own balanced judgment and the principles of scientific history to his work, and thus is able to distinguish between fact and legend. His lengthy articles in *The Catholic Encyclopedia* (New York, 1908) and the *Dictionnaire de Théologie Catholique* (Paris, 1905) are excellent résumés of Carmel's history. A collection and careful evaluation of the historical documentation about the beginnings of the Carmelite Order are contained in *Les Plus Vieux Textes du Carmel* (Paris, 1945) by François de Sainte Marie, O.C.D. The Elijahan tradition in the Order is discussed at great length in a two-volume edition of the 1956 *Études Carmélitaines* entitled *Élie le Prophète*. A number of fine critical studies about the early period of the Order can be found in the various issues of four magazines: *Mount Carmel*, published by the Irish province of Discalced Carmelites; *The Sword*, published by the American Calced Carmelites; and *Le Carmel* and *Études Carmélitaines*, both published by the French Discalced Carmelites. The historicity of the scapular is discussed scientifically and soberly by Bartholomew Ziberta, O.CARM., in his *De visione sancti Simonis Stock* (Rome, 1950); and by Élisée de la Nativité, O.C.D., in his *Le Scapulaire du Carmel* (Tarascon, 1958). A splendid review of the intellectual life of the Order is contained in "La Vie Intellectuelle des Carmes," a long study in the 1935 edition of *Études Carmélitaines*. The case of Filippo Lippi is expertly documented in *Fra Filippi Lippi* (Burgos, 1952) by José María de la Cruz, O.C.D.

Silverio of St. Teresa's monumental *Historia del Carmen Descalzo* (Burgos, 1927–1951) contains a full history of the Spanish congregation of Discalced Carmelites; however, he does not always evaluate his material critically and he must therefore be read carefully and judiciously. E. Allison Peers's *Handbook to the Life and Times of St. Teresa and St. John of the Cross* (Westminster, 1954) is largely based on Silverio's work, but Peers makes a more sober appraisal of the material and thus presents an excellent study of the first thirty years of the reform. Marcelle Auclair's *Saint Teresa of Ávila* (New York, 1953) is a provocative contemporary biography, and John Beevers' *St. Teresa of Ávila* (New York, 1961) is an excellent short study of the saint's life with all the unusual insight that Beevers ordinarily brings to his work. *The Life of St. John of the Cross* (New York, 1958) by Crisogono de Jesus, o.c.d., and *St. John of the Cross* (New York, 1932) by Fr. Bruno, o.c.d., are the two modern classical works on the saint. *The Letters of Saint Teresa of Jesus* (Westminster, 1950) and *The Complete Works of Saint Teresa of Jesus* (New York, 1949) were both translated by E. Allison Peers from the critical edition of Silverio of St. Teresa, while *The Collected Works of St. John of the Cross* (New York, 1964) were translated by Kieran Kavanaugh, o.c.d., and Otilio Rodríguez, o.c.d., from a comparative reading of a number of texts.

The development and expansion of the Discalced Carmelites is described in *Santa Teresa de Jesus por las Misiónes* (Vitoria, 1959) by Severino de Santa Teresa, o.c.d., and in the large commemorative volume *Zelo Zelatus sum* published at Rome in 1952 by the superior general's office. The *Nomenclator missionariorum ordinis Carmelitarum Discalceatorum* (Rome, 1944) contains statistical data about almost all the Discalced friars who worked in mission territories between 1582 and 1942. And the *Généalogie des Couvents de Carmélites de la Réforme de Sainte Thérèse* published by the Carmelite convent at Cherbourg in 1962 presents forty-five charts which delineate the nuns' expansion throughout the world during the four hundred years of their history. Bruno de Jesus-Marie's *La Belle Acarie* (Paris, 1942) is the finest study on Madame Acarie, but Lancelot Sheppard's *Barbe Acarie, Wife and Mystic* (New York, 1953) is an interesting popular work. *Carmel in Ireland* (Dublin, 1903) by James Rushe, o.c.d., describes the reform in Ireland, while Lancelot Sheppard's *The English Carmelites* (London, 1943) relates the history of the English province. *English Carmelites in Penal Times* (London, 1936) by Anne Hardman recounts the story of the English Carmelite convents in the Lowlands. The history of the Carmelite deserts is contained in *Les Saints Déserts* (Paris, 1927) by Benedict Zimmerman, o.c.d., and in *La Soledad Fecunda* (Madrid, 1961) by Felipe de la Virgen del Carmen, o.c.d. The story of Louise de la Vallière is given in *Louise de la Vallière de la Cour au Carmel* (Paris, 1931) by J. B. Eriau. *The Infant of Prague* (New York, 1958) by Ludvik Nemec presents the full history of devotion to the Infant of Prague, but the material is uncritically evaluated.

The complete story of the nuns of Compiègne is recounted brilliantly by Bruno de Jesus-Marie, o.c.d., in his *Le Sang du Carmel*

(Paris, 1954). The *Life of the Reverend Father Hermann* (New York, 1925), a translation from the original French work by Charles Sylvain, is still the only full account of Hermann Cohen's life, but I have been given supplementary data by his great-nephew, Jean-Marie Beaurin, a Benedictine priest at the Abbey de la Source in Paris. The case of Hyacinth Loyson was taken from the general archives of the Order in Rome. The story of Raphael of St. Joseph is based upon the *Processus* for the cause of his beatification at Rome, although a popular book has recently been published about his life, *Al Carmelo Attraverso la Siberia* (Rome, 1960) by Jole Galofaro. *Alessandra di Rudini Carmelite* (Paris, 1961) presents the full story, with documentation, about that interesting character, but in a rather baroque style. Philipon's *The Spiritual Doctrine of Sister Elizabeth of the Trinity* (Westminster, 1955) still remains the best book on the subject. The facts about St. Thérèse have been taken largely from my own book, *The Search for St. Thérèse* (New York, 1961). The story of Carmel in America has been gathered mostly from official archives, but *Catholics in Colonial America* (Baltimore, 1964) by John Tracy Ellis offers additional information about the early Carmelites in the United States.

The grim story of the Carmelites during the Spanish civil war is presented in great detail by Silverio of St. Teresa in the fifteenth volume of his *Historia*. Edith Stein has been the subject of a number of books, the best of which are: *Edith Stein* (Staten Island, 1965), by Jean de Fabreques; *Edith Stein, Thoughts on Her Life and Times* (Milwaukee, 1959), by Henry Bordeaux; and *Writings of Edith Stein* (Westminster, 1956), by Hilda Graef. Père Jacques's story has been brilliantly told by his former provincial, Philippe de la Trinité, in *Le Père Jacques, Martyr de la Charité* (Paris, 1947), but the English translation of Michel Carrouges' book, *Père Jacques* (New York, 1961), is a moving account of the heroic friar's life.

Two contemporary French books offer short but highly readable accounts of Carmel's history: *Histoire du Carmel* (Paris, 1957), by Henri Peltier; and *Carmel Vivant* (Paris, 1963), by Anne Steinmann. Peltier's book is a slightly credulous account, but Steinmann's (the family name of a Carmelite nun, Sister Anne-Elizabeth) book shows a bright and critically alert mind at work.

I have made copious use of unedited material gathered from the general archives at the *Casa Generalizia* in Rome and also from the library of the *Teresianum*. Other libraries have supplied invaluable data: the provincial library for the Paris province at Avon-Fontaine-bleau, and the provincial library for the Avignon province at Monaco. And libraries in the Carmelite monasteries at Madrid, Ávila, Burgos, and London. Interesting information was also gathered at the British Museum in London and the Biblioteca Nacional in Madrid.

Otilio Rodríguez, o.c.d., archivist for the American province of the Immaculate Heart, has compiled a massive, unedited file of statistical and biographical data about the Carmelite reform, and he was gracious enough to allow me to consult it.

INDEX

INDEX

Abstinence from meat: prescribed by rule, 43; exemption granted for travelers, 63; prescript mitigated, 112; prescript re-instated, 148, 152
Acarie, Barbe, 238ff., 252
Adeodatus of St. Joseph, 345
Agapitus of the Holy Spirit, 281
Ahab, 18, 23, 24, 26, 27, 29, 30
Ahaziah, 30, 31
Albert of Avogadro, 19, 41f.
Albert of Sicily, St., 81f.
Alcalá, Chapter of, 200–2
Aloysia of the Blessed Trinity, 332
Aloysius of St. Mary, 344
Alpargatas, 153
Álvarez, Alonso, 160
Álvarez, Baltasar, 148
Álvarez, Francisco, 139
American Provinces. *See* Carmelite Order
Amilian, Peter, 76
Andrew of the Assumption, 327
Andrew of Jesus and Mary, 300
Angela of St. Teresa, 333
Ángel de Salazar, 151–52, 199
Angelus, St., 55
Angelus of St. Joseph, 281
Anne of the Angels, 197
Anne of the Ascension, 249
Anne of the Blessed Sacrament, 246
Anne of Jesus, 213, 215f., 221, 225, 236, 242, 244, 248, 249
Anne of St. Bartholomew, 202–3, 204, 242, 244, 248
Anselm of St. Mary, 275
Anthony of the Ascension, 327

Anthony of Jesus, 158, 161, 164, 166, 167–68, 200, 203–4, 224
Anthony of the Mother of God, 264
Athanasio of the Sacred Heart, 349
Audet, Nicholas, 71, 117, 156
Augustine of the Blessed Sacrament, 278, 310–14
Augustine of St. Joseph, 331
Avignon Papacy, 102–3
Ávila, 133f., 137–53, 175–79, 193, 203, 215, 315
Aymeric of Malifaye, 37, 85
Azaro, Mariano, 165–67, 205

Baconthorpe, John, 47, 84
Baldwin I, 34, 37
Bale, John, 119, 122
Balthasar of Jesus, 184, 192
Balthasar of St. Catharine, 263
Basil of St. Francis, 268
Bathilde of the Infant Jesus, 309
Beaterio, 131, 133, 134, 144
Bede of the Blessed Sacrament, 275
Bede of St. Simon Stock, 277
Beguines, 126, 128, 129
Bencesi, Natale, 110
Benjamin of Tudela, 37
Bernadina of St. Joseph, 332f.
Bernard of St. Joseph, 250, 251
Bernard of St. Teresa, 268–69
Berthold, St., 37–38
Bibars, 35, 53
Billick, Eberhard, 122
Black Death, 97f.
Blaise of the Conception, 264
Blankart, Alexander, 122